KENT HISTORY PROJECT

4

FAITH AND FABRIC

A HISTORY OF
ROCHESTER CATHEDRAL
604–1994

KENT HISTORY PROJECT

ISSN 1352–805X

Already published

Traffic and Politics: The Construction and Management of Rochester Bridge, AD 43–1993, ed. Nigel Yates and James M. Gibson

Religion and Society in Kent, 1640–1914, Nigel Yates, Robert Hume and Paul Hastings

The Economy of Kent, 1640–1914, ed. Alan Armstrong

Volumes in progress

Kent to AD 800, ed. Alec P. Detsicas

Kent 800–1220, ed. Richard Eales

Kent 1220–1540, ed. Nigel Ramsay

Kent 1540–1640, ed. Michael Zell

The Government of Kent 1640–1914, ed. H. C. F. Lansberry

Kent in the Twentieth Century, ed. Nigel Yates and Ian Coulson

FAITH AND FABRIC

A HISTORY OF
ROCHESTER CATHEDRAL
604–1994

EDITED BY

NIGEL YATES

with the assistance of
PAUL A. WELSBY

THE BOYDELL PRESS
FRIENDS OF ROCHESTER CATHEDRAL

First published 1996
The Boydell Press, Woodbridge, and
Friends of Rochester Cathedral

ISBN 0 85115 581 2

The Boydell Press is an imprint of Boydell & Brewer Ltd
PO Box 9, Woodbridge, Suffolk IP12 3DF, UK
and of Boydell & Brewer Inc.
PO Box 41026, Rochester, NY 14604–4126, USA

British Library Cataloguing in Publication Data
Faith and fabric : a history of Rochester Cathedral,
   604–1994. – (Kent history project ; 4)
   1. Rochester Cathedral – History   2. Cathedrals –
   England – Rochester – History   3. Church architecture
   – England – Rochester
   I. Yates, Nigel, 1944–   II. Welsby, Paul A. (Paul Antony)
   III. Rochester Cathedral. Friends
   726.6'5'09422323
   ISBN 0851155812

Library of Congress Cataloging-in-Publication Data
Faith and fabric : a history of Rochester Cathedral, 604–1994 / edited
by Nigel Yates with the assistance of Paul A. Welsby.
      p.   cm. – (Kent history project, ISSN 1352–805X ; 4)
   Includes bibliographical references (p.   ) and index.
   ISBN 0–85115–581–2 (alk. paper)
   1. Rochester Cathedral (Rochester, Kent, England) – History.
   2. Rochester (Kent, England) – Church history.   3. England –
   Church history.   I. Yates, Nigel.   II. Welsby, Paul A.   III. Series.
   BX5195.R637F35   1996
   283'.422323–dc20   96–12441

This publication is printed on acid-free paper

Printed in Great Britain by
St Edmundsbury Press Ltd, Bury St Edmunds, Suffolk

Contents

Plates

Plates appear between pages 48 and 49, 80 and 81, 96 and 97, 176 and 177

Illustrations on dust jacket

Acknowledgements

This volume was jointly commissioned in 1982 by Paul A. Welsby, then Canon Librarian of Rochester Cathedral, and Nigel Yates, then County Archivist of Kent, with the enthusiastic and whole-hearted support of the Dean and Chapter. In 1989, with the consent of the Dean and Chapter, it was incorporated into the Kent History Project, launched by Kent County Council, to provide the county of Kent with its first comprehensive history since the publication of Hasted's *History and Topographical Survey of Kent* in the late eighteenth century.

The editors and contributors would like to thank the following individuals and corporate bodies who have made the publication of this volume possible:

The Friends of Rochester Cathedral who provided the major financial support for the volume.

The Trustees of the British Library for permission to reproduce two illustrations in their collections (plates 6 and 12).

The Royal Commission on the Historical Monuments of England for permission to reproduce a photograph in the National Monuments Record (plate 11).

The Very Revd John Arnold, formerly Dean of Rochester, now Dean of Durham, for assistance and encouragement at various stages.

Mary Covert and Tim Tatton-Brown for much assistance to the authors of chapters seven and eight; also to Mrs Enid Godfrey, for help with her late husband's papers, and for her generous hospitality.

Suffolk Record Office, Bury St Edmunds, for accepting temporary deposit of archive material for use by Dr C.S. Knighton.

The Research Leave Committee of the University of Durham for the provision of sabbatical leave and financial assistance to Patrick Mussett; to Alan Piper and Ann Robinson in Archives and Special Collections at Durham University Library, for assistance and support; and to Denis and Jeanette Hitchings and to Gilbert and Dorothy Johnson whose splendid hospitality made research in Kent a delight.

Last, but by no means least, the editors and other contributors are deeply indebted to Dr C.S. Knighton for agreeing to undertake the mammoth task of indexing this volume.

Foreword

Any cathedral founded in 604 must be in need of a history. This volume brings together the most recent research set in a broad historical context.

A cathedral, such as Rochester, founded only seven years after St Augustine established at Canterbury his mission to the English, has a story to tell and a significant place in the history not only of Kent but also of the English Church.

The title *Faith and Fabric* aptly reflects the commitment of the present Dean and Chapter of Rochester to both the mission and maintenance of the Cathedral Church of Christ and the Blessed Virgin Mary, as an epitome of English spirituality and a place in which both church and community have a stake.

Rochester Cathedral is more visited today than at any time in its history, its fabric better conserved, its engagement with the community more vigorous and its spiritual heritage more widely appreciated.

With this volume, it is also better recorded.

Edward Shotter
Dean of Rochester

Notes on Contributors

Martin Brett was Lecturer in History at the University of Auckland 1964–70 and has been Fellow of Robinson College, Cambridge since 1978. His published work includes *The English Church under Henry I* (1975) and collaborative editions of *Councils and Synods relating to the English Church 871–1204* (1981) and *History of the Archbishops of York of Hugh the Chanter* (1990). He is currently editing the charters of the archbishops of Canterbury 1070–1161 and bishops of Rochester 1076–1143.

Diana Holbrook took her graduate diploma in architecture from North-East London Polytechnic in 1976, became a Chartered Architect in 1983 and obtained the Architectural Association's graduate diploma in conservation in 1986. Her contribution to this volume is a condensed version of a project, jointly financed by the Royal Institute of British Architects and English Heritage, to establish an accurate record of all repairs, alterations and restorations of Rochester Cathedral since 1540.

C.S. Knighton holds degrees from the Universities of Cambridge and Oxford and has been an Editor at the Public Record Office since 1974. He compiled the *Catalogue of Pepys Library at Magdalene College, Cambridge: Modern Manuscripts* (1981), co-edited *Close Encounters: English Cathedrals and Society since 1540* (1991), and edited *Calendar of State Papers, Domestic Series, Edward VI* (1992).

Philip McAleer completed his doctoral thesis on 'The Romanesque Church Facades in Great Britain' at the Courtauld Institute of Art, University of London, in 1963. He has taught at the Universities of Columbia and California and, since 1975, the Technical University of Nova Scotia, where he is a tenured professor. He has contributed papers on architectural history, including several on that of Rochester Cathedral, to learned journals in both Britain and North America.

Patrick Mussett has for many years been on the staff of the University of Durham where he is now a Senior Assistant Keeper of Archives and Special Collections in the University Library. He has published papers on Norwich and Durham Cathedrals and is currently working on the seventeenth century woodwork in parish churches that is associated with Bishop John Cosin and his colleagues.

Anne Oakley is Senior Research Archivist at the Canterbury Cathedral Archives, having been Archivist to the Chapter, City and Diocese of Canterbury between 1970 and 1989. Previously, as an Assistant Archivist in the Kent Archives Office, she had been responsible for the cataloguing of the archives of Rochester Cathedral. She has published *Actes du Consistoire de l'Eglise Francaise du Threadneedle Street, Londres* (1969), *The Freemen of Canterbury 1800–1835* (1990) and several articles on aspects of Huguenot and Kentish history.

Paul A. Welsby   was Rector of Copdock in Suffolk 1952–66; Residentiary Canon and Librarian of Rochester Cathedral 1966–88; Prolocutor of the Lower House of the Convocation of Canterbury and Joint Chairman of the House of Clergy of the General Synod 1973–80; and Chaplain to The Queen 1980–90. He has published, among other works, biographies of *Lancelot Andrewes* (1958) and *George Abbot* (1962) and, more recently, *A History of the Church of England 1945–1980* (1984).

Nigel Yates   has been General Editor of the Kent History Project since 1989 and was Visiting Senior Research Fellow in Economic and Social History at the University of Kent 1991–5. He was City Archivist of Portsmouth 1975–80 and County Archivist of Kent 1980–90. He has published more than forty books and articles on religious and social history, including *Buildings, Faith and Worship: The Liturgical Arrangement of Anglican Churches 1600–1900* (1991), and is currently working on a major study of ritualism in Britain since the early seventeenth century.

Abbreviations

(1)   Records of the Cathedral Priory held at Medway Studies Centre, Strood
        (DRc)

T   Charters, title deeds and leases
F   Financial records
L   Legal records
Z   Miscellaneous records
R   *Textus Roffensis* and *Custumale Roffense*

(2)   Records of the Dean and Chapter held at Medway Studies Centre, Strood
        (DRc)

Ad	Charters and Letters Patent	Az	Other chapter appointments
As	Cathedral statutes	Apd	Appointments of proxies: deans
Arb	The Red Book	App	Appointments of proxies: prebendaries
Ac	Chapter minutes		
Aca	Agenda books	Alp	Presentations to chapter livings
Acd	Duplicate chapter minutes	Alz	Miscellaneous records
Acn	Note books	Apa	Patronage papers
Acz	Miscellaneous records	Ac	Convocation papers
Aq	Quindenum chapter order book	AO	Official, royal and decanal orders
Aa	Audit bundles	AR	Residence papers
Abe	Elections and inthronisations of bishops	AV	Episcopal visitations
		AZ	Miscellaneous records
Abz	Miscellaneous records	EC	Records of Ecclesiastical Commissioners
Aod	Appointments and elections of deans		
		Esp	Parliamentary survey
Aok	Installations of archdeacons	Elb	Lease books
Aop	Installations of prebendaries	Elc	Leases and related correspondence
Aoc	Appointments of chapter clerks	Elt	Land tax
Aos	Appointments of stewards and understewards	Ela	Augmentation
		Els	Schedules of chapter leases
Aoa	Appointments of auditors	Elr	Orders relating to fines and land tax
Aoh	Appointments of schoolmasters	Elf	Inventories
Aom	Appointments of minor canons	Elp	Deanery records
Aob	Appointments of lay clerks	Elz	Miscellaneous records
Aoo	Appointments of organists	Est	Surveys and terriers
Aov	Appointments of vergers, etc.	Es	Surveys of chapter estates
Aob	Appointments of bedesmen	Et	Timber returns

Eb	Bricks, ballast, etc.	FAs	South Sea Company
Egz	Miscellaneous records	FAv	South Sea Company
Emf	Repair and maintenance: fabric	FD	Deanery records
Emp	Repair and maintenance: property	FF	Financial files
EP	Estate maps and plans	LA	Legal records
FRb	Receivers' books	LP	Legal records
FRd	Deputy receivers' books	C	Charity records
FRm	The Manor Courts	S	Sacrists' records
FR	Financial records	SZ	Parish records
FTb	Treasurers' books	KS	King's School records
FTv	Bills and vouchers	CC	Chapter clerks' papers
FA	Auditors' books and papers	CCZ	Chapter clerks' papers
FAb	Bailiffs' accounts		

(3)   Records of the Diocese of Rochester held at Centre for Kentish Studies, Maidstone (DRb)

Ar   Bishops' registers

(4)   Abbreviations used by Martin Brett in Chapter One

Bethell, 'Miracles'   D. Bethell, 'The Miracles of St Ithamar', *Analecta Bollandiana*, lxxxix (1971), 421–37

Brett, 'Forgery'   M. Brett, 'Forgery at Rochester', *Fälschungen im Mittelalter*, Monumenta Germaniae Historica, Schriften, xxxiii (1988), iv, 397–412

Brooks, *Canterbury*   N. Brooks, *The Early History of the Church of Canterbury*, Leicester 1984

Campbell   *Charters of Rochester*, ed. A. Campbell, British Academy Anglo-Saxon Charters, i, London 1973

CS   *Cartularium Saxonicum*, ed. W. de G. Birch, London 1885–99, cited by number of document

Custumale   *Custumale Roffense*, ed. J. Thorpe, London 1788

DMon   *The Domesday Monachorum of Christ Church Canterbury*, ed. D.C. Douglas, Royal Historical Society, London 1944

Ecclesiastical Courts   *Select Cases from the Ecclesiastical Courts of the Province of Canterbury c.1200–1301*, ed. N. Adams and C. Donahue, Selden Society, xcv, 1981. For the edition see Brett, 'Forgeries', 399–400. The text is compared with the originals, Canterbury Cathedral Lib. Cartae Antiquae R 70, R 70a where necessary

Everitt, *Continuity*   A. Everitt, *Continuity and Colonization: the Evolution of Kentish Settlement*, Leicester 1986

Fasti   J. Le Neve, *Fasti Ecclesiae Anglicanae 1066–1300*, edn
                                 revised D.E. Greenway, London 1968–

Flores   *Flores Historiarum*, ed. H.R. Luard, Rolls Series, London
                                 1890. The Rochester MS of this chronicle (BL Cotton
                                 Nero D ii, R in Luard's apparatus) includes a series of
                                 interpolations on the history of the church, the bulk of
                                 which are derived from the annals in BL Cotton Vespasian
                                 A xxii, and from the list of benefactions in the same MS.
                                 H. Wharton, *Anglia Sacra*, London 1692, i, 341–55 prints
                                 an incomplete and inaccurate version of the same annals,
                                 attributed to Edmund of Haddenham

Gervase   *Historical Works of Gervase of Canterbury*, ed. W. Stubbs,
                                 Rolls Series, London 1879–80

Regesta   *Regesta Regum Anglo-Normannorum 1066–1154*, ed.
                                 H.W.C. Davis *et al.*, Oxford 1913–69

Registrum   *Registrum Roffense*, ed. J. Thorpe, London 1769

Richards, *Texts*   M.P. Richards, *Texts and their Traditions in the Medieval
                                 Library of Rochester Cathedral Priory*, Transactions of the
                                 American Philosophical Society, lxxviii/3 (1988)

Robertson, *Charters*   *Anglo-Saxon Charters*, ed. and trans. A.J. Robertson, 2nd
                                 edn, Cambridge 1957

Textus   *Textus Roffensis, Rochester Cathedral Library MS A 3 5*,
                                 ed. P. Sawyer, Early English Manuscripts in Facsimile vii
                                 (1957), xi (1962). The printed version, *Textus Roffensis*,
                                 ed. T. Hearne, Oxford 1720, was taken from an incomplete
                                 transcript. The manuscript is now in Medway Studies
                                 Centre DRc/R1. In the manuscript the documents are
                                 numbered, and the numbers were used by Hearne;
                                 passages cited by folio and number to allow either printed
                                 copy or facsimile to be used

Vita   *The Life of Gundulf, Bishop of Rochester*, ed. R. Thomson,
                                 Toronto Medieval Latin Texts, vii (1977)

(5)   Abbreviations used in other chapters

Arch. Cant.   *Archaeologia Cantiana*
BL   British Library
CPR   *Calendar of Patent Rolls*
CSPD   *Calendar of State Papers, Domestic Series*
DNB   *Dictionary of National Biography*
LP   *Letters and Papers, Foreign and Domestic, of the Reign of
                Henry VIII*
PRO   Public Record Office
TRHS   *Transactions of the Royal Historical Society*

1

The Church at Rochester, 604–1185

MARTIN BRETT

I. The Creation of the Diocese

The smallest of the dioceses of medieval England has a long history, but until the eleventh century it is also an obscure one. For the first century of its existence our only source is Bede's *Ecclesiastical History*, finished in 731. In the third chapter of the second book he records the foundation of Rochester with that of London:

> In the year of our Lord's incarnation 604 Augustine, archbishop of Britain, consecrated two bishops, namely Mellitus and Justus . . .
> Augustine consecrated Justus in Kent itself, in the city of *Dorubrevis* which the English call *Hrofaescaestrae*, after one of their former chiefs whose name was Hrof. It is about twenty-four miles west of Canterbury, and in it King Aethelberht built the church of the apostle St Andrew; he later bestowed many gifts on the bishops of each of these churches and that of Canterbury; and he also added both lands and possessions for the maintenance of those with the bishops.[1]

Elsewhere Bede tells us that Mellitus and Justus had not been among Augustine's original companions, but were part of the second mission sent by Pope Gregory I in 601 to follow up the early success. In due course each in turn succeeded to Augustine's seat at Canterbury.

Bede also supplies a brief succession of the bishops from Justus until his own time. Of most we know little more than the name, though Paulinus, later the third bishop, had been sent to preach the gospel in the kingdom of Northumbria, whence he fled after the death of King Edwin in 633. His successor, the Kentish Ithamar, was the first native English bishop. Both were subsequently the objects of a modest cult, though the surviving *Life* of Paulinus contributes nothing substantial to our knowledge. Ithamar was succeeded by Damian, a South Saxon, and Damian by Putta, celebrated for his skill in chanting 'after the Roman manner'. When Aethelred of Mercia ravaged Kent and destroyed his city in 676 Putta withdrew, and died in exile

---

[1] *Bede's Ecclesiastical History of the English People*, ed. B. Colgrave and R.A.B. Mynors, Oxford Medieval Texts 1969, i, 142–3, slightly adapted; Bede's etymology is disputed. When Paulinus, the third bishop, died in 644 he was buried in the *secretarium* of the church which King Aethelberht had built 'from its foundations', *ibid.*, 256–7.

among the Mercians. Archbishop Theodore consecrated three bishops to Rochester, Cwichhelm, who abandoned his impoverished church after a short time, Gebmund, and lastly Tobias, who had studied with the archbishop and Abbot Hadrian of Canterbury. Bede calls him a man of wide learning in general and church literature, who was as familiar with Latin and Greek as his own tongue. He died in 726, and was buried in the *porticus* of St Paul 'which he had built within the church of St Andrew as his own burial place'. When Bede wrote Rochester was ruled by Ealdwulf.[2]

So much is relatively clear, but almost every other aspect of the early history of the church is dark. Bede had no doubt that Canterbury and Rochester were both in Kent, both founded by the same king, but the creation of a second bishopric within a single kingdom is otherwise unexampled at so early a date. Elsewhere the assumption that there should be one bishop for each kingdom prevailed until the time of Theodore.

Several explanations may be offered. The simplest is that Augustine began his mission armed with the plan of Pope Gregory, itself derived from material from the time of the Roman empire in Britain. This called for the creation of two provinces, centred on London and York, of twelve bishops each. On this view Augustine took the earliest opportunity to establish bishops in the most substantial Roman cities within the sphere of influence of Aethelberht, in the hope that a number of similar small dioceses would follow. In the event, the archbishops of the southern province never moved from Canterbury to London, and the dioceses of Canterbury and Rochester, each with only half a shire, were to be the smallest in England until the Reformation. Their size would occasion no remark however in the Italy of Gregory and Augustine. On such a view they represent the only enduring trace of the pope's original design for the English church.

Local factors may have played a larger part. It has long been remarked that the archaeology and settlement of East Kent and West Kent show a marked division. In the more fertile east, with a long history of settlement, the characteristic grave-goods of the pagan burials of the pagan Saxon period include the lavish jewellery once described as 'Jutish', with its closest English parallels in the Isle of Wight and its neighbouring coast. From the Medway westwards the evidence for early settlement is more restricted, and the closest parallels to its poorer grave-goods are found in Surrey, or even Essex, rather than eastwards.[3]

---

[2] *Ibid.*, 158–67, 204–5, 254–7, 278–9, 334–7, 368–9, 474–5, 556–9; for the Life of Paulinus see John Capgrave, *Nova Legenda Angliae*, ed. C. Horstman, Oxford 1901, ii, 312–15; for two copies of a lost Life of Ithamar in the catalogue of the priory library of 1202, Richards, *Texts*, p. 38 no. 169; for the cult of Ithamar see Bethell, 'Miracles', 421–37.

[3] Everitt, *Continuity*. Though it is an essential element of this fundamental study that the true topographical divisions of Kent run East–West, not North–South, see esp. pp. 22, 190. For the Roman background A. Detsicas, *The Cantiaci*, Gloucester 1983, esp. pp. 1–10, for the pagan English material S.C. Hawkes, 'Anglo-Saxon Kent c.425–725', *Archaeology in Kent to AD 1500*, ed. P.E. Leach, London 1982, p. 74, citing the earlier literature; N. Brooks, 'The creation and early structure of the kingdom of Kent', *The Origins of Anglo-Saxon Kingdoms*, ed. S. Bassett, Leicester 1989, pp. 68–9.

This contrast of geography and settlement may illuminate another aspect of early Kentish history. Kent seems to have been ruled by two kings for much of the period of the independent kingdom. Even in the ninth century there were at least sometimes ealdormen for each half of the shire. Further, there is some evidence that one of these two kings, and that apparently the 'junior', had a special connection with Rochester throughout the seventh century.[4] On this view West Kent was under some aspects a distinct kingdom, and possibly one which had been acquired by the house of Aethelberht only shortly before Augustine's arrival.

Another uncertainty surrounds the emergence of this miniature diocese, for its original boundaries are unknown. The border with Canterbury is not described precisely until the twelfth century, but it is likely than it more or less followed the later course from very early times. Before and after the conversion of the South Saxons the southern limit of the diocese presumably lay through the forest of the Weald. The western boundary presents more difficult problems. For several reasons it has been suggested that the realm of the Kentish kings once extended beyond the boundaries of the modern shire, and it is possible that it may have lain even as far west as the *Fullingadic*, the long dyke whose course can be traced from Weybridge southwards to pass three miles west of Woking. The emergence of the later shire of Surrey is wrapped in obscurity, but it may well be that West Kent and so the diocese of Rochester were confined to something approaching their later limits only towards the end of the seventh century.[5]

The surviving records beyond Bede scarcely allow a glimpse of the life or endowment of the diocese in its first century. Only one surviving charter for Rochester purports to belong to these early years, a grant in the name of Aethelberht dated 604 granting the church of St Andrew, and Justus the bishop, the south-western quarter of the city. Clearly the land for the church in the south-east must also have been handed over when it was built, as a later list of benefactors suggests. No other grant of these lands is recorded, but the surviving charter is most unlikely to represent the gift of Aethelberht in any formal sense. When it was written, and what earlier material, if any, lies behind it, remain thoroughly obscure.[6]

---

[4] B.A.E. Yorke, 'Joint kingship in Kent c.560 to 785', *Archaeologia Cantiana*, lxcix (1983), 1–19. See particularly p. 5 for the suggestions that Aethelberht's charter for Rochester, Campbell no. 1 (*CS* 3), preserves an authentic early element in its address to Eadbald, the king's son, and that Justus was responsible for converting an otherwise unknown brother of Eadbald rather than Eadbald himself. A double kingship was not, of course, unique to Kent in the early period.

[5] K.P. Witney, *The Kingdom of Kent*, Chichester 1982, p. 116; N. Brooks, *op. cit.*, pp. 57–8, 68–9, 73–4.

[6] The lands in the south-eastern quarter are treated as the gift of Aethelberht in *Textus*, f. 177 no. 92, an addition to the original manuscript (compare the earlier list on f. 215 no. 209), derived in large part from Bede. Elsewhere the list gives no clear sign of being based on lost earlier material. See too Campbell no. 1 and p. xxii, G. Ward, 'A note on the Mead way, the Street and Doddinghyrnan in Rochester', *Archaeologia Cantiana*, lxii (1949), 37–44 and the literature discussed by Yorke, *op. cit.*, p. 5. On the archaeology of Rochester see T. Tatton-Brown, 'The towns of Kent', *Anglo-Saxon Towns in Southern England*, Chichester 1984, 12–16, and 'The Anglo-Saxon towns of Kent', *Anglo-Saxon Settlements*, ed. D. Hooke, Oxford 1988, 221–4. The annalist of the 'Registrum Temporalium' in *Registrum*, p. 4 concluded from the archives he studied that Rochester held no manors for a hundred years after its foundation.

It sometimes seems possible to identify the earliest endowments of an ancient church by comparing the record of known acquisitions with the lands in its possession later. Where there is no evidence for a grant, it may be presumed with caution that the land had been in the hands of the church from early times. On this principle two estates may have been granted in the first years of the cathedral, for there is no sound evidence on the origin of the bishop's substantial rights in Southfleet or Stone-next-Dartford, and both were in areas of very early settlement.[7] It must be supposed that the bishop did have a group of clergy about him, and some lands to support them, but their extent remains conjectural.

What is striking on a wider view is the absence of early minster churches in the diocese which can be shown to have had any connection with the cathedral. It is clear that these minster churches, served either by communities of clerks or by monks, were the secondary centres from which the Christian life of the countryside was fostered and served in the generations after the conversion. Only one such minster apart from the cathedral is recorded for Rochester, the community at Hoo St Werbergh, but St Werbergh was a saint more of the Mercian royal house than of Kent. The monastery appears to have been subject to Peterborough for some time, and almost everything we know of it comes from the archives of Peterborough. The house is last mentioned in a charter forged in the early ninth century, after which it vanishes from sight.[8]

The minsters in East Kent retained a number of important rights and functions up to the end of the eleventh century and beyond. The comparable evidence in West Kent reveals nothing similar.[9] Further, Everitt used a wide range of criteria to reveal the presence of a number of other 'primary' mother churches in the diocese for which there is no direct evidence. These fall into two categories, the well-established and the probable. Not one of the well-established churches was attached to the cathedral at Domesday, and only Trottiscliffe of the probable ones. Even Trottiscliffe may be a later acquisition, for the estate is not thought to have passed into the hands of the bishop until the grant by Offa of Mercia in 788. If any of the earliest churches of the diocese had been attached closely to the cathedral at the outset, Rochester retained no memory of it.[10]

One explanation of the obscurity of Rochester's early organization may be found in frequent invasions. Bede touched on a devastating attack by the Mercians under 676, and the Anglo-Saxon chronicle describes further invasions by the kings of

[7] Everitt, *Continuity*, pp. 99, 114. Stone and Southfleet both contributed among the bishop's estates to the repair of Rochester bridge c.975 in *Textus*, f. 166v no. 82 (Robertson, *Charters*, no. lii, and below n. 19), but there is no suggestion of the origin of Rochester's title before the thirteenth century – *Registrum*, pp. 2, 116 (both untrustworthy). Pinden also contributed with the bishop's estates, but it was not in the hands of the bishop in 1086. Compare Brooks, *Canterbury*, pp. 100–7.

[8] *CS* 89, 91. For *CS* 91 see Brooks, *Canterbury*, pp. 191–7. It is not clear whether the draftsman thought Hoo should be subject to the bishop of Rochester or the archbishop; the latter seems more probable. It is worth note that no other church in Kent was dedicated to St Werburgh (Everitt, *Continuity*, p. 240).

[9] Below p. 19; Brooks, *Canterbury*, pp. 187–91; Everitt, *Continuity*, pp. 181–94. J. Blair, 'Minster churches in the landscape', *Anglo-Saxon Settlements*, ed. D. Hooke, Oxford 1988, pp. 35–58.

[10] Everitt, *Continuity*, pp. 194–6; Campbell no. 12 (*CS* 253); for the estates at Domesday see below.

Wessex under 686–7. It was probably at about this time that Kent lost its westernmost elements. Mere geography ensured that any invasion of Kent would fall first, and perhaps most heavily, on Rochester rather than Canterbury. The church was to suffer many later disasters, but it is tempting to look to these early wars as the agents for the destruction of much of the original character of the diocese.

II. Rochester from the Death of Bede to the Norman Conquest

If the narrative sources for the history of Rochester after Bede are slight, the loss is partly made good by the survival of a series of more than thirty documents dealing with the rights of the church between 734 and 1012. In these one can trace, if imperfectly, the growth of the endowment and the political fortunes of the diocese until the coming of Bishop Gundulf in 1077 and a new beginning.

Between 738 and 841 the charters record a series of substantial gifts within the diocese, made by independent kings of Kent with or without the consent of the Mercian king, then by the Mercian kings alone, and finally by the kings of Wessex who incorporated Kent in their lordship decisively after 827. The shifting pattern of grantors reflects the long struggle for hegemony in Kent, and one or two of the charters hint at the losses that Rochester suffered from the wars.[11]

More generally, however, the impression is that these were years of growing prosperity. The number of sulungs granted is around sixty. It is pretty clear that all these assessments had changed considerably before Domesday, usually downwards, but the total is five times greater than the twelve sulungs at which the probable earlier endowments of Southfleet and Stone were valued in 1066. Some of the apparent grants may be restorations, some of the earlier endowments may have been lost without trace before the conquest, but the surviving evidence suggests that it was only between 738 and 841 that Rochester secured an endowment remotely appropriate to its episcopal rank. It is the more frustrating that all that can be inferred about the nature of the community at Rochester in these years is that there was already a cult of St Paulinus before the end of the eighth century.[12]

The Danish invasions brought this period of growth to an end. In 835 the Anglo-Saxon Chronicle reports an attack on Sheppey, in 841 there was severe fighting in Kent and in 842 'there was a great slaughter in London and Quentavic and in Rochester'. Between 851 and 865 the Danish army frequently wintered in Thanet or Sheppey, and there were determined attacks on Canterbury and East Kent.

---

[11] Campbell nos 2–20. According to Campbell no. 34 Wouldham had also been granted to Rochester by King Aethelberht (probably the king in Kent 725–62), but had been lost again before the reign of King Edmund (939–46). Compare below pp. 6–7. Brooks, *Canterbury*, pp. 111–49, esp. p. 115, suggests that Campbell nos 13–14 are restorations of the gifts recorded in nos 5, 9–10 after a confiscation, rather than fresh grants.

[12] Campbell nos 12, 18. The rather later lists of resting-places of the English saints have only Paulinus in the diocese, D.W. Rollason, 'Lists of saints' resting-places in Anglo-Saxon England', *Anglo-Saxon England*, vii (1978), 88, 91.

After a lull the Danes returned and laid siege to Rochester in 885, though they were driven off by King Alfred. In 892 an army under Haesten came up the Thames with eighty ships and wintered at Milton, but was defeated at Benfleet the next year; some of his ships were taken to Rochester.[13]

In the context of these long wars it is not surprising that the flow of gifts to Rochester slowed down. In 855 Aethelwulf of Wessex granted a ten sulung estate south of Rochester to Dunn, which Dunn later left to the church, but the remaining grants directly to Rochester of Cuxton and other lands command little confidence in their present form.[14] A late tradition claimed that King Alfred gave Bishop 'Burhic' the first lands of the see beyond the diocese, in Freckenham and Isleham in 895. Although Rochester seems to have acquired some rights there before 1076, the extant charter of Alfred is a crude forgery, and the earliest efforts to provide some account of the origins of the claim do not appear before the end of the twelfth century.[15]

Between 942x6 and 1012 the records of Rochester become substantial again, and in some ways they are a good deal more informative. The first and simplest of the sequence is a grant of three sulungs at Malling.[16] The second is a complex account of the estate at Wouldham, which Rochester claimed to have lost in the time of King Edmund, to have been given again under the will of Aelfege, and to have recovered from Aelfege's kin at a great plea at Erith in the presence of the communities of London, Christ Church and Rochester with their bishops and the shire reeve before 988. In 995 a solemn diploma of King Aethelred II recorded his grant of the estate to Bishop Godwine in perpetuity. The text suggests that this was an act of penitence for former misdeeds, and may indicate that Rochester had temporarily lost Wouldham again in 986, when the Anglo-Saxon Chronicle records that 'the king laid waste the diocese of Rochester'.[17]

A further cluster of texts concerns the confused history of the largest single benefaction ever made to Rochester. Most present some difficulties, but the essential document is the will of Byrhtric and Aelfswith his wife, written soon after the death of King Edgar. They made a long series of gifts to the king and other men and churches, but Rochester received the lion's share. The church was to have two sulungs at Denton, two at Longfield, and the reversion of Fawkham (later reckoned

---

[13] *Anglo-Saxon Chronicle* s.ann.; *Alfred the Great: Asser's Life of King Alfred and Other Contemporary Sources*, trans. and ed. S. Keynes and M. Lapidge, London 1983, pp. 86, 116 and nn.

[14] Campbell, pp. xxiii–vi, nos 21–7. For some recent comment see Brooks, *Canterbury*, p. 168 and nn.

[15] For the good evidence of earlier title see below, n. 21. Alfred's charter is *CS* 571 (omitted by Campbell); for other late tradition *Registrum*, pp. 5, 358–9. For later Freckenham forgeries see Brett, 'Forgery', 405–7.

[16] Campbell no. 28; Rochester later claimed it had lost the larger estate at Wouldham in his reign, Campbell no. 34.

[17] The fullest account of this attack is given by Sulcard in B.W. Scholz, 'Sulcard, "Prologus de construccione Westmonasterii" ', *Traditio*, xx (1964), 89; Osbern in *Memorials of St Dunstan*, ed. W. Stubbs, Rolls Series, London 1874, p. 117 and *The Chronicle of John of Worcester*, ed. R. Darlington and P. McGurk, Oxford Medieval Texts 1995, i, 424–5, all supporting S. Keynes, *The Diplomas of King Æthelred 'the Unready'*, Cambridge 1980, pp. 178–80 against Campbell no. 31 and p. xxi.

at two sulungs), Snodland (a six sulung estate in Domesday, which had apparently been granted to Rochester by Ecgberht of Wessex in 838, but had presumably since been lost), Bromley (apparently a ten sulung estate in the mid-tenth century, though later rated at six), and Darenth, as well as valuable rents for the celebration of their obit and a sum of gold with plate in gold and silver. Snodland, Fawkham and Bromley were said to have been first given in the reign of Edgar, but to have been recovered by the family in the troubled times after Edgar's death.

The year after he laid waste the diocese Aethelred II granted Bromley to one of his thegns, but in 995, the same year that he restored Wouldham, he restored Bromley to Bishop Godwine. Then or soon afterwards the bishop also recovered Snodland by a judgement of East and West Kent at Canterbury.[18] Though no charter records the return of the other lands, all but Darenth appear in Domesday as in the lordship of the bishop.

It is probable that a list of estates liable for the maintenance of Rochester bridge belongs to about this period. If so it may provide some indication of the extent of the church's endowment; it shows the bishop contributing from Borstall, Cuxton, Frindsbury, Stoke, Halling, Trottiscliffe, Southfleet, Stone, Fawkham and Pinden. However, Wouldham is entered under the king's land and Snodland under the archbishop; some of the other disputed estates may have been subsumed under more general headings. Whatever the date of the document, it is clearly likely that the distribution of duties reflects yet earlier conditions, but it does suggest at least the core of the Rochester estates before the conquest.[19]

In 1012 Bishop Godwine went beyond the recovery of lost estates, for King Aethelred granted him a considerable estate of fifteen hides at Fenstanton in Huntingdonshire. What lay behind this gift is unknown, and it seems to have been short-lived. At any rate the land had passed to one Ulf by 1066, and Rochester's claims seem to have been forgotten after Aethelred's charter was entered in the *Textus Roffensis*.[20]

The loss of Fenstanton was probably only one, and not the worst, of the losses suffered by Rochester over the next two generations. By the time the first Norman bishop was appointed in 1076 the church was said to have lost control of Freckenham in Suffolk and a number of estates nearer home, including Fawkham and Stoke, and to have been reduced to extreme poverty.[21]

The explanation of this apparent decline may lie partly in the second wave of

---

[18] Campbell pp. xx–xxii, nos 29–37; Robertson, *Charters*, nos lix, lxix; E.E. Barker, 'The Bromley Charters', *Archaeologia Cantiana*, xciii (1977), 179–85.

[19] Robertson, *Charters*, no. lii; recently N.P. Brooks, 'Church, Crown and Community: Public Work and Seigneurial Responsibilities at Rochester Bridge', in *Warriors and Churchmen in the High Middle Ages. Essays presented to Karl Leyser*, ed. T. Reuter, London 1992, 1–20 has shown how rash it would be to draw conclusions from the list on the lordship of pre-conquest estates.

[20] Campbell no. 33; *Domesday*, i, 207.

[21] Compare J. Le Patourel, 'The reports of the trial on Penenden Heath', *Studies in Medieval History presented to Frederick Maurice Powicke*, ed. R.W. Hunt, W.A. Pantin and R.W. Southern, Oxford 1948, 24–6; D. Bates, 'The land pleas of William I's reign: Penenden Heath revisited', *Bulletin of the Institute of Historical Research*, li (1978), 1–19. The records of Penenden Heath and the related documents make it clear that Rochester had a long-standing claim to Freckenham. According to

Danish attacks on Kent, first recorded in 980 and frequent between 991 and 1016. In 999 the army laid siege to Rochester for some days, and a force from Canterbury was heavily defeated when it attempted to bring relief. In 1012 Bishop Godwine himself was captured with his archbishop.[22]

If these wars did not prevent some benefactions to the church, they must have weakened the bishop's resources for defending or enlarging the endowment further.[23] It is possible that Denton had never been effectively under Rochester's control, though Domesday gives no indication that there were other claimants. With Stoke on the other hand we have more detail, for the Domesday entry records that Earl Godwin had bought the estate from two men of the bishop without his consent or that of the community. It seems to have been yet another example of the heavy hand of the earl on the churches of Kent which lies behind many of the pleas of Lanfranc against Odo of Bayeux as Godwin's successor in title after the conquest[24]

Remarkably little can be known of the character of the life of the cathedral clergy before the Norman conquest. Bede tells us that King Aethelberht provided support for a community, though nothing of its character, and after that near complete darkness falls until the conversion to a monastic chapter under Bishop Gundulf. In 1077 it appears that there were no more than five canons at Rochester, one of whom, the priest Aethelric, was priest of Chatham and gave a tenement in Rochester to the cathedral for the soul of his wife Godgyva.[25] On general grounds it is likely that the original clerks lived under some form of common life. The dedication to St Andrew may well reflect the patronage of Gregory the Great's own monastery, though a monastic community within the cathedral itself is scarcely credible at this date. It is possible to read Gregory I's letters in such a way as to make Justus, the first bishop, a monk, but the origin of most of the other pre-conquest bishops is thoroughly obscure. The last before the conquest was later said to have been a former abbot of Chertsey, and many of his predecessors probably had been monks, as virtually every bishop of every see in England was between 980 and 1032, but it cannot be proved, and there is certainly no evidence that any of them sought to introduce monastic observance either at their cathedral or elsewhere in the diocese.[26]

For the rest we have only two charters to give even a hint of the character of the

the thirteenth century *Registrum*, p. 5 Rochester acquired the title under Alfred (cf. above n. 15) and lost it under Bishop Aelfstan [after 955 x before 995].

22 *Anglo-Saxon Chronicle* s. ann.; *Chronicle of John of Worcester*, i, 448–9, 468–9.

23 Brooks, *Canterbury*, pp. 282–7.

24 *DMon* p. 98; D. Bates, 'The character and career of Odo, bishop of Bayeux 1049/50 – 1097', *Speculum*, l (1975), 9–10; Brooks, *Canterbury*, pp. 300–2; Odo was remembered at Rochester as a benefactor, not a predator, *Custumale*, p. 37, *Textus*, f. 211v no. 203.

25 *Textus*, ff. 172 no. 86, 190v no. 158; compare *Vita*, pp. 40–1, Bethell, 'Miracles', 429, *Eadmeri Historia Nouorum in Anglia*, ed. M. Rule, Rolls series, London 1884, p. 15.

26 *Registrum*, pp. 3–4; F. Barlow, *The English Church 1000–1066*, London 1979, pp. 62–6; *Flores*, i, 578 (following BL Cotton ms. Vespasian A xxii, f. 27); R.A.L. Smith, 'The early community of St Andrew at Rochester 604 – c.1080', *English Historical Review*, lx (1945), 289–99. Monks at the dependency of St Peter Ghent at Lewisham, granted in the tenth century, are first clearly attested in 1193 or so; *Heads of Religious Houses England and Wales 940–1216*, ed. D. Knowles etc., Cambridge 1972, p. 105. *Chartes et Documents de l'abbaye de . . . Gand*, ed. A. van Lokeren, Ghent 1868–71, no. 308 should be dated 1229, not 1167.

cathedral community. The first is an edict of the Council of *Clofesho* of 803, attested by thirteen bishops, each with some of their clergy, often six. Bishop Waermund here appears with five priests and a deacon; his successor, Beornmod, is probably the priest who appears among the clergy of Archbishop Aethelheard.[27]

A second charter is of greater interest, for it is the only surviving charter in the name of a pre-conquest bishop of Rochester. It is a grant by Swithwulf and the *higan* at Rochester of half a sulung in Frindsbury to the priest Beorhtwulf. It survives in a contemporary single sheet written by a local scribe, who also produced a charter of King Aethelberht of Wessex granting Bromley to Dyryhtwald in 862 and a blundered version of another grant of Aethelberht to Rochester itself.[28] It is witnessed by the bishop, ealdorman Sigehelm,[29] Eallhere the *minister*, three priests, Ceolmund the archdeacon and one deacon. It is reasonable to suppose that the clergy are members of the community at Rochester. Archdeacon Ceolmund is particularly interesting, for the office is first attested at Canterbury in the early ninth century, only to vanish again after 870 until the Norman conquest. Ceolmund, presumably Swithwulf's successor at Rochester, is the only clear case of an archdeacon known outside Canterbury throughout the Anglo-Saxon period.[30] The tiny glimpse into the community is striking, as is the suggestion that at least one bishop was drawn from within the community.[31]

Of the books of Rochester before the conquest only a handful survive, certainly a grand two volume set of homilies in English of the early eleventh century, possibly a second English homiliary, a tenth-century copy of Statius and another set of Latin homilies, just possibly a copy of Juvenal. The two-volume homiliary may not have been written at Rochester, but it was annotated and supplemented there.[32] The catalogue of the monastic library of 1123–4 in the *Textus Roffensis* does not suggest that a much larger number of pre-conquest books survived in the twelfth century.[33]

---

[27] *CS* 312, though the witness list in this elaborate form is found only in copies, not the contemporary single-sheet version.

[28] *CS* 562; the script is identified as that of Campbell nos 24–5 in Brooks, *Canterbury*, pp. 168–9.

[29] Presumably the same as the Sigehelm whose death with many of the men of Kent is recorded in the Anglo-Saxon Chronicle under 904/5.

[30] Brooks, *Canterbury*, p. 162, citing particularly M. Deanesly, 'The Archdeacons of Canterbury under Archbishop Ceolnoth', *English Historical Review*, xlii (1927), 1–11; C.N.L. Brooke, 'The Archdeacon and the Norman Conquest', *Tradition and Change. Essays in honour of Marjorie Chibnall*, ed. D. Greenway etc., Cambridge 1985, 1–19.

[31] Compare case of Tobias above (p. 2).

[32] Oxford, Bodl. Lib. mss. Bodley 340, 342 (N.R. Ker, *Catalogue of Manuscripts Containing Anglo-Saxon*, Oxford 1957, no. 309). BL Royal ms. 15 C x is a tenth-century copy of Statius written outside England; it was certainly at Rochester in the thirteenth century, but it is not clear when it got there. An eleventh-century copy of Juvenal (Oxford Bodl. ms. Wood B.3) cannot be shown to have been at Rochester before the fourteenth century. K. Waller, 'Rochester cathedral library, an English book collection based on Norman models', *Les Mutations Socio-culturelles au tournant des XIe–XIIe siècles*, ed. R. Foreville, Paris 1984, p. 240, would add the collection of Latin homilies in BL Royal ms. 2 C iii. Richards, *Texts*, pp. 2–3, 86–110 treats the Latin homilies as post-conquest, but would add Cambridge, Corpus Christi College ms. 162.

[33] *Textus*, ff. 224–30, printed in Richards, *Texts*, pp. 23–32; compare Waller, *op. cit.*, p. 240. To identify a pre-conquest book from the summary titles of the catalogue is however more or less impossible.

Relations with Canterbury before the Norman Conquest

Between the time of Gundulf and the early thirteenth century Rochester stood in a position of unique dependence on Canterbury. It is difficult to determine how far this dependence had ancient roots. In general, one would not expect to find more than the characteristic subordination of any bishop to his metropolitan, and Rochester later asserted that the conquest brought about a revolution. The post-conquest subordination of Rochester was closely related to the function of the bishop as standing deputy to an archbishop whose estates and travels extended far beyond the diocese. Before the time of Lanfranc this function seems to have been performed, at least occasionally, by a *chorepiscopus* based at St Martin's.[34]

However, Rochester's position clearly had anomalous qualities well before the conquest. According to Eadmer, Lanfranc appointed the first Norman bishops in the chapter of Canterbury 'according to custom'.[35] While this may be a piece of twelfth-century anachronism, even the earliest Lives of St Dunstan seem to represent Rochester as bound to Canterbury by exacting if unspecified ties.[36] The only surviving pre-conquest profession of obedience of a bishop of Rochester to Canterbury (Beornmod to Aethelheard in c.804) may also indicate something of the sort. Most of these early professions use more stringent terms of submission than was usual later, but that for Beornmod includes a promise not made by other suffragans in the ninth century:

> Should I transgress any of these promises . . . you will strive to correct this with all your mind and strength according to the authority of your office, while you will not cease to be a teacher and support to my weakness.[37]

There is no other substantial or continuous evidence for this subjection before the conquest. It probably derived such content as it had from the great gulf that divided the wealthy archbishop and his powerful community from the impoverished bishop and the few canons of his church. In Domesday the archbishop held extensive estates in West Kent; they exceeded the value of those of Rochester even within the diocese, and they included a number of ancient churches which one would expect to have had closer relations with the diocesan.[38] In later years the Canterbury lands and churches were defined as peculiars, outside the jurisdiction of Rochester, and they covered half the diocese. Well before the conquest the bishop was scarcely master of his own house.

---

[34] *Vita Lanfranci*, ed. M. Gibson, in *Lanfranco di Pavia e l'Europa del Secolo XI* (Italia Sacra 51, 1993), p. 708; *Gervase*, ii, 361; for later tradition compare *Anglia Sacra*, ed. H. Wharton, London 1691, i, 150 from Canterbury with the Rochester versions in 'Registrum Temporalium', DRb/Ar 2, f. 2v and *Registrum*, p. 51.

[35] *Eadmeri Historia Nouorum*, ed. Rule, p. 2.

[36] *Memorials of St Dunstan*, ed. Stubbs, pp. 61, 108, 200, 293; F. Barlow, *The English Church 1000 – 1066*, London 1979, pp. 221–2.

[37] *Canterbury Professions*, ed. M. Richter, Canterbury and York Society lxvii (1973), no. 6, freely translated. It may be significant that Beornmod had been a priest of the archbishop (above, p. 9).

[38] E.g. Wrotham, Northfleet, Crayford, Eynsford (Everitt, *Continuity*, p. 194).

III. The Norman Conquest and the Foundation of the Monastic Chapter

Siward, the last Anglo-Saxon bishop of Rochester, survived the wholesale deprivations in the years after the conquest, and died in office in 1072x4. He was succeeded briefly by Arnost, a monk of Bec who had been prior of Archbishop Lanfranc's former abbey at Caen, but Arnost died within months, and was succeeded in turn by Gundulf.

Gundulf is the first bishop of Rochester of whom we can know anything substantial, and in many ways the most influential. Born c.1023 of a modest family in the Vexin, he entered the monastery of Bec around 1058, at the same time as Anselm, the later archbishop. The friendship they formed there was to last for the rest of their long lives. Gundulf followed Lanfranc to the new ducal monastery at Caen, and when Lanfranc became archbishop in 1070 Gundulf seems to have accompanied him to Canterbury, where he played a leading part in his household. His relations with Lanfranc and Anselm after him seem to have been exceptionally close.[39] Gundulf must have been over fifty when he became bishop, but he was to display great energy over the next thirty years. His biographer is concerned almost exclusively with his monastic life, his impassioned devotions and paternal care for the monks. Though the biographer may well have been engaged, at least in part, in a polemic against some of Gundulf's successors, his account is amply confirmed by the evidence of the reconstructed cathedral, and Gundulf's regular attendance at the translation of saints outside the diocese.[40] He was also clearly a man of marked ability in the world beyond the cloister. Though he seems to have been a uniquely loyal supporter of Anselm in his disputes with William Rufus and Henry I, it is remarkable that both kings treated him with quite uncharacteristic consideration. The flood of benefactions from his neighbours shows that he could also attract the goodwill of a much larger circle. In the great revolt against William II in 1088 we are told that Gundulf was able to mediate between the parties with exceptional success.[41] In two celebrated passages from the *Textus Roffensis* we are also told that Gundulf was unusually skilled in building, for he played an important part in the work of the two great royal fortresses of London and Rochester.

Though the collected letters of Anselm include more addressed to Gundulf than to anyone but king and pope, only one surviving letter to him is attributed to Gundulf, and that on slender grounds.[42] The most powerful evidence of his exceptional talents is found in the circle of his friendships and the magnitude of his achievements.

---

[39] *Vita*, pp. 25–38, 69; *Memorials of St Dunstan*, ed. Stubbs, pp. 413–4; M. Gibson, *Lanfranc of Bec*, Oxford 1978, pp. 155–6; R.W. Southern, *St Anselm; a Portrait in a Landscape*, Cambridge 1990, pp. 14–18, 31, 107, 144–7 and the literature there cited. The chronology of the *Vita* is partly confirmed by the Bec profession list in A.A. Porée, *Histoire de l'abbaye du Bec*, Evreux 1901, i, 629.

[40] Compare *Acta Sanctorum*, May vi, 413, 422; *Lives of Edward the Confessor*, ed. H.R. Luard, Rolls Series, London 1858, p. 156 line 4645 and below, p. 16 and n. 69.

[41] *Vita*, pp. 49–51.

[42] *Sancti Anselmi Cantuariensis Archiepiscopi Opera Omnia*, ed. F. S. Schmitt, Edinburgh 1946–61, v, no. 365.

Once in office, archbishop and bishop together set about a fundamental reconstruction of the impoverished see. By the time Gundulf died, after thirty years in office, his church had been transformed. The five canons of the old foundation had given way to some sixty monks under the Benedictine rule,[43] the estates of the church had been much extended, and a new cathedral far larger then the old one had risen beside the walls of the Norman castle. Thanks to the rich detail incorporated in the *Textus Roffensis*, compiled a generation after Gundulf's death, Rochester, formerly so ill-recorded, becomes perhaps the best documented cathedral community of its time.

The Lands of the Church

The first stage of the reshaping of the church began even before Gundulf's arrival, with a series of pleas conducted by Lanfranc against those who detained lands of the church throughout Kent. The records of the pleas of Penenden Heath present many difficulties, but the earliest versions agree that Rochester regained control of lost estates at Stoke and Denton somewhere between 1072 and 1076, and probably other rights too.[44] Once Gundulf and Lanfranc established monks at the cathedral new acquisitions followed in rapid succession.

The *Textus* records a great number of grants from this time, of several different kinds. For the first time the cathedral acquired a number of important estates and rights outside the diocese, in Canterbury,[45] in Chichester, where Gilbert of Clare gave the church of Rotherfield in Sussex, apparently in compensation for the outliers of Rochester manors incorporated in his league of Tonbridge, [46] and in Suffolk, where Roger Bigod gave the church and land of Walton, later to become a small dependent priory, and Ranulf fitz Walter gave tithes and a render of eight thousand eels from Saxmundham.[47]

Two manors which were to be major elements of the endowment were acquired under William Rufus. The first was the forty hide manor of Haddenham in Buckinghamshire, valued in Domesday at £40 with land for forty ploughs, and there said to be in the hands of Archbishop Lanfranc. He had acquired it for life from William I, reputedly with the intention of granting it to Rochester. King William II

---

[43] *Vita*, pp. 40–1; Bethell, 'Miracles', 429.

[44] For the records see above p. 7 n. 21. The date is uncertain, for all the versions agree on the presence of Bishop Arnost, which seems to place the plea in 1076. On the other hand the 'Acta Lanfranci' in *Two of the Saxon Chronicles Parallel*, ed. C. Plummer, Oxford 1892–9, i, 289 and several later texts date the plea 1072. Though the Penenden records seem to attribute the recovery of Freckenham to this period the date is obscure. A purported charter of King William II in DRb/ Ar 2, f. 17v (unprinted) is spurious. It claims that Rochester had lost virtually all its estates before Penenden. *Textus*, f. 174v–5 no. 89 (*Registrum*, p. 27, *Regesta*, i, no. 248) may be a genuine if unspecific confirmation by King William I consequent on the plea.

[45] *Textus*, ff. 185v no. 121, 188r–v nos 132–3 (*Regesta*, ii, no. 901), 134–6; *Registrum*, pp. 168, 342–3, 402.

[46] *Textus*, ff. 175 no. 90, 182v no. 100 (*Regesta*, i, no. 450); *Registrum*, pp. 590–6; J.C. Ward, 'The Lowy of Tonbridge and the Lands of the Clare Family in Kent, 1066–1217', *Archaeologia Cantiana*, xcvi (1980), 124–5; Brett, 'Forgery', 405.

[47] *Textus*, ff. 182r–v no. 100 (*Regesta*, i, no. 452), 185v no. 120.

demanded £100 for a royal charter of confirmation to Rochester in 1088, but remitted the money in return for Gundulf's work in building the castle at Rochester.[48]

The second case is more complex. In Domesday the church of Lambeth is said to have land for twelve ploughs held directly from the king. It had formerly been in the lordship of the Countess Goda, Edward the Confessor's sister, whose second husband had been Count Eustace of Boulogne; she was probably dead well before 1066.[49] In 1088 King William confirmed Lambeth to Rochester as the countess had had it, and he had held it in demesne since, in part as compensation for the damage done at the siege of Rochester that year. However, later Rochester tradition treated the countess herself as a great benefactor, and the first keeper of the manor for the monks brought a great number of the treasures of the countess to the cathedral, including her celebrated gospel-book which still survives.[50] It is likely that Goda made the original grant before the conquest, and that the king did no more than confirm it after a long delay, though many problems remain.

These grants show Gundulf and his monks acquiring lands on a considerable scale outside the diocese from the king, the archbishop and great men among the new Norman settlers. The numerous smaller benefactions within the diocese reveal a more complex pattern of relationships. The king was still important both as donor and guarantor of the gifts of others; before Gundulf's death Henry I granted four valuable royal churches,[51] Archbishop Anselm gave the church at Northfleet, and Haimo the king's steward gave the church of Dartford.[52] Other rights were given by Normans of more modest rank, Robert of St Amand and Gosfrid Talbot.[53]

It is clear from a large number of lesser gifts that the cathedral also attracted the benefactions of many Englishmen. When Gundulf was working on the Tower of London he lodged with Eadmer one-hand, who gave Rochester his valuable fish-weir at Gillingham; the forty-shilling rent due to the archbishops was subsequently remitted by Anselm and his successors.[54] A stream of grants of town property in Rochester, tithes and portions of marsh in the Isle of Grain came from other Englishmen. Most are said to make their grants in return for fraternity with the house, but several, such as Aethelnoth of Hoo, Eadmer of Darenth, Goldwin the Greek or Goldwin the priest made their gifts with their sons who became monks in the priory.[55]

A striking case is provided by Robert Latimer and his family, who were closely involved with the church. Robert was a servant of sheriff Haimo, and appears often in the Domesday survey of Kent, holding manors at farm from Bishop Odo of

---

[48] *Textus*, ff. 173–4v no. 88, 212–3 no. 205 (*Regesta*, i, no. 301); *Vita*, p. 50; Brett, 'Forgery', 403 and note.

[49] *The Carmen de Hastingae Proelio of Guy, Bishop of Amiens*, ed. C. Morton and H. Muntz, Oxford 1972, pp. xxxix–xli, 123 rehearses the earlier literature.

[50] *Domesday*, i, 34; *Textus*, f. 211 no. 202 (for later manipulation of the text see Brett, 'Forgery', 403); *Custumale*, p. 37; *Registrum*, pp. 2, 119 (showing that many of Goda's treasures were still at Lambeth when Rochester acquired it); BL Royal ms. 1 D iii.

[51] *Textus*, ff. 177v–8 no. 92, 186v–7 nos 127–8 (*Regesta*, ii, nos 516–7).

[52] *Textus*, ff. 179–80 nos 93–5, 181v–2 nos 97–8 (*Regesta*, i, 451); these entries are all on added leaves.

[53] *Textus*, ff. 185 no. 116, 187r–v no. 130 (*Regesta*, ii, no. 647), 189v no. 146.

[54] *Textus*, ff. 210v no. 201, 179r–v nos 93–4, 181v no. 98, 187 no. 129 (*Regesta*, ii, no. 776).

[55] *Textus*, ff. 182v–86v nos 101–26, 188v–92 nos 134–64.

Bayeux and a small tenement from the abbot of St Augustine; he may also have
farmed Otford, the archbishop's chief manor in West Kent. His wife held land from
the bishop of Rochester in Frindsbury, his brother Aelfwine was the royal reeve of
Chatham and father of Godric the reeve and Aelfric the priest, his daughter married
Brodo the priest. All these appear as witnesses to priory transactions, and several
were modest benefactors of the church. It would be hard to find a better example of
an English family which quickly came to terms with the conquest and contributed
to the prosperity of the reformed cathedral.[56]

The increase in the wealth of the church should not be exaggerated; it is impossible
to tell whether the new revenues provided an income proportionate to the greater
expense of the enlarged community. Calculations of the wealth of cathedrals at
Domesday are fraught with uncertainties, particularly since they largely omit the
return from ecclesiastical renders, notably tithes, and from churches. The survey of
the lands of Rochester also gives no value for the property of the church in the city
of Rochester, though this was certainly substantial.[57] Even so, the lands of the bishop
and monks of Rochester in 1086, adding in Haddenham and Lambeth, were valued
at some £250 in all. This still left Rochester among the poorest of English dioceses.[58]
Christ Church and St Augustine at Canterbury were both far richer. Even so, the
bishop and monks now enjoyed rights in a much greater number of churches, and
had far wider interests than their predecessors.

The creation of a large cathedral priory necessarily involved some arrangements
for dividing the revenues of the church between bishop and monks; the bishop had
duties which took him far from the church for long periods, and required some
distinct provision for his household.[59] Such divisions were being undertaken widely
by Gundulf's contemporaries, abbots as well as bishops, and most proved
contentious.[60] At Rochester it became a burning issue in the century after Gundulf's
death. An unfortunate consequence is that the later testimony on the arrangements
under Gundulf is at best polemical, at worst manifest forgery. There is general
agreement that Gundulf did make such a division, but the only evidence of its nature
that seems trustworthy is that in the *Textus Roffensis*, and this is ambiguous. A charter
of King Henry I appears to confirm to the monks roughly half the lands of the church
(according to Domesday values) and all the lands and revenues acquired by Gundulf

56 The dynasty can be reconstructed from: *Textus*, ff. 182v no. 101, 198v–9v no. 183, 200 no. 186,
    200v–1 no. 187, 211v–2 no. 204; *Registrum*, pp. 370–1; *Domesday*, i.6b–8b, 11b–12; *DMon* pp.
    87, 101.
57 There are three early versions of the 1086 survey of the Rochester lands, the Exchequer and
    Canterbury versions (printed together in *DMon* pp. 95–8), and that in *Textus*, ff. 209–10 no. 199.
    There are enough minute variations of content and arrangement to show that each is independent.
    The first indication of the importance of the revenues of the city is in *Textus*, f. 196 no. 176, where
    Gundulf assigned £11 10s to the clothing of the monks from Rochester and its mill; no other estate
    rendered half as much for the purpose.
58 M. Brett, *The English Church under Henry I*, Oxford 1975, p. 103 n. The Rochester calculation
    there is too high, for it certainly includes some income devoted to the monks.
59 See the instructive example of the bishop's baker and the monks in *Custumale*, p. 28.
60 M. Howell, 'Abbatial vacancies and the divided *mensa* in medieval England', *Journal of
    Ecclesiastical History*, xxxiii (1982), 173–92.

during his pontificate. The original form of this grant is apparently genuine, though it was later altered.[61] The *Textus* also includes a list of revenues amounting to some £50 which Gundulf assigned to the clothing of the monks. The income was derived from manors, churches, and tithes, so it cannot readily be compared with the Domesday figures. Nor is it clear whether Gundulf made similar provision for the other needs of the priory, such as food, the sacristy and so on. The apparent incompatibility of the list and the charter must raise a doubt whether Gundulf did make a formal division of either the estates or the churches, at least in the form the monks were later to claim.[62]

A similar doubt attends the remarkable arrangement for the celebration of the patronal feast, the *xenium*. This appears first in a very dubious charter said to be the product of the last year of Gundulf's life. It provides that the manors (except Lambeth and Haddenham) listed in the charter of King Henry for the monks should contribute to the bishop or his successors celebrating the feast each year sixteen sucking pigs, thirty geese, three hundred hens, a thousand lampreys and a thousand eggs, four salmon, sixty bundles of wheat and a load of oats, of which the monks should have half the eggs and fish. The monks were also to have five hundred lampreys from Lambeth and twenty shillings of fish from Haddenham for their cellar. This abundant provision would then be divided equally between the bishop and the monks. Should the bishop be absent for any reason the render was to be dispensed by the monks for alms and hospitality.[63] This arrangement gave rise to passionate dispute at the end of the century between the monks and Bishop Gilbert, but by then some version of it seems to have been accepted as long current. It is clearly likely that Gundulf did make some special provision for the feast of St Andrew, though the earliest surviving form can scarcely represent it precisely.

The Monastic Community

It is said that Gundulf and Archbishop Lanfranc determined to establish monks at the cathedral soon after 1077. The *Life of Gundulf* places the change before the death of William I in 1087, and the thirteenth-century Vespasian annals date it 1083.[64] Since Lanfranc had been abbot of the recently founded house of St Stephen at Caen, and Gundulf was a monk and possibly prior there too, the decision might not cause much surprise. However, it was a remarkable event. The monastic chapters at

---

[61] *Vita*, p. 60. The altered original of Henry's charter is DRc/ T50, the earlier form is *Textus*, ff. 218–20 no. 211 (*Regesta*, ii, no. 636, dated 1103, mostly in the original hand of the cartulary), cited in *Vita*, pp. 49, 60. See further Brett, 'Forgery', 402–3, 408–9.

[62] *Textus*, f. 196 no. 176, undated but it must have been drawn up after the grant of Northfleet by Anselm. The sources of the revenues in the list do not coincide with those of the king's charter. Perhaps Gundulf made the different provision of 1103 later, but if so it is hard to explain the survival of the earlier one in the *Textus*, written well after his death.

[63] *Registrum*, pp. 6–7, for which see below p. 19 n. 89. The text is often ambiguous, possibly because it represents a later rehandling of an earlier and shorter grant; *Custumale*, pp. 35–6.

[64] *Vita*, pp. 40–1 and n. The same date reappears in *Flores*, ii,12. For William I's only charter for the church see above p. 12 n. 44; he left valuable treasures to the church at his death, *Textus*, f. 177v no. 92.

Canterbury, Winchester and Worcester in 1066 had no contemporary parallels in Europe, and a variety of sources suggest that the first instinct of the new Norman bishops was to dismantle them.[65]

In the event all survived, and over the next two generations they multiplied. In most cases this happened because an existing see was moved to, or new one established at, an older monastery. Norwich was the exception, where the see was moved to a new site designed from the outset for a monastic community. The only true parallel with Rochester is at Durham, where Bishop William, the former monk of St Carilef, replaced the earlier clerks of St Cuthbert with monks in the very year that Rochester is said to have been changed. The influence of Canterbury was to be powerful in both houses, and the change must owe a good deal to Lanfranc's own wishes. Certainly the archbishop played a key role in carrying through the plan; even in the thirteenth century the monks of Rochester remembered him as their joint founder.[66]

No body of monastic customs specific to Rochester has been preserved, but it seems overwhelmingly likely that the liturgical cycle was modelled closely on that of Canterbury. The customary of Lanfranc is well-known, and Rochester almost certainly owned a copy in 1123–4.[67] If this was what Gundulf introduced, then his monks lived under a version of the rule very close indeed to that practised at Cluny, the most powerful and influential of Latin monasteries of the age. More direct, if flickering, light is cast on the character of the new community in a number of other sources.

Gundulf himself was accustomed to celebrate two masses a day in the cathedral, the mass of the day and the mass for the dead. The *Life* of Gundulf reports that the bishop excluded from the second all but the monks and novices, with the interesting implication that the High Mass was commonly attended by a much wider congregation.[68] The *Life* also records the solemn translation of St Paulinus, Rochester's only well-known saint, from the old church to the new; over the years Gundulf was to become a leading authority on the translation of saints.[69]

The original foundation is said to have been for twenty-two monks, apparently not formerly professed.[70] One or two of the monks of the new house seem to have been former canons of the older foundation,[71] but it is likely that there was a core of experienced monks who had been professed elsewhere. The first recorded prior,

---

[65] R.M.T. Hill and C.N.L. Brooke in *A History of York Minster*, ed. G.E. Aylmer and R. Cant, Oxford 1977, pp. 24–8.

[66] *Textus*, ff. 171–2v no. 86; *Vita*, p. 48n; *Custumale*, p. 37; *Registrum*, p. 120; Horstman (as n. 2 above), ii, 314.

[67] *Decreta Lanfranci Monachis Cantuariensis Transmissa*, ed. D. Knowles, *passim* and *Consuetudines Beccenses*, ed. M.P. Dickson, pp. xxx–xxxiv, Corpus consuetudinum monasticarum, iii/iv (1967); Richards, *Texts*, p. 31 no. 71: 'Item martyrologium de nataliciis sanctorum, et regula sancti Benedicti, consuetudinesque Lanfranci archiepiscopi in uno uolumine'.

[68] *Vita*, pp. 45–6.

[69] *Vita*, pp. 48, 53 and nn.; Horstman (as n. 2), ii, 314; St Ithamar was also moved to a position of new importance, Bethell, 'Miracles', 430.

[70] *Textus*, f. 172 no. 86, though Colin Flight has pointed out (see n. 117 below) that the number is over an erasure in another hand.

[71] *Vita*, pp. 40–1 and n.

Ernulf, was a Frenchman, if we may judge by his name.[72] Certainly the second, Ralph, was a monk of Caen who like Gundulf had been summoned to England by Lanfranc. In 1107, at the age of sixty, he became abbot of Battle, where he ruled with notable success until 1124.[73] A small number of his works survive, showing the strong imprint of the teaching of Anselm, and all seem to have been written while he was at Rochester.[74] He was succeeded in turn by Ordoin, in whose time we have a list of leading members of the community. Dunstan, a skilled craftsman, bears an English name, Paulinus the sacrist might be of either race, but William the sub-prior, Baldwin the cantor, Reginald the 'oeconomus', Richard de Clovilla, Ansketill 'de quo gaudent angeli' and Robert the chamberlain sound French. By this time however such tests are thoroughly unreliable.[75]

Something more is known of Baldwin the chanter, if he can be identified with Baldwin the monk who occurs elsewhere, for he was the brother of Adelold of Chelsfield, a minor tenant who gave the priory some tithes in his lifetime and his horses and arms at his death.[76] Adelold and Baldwin may have been either English or French, but Richard de Clovilla was almost certainly French, for his father William was a tenant of Gosfrid Talbot in Oakleigh who gave some tithes with his son.[77] At a similarly modest level Thurstan the monk was the son of Gerold, probably the man of Haimo the sheriff.[78] Others were of higher birth: the brothers of Haimo fitz Vitalis, a substantial land-holder in East Kent, and of Ansfrid the sheriff were the most notable.[79] There were clearly also a considerable proportion of monks of English birth.[80] Not all these were confined to the lesser offices, for Peter, son of Goldwin the Greek and brother of Goda of London, in due course became cantor; he was remembered for good works in the church, and his sister provided several vestments.[81] The survival of several books in the vernacular copied at Rochester after the conquest is no surprise.[82]

It is a special virtue of the Rochester sources that they provide brief histories of the lesser secular officers of the priory, the bakers, porters, infirmary servants and

---

[72] *Heads of Religious Houses England and Wales 940–1216*, ed. D. Knowles etc., Cambridge 1972, p. 63; the doubt suggested there may be resolved by the appearance of Prior Ernulf in the list of Rochester monks in BL Royal 5 B xvi f. 187 (early xii c.).

[73] *Chronicle of Battle Abbey*, ed. E. Searle, Oxford Medieval Texts 1980, pp. 116–33.

[74] R.W. Southern, *Saint Anselm. A Portrait in a Landscape*, Cambridge 1990, pp. 372–6.

[75] *The Vita Sancti Malchi of Reginald of Canterbury*, ed. L.R. Lind, Illinois Studies in Language and Literature, xxvii (1942), pp. 37–8. For Dunstan, Paulinus, Robert and William see further *Textus*, ff. 198r–v no. 181 (1107x8), 200v–1 no. 187, *Registrum*, p. 119. For Englishmen with French names compare among many Robert Latimer (above pp. 13–14), or the monk Richard, son of Goldwin the priest, *Textus*, ff. 199v–200 no. 184.

[76] *Textus*, ff. 184v–5v nos 114, 118, 121; f. 196 no. 176.

[77] *Custumale*, p. 12; *Textus*, f. 186 no. 123.

[78] *Textus*, f. 185 no. 117, 189v no. 145, 196 no. 176. *Textus*, f. 194v–5 nos 173–5 show that another monk was the son of Gausfrid, a man of Walter Tirel.

[79] *Textus*, f. 185v no. 121; *Registrum*, p. 119

[80] Among the early monks were the sons of Eadmer of Darenth, Goldwin the priest, and Goldwin son of Edith *Textus*, ff. 183v–4 no. 106, 191v–2 no. 164, 192v no. 167. Another, Nicholas, was the brother of Eluiua of Winchester, *Registrum*, p. 123.

[81] *Textus*, ff. 191v–2 no. 164, *Registrum*, pp. 123–4.

[82] Richards, *Texts*, pp. 90–4, and of course the *Textus* itself.

so on. Here too a jumble of English and French names from the earliest times suggests a blending of the two races from the outset.[83]

No other church in England provides so clear a picture of the way in which a monastery put down deep roots in local society in these years; though the sources are exceptionally rich, it need not be supposed that they record an unusual situation. With sources of equal scope one might expect to find a similar position at many other post-conquest monasteries.

The monks were probably more respectable than distinguished, for only two of them were promoted elsewhere in its early years, though both were remarkable. Ralph of Battle has already been mentioned; the other was Hugh of Trottiscliffe. Like a number of other monks who were keepers of priory estates, Hugh was remembered as a notable benefactor of the church. He had all the demesnes of the church marled, gave a number of vestments, built the infirmary chapel, and established a church for lepers dedicated to St Bartholomew. In 1126 he became abbot of St Augustine, Canterbury, where he ruled until 1151.[84] By 1095 or so the community was sufficiently secure and well-regarded for Eudo the king's steward to summon two of their number to help found his priory at Colchester, though with little success.[85] For the rest, the priory later remembered the early monks as diligent administrators, men who tended their lands and enriched their house with books and vestments, rather than teachers or actors on a larger stage.[86]

The Bishop and the Diocese

In the nature of his office, the bishop had to look further. In a widening circle of obligations, he had responsibilities to the clergy and people of his diocese, to the archbishop of Canterbury, and to the king.

The *Life of Gundulf* has its focus squarely on the relation of bishop and monks, yet it touches on his work elsewhere from time to time. We are shown Gundulf travelling about his diocese from manor to manor, even when infirmity reduced him to the use of a two-horse litter, or preaching to his people.[87]

The Norman conquest was followed by some re-organisation of diocesan life in every see of England. Apart from changes at the cathedral, the most characteristic signs of this are the appearance of archdeacons as agents of the bishop's disciplinary powers, the widespread celebration of synods of the diocese, increased concern with the regulation of the relations between local churches, and a multiplication of copies

---

[83] *Custumale*, pp. 28–30.

[84] *Registrum*, p. 119; *Custumale*, p. 37: *Heads* (as n. 72), p. 36; an infirmary chapel is already mentioned before Gundulf's death in *Vita*, p. 67. Compare too 'Registrum Temporalium', DRb/Ar 2, f. 2, where Gundulf 'Fundauit etiam hospitale sancti Bartholomei extra Roffam'.

[85] *Ungedruckte Anglo-Normannische Geschichtsquellen*, ed. F. Liebermann, Strassburg 1879, pp. 159–61.

[86] A judgement reinforced by a detailed study of its library, summarized in Richards, *Texts*, pp. 122–3.

[87] *Vita*, pp. 56, 63.

of the authoritative laws of the church.[88] Many of these changes can be shown to have occurred at Rochester under Gundulf.

The first recorded archdeacon of Rochester after the conquest was Asketill, who occurs twice by that name towards the end of Gundulf's rule.[89] He may have been in office for some time, for later Rochester tradition claimed that Gundulf assigned Longfield to the archdeacon's support, and Asketill the priest appears as the bishop's tenant of Longfield in 1086.[90] He is presumably not the same man as Ansketill the archdeacon of Canterbury, a benefactor of Rochester, who first occurs in 1075 and had left office by 1100.[91] There is, however, no direct evidence of the archdeacon at work in the diocese for a century or more.[92]

Evidence for bishop's synods does not survive under Gundulf, and no charters regulating the relations between local churches survive in his name. Other developments are better attested. Though Rochester is not proved to have possessed a copy of the *Collectio Lanfranci*, this was a law book found so widely in English dioceses that one may suppose there to have been one there too.[93] The library catalogue in the *Textus* does reveal the presence of several other law-books, suggesting an informed interest in the subject.[94]

The *Textus Roffensis* contains a list of the churches of the diocese, with a list of payments from them, either ninepence or sixpence in each case. The sums refer apparently to the annual payments for chrism from the parish clergy to the bishop at the annual blessing of the oils on Maundy Thursday.[95] A similar list survives for Christ Church, Canterbury, of about the same date, and the comparison is instructive. The Canterbury list is based on a basic rate of sevenpence a church, but there are many exceptions. It is also clear that the older churches still preserved some of their earlier rights, for they answer for multiples of sevenpence, and apparently distributed the chrism to their dependencies. In Canterbury, in short, the system around 1100 bears all the marks of long use and ancient origins.[96] The Rochester list, on the other

---

[88] See in general F. Barlow, *The English Church 1066–1154*, London 1979; M. Brett, *The English Church under Henry I*, Oxford 1975.

[89] *Textus*, f. 179 no. 93 for Archdeacon William of Canterbury (before 1107 from occurrence of Prior Ernulf). Compare *Registrum*, pp. 6–7, a charter of Gundulf of 1107x8, where the witness list commands a good deal more confidence than the text – Brett, 'Forgery', 403–4. Asketill the archdeacon occurs without territorial title in *Textus*, f. 184 no. 107. See further *Fasti*, ii, 12, 81.

[90] 'Registrum Temporalium', DRb/ Ar 2, f. 2: Gundulf 'dedit etiam manerium de Langefelde archidiacono'; *DMon* p. 96.

[91] *Textus*, f. 184r–v nos 109–10. Ansketill had been replaced at Canterbury by 1099x1100, *Fasti*, ii, 12.

[92] But see below p. 25.

[93] Z.N. Brooke, *The English Church and the Papacy*, 2nd edn, Cambridge 1989, pp. xx–xxi, 57–83; Richards, *Texts*, p. 29 no. 56: 'Canones et decreta pontificum in uno uolumine' reverses the usual order of the Lanfranc collection, but otherwise describes it well. A short series of excerpts from Lanfranc's collection appears in the *Textus Roffensis*: Sawyer in *Textus* i, p. 17, fos 81v–87.

[94] Richards, *Texts*, pp. 28–9, 32 nos 40 (Letters of Gregory I), 57, 98 (an addition).

[95] G. Ward, 'The list of Saxon churches in the Textus Roffensis', *Archaeologia Cantiana*, xliv (1932), 39–59; Brett, *English Church*, pp. 164–6.

[96] *DMon* pp. 5–15, 78–80; *Textus*, ff. 220v–2 no. 213 (not in the original hand); G. Ward, 'The lists of Saxon churches in the Domesday Monachorum and White Book of St Augustine', *Archaeologia Cantiana*, xlv (1933), 60–89; T. Tatton-Brown, 'The churches of Canterbury

hand, suggests a single unified pattern, and it is easiest to understand as the product of a recent reform. There is at least a hint that Gundulf's impact was as profound on the diocese as on his cathedral.

There had never been, so far as we know, any monastery in the diocese except the obscure house at Hoo, long forgotten by 1066; a similar shortage of religious houses of formal observance is almost without parallel elsewhere in England, though monastic observance in the stricter sense had largely died out north of the Humber in the later years of the Old English kingdom. Only the diocese of Sussex seems to have had so slight a monastic presence throughout the pre-conquest centuries. Here too the rule of Gundulf marked a break; some time before 1100 he established Benedictine nuns at Malling.[97] The early archives of the house suffered heavy losses, and those that survive present some problems.[98] On any view the original endowment was modest. If we may trust a charter of Archbishop Theobald it comprised at best Little Malling given by Archbishop Anselm, two churches, a number of tithes and some small parcels of land, though the surviving church gives a more substantial impression.[99] Gundulf kept the house under tight supervision until the last year of his life, when he installed Avice as first abbess.[100]

Relations with Canterbury

The dependence of Rochester on Canterbury after the conquest was wholly exceptional in the English church; it was a central fact in the revival of the diocese under Lanfranc and Gundulf, but it was to give rise to a multiplicity of difficulties later. This dependence had three strands: from the time of Bishop Arnost until the consecration of Bishop Richard Wendene in 1238 the archbishop and monks of Canterbury claimed a part in the election, as the king did elsewhere;[101] from the time of Gundulf the bishop had a special duty to act on behalf of the archbishop throughout his diocese during the metropolitan's frequent absences and during vacancies; for a long period the bishopric was held of the archbishop, and not of the king.

Bishop Arnost was appointed by Lanfranc in the chapter of Canterbury, and the same form was observed for all his successors until Bishop Waleran in 1182, who was appointed by the archbishop but in the chapter of Rochester, to the great indignation of the monks of Canterbury.[102] By then the monks of Rochester were

diocese in the eleventh century', *Minsters and Parish Churches: the Local Church in Transition*, ed. J. Blair, Oxford 1988, pp. 105–118.

[97] *Vita*, pp. 58, 60, 65. The passage on p. 60 might suggest that the nunnery was founded under Henry I, but a curious writ of William II, dated 1099–1100 if genuine, pushes the foundation earlier (*Registrum*, p. 486, *Regesta*, i, no. 485).

[98] *Registrum*, pp. 480–1 claim that almost all were destroyed by fire by the time of bp Waleran, but a fair number appeared later in *Calendar of the Charter Rolls*, v, 55–63 of 1347 and A. Saltman, *Theobald, Archbishop of Canterbury*, London 1956, pp. 395–9.

[99] Saltman, *op. cit.*, pp. 395–7 no. 173; *Textus*, f. 198r–v no. 181.

[100] *Vita*, pp. 65, 82–3 (*Textus*, f. 198r–v no. 181).

[101] *Flores*, ii, 215–26; Brett, 'Forgery', 412.

[102] 'Acta Lanfranci' in *Two of the Saxon Chronicles Parallel*, ed. C. Plummer, Oxford 1892–9, i, 289; in *Canterbury Professions* no. 38 Arnost addresses Lanfranc as 'a te electus', and compare

beginning to assert their claim to elect their own bishop in their own church, as every other English chapter would demand; they made the symbolic protest of refusing to deliver the staff of Bishop Walter to Canterbury. Waleran's successor, Gilbert, was appointed by Archbishop Baldwin in 1185, and again the monks of Canterbury protested that the monks of Rochester had failed to deliver the staff of their late bishop to Christ Church. After much debate the prior of Rochester delivered the staff to the archbishop, he handed it over to the prior of Canterbury, and the prior placed it on the high altar of the cathedral.[103] The dispute was set to continue for many years. Throughout the period, however, the bishops all had close connections with the archbishop before their election, and none was in the first instance the choice of the monks of Rochester.

The functions of the bishop as deputy to the archbishop are widely attested. An added leaf in the *Textus Roffensis* sets them out as Rochester understood them in the mid-twelfth century; whenever required by the archbishop, or during a vacancy, the bishop should perform all the duties of the archbishop, whether as a diocesan himself or in the consecration of kings and bishops, and should receive either twenty shillings a day or a handsome provision for all his needs.[104] Incidental references provide a number of glimpses of Gundulf and his successors performing these duties, though the bishops of Rochester had to contend with the bishops of London and the monks of Canterbury in making good their rights on the more dignified occasions.[105]

The feudal dependence of Rochester on Canterbury seems to have been of slower growth. In Domesday the bishop is entered as a tenant in chief, answering directly to the crown. However, a little later the only lands surveyed in the Canterbury *Domesday Monachorum* which do not belong to Canterbury are those of Rochester. Further, the ten knights of the fee of Rochester were entered among the knights of the archbishop at about the same time.[106] A charter of King William II of 1093 or shortly after grants the abbey of Selby to be held in perpetual right by York 'as the archbishop of Canterbury has the bishopric of Rochester'.[107] Before the end of the century then Rochester's lands were treated as a fief of Canterbury. Bishops Ralph, Ernulf, Walter and Waleran are all recorded as swearing a vassal's oath of allegiance

no. 89; *Eadmeri Historia Nouorum*, ed. Rule, pp. 2, 196, 225; *Gervase*, ii, 385; *Radulfi de Diceto . . . opera historica*, ed. W. Stubbs, Rolls Series, London 1876, ii, 13–14.

[103] *Gervase*, i, 302, 306–7, 326–31; *DMon*, pp. 106–7.

[104] *Textus*, f. 220 no. 212.

[105] *Eadmeri Historia Nouorum*, ed. Rule, p. 37; *Gervase*, i, 97, 168–71, ii, 380; *Registrum*, p. 51; in general R.A.L. Smith, 'The place of Gundulf in the Anglo-Norman church', *English Historical Review*, lvii (1943), 262–4; I. Churchill, *Canterbury Administration*, London 1933, i, 279–87; M. Brett, *English Church under Henry I*, pp. 67–8, 164n; F. Barlow, *The English Church 1066–1154*, London 1979, p. 41.

[106] *DMon*, pp. 95–8, 105; compare 'Registrum Temporalium', DRb/Ar 2, f. 2v: 'Archiepiscopus [sc. Lanfranc] . . . decenciorem sibi uicarium prouidere desiderans, Gundulfum . . . conuenit ut officium illud in se susciperet, necnon et de septem militibus seruicio regi principaliter debito de ipsius regis assensu ei quasi medio responderet.'

[107] *Registrum Antiquissimum of . . . Lincoln*, ed. C.W. Foster, i, Lincoln Record Soc., xxvii (1931) no. 4 (*Regesta*, i, no. 341); compare *Hugh the Chanter. The History of the Church of York*, ed. C. Johnson, 2nd edn, Oxford 1990, pp. 14–17.

to the archbishop as well as their conventional profession of obedience.[108] In 1166 the bishop made no separate return to the inquest on knights' fees. In 1182 Archbishop Richard took the lands of Rochester into his own hands on the death of Bishop Walter, and maintained his right to do so against the king's justiciar.[109] In a record of 1182/3 it was stated formally that the bishop elect, immediately after his election, should perform his homage to the archbishop in the chapter at Canterbury 'for the fief of his bishopric which he holds especially from the archbishop and chapter of Canterbury'.[110]

More strikingly, during the vacancy at Rochester of 1184-5, the keepers of the lands of the bishopric answered to the king until the feast of St John the Baptist 'because the archbishopric of Canterbury was then in the king's hand', and after the feast of St John they answered to the new archbishop, Baldwin.[111]

In a celebrated charter King John granted the patronage of Rochester to Archbishop Stephen Langton in 1214, but in effect this was at most a restoration, not a substantial new concession.[112] The question was to become a matter of fierce dispute later with the king and the archbishop, and Rochester tinkered with its early muniments in support of a claim to hold directly of the crown, but the relationship seems to have been largely uncontentious before 1185.

IV. Rochester between 1108 and 1185

The work of Gundulf and Lanfranc determined the essential development of the cathedral priory until the end of the reign of Henry II. The pattern of endowment changed little, and many of the changes that occurred were either a natural development or were responses to local crises. Nevertheless, much remained to be done.

Almost nothing is recorded of the brief pontificate of Ralph, the former abbot of Séez who became bishop in 1108 and was translated to Canterbury in 1114.[113] His successor, Ernulf, can be seen at work more clearly. He was a scholar of wide learning, as his short works written as prior of Christ Church show, and it is not surprising that the library grew considerably during his rule. There is very good reason to attribute the compilation of the *Textus Roffensis* to his time as well, and

---

[108] *Eadmeri Historia Nouorum*, ed. Rule, pp. 196, 225; *Gervase*, i, 132–3, ii, 399.

[109] *Red Book of the Exchequer*, ed. H. Hall, Rolls Series, London 1896, i, 193–4; *Gervase*, i, 302; H.M. Chew, *The Ecclesiastical Tenants-in-Chief*, Oxford 1932, pp. 7, 184–5. There is no account in the Pipe Rolls for the estates of Rochester in the few months after Walter's death; for the vacancy after Waleran's death see below, n. 147.

[110] *DMon*, pp. 44–5, 106. Compare *Gervase*, i, 132–3.

[111] *The Great Roll of the Pipe for the thirty-first year of the Reign of King Henry the Second, A.D. 1184–5*, Pipe Roll Soc., xxxiv (1913), pp. 239–40; *Gervase*, i, 312.

[112] M. Howell, *Regalian Right in Medieval England*, London 1962, pp. 61–2, 201–3; compare *Acta Stephani Langton*, ed. K. Major, Canterbury and York Soc. 1 (1950), pp. 19–21, 158–9 and *Registrum*, p. 2, 'Iohannes dedit et reddidit ecclesie Kantuar' patronatum ecclesie Roffens'.

[113] He was remembered and celebrated as a benefactor in *Custumale*, pp. 11, 37; *Registrum*, pp. 7, 120; *Ecclesiastical Courts*, p. 42; *Flores*, ii, 44; *Textus*, f. 179v no. 94.

the work is a notable one under several aspects. Nothing quite like the collection of charters and narrations of the second part is known for any other English house so early, and the collection of Anglo-Saxon laws in the first part is also distinctive in conception.[114]

He was later remembered at Rochester with the same honours as Gundulf and Lanfranc, and as 'pater noster post Gundulfum',[115] less one imagines for his encouragement of scholarly work than for his building and his lavish gifts of vestments, plate and service-books. Presumably Gundulf had provided a provisional dormitory, refectory and chapter house, but Ernulf was credited with constructing something more enduring.[116] How far the church was enlarged or altered in his time remains controversial.[117]

Ernulf's more formal regulations for the house are recorded in some provisions for the anniversary of Gundulf,[118] and in two charters. One grants the church of Haddenham to the priory for the provision of lights, the other grants the monks the chrism pennies of the diocesan clergy and their synodal pennies for the maintenance of the conventual buildings. The clergy had almost certainly been paying for the consecrated oils earlier, and may well have been attending synods under Gundulf, but Ernulf's charter is the first proof of both practices.[119]

Bishop Ernulf died at a great age in 1124, shortly after the contentious election of the regular canon William of Corbeil to Canterbury, and was succeeded by John, a nephew of the late Archbishop Ralph and his archdeacon at Canterbury.[120] John was the first bishop of Rochester since before the conquest who was not a monk, but this does not seem to have provoked the kind of disputes which were common enough elsewhere under similar conditions.[121]

In 1130 Bishop John was able to have the cathedral church consecrated on 8 May by the archbishop and several suffragans, and in the presence of the king, though the ceremony must have been overshadowed by a fire which ravaged the city the previous day. The king's contribution to the festivities was a grant of the royal church of Boxley.[122] Bishop John was remembered as a benefactor in his own right,

---

[114] Richards, *Texts*, pp. 5–6, 43–60; P. Cramer, 'Ernulf of Rochester and the problem of remembrance', *Anselm Studies*, ii (1988), 143–63 and 'Ernulf of Rochester and early Anglo-Norman canon law', *Journal of Ecclesiastical History*, xl (1989), 483–510; Waller (as n. 32 above), p. 240 believed that the overwhelming bulk of the surviving books listed in the catalogue of 1123–4 were produced after 1107.

[115] *Registrum*, p. 120.

[116] *Custumale*, pp. 31, 37; *Registrum*, pp. 7, 120; *Ecclesiastical Courts*, p. 43; *Flores*, ii, 45.

[117] A detailed study of the issues by Colin Flight is to appear under the auspices of the Kent Archaeological Society; I have benefited a great deal from seeing a draft of this important work, but have tried not to anticipate its conclusions.

[118] *Textus*, f. 197r–v no. 179.

[119] *Textus*, ff. 196v–7, nos 177–8. For chrism pennies see above, pp. 19–20, for synods post-conquest Brett, *English Church under Henry I*, pp. 155–61.

[120] *Fasti*, ii, 13, 76; *Gervase*, ii, 379–80.

[121] Brett, *English Church under Henry I*, pp. 192–3.

[122] *Chronicle of John of Worcester*, ed. J.R.H. Weaver, Oxford 1909, p. 30; *Anglo-Saxon Chronicle* s.a. 1130; *Registrum*, pp. 34–5 (= DRc/ T 51, *Regesta*, ii, no. 1867, of dubious authenticity), 177 (*Regesta*, ii, no. 1728); *Textus*, f. 177v no. 92.

translating St Ithamar to a new shrine, giving vestments and plate, and granting the church of Frindsbury with its chapel of Strood to the priory for lights and his own obit.[123] If another charter, first recorded in the thirteenth century, may be believed, he also restored to the monks the manors of Haddenham, Stoke and Lambeth, which he had held at farm.[124]

Bishop John's last year was marked by a notable disaster, for there was another fire at Rochester on 3 June 1137 which destroyed much of the church, conventual buildings and city. Fires were common enough, and in the same year there were similar blazes at York, Winchester, Bath, Arundel and Leicester, but the damage at Rochester is supposed to have been so severe that the community was temporarily dispersed. A fortnight later the bishop died.[125]

The difficulties of the church were now considerable; to the dispersal of the community was added the likelihood of a long vacancy, for the archbishopric had also been vacant since the previous November. The curious status of the bishopric may explain why King Stephen seems to have entrusted it to Bishop John of Séez, a notable supporter of his cause. The priory later claimed that he had been installed 'more as a plunderer than a keeper', and held it for three years.[126] The only charter clearly issued in his name describes him as bishop 'by the grace of God, holding the episcopal office by apostolic precept, having secured the privilege of complete authority'.[127]

This suggests that John of Séez had more than royal warrant for his office, but it is unlikely that he was formally installed as bishop. He did not resign his own see, and there is no profession of obedience to the church of Canterbury in his name. His status may have been as ambiguous then as it has been for modern scholars.

On 9 January 1139 Archbishop Theobald was consecrated to Canterbury, and in April he received his pallium from Pope Innocent II at the Lateran Council. Bishop John may have accompanied him.[128] Meanwhile the landing of the Empress Matilda at Arundel in September and the weakening position of Stephen in Normandy precipitated the outbreak of civil war in England and must have weakened the hold of Bishop John on the diocese. He is last recorded in England, as the only bishop in attendance on the king, at Whitsun 1140.[129]

---

[123] Bethell, 'Miracles', 432; *Registrum*, pp. 7–8, 121; *Ecclesiastical Courts*, p. 43; *Flores*, ii, 50.

[124] BL Cotton ms. Domitian x, f. 123r–v no. xxxvii. For the cartulary see Brett, 'Forgery', 402 and n. Printed by Saltman in *English Historical Review*, lxvi (1951), p. 73.

[125] *Chronicle of John of Worcester*, ed. Weaver, p. 43; *Ungedruckte Anglo-Normannische Geschichtsquellen*, pp. 80, 95; *Gervase*, i, 100; *Registrum*, p. 8; *Ecclesiastical Courts*, p. 43; *Flores*, ii, 60 (dating 1138, but 1137 is confirmed by the earlier references).

[126] *Ecclesiastical Courts*, p. 43; *Registrum*, p. 8. C. Flight, 'John II, Bishop of Rochester, Did not Exist', *English Historical Review*, cvi (1991), 921–31

[127] *Registrum*, pp. 370, 412–13. The charter mentions a John as his predecessor, and is in favour of Hugh of St Clare. It was not preserved at the priory, and there seems no motive for forgery, in spite of the fourteenth-century date of the known copy.

[128] *Gervase*, i, 109; *Fasti*, ii, 4.

[129] John of Séez was in England in 1136, in Normandy with Stephen in 1137, appears to be the unnamed bishop of Rochester mentioned by Richard of Hexham at the Lateran Council of April 1139, and died in 1144 – *Regesta*, iii, nos 46, 69, 335, 608, 843, 919, 979; *Chronicles of the Reigns of Stephen, Henry II and Richard I*, ed. R. Howlett, Rolls Series, London 1884–9, iii, 176–7; iv,

The capture of King Stephen at Lincoln in February 1141 and the ensuing confusion may have delayed a decision at Rochester. Though Kent saw relatively little fighting, it is clear that the civil war was a period of difficulty for Rochester. At some point the priory fell heavily into debt to William of Ypres, Stephen's chief captain in the South East, and some of their men were imprisoned by Stephen's queen for treason.[130] Whatever the reason for the delay, Theobald did not appoint a new bishop until 1142, when his choice fell on the monk Ascelin, formerly sacrist of Christ Church and prior of Dover.[131]

Ascelin ruled for only six years, but they were filled with dispute. The first quarrel involved Rochester in a much wider world. At a point which is quite obscure Robert Pullen became archdeacon of Rochester. Pullen had taught at Oxford, possibly when already archdeacon; it is said that Henry I had offered him a bishopric, but failed to tempt him. Later he went to Paris, where the fame of his teaching spread widely.[132] When Ascelin came to Rochester he found his archdeacon far away, but enjoying the revenues of the churches of Boxley, Aylesford, Southfleet, and the Rochester parish altar of St Nicholas in the cathedral. It seems that the bishop suspended his archdeacon, and Pullen appealed to Rome. At any rate by November 1143 the bishop and some monks were at Rome to answer an appeal by the archdeacon. Pullen himself failed to attend, so the bishop and monks initially enjoyed a complete success. Pope Celestine II restored the disputed churches to the bishop and commanded the archdeacon to appear before his bishop by Whitsun 1144 to take up his duties or resign. The bishop returned and restored the churches to the monks, but his success was frail; Pullen had powerful friends.

St Bernard of Clairvaux had already written to Ascelin on behalf of Pullen, but worse was to follow. Soon after the death of Celestine II in March 1144 the archdeacon was summoned to Rome by Lucius II and became a cardinal; by early 1145 he was papal chancellor. According to a pathetic letter of Ascelin to Lucius' successor, Eugenius III, Pope Lucius first compelled him to restore the churches to the new cardinal, and later to entrust both the churches and the archdeaconry, with its attendant revenue, to the chancellor's nephew, Master Paris. Pullen died in the

---

149; John of Hexham in *Symeonis Monachi Opera Omnia*, ed. T. Arnold, London 1882–5, ii, 300; *The Historia Novella of William of Malmesbury*, ed. K.R. Potter, Nelson Medieval Texts, London 1955, p. 44. For his family and career see *The Letters of Arnulf of Lisieux*, ed. F. Barlow, Camden 3rd Series, lxi (1939), pp. xi–xii, xxxiii–iv, 55–6.

[130] *Registrum*, p. 123; Bethell, 'Miracles', 435; R. Eales, 'Local loyalties in Norman England: Kent in Stephen's reign', *Anglo-Norman Studies*, vii (1985), 99–101.

[131] *Fasti*, ii, 76.

[132] *Ecclesiastical Courts*, p. 43, *Registrum*, p. 8 claim that Robert was appointed by John of Séez, but this is late and partisan evidence. An Archdeacon Robert attests two charters of a Bishop John, *Registrum*, p. 177 and BL Cotton ms. Domitian x, f. 123r–v no. xxxvii (above p. 24 n. 124). One confirms Boxley to the monks, which one would expect to belong to 1130 or so (above, p. 23); the second lists his predecessors to Ernulf, without mentioning another John. Both seem more probably charters of John I. If so, and if the charters are genuine, either there were two consecutive archdeacons called Robert, or Pullen was appointed before 1137. An Archdeacon Robert gave Rochester an alb, *Registrum*, p. 124. For Pullen see F. Courtney, *Cardinal Robert Pullen*, Analecta Gregoriana, lxiv (1954), B. Smalley, *The Becket Conflict and the Schools*, Oxford 1973, pp. 39–46, A. Morey and C.N.L. Brooke, *Gilbert Foliot and his Letters*, Cambridge 1965, 53–5.

autumn of 1146, while Ascelin was still trying to recover the churches, but Paris maintained his position, and remained in office until 1190 or later. This was Rochester's first experience of the curia, and it was both unhappy and expensive.[133] Meanwhile, however, the bishop had also fallen foul of the priory.

At London in May or June 1145 the papal legate Imar of Tusculum and Archbishop Theobald heard an appeal of the monks against their bishop, who had taken into his hand the manor of Lambeth and a ten pound rent from Haddenham. The monks paraded a series of charters of kings and archbishops in support of their claim, and the bishop admitted defeat.[134] Later sources claim that a second issue was at stake, the bishop's claim to appoint the priory servants, and specifically the chief lay servant of the infirmary. Again, the legate commanded the bishop on his obedience to restore the monks' candidate.[135]

In the event the quarrel was still not over, for the bishop complained that the monks had involved him in great expenses over the Pullen affair. Later in the year monks and bishop were finally reconciled by Archbishop Theobald at Canterbury; the bishop confirmed the monks in their possession of all the manors and churches they claimed, and the monks agreed to pay the bishop a hundred marks over five years as a contribution to his costs.[136] These warmer relations seem to have lasted until Ascelin's death on 24 January 1148, for he made valuable gifts to the priory, and was remembered with some formality later.[137]

Within three days of Ascelin's death Archbishop Theobald appointed his own brother, Walter archdeacon of Canterbury, as his successor.[138] Walter's thirty-three year pontificate has left little trace in the records. All about him there were great events, not least the dramatic life and death of Archbishop Thomas, but Walter's part in them appears slight or conventional.[139] Compared to his fellow bishops, he appears to have issued remarkably few charters for any beneficiary; only nineteen survive, little more than one every two years, of which six are for his own church.[140] Of his contemporaries, Bishop Hilary of Chichester left twice as many in a twenty-two year pontificate in a small diocese; Robert Chesney of Lincoln produced some 220 in sixteen years.[141]

---

[133] *Ecclesiastical Courts*, pp. 43–4; *Registrum*, pp. 8–10, 39–41; B. Zenker, *Die Mitglieder des Kardinalkollegiums von 1130 bis 1159*, Würzburg 1964, pp. 89–92; *Fasti*, ii, 81.

[134] *Textus*, ff. 203v–5v nos 196–7; *Registrum*, p. 384; for the chronology see *Councils and Synods I*, ed. D. Whitelock etc., Oxford 1981, ii, 810–3. The settlement was confirmed in a bull of Eugenius III of 25 February 1146, *Textus*, ff. 206–8 no. 198 (JL 8870).

[135] *Custumale*, p. 30; *Flores*, ii, 64.

[136] *Registrum*, pp. 39, 41 (Saltman, *Theobald*, no. 223), 40–1 (Ascelin's remission of the outstanding balance).

[137] *Registrum*, pp. 41, 121 (*Flores*, ii, 64), 384; BL Cotton ms. Domitian x, f. 126r–v no. xlii; Richards, *Texts*, pp. 33–4 nos 65–6, 87.

[138] *Gervase*, i, 132–3; Saltman, *Theobald*, pp. 103–5; *Fasti*, ii, 13, 76.

[139] D. Knowles, *The Episcopal Colleagues of Archbishop Thomas Becket*, Cambridge 1951, pp. 16–17.

[140] *English Episcopal Acta*, Rochester (forthcoming). I am grateful to Margaret Blount for showing me a draft of her edition, on which I depend for this paragraph.

[141] *The Acta of the Bishops of Chichester 1075–1207*, ed. H. Mayr-Harting, Canterbury and York Soc., pt. cxxx (1964), nos 20–55, of which one or two are forgeries, but not all Walter's are secure either; *English Episcopal Acta, Lincoln*, ed. D.M. Smith, London 1980, nos 67–284.

At his cathedral Bishop Walter was remembered with affection; he is said to have confirmed the priory in its privileges with an open hand, and he gave them an abundance of vestments, plate and books. Only one dispute seems to have marred their relations near the end of his life, when they quarrelled over the patronage of Dartford church. Both parties appealed to Rome, where the monks claimed that they triumphed, and reconciliation followed quickly.[142] The principal event of his pontificate may well have been a second great fire at the cathedral, which reduced the church, conventual buildings and city to ashes on 11 or 12 April 1179.[143] It is unclear how far the work of reconstruction had gone before Walter died on 26 July 1182.[144]

On 10 October Archbishop Richard presided over the election of his successor Waleran, archdeacon of Bayeux, who had been the archbishop's constant companion over many years.[145] Waleran's rule was brief – he died less than two years later – but these were ominous years for the priory. Archbishop Richard, the former monk of Canterbury, died at the Rochester manor of Halling on 16 February 1184, and the king refused to accept any of the candidates offered by the monks of Canterbury. It was widely believed that the king's clerks intended a frontal assault on the monastic order. At any rate Bishop Waleran was appointed to head an embassy to Rome, and at Canterbury they believed he had his own plan to replace his monks with secular clerks. In the event he died at Rochester before setting out.[146]

The truth behind these rumours is hard to discern. Waleran was clearly no out-and-out opponent of his monks; he gave them a number of valuable vestments and books, the prior of Rochester was one of his executors, and a few years later the monks remembered him as a friend to their liberties.[147] Nevertheless, at both Canterbury and Rochester the skies were already threatening. With the election of Baldwin at Canterbury and Gilbert at Rochester the storm broke.

---

[142] *Ecclesiastical Courts*, p. 44; *Registrum*, pp. 10–11, 121; *Flores*, ii, 67–8.

[143] Rochester annals printed in *Ungedruckte Anglo-Normannische Geschichtsquellen*, p. 49; *Gervase*, i, 292; *Flores*, ii, 89 (dating 1177, but the annal in BL Cotton ms. Vespasian A xxii, on which the *Flores* text is based, agrees with Gervase and the earlier annals of Rochester).

[144] Prior Ralph, who left office 1203 x 1214 (*Fasti*, ii, 79) was credited with roofing and partially leading the church, presumably as a consequence of a rebuilding after the fire, *Registrum*, p. 122.

[145] *English Episcopal Acta*, ii, Canterbury 1162–1190, ed. C.R. Cheney and B.E.A. Jones, London 1986, *passim*; *DMon*, p. 107; *Flores*, ii, 94; *Gervase*, i, 302; *Chronicle of Battle Abbey*, ed. E. Searle, Oxford Medieval Texts 1980, pp. 328–31.

[146] *Gervase*, i, 308–13; *Radulfi de Diceto*, ed. Stubbs, ii, 21–4.

[147] *Ecclesiastical Courts*, p. 44; *Registrum*, pp. 11, 121; Richards, *Texts*, pp. 33–4 nos 65–6, 71; *The Great Roll of the Pipe for the thirty-first year of the Reign of King Henry the Second*, pp. 239–40; *Flores*, ii, 94.

2

Rochester Priory, 1185–1540

ANNE OAKLEY

(1) General Introduction

Monastic chapters were very much an English institution. In grafting Benedictine houses of monks on to existing cathedrals Archbishop Lanfranc had created problems for the future which proved difficult to resolve. The status of these houses was always in doubt, and the estates with which they were endowed were never clearly sorted out. The original conception of a bishop as abbot living in common with his monks was rapidly dispelled. The increasing use of bishops by the crown on embassies and in other offices of state meant that the bishop was often absent, leaving his work as abbot in the hands of his deputy, the prior. Within a hundred years of the conquest most bishops, if not all, had separate establishments away from their monks.[1] Over the years the prior in his turn also set up separate rooms for himself;[2] and occasionally, in the same way, obedientiaries sought to set up their own households.[3]

The life of the Benedictine monk was based on the rule of St Benedict, and however loose this observance might have become since the re-establishment of the Benedictine order in England by Archbishop Lanfranc, the rule was still at the root of every monk's life in the monastery. It provided for an organised day where prayer, work and study had their place, but these secure elements had become disturbed by the end of the twelfth century for several reasons.

Because the monks had to act for the bishopric during a vacancy they were pushed much more into the real world of politics. The ever increasing demand for communal masses and private masses complicated the round of liturgical observance throughout the day. The huge numbers of visitors to the shrines had to be allowed for and to a certain extent catered for. Processions attracted local people and

---

[1] M. Howell, 'Abbatial vacancies and the divided *mensa* in medieval England', *Journal of Ecclesiastical History*, xxxiii (1982), pp. 173–92; and E.V. Crosby, *Bishop and Chapter in Twelfth-Century England*, Cambridge 1994.

[2] W. St John Hope, 'The Architectural History of the Cathedral Church and Monastery of St Andrew at Rochester', *Archaeologia Cantiana*, xxiv (1900), p. 58 where he mentions separate buildings for Ralph de Ros, Osbern de Sheppey and Helyas.

[3] See B. Dobson, 'The English Monastic Cathedrals in the Fifteenth Century', *Transactions of the Royal Historical Society*, sixth series, i (1991), pp. 151–72; William Ingram, the sacrist at Canterbury attempted to set up his own household, *ibid.*, p. 171.

particularly women into the enclosure. Important and influential landowners had to be entertained. The obedientiary system which had been designed to provide for the smooth running of the house by placing specific jobs in the hands of a few monks, expanded to include larger numbers of monks who often had to be excused attendance at some of the monastic hours.[4] The income of the obedientiaries ceased to be adequate for their increasing tasks. Problems over the running of the estates and the collection of rents and dues meant the placing of this work in the hands of lay persons. And there was also the problem of corrodies, where sometimes influential and rich lay persons sought provision for their old age within the walls of a monastic house.

(2) Relations between the Bishop and the Prior and Chapter

At the end of the twelfth century Rochester priory was a very different place from what it had been in the early years of Bishop Gundulf (1077–1108). The monks were much more politically, and increasingly legally, aware. As a body with legal rights, they were prepared to fight for those rights and go to law for their protection. Like many of their contemporaries in England, they had acquired a legal consciousness, and never was this more apparent than in their battle with their bishop Gilbert Glanville.

The election of Gilbert Glanville, archdeacon of Lisieux, as bishop of Rochester in September 1185 was an event of some moment in his diocese.[5] The new bishop was a scholar and a lawyer, and significantly, very much a member of the anti-monastic faction. He was a native of Northumberland and a kinsman of Ranulf Glanville, and as a young man had joined the group of scholars attached to the household of Archbishop Thomas Becket. Herbert of Bosham says he was learned in both civil and canon law, and that he several times visited the court on Thomas's behalf. After the death of Thomas Becket, Gilbert may have worked with John of Salisbury who certainly knew him. In 1184 Gilbert became Archdeacon of Lisieux, but nevertheless accompanied Baldwin, bishop of Worcester as a member of his household when he was elected Archbishop of Canterbury in December 1184. In the July following Gilbert was elected bishop of Rochester.[6]

Gilbert's predecessor, Waleran, had also been a member of the anti-monastic faction and, unfortunately for the monks at Rochester, his tentative plans for their

---

[4] Archbishop Winchelsey, in his 1299 injunctions, addressed this problem, even while accepting that some of the monks were prevented by their duties from attending some services. *Registrum Roberti Winchelsey Cantuariensis Archiepiscopi*, ed Rose Graham, Canterbury and York Society, lii (1956), p. 839.

[5] Gilbert Glanville was elected bishop of Rochester 16 July 1185 according to, *John Le Neve, Fasti Ecclesiae Anglicanae 1066–1300: Monastic Cathedrals*, ed. D.E. Greenway, London 1971, p. 76.

[6] Baldwin became bishop of Worcester in 1180. It is possible that Gilbert may have joined his household then as a clerk. C.R. Cheney, *From Becket to Langton*, Manchester 1956, p. 27.

eviction had already won royal approval.[7] Despite the setback that the murder of Archbishop Thomas Becket may have been to King Henry II's plans for the reformation of canon and civil law, the king still hoped in some way to curb the power of the regular orders which he felt were too independent of the crown. To implement such a plan, Henry chose his friends Baldwin, archbishop of Canterbury, Hugh Nonant, bishop of Coventry, and Archbishop Baldwin's protégé, Gilbert Glanville, to work with him in suppressing the regular orders. With royal support they were to use Canterbury, Coventry and Rochester as experimental sites for the establishment of colleges of secular canons.

Such attempts to de-monachize chapters like Rochester had been successful in Ireland and Scotland, but in England, except at Coventry, where force was used to set up a college of secular canons, the idea came to nothing. Baldwin's proposed establishment at Harbledown was so unpopular with his own monks that papal influence was used to halt the plan. Gilbert was likewise unsuccessful, and even though his plans had barely matured, the king's death in July 1189 put an end to all his hopes of success. It was an inauspicious beginning which did nothing to ease relations between the new bishop and his monks.[8]

Bishop Gilbert remained in favour with the new king, Richard I. He had preached the crusade with Archbishop Baldwin at Geddington in 1188, and may have been with Richard in 1190 when he issued a charter to the city of Rochester in connection with the third crusade.[9] He was certainly with the king in Germany in 1193. When Richard was captured and later imprisoned there, the bishop worked with a will to secure his release. His principal contribution was the establishment of the Hospital of the New work of St Mary in Strood founded between December 1192 and February 1194.[10]

This was a small house whose primary purpose was to pray for the restoration of Christianity in the kingdom of Jerusalem and for the king's release from captivity; and secondarily to provide for the poor and travellers. However small, such a house needed an endowment. Had the bishop won the monks' goodwill, all might have been well. He seems, however, to have behaved with high-handed tactlessness and, without consulting them, appropriated the churches of Aylesford and St Margaret, Rochester, for the support of his new foundation. He also bribed their prior, Ralph de Ros, to give a piece of meadow land in Strood to the hospital in return for money to finish the cloister stonework and for a pair of organs.[11] The two churches had only recently been won back from Gilbert's predecessor at vast expense. The angry monks

---

[7] But see M. Brett's conclusion, p. 27 above, and his doubts that Bishop Waleran ever really intended to replace his monks with secular clerks.

[8] John Denne, *The History and Antiquities of Rochester and its Environs*, ed. T. Fisher, 1817, pp. 112 15.

[9] Ronald Marsh, *Rochester: The Evolution of the City*, Rochester 1974, pp. 19–20.

[10] A.C. Harrison, 'Excavations on the site of St Mary's Hospital, Strood', *Archaeologia Cantiana*, lxxxiv (1969), pp. 139–60. For the date of the foundation see the collection of charters for the hospital with full texts and discussion in *English Episcopal Acta III Canterbury 1193–1205*, ed. C.R. Cheney and E. John, London 1986, nos 591, 623–9, pp. 245, 272–8. King Richard I confirmed Bishop Glanville's foundation at Strood while in captivity at Worms 14 August 1193.

[11] T572/1–15.

appealed unsuccessfully to the pope for help, and the bishop forced them into an agreement to maintain his foundation together with its endowment.[12]

This agreement remained more or less in force until 1239 when a further dispute with the bishop arose. In 1256 the pope declared that the two churches appropriated to the hospital should be returned to the monks. Gilbert was long since dead, buried in haste during the Interdict, and Bishop Lawrence of St Martin refused to comply. The quarrel simmered and finally came to a head at some time towards the end of the thirteenth century when the Rochester monks were ambushed and assaulted by the brothers of Strood while they were attempting to pass in procession through the hospital grounds.[13] After this débâcle, the Rochester monks gave up what was obviously an unequal struggle but used the results of the 1264 siege of Rochester to remedy some of their difficulties.[14]

The monks' quarrels with Bishop Gilbert and his successors went far beyond Strood Hospital. There were other problems which caused dissension: rights of presentation to benefices; the bishop's *xenium*; and appointments of priory servants.

In 1207 the monks possessed at least eleven churches within and seven outside the diocese of Rochester, but they also laid claim to present to others which belonged to the bishop. On his part Bishop Gilbert laid claim to none of the monks' churches. He merely stated that when John of Séez was bishop he had always presented and instituted incumbents to all vacant livings both inside and outside the diocese, but had secured to the monks their rightful pensions which he believed was their sole entitlement. Gilbert said that he proposed to do likewise, with the sole concession that those so instituted should do fealty to the monks as well as to himself.[15]

This was a meaningless concession on Gilbert's part, and although the monks gave way on this point, they always insisted that the bishop had no right to present to priory livings within the diocese. They did, however, reach agreement over the right of presentation to priory livings outside the diocese. They allowed the bishop's claim to joint right of presentation to Norton, Boxley and Stourmouth, although they knew he had none, and they maintained this agreement with ten of Gilbert's successors throughout the following 150 years.[16]

The quarrel was not only one of influence and authority, but also a question of fees. The bishopric was one of the smallest and poorest dioceses in the country and depended for support on the personal wealth of its bishops. In 1256 Bishop Lawrence of St Martin claimed his income was barely £40[17] whereas a later bishop, Hamo, used his own wealth to embellish the cathedral church.[18] Income could be derived from presentations to such a benefice as Northfleet, for instance, which was a

[12] L3.
[13] William Lambarde gives a spirited account of this incident in *Perambulation of Kent*, 1826 edn, pp. 328–31.
[14] T53; and F.F. Smith, *History of Rochester*, London 1928, pp. 18–21; *Chronicles of William Rishanger*, Rolls Series, 1865, p. 22. See also T63.
[15] L3.
[16] L10.
[17] Ar 1/1, ff. 16v–18v.
[18] T320 and Elb 1A, ff. 7v–10r.

relatively wealthy one and paid an annual pension of 60 shillings to the priory as well as a large part of the tithes.[19]

The disagreement over the bishop's *xenium* or hospitality allowance is an interesting one, not only in itself but because it throws some light on the careers of the various bishops. The allowance was particularly lavish, and from the date of its ordination in 1107 had always carried the significant proviso that if the bishop was away from Rochester on the patronal festival, then the *xenium* should be given to the poor.[20]

The monks appear to have resented making the gift, and refused to bring it on many occasions when the bishop was away. They argued that this was contrary to the ordinance, and that moreover, the *xenium* was an imposition. This may have been true, but it is even more true that successive bishops of Rochester spent more and more time away from their diocese. As an expert in canon and civil law, Gilbert Glanville was frequently used by the court as a judge and adjudicator as well as an ambassador. He travelled widely in England and Europe on royal business. In 1186 and 1189 he was in France and Normandy; and in 1190 in Worcester and Coventry. In 1191 he escorted the Chancellor Longchamps when he fled to Dover. In 1193 he was with King Richard in Germany. In 1206 he was at Evesham, and in 1207 fled to Scotland for a few months to escape from King John's persecution.[21] Gilbert argued that he could not always arrange to be in Rochester when he wished, and, in opposition to the monks, claimed the *xenium* as his right wherever he might be on St Andrew's day.[22]

By 1207 the monks surrendered to Bishop Gilbert's demand and this doubtless led his successors to abuse the system. In 1329 the monks accused Bishop Hamo (1319–1352), who spent more time in his diocese perhaps than any of his predecessors or successors, of abusing the system. They claimed he ought by ancient custom to celebrate St Andrew's day in the cathedral and in the hall adjoining, and there receive a present of ten pounds (to which the *xenium* had been commuted in 1320) from the prior and chapter towards his expenses, but that each year he received the present without performing the ceremony, and had left the prior both to do it and pay for it as well.[23] Thomas Brinton who died in 1389, John Kempe (1419–1421), Thomas Brouns (1435) and Thomas Rotherham (1468–1472), all of whom spent long periods abroad as ambassadors or at court pursuing their own interests, were hardly ever in Rochester to receive the *xenium*. It was, however, still being paid in the eighteenth century.[24]

Interference in the appointment of priory servants had always been a cause of friction at Rochester. Their number included the master baker, the second baker, brewers, cooks, the steward, janitor, guestmaster, granger, tailors and launderers.

---

[19] T55, T57/7.

[20] T47 and see above, p. 15.

[21] See *Dictionary of National Biography*, xxi, p. 411.

[22] L3.

[23] *Registrum Hamonis de Hethe Diocesis Roffensis AD 1319–1352*, ed. C. Johnson, Oxford 1948, pp. 424–31 and introduction.

[24] FTv 34.

The work of each servant was carefully laid down, but perhaps more than this, so also were their wages and perquisites. It was these perquisites, often free food and drink and livery, which made the offices so popular. Nepotism was rife. Servants were often related to monks and higher officials, and in some cases offices were handed from father to son.[25]

The monks complained to Bishop Gilbert that he interfered in the appointment of servants.[26] Gilbert Glanville doubtless had many relatives for whom he wished to provide, but even he cannot have had more than Bishop Hamo who was a major offender in this matter. It must be admitted that neither Hamo, nor Rochester priory was peculiar in this respect, but in this particular case, evidence against the bishop is abundant.

When Simon Meopham made his archiepiscopal visitation in 1329 the monks of Rochester made 25 complaints against Bishop Hamo, four of which related to this problem. They complained that he appointed to twenty or more offices in the priory when he was entitled to only four, or at most five; that he appointed his own kinsmen and others to priory offices who did their work by deputy and at half wages, too ill paid to be honest; that the officers and their deputies were insubordinate and, according to them, irremoveable; and specifically, that he had appointed a brewer who was inefficient and of ill repute.

Most of these charges against Bishop Hamo were dismissed, but the monks' allegations of nepotism were not unfounded. The bishop's family name was Noble, and there are a great many appointments of persons of that name in his register.[27]

(3) Relations between the Priory and Other Bodies

Apart from their contentions with their bishops, there were also three major areas of conflict, which affected the monks, all of them outside their own walls. These were the position of the priory in relation to the crown and the castle; relations with the citizens of Rochester; and relations with the neighbouring diocese of Canterbury.

There were many skirmishes involving the castle over the years, but no serious sieges until 1215 when the castle and priory were pillaged by King John and his followers.[28] The most spectacular siege, however, and the one which the monks turned most to their advantage, was that of 1264. In that year, says the chronicler Rishanger, Simon de Montfort and the rebel barons brought great siege engines and fire ships to Rochester, and prosecuted the siege of the castle and the nearby priory

[25] *Custumale Roffense*, ed. John Thorpe, 1788, ff. 53–60.
[26] L3 'Ordinatio Gilberti episcopi Roffensis super querelis monachorum sancti Andreae Roffensis'.
[27] Hamo, *Registrum*, p. 425 and introduction.
[28] See I.W. Rowlands 'King John, Stephen Langton and Rochester Castle 1213–15', *Studies in Medieval History presented to R. Allen Brown*, eds C. Harper-Bill, C. Holdsworth and J.L. Nelson, Woodbridge 1989, pp. 267–79.

with great violence. Some of the priory buildings were badly damaged, and Simon and his soldiers broke in to the prior's chapel and stole the priory muniments.[29]

The story of the theft is told on the dorse of one small deed, and of how, when they had been carried off to Winchester, the prior John de Rainham won them back from the robbers, but with their seals broken and the charters torn and damaged.[30] Fearful of the danger in which this loss might place his house, at great labour and expense, Prior John de Rainham persuaded King Henry III to reconfirm all the damaged charters with a new one in 1265.[31] It says much for the prior's perspicacity that he was able to appeal to the crown in this way, but even more so to realise that the monks took due note of the defects of their damaged charters, and forged others to supply them, a few of which were incorporated into the new confirmation of 1265.[32]

Disagreement between the monks and the citizens of Rochester was also rife. The people had no parish church of their own, and as was usual in such circumstances, worshipped at the altar of St Nicholas which stood before the rood screen in the nave of the cathedral church.[33] The monks disliked this because it brought them into closer contact with the people than they preferred; it disturbed their peace, and meant that their church was not their own. They tried by every means in their power to prevent the citizens using the church. They shut the doors at night and refused the sacrament to the sick; they denied services;[34] and in 1327 they locked the doors of the nave and took away the key. Their quarrel was also with Bishop Hamo who had much sympathy for the citizens. He forced the monks to come to a compromise with them on 14 June 1327 and to agree to build an oratory for them in the corner of the nave near the north door, with both a door and a window on the outside of the church. Here the people were to have access to the sacrament for the sick during the night, and free entry and exit at all times. They were also guaranteed all the usual daily services.[35] Bishop Hamo and his successors made strenuous efforts to have a separate

---

[29] On this siege see *The History of the King's Works, vol. II, The Middle Ages*, eds R.A. Brown, H.M. Colvin and A.J. Taylor, London 1963, pp. 809–10.

[30] T53 and F.F. Smith, *History of Rochester*, pp. 8–19 '. . . et sciendum quod hec carta cum aliis multis tempore Gwerre in obsidione et irruptione Civitatis et Castri Roffensum ante Bellum Lewense in capella prioris depredata fuit et per hostes asportata usque ad partes Wynton' de quibus partibus frater Johannes tunc Prior hanc cartam cum multis aliis multo precio a predonibus redemit et eas recepit taliter confractas et lamentabiliter conculcatas . . .'. See also *The Chronicle of William de Rishanger of the Barons' Wars . . .*, ed. J.O. Halliwell, Camden Society, xv (1840), pp. 25–6.

[31] *Ibid.*; T60, although as Martin Brett has pointed out, this charter as well as T65 may be a forgery.

[32] T48, T60(1), T65(1).

[33] *Ibid.*; Emf 77. This was a long running problem which came to a head in 1327.

[34] It was one of Archbishop Pecham's complaints in 1283 that the people had no church. He ordered the prior and convent to build them a church in the cathedral precinct where one had previously been begun and since demolished. *Registrum Epistolarum Fratris Johannis Peckham, Archiepiscopi Cantuariensis*, ed. C. Trice Martin, Rolls Series, 1882–5, ii, p. 624. Archbishop Chichele sought to establish a processional route for the parishioners which he meticulously planned to avoid clashes between the monks and the parishioners in procession in the grounds. *The Register of Henry Chichele, Archbishop of Canterbury*, ed. E.F. Jacob, Canterbury and York Society, 1943–7, iv, pp. 229–30.

[35] L7.

church built for the people, but it was almost a century before this became a reality and St Nicholas' church was built beside the cathedral in 1423.[36]

Relations with Canterbury were equally bad. It was customary, as a mark of episcopal dependence on Canterbury, that on the death of their bishop, the monks of Rochester should take his staff to Canterbury and deliver it to the prior of Christ Church. There it was laid on the altar, and from there the new bishop took it after his consecration. Rivalry between the two houses grew over the years. Negotiations for the delivery of Bishop Waleran's staff dragged on into his successor's episcopate and beyond. To avoid the humiliating ceremony, the monks had buried Waleran's staff with him when he died in 1184, but the monks of Christ Church were not to be denied. For this occasion, a temporary compromise was reached under his successor, Gilbert Glanville. The monks agreed to deliver the staff, not to the prior of Christ Church who claimed to represent the church of Canterbury, and as arbiter of these affairs to have some power over them, but to the archbishop who would deliver it on their behalf.[37]

Gilbert Glanville valued his position as chaplain to archbishop Baldwin seeing it as an opportunity for advancement, and himself as chaplain to his friend and patron. His successors did not. Benedict of Sawston was consecrated at Oxford in an attempt to escape from the overlordship of Canterbury; and Lawrence of St Martin, one of the king's clerks who became bishop of Rochester in 1251, initiated litigation to try and secure some measure of independence for Rochester. He did this in the face of royal disapproval, for both Henry III and his queen favoured Archbishop Boniface in this matter. The negotiations failed, but at least they won for Lawrence a measure of favour from his monks.[38]

The pope too attempted a compromise between the prior of Rochester and the archbishop when the latter claimed rights of patronage over the election of the bishop. The prior and convent had elected Master Richard, rector of Bromley, for eight years official of the diocese, in 1235, but the archbishop refused to accept the nomination. The case dragged on for three years until the archbishop acquiesced in the pope's confirmation of the new bishop at the insistence of the prior and chapter, although he feared it would lessen the rights and liberties of his see to do so.[39]

[36] Ar 1/8, ff. 16v–18v.

[37] C.E. Woodruff and W. Danks, *Memorials of Canterbury Cathedral*, London 1912, p. 104.

[38] *Ibid.*, L2. See also H. Wharton, *Anglia Sacra*, pp. 343–351; C.E. Woodruff and W. Danks, *Memorials of Canterbury Cathedral*, p. 104. E. Hasted, *History of Kent*, folio edn, iv, p. 124 says the archbishops did not interfere after 1238. The prefix to the *Registrum Temporalium* strongly suggests that the register was compiled in connection with the litigation against the see of Canterbury in 1251–6 over authority and the would-be independence of Rochester. The register is made up in the form of a cartulary and contains copies of all documents relevant to the case against Canterbury: foundation charters, compositions relating to episcopal and priory estates, lists of temporalities, rents and dues, and also an account of the landing of Augustine in Kent. It has almost certainly been written throughout by one scribe.

[39] *Calendar of Papal Letters*, i, pp. 148,156,162,169,174.

(4) The Estates of the Priory Church

By the end of the first quarter of the twelfth century the priory held land in Kent, Surrey, Suffolk and Buckinghamshire. The original nucleus of the priory estates comprised the city of Rochester within the walls;[40] the manors and churches of Stoke, Denton, Frindsbury, Wouldham and Southfleet in Kent; Lambeth in Surrey;[41] and Haddenham with its dependent manor of Cuddington in Buckinghamshire.[42] The monks also had a two day fair on the eve and festival of Bishop Paulinus, 9 and 10 October,[43] and a fishery on the river Thames at *Niwera*.[44] Between 1087 and 1100 Roger Bigod had given to Rochester priory the church of St Felicity in Walton near Felixstowe with its tithes where the monks established an outlying cell.[45]

In 1197 the monks acquired Darenth manor and its church in Kent with the chapel of St Margaret, Helles, a sheepfold called Estmers and a number of the archbishop's tenants and their lands in Cliffe, when they gave Archbishop Hubert Walter their manor of Lambeth and its church in exchange, no doubt to help further his plans to build a secular college there.[46] The manor of Darenth had within it the subsidiary manor of Clendon. This was in the hands of the Hastings family, Earls of Pembroke, and was held by custom of gavelkind and by service of rendering 38s 2½d a year and suit of court at Darenth every three weeks.[47] Haddenham and Cuddington were managed by a reeve or steward on behalf of the priory who accounted to it.[48]

The thirteenth century was basically a period of consolidation. The estates were small and income had to be found for land acquisition and for the fabric fund. Much of this general policy of land acquisition and rebuilding coincided with the establishment of the new shrine of St William of Rochester in the north-east transept of the cathedral church.

Rochester already had two shrines, those of Bishop Paulinus (d. 644), and his successor Bishop Ithamar (644–c.655). Ithamar had become the centre of a cult in the twelfth century when his bones were translated to a new shrine in the rebuilt church, and remained so for many years, partly because he was an Englishman, the

---

[40] The gift of King Aethelberht and not mentioned in any of the post conquest royal or archiepiscopal charters. See P. Sawyer, *The Anglo-Saxon Charters of Rochester Cathedral*, 1971.

[41] The gift of Goda, sister of Edward the Confessor. See T48.

[42] The gift of William II made at the request of Archbishop Lanfranc 1087–9, T60.

[43] T66 B9 1100–7.

[44] T66 B12 1103–7. For a fuller account of the early estates see pp. 12–15 above.

[45] T66 B6 and *Calendar of Inquisitions Post Mortem, Edward I*, iv, p. 302. Felixstowe cell was in the patronage of the earls of Norfolk, and though a cell of Rochester was more or less independent. A papal enquiry of 1367, when the buildings had been destroyed by the sea, found that the bishop of Norwich had no jurisdiction over the priory. Licence was given to the cell to rebuild in Walton parish. *CPL*, iv, pp. 66, 79. Two priors of Rochester served previously as priors of Felixstowe. One other monk was prior there.

[46] T54/1–3.

[47] See *IPM Edward I*, vi, p. 322; *ibid.*, ix, p. 260; *ibid.*, x, pp. 26–34. In 1390 it was held by Richard, earl of Arundel by fealty and service of 29s a year, *ibid.*, *Richard II*, no. 967.

[48] F6.

first English bishop to have a reputation for sanctity, and partly as a protest against the Normanization of the English church.[49]

Shrines such as Ithamar's, and those of St Edward at Westminster, St Thomas at Canterbury, St Cuthbert at Durham, or the Sainte Chapelle in Paris were built to hold the relics and bones of Christ and his saints. From the point of view of the would-be pilgrim they were places to go to buttress faith, ensure victory in battle, and cure illnesses, but from the point of view of those who housed such shrines they were a highly lucrative source of finance. Just as Thomas Becket had sought to exploit the popularity of Archbishop Anselm by seeking his canonisation,[50] and a later chapter at Hereford successfully exploited the popularity of Thomas Cantilupe,[51] so Rochester priory hoped for a new and popular centre of pilgrimage in the shrine of William of Perth.[52]

William, a baker from Perth in Scotland, was murdered near Rochester in 1201 either by his adopted son or his apprentice while going on a pilgrimage to the Holy Land. He was taken up by the monks and buried in the cathedral, according to the chronicler, 'with glistening miracles' and was popularly hailed as a saint, the more so because he had been himself in the act of pilgrimage. In 1256 Bishop Lawrence of St Martin is said to have secured his canonisation while in Rome.[53] No papal bull to this effect can be found; possibly Bishop Lawrence did no more than seek leave to continue the cult of a man who was, in the popular imagination, thought to be a saint. His cult proved in the early years to be the successful manipulation of opportunity.

Offerings left at the shrine in the first quarter of the thirteenth century allowed for the extension of the east end of the church and the rebuilding of the quire which was opened in 1227.[54] Queen Philippa left 12d there in 1352, and Thomas de Wouldham 10 marks in 1360.[55] Pope Boniface IX granted an indulgence of a hundred days to those who visited the shrine and gave alms for its conservation in 1398.[56] Others left gifts in their wills,[57] all providing a steady source of income for the policy of land acquisition and fabric improvement envisaged.

Between 1200 and 1270 the many shares in Goldhawk mill in Darenth were

---

[49] *Victoria County History, Kent*, ii, p. 124. His shrine was on the east side of the high altar. See also James Bentley, *Restless Bones: The Story of Relics*, London 1985, pp. 67–8. Most of what we know of Ithamar comes from Bede's *Ecclesiastical History of the English People*.

[50] Canterbury Cathedral Archives Register N, f. 183r.

[51] N. Yates, 'The Dean and Chapter of Hereford 1240–1320', unpublished MA Thesis, University of Hull 1972, p. 183. See also *St Thomas of Cantilupe, Bishop of Hereford*, ed. M. Jancey, Hereford 1982.

[52] T289, datable between 1225 and 1239, relates to a gift of land lying the length of the burial ground where St William's gate was set.

[53] W. St John Hope, 'The Architectural History of the Cathedral and Monastery of St Andrew at Rochester', *Archaeologia Cantiana*, xxiii (1898), pp. 232–3.

[54] P.A. Welsby, 'William of Perth', typescript; and see also William Lambarde's account which he quotes.

[55] St John Hope, *Arch. Cant.*, xxiii, p. 320.

[56] *CPL*, v, p. 256.

[57] St John Hope, *Arch. Cant.*, xxiii, p. 321 mentions the following: 1474 Edmund Cherkey, gent, 6s 8d for painting the shrine; 1480 John Beaule for a light; Julian Hickes, paid 20d; 1496 John Hilles

acquired piece by piece.[58] At the same period a similar process was in operation in Frindsbury where the priory held the three manors of La Rede or Redecourt, Chattendon and Frindsbury.[59] In 1307 a further process was brought to an end when the priory acquired the manor of Ores by gift from Nicholas de Ores.[60] Other properties, particularly rents, were quitclaimed to the priory after years of payment.[61]

This process continued into the fourteenth century. Edward III gave the priory land in the city ditch from the Eastgate to the priory gate on the south to extend the church precinct in Rochester in 1344;[62] and in 1369 an exchange was effected with the same king whereby the priory gave up its right to collect the fourth penny from the hundred of Rochester and the fourth part of the issues of the constables in Rochester hundred, as well as the tithes of Eltham park which had been given to it by King Henry I. In return the priory acquired property and rents in St Bride's Fleet Street and St John Zachary in London worth £13 8s 0d.[63] Again in 1394 the priory had a special licence from the crown allowing it to benefit to the value of 100 marks a year from the properties of alien priories and other foreign religious houses in the king's hands because of the war.[64] There is no indication which ones, if any, were acquired. In 1395 the priory received Findon church in Chichester diocese from Thomas, Earl of Nottingham in return for masses for his family and descendants at the altars of St Andrew and St Ithamar.[65] Perhaps the priory's greatest acquisition during this century was the gift of the manors of Sharstead and Lidsing with their lands in Chatham, Gillingham, Rochester and Wouldham. Sir Roger de Beleknappe and his wife Amy had gradually built up the unit from about 1365 onwards, and in 1376 conveyed it to the priory.[66]

There were no further significant acquisitions, but a few gains. In 1386 the prior had laid claim to a property in Rochester lying between Dodingherne Lane and Eastgate and entered into it when it fell vacant by neglect. His claim was based on the fact that it had been part of King Aethelberht's gift which had been lost to the priory for many years. The whole of this property was not recovered until 1475.[67] In 1486 King Henry VII acknowledged the priory's right to hold the advowson of Hoo St Werburgh which Prior Simon had exchanged with the nuns of St Sulpice in Rennes in Brittany over two hundred years before in 1259, by payment of one gold mark into the wardrobe.[68]

By 1511 the priory estates had more or less achieved their final extent. The estates listed in Prior William Fressell's inventory of that year comprised the two manors of Haddenham and Cuddington with Kingsey rectory in Buckinghamshire; eleven or twelve manors in Kent including Darenth, Southfleet and Denton; Redecourt or La Rede, Chattendon and Frindsbury in Frindsbury; Stoke, Wouldham, Sharstead

---

of Strood a cow; 1516 Jane Skipwith 12d to St William's light; and 1523 Thomas Shemyng, draper 6s 8d to St William's chapel.

[58] T105–155.	[64] T66.
[59] T163–274.	[65] *CPL*, iv, p. 520.
[60] T185.	[66] T70–94.
[61] T168/2 for example.	[67] T280, 281.
[62] T62.	[68] T66A.
[63] T63.	

and Lidsing; and Almery Court in Rochester; the three rectories of Boxley, Hartlip and Hoo St Werburgh; marshland in Cooling and Cliffe; meadow land in New Hythe acquired from Malling abbey in about 1220; mills in Rochester, Strood and Darenth; as well as innumerable rents, tithes, portions, pensions and rights of advowson from all over Kent from about twenty churches. In addition there were properties and rents in London. By far the most valuable property was that in Buckinghamshire.

(5) The Management of the Estates

Unlike Durham priory where wholesale leasing of the demesne lands did not begin until the early fifteenth century,[69] demesne lands, manors and other Rochester priory properties were in lease from the beginning of the thirteenth century.[70] The leasing of property began in earnest in the priorate of John de Rainham (1262–83).[71] Receipts and undertakings, very much in the form of leases, though not so called, exist for properties in Rochester and Strood.[72] The deeds contain clauses allowing distraint for non-payment of rent, and for the repair of the property by the tenant.

John de Rainham's land acquisition and leasing policy was an attempt to compensate by alternative means for non-existent income from rents, and from sales which had produced only short term capital gains. It was in direct contrast to the system of direct management mentioned in his injunctions by Archbishop Winchelsey in operation in some of the outlying manors such as Southfleet and Cuddington.[73] The income from the shrine of William of Perth had been absorbed in the vast building programmes of the early years of the century and in acquiring new estates. The demesne estates were too small and the soil too poor for any other form of exploitation to be possible.[74] In addition the priory had incurred huge debts as a result of the legal battle with Gilbert Glanville and his successors which had lasted well into the second half of the thirteenth century. In consequence John de Rainham was accused by Archbishop Pecham of maladministration and debt, and removed from office.

The policy of leasing, however, continued, even though it was forbidden by

---

[69] B. Dobson, *Durham Priory 1400–1450*, Cambridge 1973, p. 272.

[70] T193/1.

[71] The written records, such as survive, suggest that some form of leasing had been in operation since 1214, and by inference, earlier than that. The form of the leases is certainly different in the later period. See M. Mate, 'The Farming Out of Manors: a new look at the evidence from Canterbury Cathedral Priory', *Journal of Medieval History*, ix (1983), pp. 331–43.

[72] T343, 345 refer to two properties in Strood, the first on the street between Rochester and Gravesend, and the other on the main road in Strood.

[73] See below, p. 41.

[74] Anne Brown, 'The Financial System of Rochester Priory: A Reconsideration', *Bulletin of the Institute of Historical Research*, 1 (1977), pp. 115–20. In 1316 Walter de Finchingfield had provided stock and crops to feed the monks from the manor of Southfleet during the corn famine, T324/1; and in 1328 John, son of Edmund Waryn agreed to provide wheat from lands in North Darenth over a 20-year period, T145/6. Further evidence is provided by the lease of lands by the prior to the archdeacon of Rochester of lands in Redecourt and Chattendon in Frindsbury where not all the land had been brought into cultivation, T193.

Archbishop Pecham in 1283, and again by Winchelsey in 1299 except with the bishop's consent.

The continuance of this policy also coincided with the use of lay stewards or bailiffs on the priory manors. There are several accounts[75] including one for Ralph Fayry, reeve of the manor of Cuddington in Buckinghamshire, 1448–9,[76] and another for Robert Scathebury, beadle of the manor of Southfleet, 1387–8.[77] Anne Brown suggests that bailiffs may have been in office in about 1292 when the bishop had a manorial steward[78] although Archbishop Winchelsey seems to accept the fact of monk wardens of the manors in 1299. In his injunctions he specifically enjoins that the monk wardens do not unnecessaily delay their return to the monastery after they have completed their business, nor go out to the manors in other than their monastic habits.[79] These stewards or bailiffs ran the manors and accounted for all matters relating to them including expenses, stock, profits of the courts and arrears. In 1511 the priory properties were administered by a steward and under-steward to whom five collectors of rents accounted for the manors of Sharstead and Lidsing, Frindsbury, Stoke and Denton, Southfleet and Darenth, and for the cellarer's rents.[80]

Up to the middle years of the fourteenth century properties were leased for short periods in return for services and rents in kind as well as money rents. John Pikard, for instance, owed rents and services but no money rent for a croft near the entrance to the priory wood in Darenth.[81] The leasing out of manors and properties escalated in the second half of the fourteenth century after the Black Death, and continued until the dissolution.

There seems to have been no set term of years favoured for leases. Some properties were leased for lives, as was Callebelle in Frindsbury for life and a year in 1374 to John Walshe and his son for a rent in kind;[82] and the meadow land on the banks of the river Medway at New Hythe to William atte Hall and Isabel, his wife in 1319, and to Thomas Cugg of New Hythe and his wife Agnes in 1390 for 2s 0d a year.[83]

Other properties were leased for periods varying from five to two hundred years, with leases of 99 years being fairly common. William Syncott, a citizen of London, had a 31-year lease of a tenement in St Bride's, Fleet Street for 40s a year; this lease had been alienated and it is doubtful whether the priory received other than the rent.[84] John Freere had a lease of two vacant plots in Strood for 99 years at 6d a year in 1456. This lease was transferred to Thomas Adams of Rochester city for 88 years at the same rent in 1524 despite the fact that a barn had been built on one of the plots.[85] John Bulbecke leased a shop near the church stile in Hoo St Werburgh in 1506 for sixty years at 3s 4d a year,[86] but John Bradfield, citizen of London, Thomas Bradfield, clerk, and Walter Northampton managed to secure a 200-year lease of a messuage in the city of Rochester at 28s a year in 1382.[87]

[75] F1–8.
[76] F6.
[77] F8.
[78] Anne Brown, *op.cit.*, p. 119.
[79] Winchelsey, *Registrum*, ii, pp. 840–841.
[80] F17.
[81] T141/1.

[82] T175.
[83] T274/2,3.
[84] T370/2,3.
[85] T348/1,2.
[86] T271.
[87] T286.

The rents charged for leases of the priory manors were somewhat greater than those charged for other properties. William Hilles and his family leased Darenth manor for thirteen years at £18 a year in 1488,[88] while George Brooke, Lord Cobham leased Chattendon in Frindsbury for ninety-nine years at £17 17s 0d in 1538.[89] The rent for the manor of Stoke was £20.[90] The largest rents had always come from the Buckinghamshire properties; in the 1511–12 survey these are recorded as amounting to £138 6s 8d.[91]

There is no evidence that a fine system was in operation for the renewal of leases, but if it was this would explain the low rents. Longer leases offered more security to tenants. The policy apparently pursued by the priory argues more for the stability of the tenants rather than a rich yield for the lessor. The policy did, however, free the priory from the enormous repair bills for its properties since these bills now fell almost entirely on the tenants. By 1511 even the lands and tenements belonging to the various obedientiaries were leased out so that their accounts would not be burdened with repairs.[92]

The commissioner who examined the accounts of Boxley abbey before the dissolution of that house said that the abbot and his predecessors had leased out many lands for years and had not profited.[93] Archbishops Pecham and Winchelsey had complained about the system of leasing at Rochester which they felt did not profit the priory, although admittedly in very different economic circumstances two hundred and fifty years earlier. Rents and services were not easy to collect. John Pikard surrendered a lease of a croft near the entrance to the priory wood in Darenth in 1300 because he found the services and rents tedious and onerous.[94] When Roger de Beleknappe was banished to Drogheda in 1388 for his part in subscribing to a formal Act of Council concerning the impeachment of Michael de la Pole, earl of Suffolk, the monks lost the rent from this property which was assigned to others, but later regained it.[95]

Some gifts of land entitled the donor to a corrody, perhaps of food only, but more often of a room in the priory and sustenance for life. Few corrodies appear in the accounts which have survived, which suggests that Rochester was less plagued than most houses with this problem. John, son of Edmund Waryn, did try unsuccessfully to bribe the prior in 1329 to provide one, or a marriage portion, by offering his land rent free.[96] Richard de Honeberghe and his wife Isabel gave a messuage and 20 acres of land in Frindsbury in return for a substantial corrody in the next year which was to be provided by the almoner.[97]

In 1355 a special court was held at the Almery Court manor to find out what had happened to properties on the manor during the period since the Black Death, or pestilence as it is called in the presentments, who had died, who had inherited or

---

[88] T104.
[89] T164.
[90] F17.
[91] F17.
[92] Elb 1A, f. 12r.
[93] *Three Chapters of Letters relating to the* *Suppression of Monasteries*, ed. Thomas Wright, Camden Society, xxxi (1843), p. 172.
[94] T141/1.
[95] T86–94.
[96] T103.
[97] T201.

otherwise acquired the properties, and who in consequence was liable for relief and suit of court. From the large number of presentments mentioning death from the pestilence as a cause of change of ownership after 1349, it is quite clear that deaths from the Black Death on the manor were numerous.[98] Much of the sacrist's income came from this manor.

Evidence from the manor court books also suggests that the tenants were slow in agreeing to pay their reliefs for alienations and acquisitions of property. The evidence provided by the behaviour of just one family in the court of the manor of Ambrey or Almery in Rochester will serve to illustrate this. Thomas Shemyng had failed to pay a rent owed in 1514. The beadle Edmund Estridge distrained on two pieces of woollen cloth for the debt, but Thomas stole them back at dagger point. He was fined 3s 4d. He also owed 6s 0d rent for le Horne de le Hope, an inn near Strood hospital, but said that he did not hold it of the manor but 'de foedo alieno', which was not true. When he died some ten years later, it was found that he had given away some of his properties on the same principle, for which reliefs were said to be due but had never been paid, nor rents. His son John had confirmed the gifts, notably a tenement and orchard to Agnes Clerke, and a tenement in Crowe Lane he had sold to William Warner. John owed 26s 0d relief for the inn, which he still held, and Langford, but to avoid doing fealty and paying relief, he had alienated the properties to his wife Alice. She did fealty and paid the reliefs later, but for over ten years the court had been deprived by these tenants, and by others as well, of sums legally due.[99]

(6) Worship

In accord with the psalmist's 'Seven times a day will I praise thee', and 'At midnight will I rise and give thanks unto thee', the monk's day was divided up to accommodate the seven canonical hours of matins and lauds, prime, terce, sext, none, vespers and compline. Lanfranc makes no reference to the timing of the hours because this really depended on where the monastery was situated, and the season of the year, when the monk began and ended his day. Daylight hours might be longer in the south than the north, and shorter in the winter months.[100] Generally speaking, however, the day was divided up so that, excluding the eight hours of sleep, there was a short interval of prayer every two or three hours. Each week a hebdomadarian was appointed, usually one of the young, newly priested monks, who took his turn to celebrate mass at the high altar on behalf of founders and benefactors. In the early years this would have been a short service, but the multiplication of donors over the years, and the demand for prayers made this an increasingly onerous task. All but the sick in the infirmary were obliged to attend, though obedientiaries absent on business could be dispensed from attendance. There was abuse of this privilege as is evident from

---

98 F1A.
99 Medway Studies Centre, CCRc M1, Manor of Ambrey or Almery of Rochester priory, pp. 58, 75, 120, 160, 165, 173, 192, 205, 216, 304.
100 D. Knowles, *The Monastic Constitutions of Lanfranc*, London 1951, pp. xv–xviii.

Archbishop Winchelsey's injunctions of 1299. He warned that those who knew they would be away should obtain licence of absence from a superior.[101]

The first night office, Matins, was sung around 2.30 in the morning. It began with the *Pater noster, Ave* and *Credo*, and was followed by the recitation of the fifteen gradual psalms, CXX–CXXXIV, and the reading of the lessons for the day. There might be as many as twelve, and each was read by a different monk. Matins was followed by lauds, named from the opening words of the psalm, *Laudate Dominum*. This service normally took an hour and a half and was probably the longest of the day. Prime was around daybreak, and as with the other hours consisted of a hymn, psalms and prayers. The hours of terce, sext and none followed at similar intervals with vespers and compline before the monks retired to sleep.

The most important service of the day was high mass which was celebrated in the middle of the morning by the hebdomadarian. On Sundays and festivals this service would have been celebrated by the prior, or the bishop if he was present. It began with a procession which followed a predetermined route round the cathedral church and ended in the nave before the rood screen. The purpose of this procession was the asperging of all the altars in the church. St John Hope has suggested a route that might have been followed by the Rochester monks.[102] This procession was often joined by other persons attending the service, and was particularly popular with women.[103] Although enjoining that they should not be allowed in the quire, cloister, offices and crypt, even Winchelsey could not exclude them from the mass and viewing the procession.

As well as their round of services within the community, the monks made some contribution to the spiritual welfare of the community as a whole. Some of the senior brothers, the subprior and senior obedientiaries, were regularly commissioned as penitentiaries by the bishop.[104] In 1424 Prior William Tonbridge and his successors were given permission by the pope to administer or cause to be administered any sacraments to the members of their household or their servants. As at Durham, these became a confessorial *corps d'élite*.[105] They were empowered to hear confession, grant absolution, and impose penance on monks and other persons in the diocese, and this rapidly extended their area of influence in the community outside. In 1463 the pope reindorsed the prior of Rochester's right to wear the ring and other pontifical insignia in his own and in other churches, and to give the blessing at Mass, Mattins and Vespers provided no papal legate or bishop was present. In addition he was allowed to wear the almuce and to carry a staff,[106] raising his status almost to that of a bishop.

In the period of religious turmoil created by the preaching of John Wycliffe, and

[101] Winchelsey, *Registrum*, ii, p. 839.
[102] St. John Hope, *Arch. Cant.*, xxiii, pp. 82–83.
[103] Winchelsey, *Registrum*, ii, p. 839. Winchelsey specifically mentions this popularity of processions with women.
[104] *CPL*, v, p. 564; *ibid.* vii, p. 367.
[105] Dobson, *op. cit.*, p. 166.
[106] *CPL*, xi, p. 645.

the attack on the bishop of Winchester and churchmen in general in offices of state by John of Gaunt and others in parliament,[107] the bishop of Rochester was a man of solid piety and an eminent preacher, Thomas Brinton. Rochester was one of the smallest of the dioceses, but Brinton came to hold there a position of considerable weight as a conscientious bishop and a fearless preacher. He was neither a revolutionary nor a conservative. Nor was he politically minded. But he was a resolute critic of corruption and social injustice wherever he found it, at court, in the city or in his diocese. He stood for stability when Wycliffe attacked the church and when the peasants attacked the social order in 1381 and 1382.

Intellectually able monks were trained to preach, and even if away from their convent at Oxford, they returned to preach their turns as Brinton had done at Norwich. Brinton exercised a profound influence at Rochester and beyond during his years as bishop. He took as his motto, 'the truth shall make you free' and for ten years was a public orator among the bishops putting forward his own social and political ideas in his sermons, which he left to the monks of Rochester in his will.[108]

(7) The Obedientiaries

Excluding the prior, it would appear that there were eight principal obedientiaries at Rochester: the subprior, precentor or cantor, almoner, sacrist, chamberlain, cellarer, infirmarer and warden of the chapel of St Mary. This small group is listed in the *Custumale Roffense*.[109]

The size and work of the house determined the number of obedientiaries chosen. There was only ever one subprior and not two as at St Albans and Durham, or three as at Winchester and Canterbury. There was no anniversarian as at Winchester and Canterbury; no pittancer as at Bury St Edmunds; and, despite the presence of three shrines by the thirteenth century, there was no feretrar as at Winchester and Canterbury. There was no master of the novices as at Durham and Winchester; no bartoner is ever mentioned as at Canterbury; and there was no *custos operum* as at Winchester.[110] As will be seen, there was never a treasurer.

With a small number of monks there was perhaps no need for more than one subprior whose main sphere of work was the maintenance of discipline. The work of an anniversarian and novice master was coupled with that of the almoner; that of the feretrar with that of the warden of St Mary's chapel; and that of the pittancer with that of the almoner.[111] This early doubling up of work may account for the expansion of the system, particularly the large number of subsacrists who would

---

[107] W.F. Hook, *Lives of the Archbishops of Canterbury*, London 1860–7, iv, pp. 229–30.

[108] *The Sermons of Thomas Brinton, Bishop of Rochester*, ed. Sister Mary Aquinas Devlin, Camden Society, 3rd series, lxxxv–vi, London 1954. See also G.R. Owst, *Literature and Pulpit in Medieval England*, 2nd edn, Oxford 1961.

[109] R2.

[110] R.H. Snape, *English Monastic Finances in the Later Middle Ages*, Cambridge 1926, pp. 25–6.

[111] F11, 17.

have had to deal with the increasing number of masses. By 1432 the number of obedientiaries had risen to fourteen. In addition to the original eight, there were a subcellarer, three subsacrists, a subchamberlain and a master of the guesthouse.[112]

At Durham and elsewhere the office of treasurer was one of great importance, but it did not exist at Rochester. When Archbishop Pecham visited the priory and removed the prior John de Rainham from office, it was undoubtedly his intention that three treasurers or bursars should be appointed to exercise control over the priory finances.[113] Three worthy monks were to act as receivers of all income, except that appointed to the obedientiaries, so that the independence of the prior could be curtailed. Both the prior and the three treasurers or receivers were to account three times a year. In addition a monk and a secular were instituted to oversee the monastic estates and ensure that the income from them actually passed to the treasurers. Auditors were also to be introduced to oversee the accounts.[114]

Archbishop Pecham's advice appears to have been disregarded and his injunction not put into operation at Rochester. No treasurer is mentioned in the list of obedientiaries in the *Custumale Roffense*[115] and no account roll has survived for any treasurer except for 1511 when William Fressell, the prior was acting as his own treasurer, and accounting, presumably and finally to the auditors for the entire income of the priory including sums delivered by him to certain obedientiaries. The cellarer, for instance, accounted for £129 9s 0d delivered to him by the prior to pay for most of the expenses on his account. Fressell also included the obedientiaries' accounts with his own, but kept them separate within it, thus emphasising the fact that they also were accounting for sums of money not within his sphere of duty. John Sedley of the king's treasury and John Holt, his clerk, were appointed as auditors in 1504[116] and they, or similar officers, continued to serve until the dissolution.[117]

Very few obedientiaries' accounts have survived among the priory archives; there are scattered survivals only for the chamberlain, sacrist, almoner, cellarer and infirmarer. Together they cover the mid fourteenth to early fifteenth centuries.

All the obedientiaries were appointed by the chapter, but only the elections of the subprior, cellarer, precentor, sacrist and chamberlain were approved by the bishop. He had no choice in the appointment of any of the others. This right of approval was more a custom to be continued than something worth having. At Rochester and at Worcester the bishops did not give up this right. At Durham, on the other hand, the prior and chapter were almost free from episcopal interference.[118]

Each obedientiary was treated as a distinct corporation in his own undiminished

[112] Ar 1/8, f. 33.

[113] Peckham, *Registrum*, pp. 621–5.

[114] Snape, *op.cit.*, pp. 38, 39 says that this system was in operation at Clairvaux in the early thirteenth century. Some very similar system may have been in place at Canterbury in the time of Archbishop Baldwin (1187).

[115] R2.

[116] Elb 1A, f. 19v.

[117] The *Valor Ecclesiasticus* notes the prior as treasurer, i, pp. 101–4.

[118] Ar 1/8, f. 33 and Dobson, *op. cit.*, p. 164. In 1250 the pope had suggested that the bishop should be content with the right of appointment of keepers of priory manors and sergeanties, and not with the appointment of obedientiaries, *CPL*, i, p. 259, but he does not appear to have accepted this.

right within the priory. Each had specific sums of money to spend on specific departments and spheres of activity within the house, the majority of which derived from gifts of property and rents in both kind and money which could not be used in any other way. Their income was separate from other priory income. The duties of the obedientiaries were defined by custom, and their worth as officials rested on their ability to end their year or term of office in credit. Archbishop Winchelsey ordered in 1299 that the obedientiaries should account each year to the prior and chapter for their offices, and that those who were found guilty of maladministration should be immediately removed from office and punished.[119]

Many of the property deeds belonging to the priory are not only endorsed with the name of the place concerned, and the donor, but also with a note as to which particular section of the monastic establishment the income was to be channelled. The largest number are endorsed *Ista pertinet as Elemosinarium*; others with the single word *Elemosinaria* often heavily abbreviated. Of the surviving deeds, those pertaining to the almoner number twenty-six. Two are marked to indicate that the incoming rents were paid to the sacrist; eleven to the cellarer; two to the chamberlain, three or four to the precentor; four to the infirmarer and two to the chapel of St Mary in the infirmary; and eleven to the the warden of St Mary's chapel. These numbers are taken from surviving deeds for the period 1200–84.[120] The lands pertaining to obedientiary offices suggest that there were very many more. Some of these lands had been early gifts when men became monks.[121]

Each obedientiary was responsible for his own department and for the charges on it. The cellarer looked after the kitchen. He provided food, coal, candles, wages for persons connected with the kitchen, cutlery and napery, and for some repairs to property. In 1383/4 John Dane paid £9 5s 10d for corn, 105 eggs at 8 for 1d, hay, 200 candles, 2 pounds of cotton for wicks, 13 ells of cloth for towels in the refectory and infirmary; tankards, a trivet, and six and a half quarters of coal for the kitchen. He spent £7 3s 7d on repairs to his buildings, and £6 17s 6d on horses, cows, provender and seed corn and peas, and barley for the household. His wage bill was £9 11s 0d and included cooks, porters, a pig-keeper, launderer, horse-keeper and men in the vineyards. His kitchen expenses, which are not enumerated, amounted to £144 13s 0d.[122]

The chamberlain provided clothing for the monks, rushes, pittances, the monks' salaries, liveries, wine, wages for his rent collectors, and repairs to priory property. In 1385/6 Nicholas de Frindsbury paid £6 10s 2½d towards the tiling of the granary roof, 2,000 tiles and other ridge tiles to mend priory houses, plus the wages of John the tiler for nine days at 9d a day. He also paid Geoffrey atte Donne 41s 8d. for work

---

[119] Winchelsey, *Registrum*, ii, pp. 621–4.
[120] See for instance gifts to the almoner: T168, 170, 172, 176, 177, 179, 187, 190, 191, 201, 204–206, 208, 212, 213, 215, 216, 228, 267, 269, 270, 273, 278, 346, 352.
[121] When Helyas became a monk in about 1130 he gave property in Crowe Lane, Rochester, T302. Similarly when William, son of Ernulf de Strodes, became a monk in about 1150, his father gave lands in 'Pivindene' for the almoner, T191/2.
[122] F12.

on the dormitory chapel.[123] In 1396/7 Roger de Staplehurst, the chamberlain paid for the building of the new latrines for the infirm brothers at a cost of £9 7s 7½d as well as repairs to houses costing 19s 4½d. Thomas Ealdynge, chamberlain in 1415/16 accounted for 2,000 tiles at 10s, and nails, rushes and bars of iron for the furnaces.[124]

The almoner looked after the boys in the almonry and their teaching, paid the schoolmaster, and provided for the poor. His payments for the boys include candles, herrings, and some meat on feast days in Lent and Advent; and for the poor, bread on Gundulf's anniversary. Little provision was made for the poor in the account because poor people were given food left over from meals in the refectory. Archbishop Pecham had complained in 1283 that the monks had failed to do this, and his successor Winchelsey reiterated the injunction that what was left over from meals should be reserved for the poor.[125]

Knowles, following R.A.L. Smith, says that the obedientiary system was abandoned at Rochester in the fourteenth century in more or less the same way as it was at Canterbury, the prior taking the revenues of the house into his own hands. On the surviving evidence this does not seem to have been the case.[126] The presence of the endorsements and the fact that the obedientiaries were still accounting for them in the sixteenth century argues against this.[127] It is clear too, that registers of lands existed which detailed the purpose of the various gifts. There are thirteen and fourteenth century endorsements to the effect that a deed has not been copied into the register. These registers have not survived with the sole exception of part of a priors' register kept by William Woode and Thomas Bourne, 1478–1504. This register deals almost exclusively with territorial problems or leases.[128] Nor have any registers there may have been survived for the lands and properties of the obedientiaries. Rather than abandoning the system, it could be conjectured that the obedientiaries were encouraged to accept gifts on their own initiative and to buy properties with money at their own disposal and that in doing so they made a major contribution to the welfare of the community itself.[129] Rents were still being administered by specific officials in 1511, as carefully set out in Prior Fressell's inventory, in 1526 and even in 1535. When the total value of the priory possessions was calculated, it was based on the rents allocated to the various officers.[130]

---

[123] F13.

[124] F15.

[125] Peckham, *Registrum*, ii, pp. 621–4; Winchelsey, *Registrum*, ii, pp. 839–42. Gundulf died 7 March 1107/8.

[126] D. Knowles, *The Religious Orders in England*, Cambridge 1948–59, ii, pp. 329–30. But see R.H. Snape, *op. cit.*, pp. 25, 26 and Anne Brown, *op. cit.*, pp. 115–20.

[127] F9–17.

[128] See T98/1, 190/1, 292/1, 332, 368, 372/1. Priors' register Elb 1A.

[129] See Anne Brown, *loc. cit.*

[130] *Valor*, i, pp. 101–4. Laurence Mereworth, prior and treasurer, £388 13s 9½d; Walter Boxley, cellarer £39 13s 7¾d; Anthony London, sacrist £33 17s 6d; Thomas Nevylle, chamberlain £35 0s 8d; Robert Maydestone, precentor £1 11s 8d; John Rye, warden of St Mary's chapel £1 6s 8d;

Plate 1. Illuminated capital letter from the *Textus Roffensis*, early twelfth century.

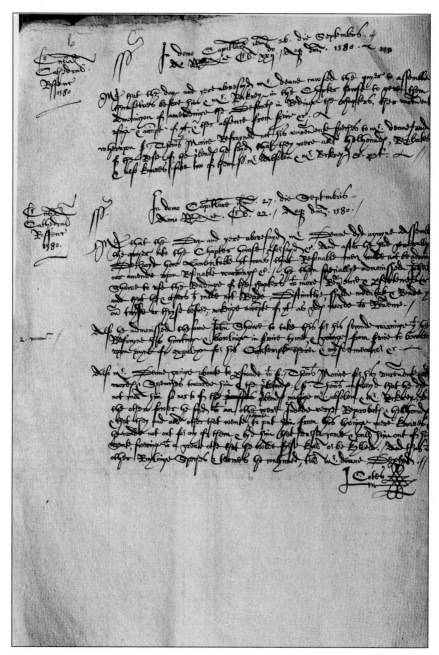

Plate 2. Extract from the chapter minutes in which the dean and canons are described as 'helhoundes', 1580.

(8) Personnel

Rochester priory had from its earliest years the privilege of electing its own priors without royal interference. In the early years men from other houses had been elected, but by the third quarter of the thirteenth century it had become standard practice to elect a prior from within the house itself who was confirmed in office by the bishop. The only exception to this arrangement was the election in 1509 of William Fressell, Prior of Bingham in Norfolk, who may have been brought in as a reformer to stabilise the finances of the priory. With the exception of those priors who were elevated to the bishopric, Thomas de Wouldham in 1291, Hamo de Hethe in 1319 and John de Sheppey in 1352, none of the priors left the house. After 1189 no monk or prior left the house to rule elsewhere. If a prior resigned his office, and at least eleven did, they remained as brothers in the house until they died.[131]

It is difficult to follow the trend of numbers of monks in the priory as the information is somewhat inadequate. The catchment area can be determined from the names adopted by the monks when they entered the house, or took their first vows. Normally this was their parish of origin. Many were local men from Rochester and its neighbouring parishes in West Kent, and particularly from priory estates and manors, but others came from Canterbury, Folkestone and Dover. A few came from even further away – London, Winchester, Mayfield, St Albans and even Ossory in Ireland.

The bishop of Rochester had the privilege of ordaining the majority of clergy both regular and secular in his diocese; and, as chaplain and assistant to the archbishop of Canterbury, throughout Kent, parts of London and southern England *sede vacante* and *sede non vacante*. Most monks were professed in their own house by their prior on receipt of letters dimissory from the bishop, usually taking their threefold vows of stability, poverty and conversion of manners after a year in the priory. Aspirants to the order of acolyte, subdeacon, deacon or priest, however, had to present themselves to the bishop in person. In the fourteenth century ordinations usually took place on the bishop's manors of Bromley, Halling or Trottiscliffe, or in Rochester or London.[132] The monks were normally presented by their own prior or some person deputed by him. When a monk took the order of subdeacon, deacon and priest he was ordained to a title in the priory.

It would appear that the number of monks entering the priory at any one time was fairly small, perhaps only three or four, and that these small groups progressed together at least through the minor orders to that of subdeacon or deacon. A Durham monk writing in the fourteenth century said that only as many novices should be recruited into a community 'as its resources can support if they are well

and Robert Rochester, almoner £5 0s 8d; total £486 11s 5d. These figures are net. F17; Elb 1A, 10v–12; and *Victoria County History, Kent*, ii, p. 124.

131 H. Wharton, *Anglia Sacra*, pp. 392–4.

132 See *Registrum Hamonis de Hethe*, ed. C. Johnson, 2 vols, Oxford 1948.

administered.'[133] If Rochester priory was not financially secure at this time, as Dobson suggests, this may account for the lower numbers in the fourteenth century.[134]

Whether a man then took priest's orders was very much a matter of personal inclination. Progression through the minor orders was fairly rapid. As is to be expected, some monks were ordained as deacons but did not progress to the priesthood. It is among this group that the majority of office holders is found. A surprisingly large number of monks were ordained as priests in the period from the late thirteenth to the end of the fifteenth century within eighteen months or two years at the most. There were of course exceptions. John de Burgam became an acolyte on 21 September 1335 but was not priested until 4 June 1341.[135]

A small number of monks went up to Oxford to study and for this purpose were granted a pension from the priory. One of the first students from Rochester was John de Sheppey who became the prior in 1333.[136] He obtained a doctorate in theology in 1332. Among the others, John de Hollingbourne was there in 1382,[137] John Ealdyng in 1387,[138] John de Shipton in 1415/16,[139] Thomas Wybarn in 1467/8,[140] Roger Pylton in 1496[141] and Anthony London in 1511.[142]

The names and in many cases the dates of profession of some 471 Rochester monks have been traced to date through the Rochester episcopal registers and other sources,[143] but this figure cannot be by any means complete. Of these, most entered the house between 1200 and 1539, and 29 of them rose to the office of prior. Many of the monks held more than one office, but as with other houses there seems to have been no standard progression from one office to another.

In the eleventh and twelfth century period of expansion monks from well established houses were often sent out to help found and replenish other houses. Monks from Rochester were sent to Christ Church, Canterbury in 1207, and doubtless others went elsewhere.[144] In the same way others came to Rochester. Ralph of Olneye transferred from Lincoln diocese in 1287.[145] The episcopal memorandum

[133] See Dobson, *op. cit.*, p. 157.
[134] *Ibid.*, pp. 157–8.
[135] Ar 1/1, ff. 165, 166, 173, 195.
[136] A.B. Emden, *A Biographical Register of the University of Oxford to AD 1500, P–Z*, Oxford 1959, pp. 1683–4.
[137] *Ibid., F–O*, Oxford 1958, p. 951.
[138] *Ibid., A–E*, Oxford 1957, p. 619.
[139] F15.
[140] Emden, *op. cit., P–Z*, pp. 2098–9.
[141] He is listed as at Oxford in the prior's certificate returned to Archbishop John Morton's visitation citation, *The Register of John Morton, Archbishop of Canterbury 1486–1500*, ii, p. 446.
[142] F15.
[143] Personal communication from Dr Joan Greatrex, who is shortly to publish monastic biographies for many of the English cathedral priories including Canterbury, Rochester and Norwich, 19 June 1994.
[144] H. Wharton, *Anglia Sacra*, p. 337.
[145] Peckham, *Registrum*, ii, p. 239.

of 1432 names thirteen officers, and this might presuppose a fairly large establishment. However, this proves not to be the case. Numbers are given for monks voting in elections which are recorded in the episcopal registers, but not all are recorded in full. There were thirty-five monks at Rochester in 1317, but the record of the disputed election of 1333, names only the senior monks. These totalled thirty. Twenty-two of this number led by the former prior voted for John de Sheppey; five, led by Richard Bledlawe the cellarer and his subcellarer, Peter de Lambourne voted for William de Ryarsh the sacrist; and the other three, said to be younger monks, voted for Robert de Southfleet. Since only professed monks could vote, the figure of thirty does not include novices or postulants, and perhaps some junior monks who are not mentioned. The final figure might be nearer thirty-five. There were only twenty-three monks present at the election of Lawrence Dan *alias* Mereworth in 1532, and twenty in the priory in 1535.[146]

The chamberlain accounted in his expenses for the number of monks in the priory. Numbers had been drastically reduced by the Black Death which raged in Rochester between 1349 and 1352,[147] and never again reached their pre-1349 levels. In November 1390 the pope issued an indult allowing the bishop of Rochester to ordain six monks as deacon at eighteen and priest at twenty-three years of age because the number of monks in the priory had been much reduced by the pestilence and there were no men of sufficient age to be otherwise ordained.[148] A few may have left, as did William Leicester who was transferred to Canwell Priory in Staffordshire in 1480, but this was rare at the time.[149] In February 1385 Nicholas de Frindsbury accounts for twenty-one brothers plus the prior and John de Hartlip, who had resigned as prior in 1380 but was still living there, and at Michaelmas for twenty-three brothers.[150] This figure may include the prior and John de Hartlip, or it may be an increase. There is no evidence either way. Roger de Staplehurst accounted for twenty-three brothers at both February and Michaelmas in 1396/7;[151] and Thomas Ealdynge for twenty-three brothers in February and twenty-one brothers at Midsummer in his 1415/16 account.[152] In 1511 there were only fourteen monks and four novices in the house, but two monks, William Rykyll and Edward Hattfield, the chamberlain, had recently died.[153]

The fluctuation in the numbers of monks in the priory between 1317 and 1540 can be summarised as follows:

[146] Ar 1/1, f. 157 and Ar 1/4, f. 173.
[147] F1A. There were a large number of deaths of tenants on the manor of Ambrey Court which covered much of the city of Rochester.
[148] *CPL*, iv, p. 366.
[149] Elb 1A, f. 6.
[150] F13.
[151] F14.
[152] F15.
[153] F17.

Year	Number	
1317	35	
1333	35	
1385–1386	23	February
1385–1386	23	Michaelmas
1396–1397	23	Michaelmas
1415–1416	23	February
1415–1416	21	Michaelmas
1432	[20]	13 officers + ?7–10 monks[154]
1496	19	November. Includes one apostate
1511	20	14 monks + 4 novices + 2 monks who had died
1532	23	
1534	20	
1535	20	
1540	16	

From the figures available of professed monks it could be postulated that in the period before the Black Death there were probably between thirty-five and forty monks in the house. In the latter half of the fourteenth century this figure dipped to twenty-three and remained fairly constant until 1535. In 1540 there were still sixteen monks, and five of these joined the new cathedral foundation in various capacities. If thirteen of the monks held office, as for instance in 1432, the community would not have been so well balanced as it had been prior to the Black Death when this figure was just over a third. At Westminster the figure was 60%, and at Canterbury forty of the fifty-nine monks present in the house in 1540 were obedientiaries.[155] Unlike the monks in the Durham cells, the monks at Rochester's Felixstowe cell were not counted as monks of Rochester because they had no vote in the election of the prior.[156] In the fourteenth and fifteenth centuries numbers of monks at other houses were larger than at Rochester. At Canterbury numbers were between seventy and eighty, at Durham around seventy, and at Ely, Norwich, Worcester and Winchester between thirty and thirty-five.[157] Rochester therefore was a small house in comparison.

(9) The Dissolution

By the late 1530s the dissolution of the smaller religious houses in Kent had been in progress for some years. Higham nunnery had been dissolved in 1521 and its possessions transferred to St John's College, Cambridge; and Lesnes and Tonbridge

---

[154] Three monks may have died in about 1426. *CPL*, vii, p. 430.
[155] Dobson, *op. cit.*, p. 170.
[156] H. Wharton, *Anglia Sacra*, i, p. 371.
[157] Dobson, *op. cit.*, pp. 156–7.

were dissolved in 1525 to help found Cardinal Wolsey's college in Oxford. Rochester priory's cell at Felixstowe was suppressed in 1528 also to provide endowment for Wolsey's college.[158] Dover and Langdon were dissolved in 1535; and five others, Canterbury St Sepulchre, Canterbury St Gregory, Monks Horton, Combwell and St Radegund's in 1536. Only the larger houses remained, and the prior of Leeds, Arthur St Leger, had no illusions about their survival.[159] Within another five years the remaining eighteen large religious houses in Kent had been dissolved[160]

Rochester priory was one of the last religious houses to go. The process was foreshadowed on 10 June 1534 when Prior Lawrence Dan or Mereworth, Robert Rochester, the subprior, and eighteen monks took the oath of acknowledgment of the royal supremacy,[161] but was not completed until the final surrender in April 1540.

In 1535 Dr Richard Layton, Cromwell's principal agent in the dissolution of the monasteries, visited the house, probably in October.[162] No account appears to exist of his findings, but his work at Rochester presumably followed instructions similar to those issued to all commissioners later on in 1536.[163] These instructions fell into three distinct parts: first to inspect the house and discover its state and indebtedness, to identify items of value, and survey the buildings, lands and possessions; second to appoint pensions for the religious and displace them and their servants; and last to sell the grain, stock and household goods, remove all items of value such as jewels, plate, lead and ornaments to London together with all useful documentation for the king's use, and to deliver the property and its lands as directed by the king. The findings of the commissioners were to be certified under their seals on an appointed day.

The work of inspection and survey continued slowly throughout the country as well as at Rochester. In 1537 Rochester was listed as one of the new cathedral churches 'to be changed according to the king's new devise', and during this and the next year at least two proposals were drawn up for the new foundation despite the fact that it was said to be £500 in debt to the crown. In the first draft proposal, beginning, 'Forasmuch as the prior and monks of Rochester, living in such sort as they now do, be not able to serve God and the Kings Highness in his graces commonwealth so well as they might', proposals were drawn up for a foundation consisting of a dean, ten prebendaries besides the archdeacon, one of whom was to be a lecturer in divinity and to have as his prebend the Hospital of Strood, and another who was to preach in the city and diocese of Rochester. There were also to be four minor canons, six lay clerks or vicars, six choristers, a master of choristers, one porter, two sextons, a verger and a schoolmaster. Ten poor men from the city were

[158] E. Hasted, *History of Kent*, folio edn, ii, p. 38 note u.
[159] In a narrative about 'Punghorst' wood Lancelot Gilbank, a former canon of Leeds priory and then warden of St Mary Chatham, wrote of rumours of dissolution and spoke of a visit from the prior of Leeds, Arthur St Leger, who had 'sayd we schuld be putt owte of owr place with in schort tyme', Egz 5.
[160] See *Victoria County History, Kent*, ii, pp. 113–240.
[161] *LP* VII, no. 921.
[162] He was in Canterbury on 23 October. See *DNB*, Layton.
[163] *LP* XI, App. no. 15.

also to be supported under this scheme who were to pray for the king and Prince Edward every Sunday and holy day, and attend mass and evensong in the cathedral.[164]

A later paper proposed a much reduced establishment of a dean and six prebendaries, one of whom was to be the archdeacon, and one the master of Strood. The master of Strood was to have the former hospital buildings and lands valued at £30 a year as his prebend. He was to be a divinity lecturer and was always to be a learned man who was to lecture on divinity in the cathedral on Mondays, Wednesdays and Fridays. There were to be four other prebendaries, one of whom may have been intended as a diocesan preacher as his salary was slightly larger than that of the other three. Four minor canons, six lay clerks, eight choristers, a schoolmaster, verger and ten poor men made up the remainder of the foundation. All the clergy were to be allowed to hold benefices and to be absent from the cathedral without licence. The bishop was to have the nomination of the dean, the regulation of discipline, and the patronage of all the livings belonging to the cathedral.[165]

The first of these proposals was lavish and would have created an establishment nearly equal in size to Canterbury where there were to be a dean and twelve prebendaries. It was monastic in outlook in some ways, in that the clergy were obviously expected to stay within the precincts, but it addressed the problem of teaching which was recognised as necessary, both in the cathedral and in the city and diocese. The smaller foundation was less monastic in outlook and more in keeping with the size of the cathedral building and available lodging space, as well as less costly. The proposal to allow the prebendaries to hold livings would have been seen as a way of increasing their regular income which was to be based on a small salary and a share of the fines and dividends as they arose each quarter. No attempt was made to create a group of diocesan preachers equivalent to the Six Preachers at Canterbury. The prebend at Strood was never established.

In the early months of 1538 events began to move forward. The prior, Lawrence Dan or Mereworth, resigned and Walter Phillips or Boxley was appointed in his place. This appointment appears to have been deliberate policy to ease the process of dissolution.[166] It also appears to have caused some resentment among the older monks, so much so that John Hilsey, the bishop, wrote to Cromwell asking him to reverse the decision to appoint Phillips and allow him to have his poor monk back because 'many things have gone amiss, as the elder brethren of the house have at divers times declared' since Prior Dan's resignation.[167] There was no reversal.

---

[164] LP XV, no. 379 (1).

[165] LP XV, no. 379 (2).

[166] An unknown writer, reminiscing about the dissolution, wrote in the reign of Elizabeth, 'He [Cromwell] placed abbottes and friers in divers great housses divers lerned men, and perswaded against these superstitiens, which men were readiee to make surrender of their houses at the kinges commaundement.' And, 'First, divers abbotes and other that could be thereunto perswaded, or were some of them four the purpose placed by the king, made surrender of their houses and conveied them to the kinge by order of lawe, and had competent pencions both themselves and their companie during their lives. . . .', Three Chapters of Letters relating to the Suppression of Monasteries, ed. Thomas Wright, Camden Society, xxxi (1843), pp. 114, 115.

[167] LP XIII (i), no. 1391.

A much later document, dated 4 July 1540, proposed a foundation of a dean, six prebendaries, one of whom was to be the archdeacon, six minor canons, an epistoler, a gospeller, six lay singing men, a master of choristers, eight choristers, a schoolmaster, usher and twenty scholars, two sextons and six poor serving men. The same document also appointed lodgings for the dean and prebendaries and other persons within the cathedral precinct where they were to live in common.[168] This was the final plan which was followed, except that Maurice Griffith, who had been archdeacon of Rochester since 1537, continued in office and did not hold a prebendal stall. A similar plan was adopted at Canterbury though on a larger scale.

(10) Conclusion

In general it might be true to say that the period 1185–1540 is one of paradox. On the one hand there is the constant conflict with some of the early bishops modified in the thirteenth and fourteenth centuries when successive Rochester monks were appointed bishops; on the other there is the steady acquisition of lands and consolidation of holdings, and the leasing out of property. Apart from its vast collection of title deeds, relatively little documentary evidence survives for Rochester priory, so that it is difficult to be positive about its development. In the late medieval period it is likely that the priory went through a difficult period, not assisted by the decline in the number of monks, but Rochester was never beseiged by so many pilgrims as Canterbury, nor at the mercy of so many rebuilding programmes. The relatively high proportion of monks progressing to the priesthood, with some studying at Oxford, argues for a fairly healthy atmosphere, and good teaching within the house. The decade of the episcopate of Thomas Brinton, an excellent administrator as well as teacher, many of whose sermons have survived, allowed the priory a period of stability in a period of profound unrest throughout the rest of the country, enabling it to pursue its way less encumbered with external problems than were other houses, but one nonetheless that was fairly typical of other smaller Benedictine houses of the time.

---

[168] St John Hope, *Arch. Cant.*, xxiv, pp. 71–3. See also T281 which bears an endorsement by Martin Cotes, the chapter clerk 'The howse nexte the grete gate leased to Mr John Simkins nuper prebendario in quo ego Martinus Cotys Inhabito.'

3

The Reformed Chapter, 1540–1660

C. S. KNIGHTON

King Henry VIII reversed the achievement of Bishop Gundulf by replacing the Benedictine chapter of Rochester with a community of secular clerks. This was in order that the cathedral might survive the abolition of the religious orders. There were some who hoped that cathedrals would be dissolved along with all other ecclesiastical corporations, but the government resisted so radical a move. In fact the number of English cathedrals was slightly increased by the transformation of (initially) six abbeys and most of the cathedral priories into secular churches. Rochester was therefore reborn into a family of new foundations, distinguished by the common form of their creation and constitution from those cathedrals which had been served by secular chapters before the Reformation. The Henrician cathedrals were intended to be ruled by deans and canons who were resident and paid fixed stipends, unlike the canons of the old foundations who resided (or, more usually, did not) as they chose, and who were supported by individual endowments ('prebends'). The new cathedrals were also promoted as centres of learning, preaching and social welfare, extending to the care of the old and the mending of roads. These aspirations, expressed in the enabling act of 1539 and repeated in the foundation charters and the statutes which followed, have been derided by one modern commentator as 'the most extraordinary collection of largely irrelevant jargon'.[1] But the dean and chapter of Rochester, in the first century of its existence, did for the most part carry out its various obligations within the limits of its modest resources.

The process by which Rochester and the other former monasteries became secular colleges was generally uniform. The evidence is not complete in any one case, and Rochester furnishes some details not found elsewhere. When on 20 March 1540 commission was issued to take surrender of the cathedral priory the bishopric lay vacant by the death of Bishop Hilsey seven months before. So six days later the King directed his *congé d'élire* to the prior and convent, who duly elected Nicholas Heath on 26 March: only then could the monastic chapter be abolished.[2] Between 4 and 16 April the Chancellor of the Court of Augmentations, Sir Richard Rich, attended to

---

[1] J. Youings, *The Dissolution of the Monasteries*, London 1971, p. 85.
[2] PRO E 322/206 (*LP* XV, no. 378(2)). *LP* XV, no. 436(83), pp. 178–9. Lambeth Palace, Reg. Cranmer, f. 257v (*LP* XV, no. 436(91)).

the surrenders of Canterbury and Rochester, along with the deputy Vicar-General, Dr William Petre, and the solicitor of Augmentations, Walter Hendle (who drew up the surrender papers).[3] Benedictine observance at Rochester came to an end on 8 April.[4] The King's officers (according to the terms of their commission) summoned the monks along with the townsfolk and explained to them the royal reasons for altering the cathedral into a secular establishment. Inventories were made, and all that was not considered necessary for the new community was removed. The monks were at once to take off their habits, and those found suitable were selected for service in the new college. Wherever possible the former prior was placed in charge with the title of warden or guardian, so at Rochester Prior Walter Boxley dispensed with his monastic *alias* along with his black robes, reverting to the family name of Phillips by which he would be known as the first dean. Otherwise a smaller number of monks was retained than elsewhere. None was considered sufficiently distinguished to become a canon. But Thomas Grey and Nicholas Spelhurst were given the posts of gospeller and epistoler, while Thomas Coxe and Owen Oxforde became high and under sexton. The remaining nine (including two described as chantry priests) were dismissed with pensions. Those chosen to be the nucleus of the refounded body were told to adopt the dress of secular clergy and to follow the Sarum rite and the customs of St George's Chapel, Windsor.[5] Some have supposed that the interval between dissolution and refoundation was a void in the cathedral's life, but it is clear from records of sister foundations that liturgical observance was unbroken. The main difference was that the place of the choir monks was taken by the lay clerks and boy choristers who had previously served the Lady Chapel.[6] New desks were made in 1541 to accommodate them.[7] As yet the liturgy was untouched by Protestant reform, and the first episcopal injunctions (1543) provided in great detail for ceremonial and polyphony.

Meanwhile constitutions were being devised for the new cathedrals, perhaps in part delayed by the fall from power of Thomas Cromwell in the summer of 1540. Even so the process was necessarily protracted. There were several draft schemes for cathedral bodies, in all of which Rochester featured, despite the general intention (never realised) of having one cathedral for each county.[8] One proposal was in a form, not found in connection with any of the other locations, of application for the King's licence to alter the house into a secular college. Although notionally a petition from the prior and convent seeking its own demise, it is almost certainly the work of the Augmentations Office. It envisaged a chapter of a dean and ten canons, the canons to be chosen and the statutes issued by the bishop (though in the event these functions would be reserved by the Crown). One of the canons was to be divinity lecturer, having Strood Hospital as his prebend; another was to be permanently

3   *LP* XVI, no. 745 (ff. 36, 38); XVIII(ii), no. 231, p. 123.
4   As 1, pp. 53–6. *LP* XV, no. 474.
5   PRO E 36/116 (*LP* XIV(i), nos 1189, 1190).
6   See F. Ll. Harrison, *Music in Medieval Britain*, 2nd edn 1963, pp. 40–5, 185–92.
7   W. St John Hope, 'The Architectural History of the Cathedral Church and Monastery of St Andrew at Rochester', *Archaeologia Cantiana*, xxiii (1898), 301–2.
8   Printed in H. Cole, *King Henry the Eighth's Scheme of Bishopricks*, London 1838, pp. 3–4, 49–51.

engaged preaching in the city and diocese. The archdeacon was to have a place in the cathedral body. There were to be ten poor men of the town present at what was still called the monastery to pray for the King and his son.[9] The eventual establishment would be on a smaller scale:

The Cathedral Body as refounded by Henry VIII

The Chapter	The dean 6 canons (including vice-dean, treasurer and receiver)
The ministers and choir	6 minor canons (including precentor and sacrist) gospeller epistoler 6 lay clerks master of the choristers 8 choristers 2 subsacrists [under-sextons]
The school	schoolmaster under master 20 scholars
Almsmen	6 paupers
Servants	butler janitor cook under cook
Non-residents	steward auditor 4 university students

During the transition period the properties of the former priory remained in the King's hands, and the cathedral clergy had no legal status. The dean-designate was in charge of internal finances, and the priory tenants were ordered by Augmentations to pay him the customary rents and dues.[10] Walter Phillips was also reimbursed for £20 spent on entertaining the dissolution commissioners.[11] Even so the house was under financial strain, and it was proposed to sell £80 worth of lands and impropriate a rectory worth forty marks to augment the revenue.[12] By March 1541, when government business was transacted there, the cathedral had become known as 'the college of Rochester'. The last of the canons-designate was chosen in April.[13]

---

[9]   PRO SP 1/158, f. 79 (*LP* XV, no. 379). Cf. above, pp. 53–4.
[10] AO 1, 2.
[11] *LP* XVI, no. 745 (f. 40).
[12] PRO SP 1/158, f. 79v (*LP* XV, no. 379).
[13] *LP* XVI, nos 644, 678(45), 693.

The charter of foundation is dated 18 June 1541.[14] After recapitulating the King's pious intentions in advancing religion, education and charity, it formally reconstituted the cathedral with the new dedication of Christ and the Blessed Virgin Mary. By the same instrument a chapter of a dean and six canons was erected and its first members appointed. Dean Phillips was joined by six outsiders. The senior canon was Hugh Aprice ('Dr Hewes' as he was commonly called), treasurer of St David's Cathedral and subsequently founder of Jesus College, Oxford. John Symkyns had been prior of St Gregory's, Canterbury; John Wildbore was the last master of Strood Hospital. Also named were Robert Johnson, Vicar-General of the diocese, Richard Engest, principal of Magdalen Hall, Oxford, and Robert Salisbury. Two days later the new chapter received its endowment: eleven manors in Kent which had belonged to the cathedral priory and ten which had been owned by Leeds Priory; Strood Hospital; properties in Rochester, London, Canterbury and Maidstone from the priory and from Leeds; eight Kent and three Buckinghamshire rectories which had belonged to the priory and fourteen more from Leeds, all but one of which was in Kent.[15] There followed on 4 July a commission to Lord Cobham and other local worthies to install the dean and canons in quire and chapter, a notable exhibition of the royal supremacy, for the cathedral body was thus inaugurated without reference to ecclesiastical authority (though subsequent royal nominees were presented to the bishop). The same commissioners were then required to allot houses to the clergy.[16] This was more difficult at Rochester than in other locations because the dean and chapter did not have at its disposal the domestic buildings of the monastery. These were retained by the King with the intention of erecting there a palace for his own use. Much construction took place there over the next two years, but the project was then abandoned and the property sold in 1551 to Lord Cobham. He in turn made it over to the dean and chapter in 1558 for £100.[17] It is likely that the site was already in disrepair, and that materials from it were used to augment the clerical housing which had been provided in 1541. Nevertheless these houses seem to have been in frequent need of repair; in 1584 the chapter had to put a limit of 5 shillings on work done on any one house within a year, and at the end of the century two canons were said to be without houses.[18]

The first major occasion for the refounded cathedral was the enthronement (by proxy) of Bishop Heath in April 1542.[19] The bishop's visitation articles of the following year suggest that the dean and chapter had as yet imperfectly ordered their affairs. The dean was told to collect all the archives, including the deeds of foundation and endowment. Particular attention was needed for records of properties newly come to the cathedral from Leeds. The dean was not to make leases without consulting his chapter colleagues, whom he was to meet every Saturday to discuss

[14] *LP* XVI, no. 947(36).

[15] *LP* XVI, no. 947(42).

[16] As 1, back fly-leaf. PRO SP 1/243, ff. 226–9 (*LP* Add, no. 1502). Cf. above, p. 55 and n. 168.

[17] Hope, *Arch. Cant.*, xxiv (1900), pp. 67–81.

[18] Ac 1, p. 31. As 3, p. 8.

[19] Ar 1/15, ff. 13v–15. J. Le Neve, *Fasti Ecclesiae Anglicanae 1541–1857*, iii, *Canterbury, Rochester and Winchester Dioceses*, comp. J.M. Horn, London 1974, p. 50.

business, committing to individuals particular duties. A complex liturgical regime was prescribed. Priests and clerks were to be present at the start of every service, or at least by the first *Gloria Patri*, on pain of forfeiting ¼d, and not to depart before the end, or lose ½d. The dean and canons were to be fined 10 shillings if they did not preach once a fortnight. An inventory of the church's goods was to be made and kept by the sextons, one of whom was to keep guard at night. The modest size of the cathedral body entailed some doubling of parts, the porters acting as vergers and the boys of the school as lectors and servers.[20]

These regulations were followed and in some respects modified by statutes issued in common form to the new foundations during 1544. Rochester's are dated 30 June.[21] They were not authenticated by the great seal, a fact of which the dean and chapter would later attempt to take advantage. They laid great emphasis on residence, communal life and obedience to the dean. He was supposed to be a Doctor of Divinity or Law, or at least Bachelor of Divinity (which Phillips, *in situ*, was not) and to be perpetually resident, with an allowance of one hundred days' leave each year to visit his other benefices or attend to private business. He might also be absent on affairs of church or state, but otherwise would suffer financial penalty. The canons were similarly bound. None but the sovereign's chaplains were to hold places in the chapters of any other royal foundation. Each canon was to preach four times a year, and the dean on major festivals (Christmas, Corpus Christi and Easter). All canons with income of £40 or more from other sources were to maintain households with four servants, and only those who so did were to be accounted resident. Others were to have meals at their own expense, and to take no share in forfeit money or sealing fees. The payment of the dean and canons comprised a fixed sum and a daily allowance based on church attendance. The precentor was supposed to keep a register of those present, and every quarter deductions from unlawful absentees were to be shared among the rest. There is no evidence at Rochester that this complicated system ever operated. The treasurer invariably assigned to each member of the chapter the sum for which he qualified by full residence: but for the purpose of discharging his account liability this was all that was required, since the total expended was unaffected by juggling between residents and non-residents. There is some indication of daily allowances being computed for the chapter of Westminster Abbey.[22]

Each year three of the canons were chosen as vice-dean, receiver and treasurer. The receiver collected the revenues and generally handled external affairs; the bulk of his receipts he then passed on to the treasurer for internal expenditure. The random survival of these officers' accounts precludes statistical analysis, but allows occasional glimpses of different details of the cathedral's history at various times.

---

[20] Ar 1/15, ff. 23a–24v. Printed in *Visitation Articles and Injunctions of the Period of the Reformation*, ed. W.H. Frere, Alcuin Club, London 1910, ii, pp. 91–7.

[21] Original copy now Bodleian Library, Oxford MS e Musaeo 51, cited as Statutes. Three later copies in As 1, 2 and 3. Printed in [R. Rawlinson], *History and Antiquities of the Cathedral Church of Rochester*, London 1717, pp. 60–115. Collated with other new foundation cathedral statutes in *The Statutes of the Cathedral Church of Durham*, ed. A.H. Thompson, Surtees Society, cxliii (1929).

[22] Westminster Abbey Muniments 33624–9, 33631.

The series of receivers' books now begins in 1542 but is complete only for the first twenty years of the seventeenth century.[23] Treasurers' accounts exist from 1548, though the only substantial sequence is from 1559 to 1574. In those years the amounts at the treasurer's disposal ranged from £806 to £1,030. To this was normally added the arrears of the previous year's account, leaving an average liability of around £1,000. Just over half of this (£536 13s 4d) went on the stipends of the resident cathedral body, from the dean's £100 and the six canons at £20 each down to the under cook (£3 6s 8d). These figures varied only slightly during the century, in relation to minor changes in the composition of the staff: thus in 1571/2 it was £526 13s 4d because one minor canonry was vacant; in the following year a deputy was employed and the salary bill rose by £8.[24] The treasurer also paid fees to non-resident officials such as the steward and his deputy, the auditor and woodward, and retainers to legal counsel. The dean and chapter were enthusiastic litigants; in one year (1550/1) they were involved in proceedings at the Courts of King's Bench, Common Pleas, Chancery, Exchequer, Requests and Quarter Sessions at Canterbury and Maidstone.[25] After salaries taxation was the largest single item of expenditure: a regular annual payment to the Crown of £124 6s 8d, to which were added occasional subsidies or benevolences, e.g. £44 in 1590/1.[26] About £30 was also paid out in ecclesiastical dues and pensions to the archbishop, bishop and others. Once all the expenses of the church had been met there was occasionally a surplus which the dean and canons shared among themselves; this happened four times between 1559 and 1576, when as much as £90 6s 3d was available. In 1621 the dean received dividends of £40 and £1, each of the canons £13 6s 8d and £1 4s 9d.[27] Rents in kind, mostly corn and fuel, were also shared in this way. So too were receipts from sealing fees and entry fines, though the former were rarely recorded, the latter never. In 1591 and again in 1634 the dean and chapter maintained that they had received no fines or dividends for many years.[28]

Occasionally the chapter awarded extras to their junior colleagues: twelve quarters of rent corn to the minor canons, fines from absentees to the scholars.[29] All the inferior members of the community were encouraged to maintain a common life. But it was envisaged from the outset that the masters of the boys and the lay clerks might be married, in which case they were to have allowances in lieu of commons. Marriage of the clergy, allowed from 1549 onwards, would further de-stabilize the community spirit, despite a futile attempt by Queen Elizabeth to exclude women from cathedral closes. At Rochester women were not allowed in the quire except at

[23] FRb 1–12, 173.
[24] FTb 3–8A.
[25] FRb 1.
[26] FTb 6.
[27] FRb 11.
[28] Emf 1. House of Lords Record Office, Main Papers H.L.1634, Archbishop Laud's Visitation (no pagination). Printed (and hereafter cited) as V.J. Torr, 'Rochester Cathedral in 1634', *Archaeologia Cantiana*, lxxviii (1963), p. 54.
[29] AV 2.

sermons and 'sacring times' and even then were segregated.[30] But women were not absolutely restricted to washing and cleaning in the service of the cathedral, for in 1617 Goodwife Round was on the foundation as a porter.[31] Otherwise the cathedral was not only a masculine domain but one in which the lay staff outnumbered the clergy. The dean and canons were set apart from the rest not merely by their superior education and remuneration, but also because they were almost always outsiders, often at Rochester for a short time before moving on to more lucrative posts. By contrast the lesser clergy and lay staff would have been mostly local people whose entire careers were spent in the service of the cathedral. It was rare for a minor canon to be advanced to the chapter, as may have been the case of John Ready (canon in 1610) if he is to be identified with one of the same name as minor canon in 1587.[32]

It has been said that the Rochester chapter was 'perhaps less distinguished than some others'.[33] This may have been inevitable because of its size (Canterbury had twice as many canons). Of forty-four canons who held stalls in this period forty were graduates, seven of them holding doctorates while a further fifteen were Bachelors of Divinity. Eight would find a place in the *Dictionary of National Biography*. As in all the new foundations the chapter members were appointed by the Crown, save for a short time when Queen Mary transferred patronage of the canonries to the bishops.[34] At Rochester Bishop Griffith had only one opportunity to exercise this right. Thus all the other deans and canons were royal appointees, and aspirants needed a friend at Court. In 1545 Archbishop Cranmer obtained a stall for his chaplain Richard Collier, although he was never admitted.[35] In 1546 Sir Thomas Cawarden's favour secured a stall for Edward Culpeper.[36] Less successful was John Heron, master of the King's School, whose repeated approaches to Sir John Cheke and Sir William Cecil, Edward VI's principal secretaries, failed to bring him the canonry he sought.[37] Royal presentation was not always a guarantee of admission to the chapter. Elizabeth's reign saw a protracted squabble between Walter Hayte and John Wolward, both of whom were legitimately presented in 1576, though only Wolward was nominated to a particular stall. In the Court of Requests Wolward alleged Hayte had substituted his own name on Wolward's deed, to which it was countered that the Queen herself had altered the document at the request of another. Wolward retained possession for some time, but in 1586 the bishop instituted Hayte in succession to the original vacancy, implicitly nullifying Wolward's tenure.[38] There was also a dispute over the third prebend, held since 1569 by Robert Johnson. Thomas Bell had a presentation to the next vacancy, and Sir Francis Walsingham

[30] A V 2. J. Thorpe, *Custumale Roffense*, London 1788, p. 225.
[31] FRb 9.
[32] Ar 1/16, f. 36v.
[33] Le Neve, *Fasti*, p. 47.
[34] *CPR 1554–5*, p. 53. Cf. Le Neve, *Fasti*, pp. 3, 75; P. Mussett, *List of Deans and Major Canons of Durham 1541–1900*, Durham 1974, p. iv.
[35] *LP* XX(ii), no. 418(100).
[36] *LP* XXI(i), no. 963(79).
[37] PRO SP 10/15, no. 54 (*CSPD Edward VI*, no. 766).
[38] *CSPD Addenda 1566–79*, p. 541. Le Neve, *Fasti*, p. 69.

requested the chapter to admit Bell in place of Johnson's long dead predecessor. The chapter pointed out that there was no vacancy, and took the singular step of issuing a *caveat* in the chapter acts to protect Johnson's place.[39] The Crown on occasion appointed canons whom it wished to serve elsewhere. In 1552 George Burden was presented with specific allowance of daily distributions whether he was resident or not, provided only he preached in person or by deputy at the appropriate times.[40] Percival Wiborne was dispensed from residence while preaching in Guernsey in 1575.[41] Keenly as Rochester canonries might be sought, their occupants sometimes found the rewards inadequate. In 1579 Edmund Rockrey disparagingly referred to the 'small prebend' for which, as he complained to Lord Burghley, he was being 'molested' over his fellowship at Queens' College, Cambridge.[42] Some protestant divines accumulated cathedral benefices as hungrily as their medieval predecessors. Archbishop Parker observed tartly that Robert Johnson evidently had no difficulty in reconciling his puritan fervour with retention of four canonries (Rochester, Norwich, Peterborough and Windsor).[43] During the sixteenth century the archdeacon of Rochester had a place in the cathedral body only if he happened also to be a canon. In 1546 Maurice Griffith, who had been archdeacon since 1537, was appointed to the fifth stall. This he retained *in commendam* when advanced to the bishopric of the diocese in 1554. This was probably purely a financial perquisite. In 1637 the then archdeacon, Elizeus Burgess, was presented to the next vacant canonry, to which he duly succeeded, whereafter the archdeaconry was permanently annexed to the sixth stall.[44]

The epistoler and gospeller remained on the foundation until the 1570s, but had disappeared by 1590.[45] These posts had strictly been redundant since the introduction of the 1552 Prayer Book which made no provision for a choral celebration of communion. The other members of the musical establishment survived, although from time to time order had to be taken to make up the complement. At first the choristers seem not to have been boarders, and a place for them to sleep was still unprovided in the mid-sixteenth century.[46] When Peter Rowle was appointed master in 1560 he was required to board and clothe the boys at his own expense, while the chapter was thereafter to provide their gowns.[47] But it appears that by the next century the boys were again living at home, their parents complaining of the expense of maintaining them.[48] In addition to their musical training they were catechised by one of the canons in 1634.[49] The master of the choristers or another of the lay clerks was

[39] Elb 1, ff. 34v–35. Ac 1, p. 20. Le Neve, *Fasti*, p. 64.
[40] *CPR 1550–3*, p. 270.
[41] *CPR 1572–5*, p. 516 (no. 3089).
[42] *CSPD 1547–80*, p. 616.
[43] *DNB. Correspondence of Matthew Parker, D.D. Archbishop of Canterbury*, ed. J. Bruce and T.T. Perowne, Parker Society, Cambridge 1853, p. 450.
[44] Le Neve *Fasti*, pp. 45, 58.
[45] FTb 4, 6.
[46] AV 2.
[47] Aoo 1. S.E. Lehmberg, *The Reformation of Cathedrals*, Princeton 1988, p. 201.
[48] Azo 3.
[49] Torr, *Arch. Cant.*, lxxviii, p. 49.

paid for playing the organ. An organ builder was also retained for £2 a year. Deputies were often employed for absent clerks, sometimes being promised the next vacant place.[50] Cathedral music was becoming a family profession: in 1581 Philip Heath received a reversion of his father's clerkship.[51] The men were paid £8 a year, less than those at Canterbury but on the same level as those at Westminster Abbey. Accounts of the choral performance suggest that this was on a modest scale, but orderly and competent, at a time when the choir of King's College, Cambridge was said to consist of men who could not sing and boys who were half-mute.[52]

With the refoundation of the cathedral the ancient school became an integral part of the collegiate body. The 1544 statutes required the twenty scholars to be of humble origins but able to read and write. Former choristers were to be chosen, when suitable, in preference to others when their voices broke. They were to stay no more than five years in the school, learning Latin. As with the choristers there was some delay in providing them with adequate accommodation.[53] The 1543 injunctions gave the dean alone responsibility for admitting the scholars, and to make bargains with their families to provide their clothing. In 1576 it was necessary to stipulate that the scholars should not be taught anywhere outside the precincts, nor be away for more than one month a year.[54] It was later (1577) agreed that the dean should nominate eight scholars and two choristers, and each of the canons might name two scholars and one chorister.[55] Their day began with prayers at 6 o'clock, though in 1581, in renewing this rule, the chapter allowed an hour's later start in the winter (but with a whipping for latecomers).[56] The Rochester scholars, along with those of Canterbury, Chester, Westminster and Winchester, were given preferential advancement to Christ Church, Oxford.[57] Although a second master or usher was envisaged in the statutes, he is not recorded until 1576; in the following year he was given a chapter benefice to augment his stipend, while a later usher (1580) was one of the choir deputies. In 1576 the two schoolmasters were accorded precedence after the dean and canons and above the minor canons and all others.[58] The school seems to have been in a poor state in the early seventeenth century: in 1618 the dean complained that it was filled with 'idle oppidate boyes' who had no interest in their studies.[59] There is some support for this from a scholar called John Cobham who in 1617 had been unable to sign for his 13s 4d but could make only the mark of an illiterate.

---

[50] FRb 9. Ac 1, pp. 15, 18, 24. FA 4.

[51] Ac 1, p. 20.

[52] BL Lansdowne MS 213, f. 350v, cited in Torr, *Arch. Cant.*, lxxviii, p. 41. See S.E. Lehmberg, 'The Reformation of Choirs: Cathedral Musical Establishments in Tudor England', in *Tudor Rule and Revolution*, ed. D.J. Guth and J.W. McKenna, Cambridge 1982, pp. 62, 66. R.J. Henderson, *A History of King's College Choir School, Cambridge*, Cambridge 1981, p. 11.

[53] Statutes, p. 14. AV 2.

[54] Ar 1/15, ff. 23a–23av. Frere, *Visitation Articles*, ii, p. 93. Ar 1/16, f. 11.

[55] Ac 1, p. 9.

[56] Ac 1, p. 20.

[57] Christ Church, Oxford, MS D.P.vi.b.i, ff. 120v–121.

[58] Ac 1, pp. 6, 18, 35.

[59] Egz 18.

Maybe circumstances were not conducive to learning. Some relief came in 1621 when the chapter spent 2s 8d on mats for the boys to kneel on in the cathedral.[60]

In addition to the resident scholars, students at the universities were placed on the foundation at most of the new cathedrals. Rochester was charged with maintaining four. This scheme was abandoned at the end of Henry VIII's reign when the King founded Trinity College, Cambridge and Christ Church, Oxford, where many of the ex-cathedral students were found places. The cathedrals were obliged to surrender to the Crown lands equivalent in value to the cost of supporting the students.[61] Some cathedrals found themselves out of pocket as a result of these exchanges. Rochester surrendered a manor and received a rectory in return, notionally increasing its revenue but with a consequent rise in tax liability of £9 6s 8d.[62] The dean and chapter later regularly paid exhibitions to university students, in addition, that is, to casual gifts to students which were accounted as alms. The number of students and the sums they received varied considerably. The first record of such an award is in 1571/2, when £8 13s 4d was spent, and £10 was given in the next three years. Percival Wiborne's son John, who had been a King's Scholar, received an award when at Oxford in 1578. Another Wiborne, Nathaniel, was exhibitioner in 1590/1. In 1583 the chapter decided to limit the number of awards to three, worth a maximum of 26s 8d each. In the early seventeenth century there were several years in which no such payments were made, and in 1617 the exhibition money was used to buy books for the school. On the eve of the Civil War there were seven exhibitions held, at a total cost of £29, and the chapter was again considering reducing the payments. Two of the students currently supported were called Lorkin, and so again were probably sons of the canon of that name.[63]

The chapter made frequent (and so, one must suppose, imperfect) efforts to keep their books and papers in order. The great medieval library was plundered at the dissolution, its contents now dispersed from Berlin to Baltimore, but mostly in the British Library, thanks to Henry VIII who retained a substantial if eclectic number of Rochester books for his son's education. Only three complete volumes remained at the cathedral, including the *Textus Roffensis*, which was used by Richard Tillesley (canon 1615–21) in a work of his own.[64] It has been claimed that the dean and chapter began to stock a library suitable for their needs in 1545 when £21 was expended.[65] During 1550/1 when 2 shillings was spent on three inventories and £2 for four new account books, an iron ring and staple were fitted to the library door. Care was taken of individual documents and the chapter seal. But the officers of the church often

[60] FRb 9, 11.
[61] Statutes, p. 23. See C.S. Knighton, 'Canterbury Cathedral's University Studentships under Henry VIII', *The Cantuarian*, xlix, no. 2 (April 1985), pp. 110–13.
[62] *LP* XIX(i), no. 812(84); XX(ii), no. 1066. *CSPD Edward VI*, no. 432. [W. Shrubsole and S. Denne], *History and Antiquities of Rochester*, Rochester 1772, p. 86.
[63] Ac 1, pp. 5, 11, 18, 25. FA 2, 3, 4. FRb 9. FTb 4(9, 10, 11), 6, 7, 8, 8A.
[64] N.R. Ker, *Medieval Libraries of Great Britain,* Royal Historical Society Guides and Handbooks no. 3, 2nd edn, London 1964, pp. 160–4. R. Stockdale, 'Benedictine libraries and writers', in *The Benedictines in Britain*, BL series no. 3, London 1980, p. 63. Thorpe, *Custumale Roffense*, 227.
[65] W.H. Mackean, *Rochester Cathedral Library*, Rochester 1953, p. 14. [This entry cannot be verified, there being no extant treasurer's account for the year stated.]

kept their business papers at home, and in 1575 order was given that such material should be passed on by each officer to his successor. Two years later the chapter was still exercised over the need to house the church's books in a suitable room. In 1581, after the death of Dean Willoughby, it was decided that all college books in the deanery and elsewhere should be collected, inventoried and chained. The most appropriate place was felt to be the east end of the old vestry which had become the chapter house, where it was particularly hoped that preachers would wait and study before their sermons. Some further attention was paid to the library in 1621 when assorted ironmongery was provided for the book press. Despite all this, material still went astray. In 1621 five treasurers' accounts were sent to one of the legal counsel in London; they are among those which are no longer extant.[66] In the 1630s the most treasured manuscript, the *Textus*, had to be recovered through litigation after a borrower had failed to return it.[67] For the most part the library grew from gift rather than purchase, though members of the chapter did not necessarily bequeath their private collections. Richard Engest (d.1544) left his books to William Harrison, vicar of St Nicholas's Church, who succeeded to his stall. Dean Phillips gave most of his library to be sold to benefit poor maidens' marriages and other good causes, but left six books of Hebrew, Greek, Latin and Chaldic to the cathedral; they had disappeared by the time Thorpe compiled the *Custumale Roffense* in 1788.[68]

The main beneficiaries of the cathedral's charity were the six resident almsmen, impoverished by age, infirmity or injury in battle. They were expected to attend services and help (as far as they were able) in the arrangement of them. The Crown reserved to itself these appointments, and in several cases those chosen were in genuine need, such as George Bonner, wounded in action at Le Havre, admitted in 1564. But the Crown also used the places to reward perfectly able-bodied members of the royal household: such was John Greaves, admitted on the Queen's appointment in 1583 in place of another dismissed for absenteeism, but allowed to have a deputy because of his own service at Court. Sometimes the bishop, sometimes a courtier would make recommendations. In 1575 the chapter decreed that the almsmen's places should be assigned by their united decision, though the dean personally ordered the admission of one in 1579. At the visitation of 1599 four of the six almsmen were absent, being blind or lame, and in 1634 none was resident, it being explained that the places were given to men who had never lived near the church and were unwilling to move there. Nevertheless they continued to receive 6s 8d apiece above their annual stipends for the fictitious duty of sweeping the church.[69]

The dean and chapter were also under statutory obligation to spend £20 a year in alms to the needy of the city and their estates, and a further £20 on the repair of roads and bridges. In 1545 all the new cathedrals were asked to account for the sums they

---

[66] Ac 1, pp. 8, 21. AO 12. As 3, p. 115. AV 2. FRb 1, 11. Ar 1/16, f. 12.

[67] Mackean, *Cathedral Library*, pp. 18–19.

[68] A.B. Emden, *A Biographical Register of the University of Oxford, A.D. 1501 to 1540*, Oxford 1974, p. 191. Thorpe, *Custumale Roffense*, p. 223.

[69] Statutes, p. 15. Ac 1, pp. 9, 11, 14, 17, 23, 26. Aob 1–8. AO 12. AV 1. Ar 1/16, f. 50v. *LP* XX(i), nos 148(48), 963(135). *CSPD 1595–7*, p. 458; *1598–1601*, pp. 342, 505. Torr, *Arch. Cant.*, lxxviii, p. 49.

had actually directed to these purposes. The dean and chapter of Rochester subsequently reported that their highway fund had been remitted to them for five years in order to improve their housing.[70] Thereafter roadworks never cost the dean and chapter more than a few pounds, and are often not charged at all. Paving the High Street is mentioned several times in the early seventeenth century. But almsgiving was always maintained, sums varying from £11 in 1613/14 to £39 13s 9d in 1569/70, the average of £28 being above the statutory amount. There are many indications of the chapter's benevolent disposition. In 1583 the widow of Hamlet Taylor who had been precentor for many years was discharged of all her debts. John Bunce, a labourer who had frequently been employed about the church, was allowed to settle for 6d his rent of 4d which had been undemanded for many years. A poor man who regularly received alms was given a permanent quarterly allowance of 26s 4d. The receiver's account for 1550/1 has a particularly detailed catalogue of benefactions: 2 shillings to a woman with many children, 20 shillings for purchase of books, 20 shillings to a goodwife of Strood to heal John Austen of the pox, several wedding presents, a few pence here and there to poor sailors, prisoners at Maidstone and the Bishop's Palace, itinerants with royal licence to collect for houses burned in their village, poor scholars at Cambridge, the blind and the lame, a merchant who had suffered great loss at sea, shoes and shirts to poor children. In all, seventy-four individuals are identified as recipients of aid, in addition to those benefiting from general distributions in the city, the diocese and in London.[71]

The dean and chapter also had military responsibilities. In 1544 they supplied ten footmen for the expedition to France which won Boulogne for Henry VIII. Under Edward VI the dean was perhaps to provide a light cavalryman, and the cathedral sent a man and a horse to the Scotch expedition of 1548. In the same year they bought eight suits of mail, seven sheaves of arrows, nine swords and ten daggers on the advice of a London armourer, at a cost of £7 12s 6d. In Elizabeth's reign the chapter complained of the heavy burden of military charges. Not all was for expeditionary forces: in 1621 there was 18 shillings for the muster, and on the eve of the civil war, in addition to a huge £66 13s 4d to aid the King's abortive Scottish war, £11 19s 7d was spent on military apparatus. It is possible that this last sum financed a small cathedral guard, as is known to have existed later in the century. Also in Charles I's reign the cathedral was charged for ship money. More usually the cathedral's links with the navy had been of a friendly kind. In 1550/1 the receiver had occasion to entertain one of the masters of the King's ships. The dean and chapter made recommendations of clerics to be preachers to the ships at Chatham. The navy commissioners and many individuals in naval service were among the cathedral's tenants.[72]

Such then were the various functions of the reformed chapter established by Henry

[70] Statutes, p. 23. AO 4/1, 2. *LP* XX(i), no. 1335(52).

[71] Ac 1, pp. 5, 25, 28. FA 2, 4. FRb 1, 9. FTb 4–8.

[72] AO 3, 5, 6. Emf 1. FA 3, 4. FRb 1, 11. FTb 3. *CSPD Edward VI*, no. 137. *CSPD 1635*, pp. 295, 302, 323; *1656–7*, pp. 216–17. M. Moad, '17th Century Military Equipment from Rochester Cathedral', *Report of the Friends of Rochester Cathedral*, 1986, pp. 12–13.

VIII. While the King lived there was little further change in the observances of the church. In 1545 when the dean and chapter leased a chamber to a wax chandler they demanded in rent a taper for the Good Friday sepulchre. But the elaborate ceremonies of Holy Week were among the first to be abolished after the accession of Edward VI in 1547. The first complete treasurer's account to survive tells something of the year (1548/9) which saw the appearance of the Book of Common Prayer. The master of the choristers, James Plumley, was paid for writing copies of what was still called the mass, while twenty-one new psalters were bought for 1 shilling each, and 42 shillings was spent on bibles and the *Paraphrases* of Erasmus for churches of which the chapter was patron. John Pyle and John Wattes earned 18d. for taking down the 'Jesus' (rood cross), but considerable sums were still spent on incense, wax and oil. There were relaxations, too: the Lord Protector's players were entertained, as was Lord Cobham with a bottle of Rhenish wine costing 1s 2d; 1s 8d was spent on fish for Bishop Ridley on his first visit. A less welcome guest was the receiver of the King's tenths, who ate what must have been an enormous breakfast which cost 4s 10d.[73] The more radically protestant second prayer book of 1552 presented a threat to cathedral musicians, and many organs were removed and choirs restricted to the most simple homophonic renderings. At least protestant ritual was inexpensive, at a time when everything else was costing more. 1551 was a bad year. The government decried silver coinage by 25% in a proclamation embargoed to 8 July. On 11 July the receiver of Rochester had therefore to write off 12s 2d, a quarter of a sum then in his hands. Worse followed: on 16 August the testoon was devalued by a further 25%, causing the receiver to discount £4 12s 0d, half of the midsummer rent for Darenth which he had just collected. Altogether £84 11s 1½d was wiped off the value of the cathedral's cash stock in that year.[74]

It is uncertain what might have become of the cathedral had the diocese been merged with that of Canterbury, as was considered by the privy council in 1552. After the new see of Westminster had been extinguished in 1550 its cathedral and chapter continued in being; but it is doubtful if Cranmer, who had quite enough trouble with his Canterbury prebendaries, would have wanted a second chapter in his diocese. The bishopric remained vacant after the translation of Scory in May 1552; but the Duke of Northumberland's suggestion in October that John Knox might be appointed to Rochester to deal with Kentish Anabaptists indicates that the independence of the diocese was to continue.[75] The cathedral thus survived a threat to its existence of which it had probably been unaware.

Dean Phillips continued to preside over the new foundation for almost thirty years, and Hugh Aprice held the senior canonry for even longer. To retain high position in the church through the reigns of Henry VIII and his children required some dexterity of conscience. We are told of two occasions on which the dean is said to have undergone a change of heart. In Edward VI's reign he allegedly destroyed a book given to him by Bishop Fisher, and thereafter regretted having done so. Then, in his

---

[73] Thorpe, *Custumale Roffense*, p. 174. FTb 3.
[74] FRb 1. Cf. C.E. Challis, *The Tudor Coinage*, Manchester 1978, pp. 105–6.
[75] PRO SP 10/14, no. 8; 15, no. 35 (*CSPD Edward VI*, nos 609, 747).

sole appearance on the national stage, he was one of half a dozen cathedral clergy who in the 1553 convocation opposed the reintroduction of Roman Catholicism; but it seems he took no part in the subsequent debate, and was soon reconciled to the old order.[76] Others were less pliable. Three of the canons (and one minor canon) were deprived in March 1554 when Queen Mary's government moved against those clergy who had demonstrated their protestantism by taking wives. John Symkyns and John Ellis would return to their stalls when Elizabeth became queen; Rowland Taylor was to die as a heretic in 1555 at the Suffolk town of Hadleigh where he was incumbent. Under Elizabeth, too, there were malcontents. Assent to the Elizabethan settlement was required not only of the clergy but of the whole adult cathedral body, as holders of office under the Crown. George Burden was put out of his stall in 1561, presumably for adherence to the old religion. Conversely there were three canons of strong puritan inclination: Edmund Rockrey, Percival Wiborne, and Robert Johnson, who were at various times suspended from officiating (though not deprived).[77]

The most disturbing event of the early years of Elizabeth's reign occurred in 1564 when John Springfield and others broke into the close and treasury and stole £80 belonging to Canon Hugh Aprice.[78] Financial worries of various sorts continued to beset the chapter. In 1577 the receiver was authorised to sell £50 or £60 worth of trees and wood to offset the charges of the house. In 1584 the chapter prohibited the granting of bailiffs' patents which could be passed on to others, as a consequence of which they had lost much rent. Like many landlords the dean and chapter had been tempted to make very long leases for the immediate bonus of an entry fine followed by decades of fixed income and rising prices. A yeoman of the King's pantry secured eighty years for a tenement in May 1544, just a month before the statutes sought to impose a limit of twenty-one years on country properties and no more than sixty for those in towns. This was very widely ignored. In 1571 and 1576 capitular lands were by Act of Parliament limited to leases of twenty-one years or three lives. The relevant passages were entered by the dean and chapter in their act book, and the law was generally respected. Priory Hall was leased eight times between 1546 and 1639: on the first four occasions for around forty years, while the remaining four leases, after 1570, are for twenty-one years. Even so there were exceptions: forty-nine years on Aylesford parsonage in 1576; forty years on three Rochester tenements in 1581.[79]

Walter Phillips's long tenure of the deanery ended with his death in 1570. Of his successors until the civil war only three died in office, while seven were advanced to bishoprics or grander deaneries. Edmund Freake (1570–2) was among those for whom the Rochester deanery was an intermediate appointment. During his brief

[76] Thorpe, *Custumale Roffense*, pp. 223–4. G. Burnet, *History of the Reformation of the Church of England*, ed. N. Pocock, Oxford 1865, ii, pp. 422–3; iii, p. 389.

[77] Azo 1. *DNB*. Le Neve, *Fasti*, p. 61. R. Tittler, *Nicholas Bacon: The Making of a Tudor Statesman*, London 1976, pp. 169–70, 212–13. P. Collinson, *The Elizabethan Puritan Movement*, London 1967, p. 266.

[78] *CPR 1563–6*, p. 244 (no. 1175).

[79] Ac 1, pp. 1, 5, 18, 29. Ele 2/1; 57/1; 70/1–8, and the series generally. Cf. C. Hill, *Economic Problems of the Church*, Oxford 1956, pp. 30–1, 116.

occupancy he was among those named to examine the state of Rochester bridge, by now two hundred years old and in ruinous state. Freake became bishop of the diocese in 1572, and later moved to Norwich, where he is best remembered as the victim of an overbearing wife.[80] Thomas Willoughby, who became dean in 1572, had been deprived of his livings by Queen Mary and joined the exile community in Frankfurt. On Elizabeth's accession he had returned to his benefices and received more, becoming chaplain to the Queen in 1570. The Queen visited Rochester in the year after he became dean, when £34 13s 4d was spent in what must have been very lavish festivities at the cathedral. By comparison the regular high point of the year, the audit feast, cost £8 2s 9½d that November.[81] The audits and other chapter meetings from 1575 to 1584 are recorded in the only act book to have survived from the chapter's first century. This was the work of Martin Cotes, who was sworn as chapter clerk on 16 July 1575, and was confirmed in office three years later on condition of compiling within eight years a survey of the cathedral's estates and revenues. This he never completed, alleging that his access to the documents was impeded by the clergy.[82] Nevertheless traces of his activity are found throughout the chapter records, where he habitually docketed every mention of himself. The act book seems to be a draft for or copy of a formal register now lost. It records the main meetings of the chapter in June and November, and occasional *ad hoc* assemblies at other times. Since the refoundation a vestry to the east end of the cathedral had been used for the meetings, though towards the end of Willoughby's life he was too ill to leave the deanery, so the chapter assembled there.[83] Meetings were sometimes abandoned because no quorum was present, as on 24 June 1576, when the chapter was adjourned to 16 October, and then again to 21 November. In June 1578 adjournment was necessary because of an imminent episcopal visitation, while in the following June when visitation was again due it was the absence of the bishop's officers which caused adjournment. On some occasions the assembly was postponed to accommodate a late arrival.[84] In the early pages of the act book the 'signatures' of the chapter are in fact written by the clerk; although actual signatures subsequently occur, they cannot be taken with certainty to indicate the presence of the signatories at particular meetings, since retrospective signature to such registers was not uncommon. In one instance these signatures do not accord with the list of those said to have been present.[85] It is clear, however, that in the period covered by the acts there was only one persistent absentee. William Absolon, the Queen's sub-almoner, appears only to have interested himself in the cathedral's affairs when they offered him the opportunity to exercise personal patronage: in November 1575 he made a presentation to Strood Hospital, and in April 1576 signed an act awarding reversion of a bellringer's place to one of his servants; only once thereafter was he present in chapter.[86]

---

[80] *CPR 1569–72*, pp. 278–9 (no. 2162). *CSPD Addenda 1566–79*, pp. 548, 551–2.
[81] FTb 4.
[82] Ac 1, pp. 2, 6, 8. Aoc 1. Elb 1, f. 350.
[83] Ac 1, pp. 17–20.
[84] *Ibid.*, pp. 3–4, 11, 12, 14, 15.
[85] 12 January 1583. *Ibid.*, p. 25.
[86] *Ibid.*, pp. 3, 15. AO 12.

In November 1575 the chapter found it necessary to reiterate that any who neglected to preach in person or by deputy would be ineligible for his daily allowance, and receive only his bare stipend. At the same time they gave consideration to the post of divinity lecturer, for which payment had first been made in 1572/3 when an outsider received £15 for three quarters of the year. The chapter stayed the payments until the next bishop (the see then being vacant) gave orders and the mayor provided an 'auditory', unless the dean or one of the canons chose to exercise the duty. The full payment of £20 was made in 1573/4 to 1576/7. It was not necessarily a member of the chapter who read the lecture: in 1581 it was stated merely that Percival Wiborne or one of the other canons should do so in preference to anyone else. Thereafter the lectureship seems to have lapsed, and in 1634 the chapter admitted they had no weekday sermons or lectures, nor were they obliged to offer them. There was, however, a sermon on 5 November, as envisaged in the special service for that day.[87]

The chapter was from time to time concerned with indiscipline among the lesser clergy and choirmen. Absenteeism, irreverence and drunkenness were, as so often, the problems they faced. Of serious crime or sexual misdemeanour they made no mention. The chapter showed much forbearance in the face of provocation from a few noisy individuals. Minor canons who had been deprived were even so accorded a place of precedence, albeit ignominiously between the choristers and the schoolboys. Peter Rowle, lay clerk and sometime master of the choristers, was admonished for various faults and absences in November 1576. A year later he was dismissed, along with John King, minor canon. King and another minor canon, Thomas Morrice, had earlier been told to attend to their duties or else leave the cathedral and serve their cures. Morrice and King were reprieved, only to be dismissed again in November 1578, this time specifically for frequenting taverns. Yet in November 1579 they were each awarded £5 a year because of their impoverishment. Morrice was still around in the following year, unrepentant, calling the dean and canons 'helhoundes, reprobates and also knaves' (Plate 2). Irreverent reading of the scriptures was another failing: in 1580 the dean reprimanded John Shaw for his slovenly delivery, sensibly advising readers to rehearse what they had to say. Chattering during services and unseemly behaviour in the streets came up for censure in 1581.[88] But these were timeless troubles, in no way connected with the upheavals of the Reformation. Rebelliousness of a more specifically religious character was likelier to be found among the better educated higher clergy. In 1587 it was reported that three of the canons (the puritans Wiborne, Rockrey and Johnson) would not wear the prescribed vestments in church. Twelve years later Wiborne was the sole survivor of the radicals, the dean and treasurer wishing the bishop might amend him, but admitting that this would be 'a myracle'.[89] But beyond this commonplace vestiarian protest there is no indication of how the cathedral was affected by the controversies of Elizabeth's reign. The dean and chapter may well

---

[87] Ac 1, p. 19. AO 12. FTb 4, 5, 6. FA 4. Torr, *Arch. Cant.*, lxxviii, p. 48.
[88] Ac 1, pp. 4, 5, 7, 9, 13–16, 21.
[89] Ar 1/16, ff. 36, 50v.

have been more worried by tenants behind with their rents, or such as Mr Manninge, who in 1583 cut down woods belonging to the church, or one Brian, who built himself a cottage on the cathedral's land near Sharstead; he was ordered to dismantle it and find himself a new dwelling at his peril.[90]

From 1581 to 1591 the dean was John Coldwell, a Kentish man, a protégé of archbishops Parker and Grindal, and also a royal chaplain, though more highly esteemed as a physician than a divine. But unlike Willoughby he was not content to die a dean, and having had hint of the bishopric of Salisbury, wrote anxiously to Lord Burghley lest the Queen should change her mind. Well might the Queen have hesitated, for Coldwell's regime at Rochester seems to have been untidy. At the visitation of 1587 he admitted that none of the canons preached or resided according to the statutes, and could not say for certain if they appointed deputies. He himself did not celebrate communion on the appointed days because he claimed he could not do so and also preach. The canons reported that the lesser members of the foundation did not have the relevant parts of the statutes read to them, but they did not know them well enough to be aware of any misconduct. In fact the minor canons (one dissenting) accused one man for failure to communicate and for immorality, while another was presented as a hunter and gamer. The choristers were not properly examined, and the almsmen did not come to services. At least most of the houses were in repair and the accounts in order, but money stocks were much depleted by great charges.[91] In the year that Coldwell eventually attained his promotion the cathedral was seriously damaged by fire. It is possible that the payments in 1590/1 of £5 5s 11d for a new pulpit and thirteen benches at 8d each were occasioned by this disaster.[92] Further restoration took place in 1598 when Merton College paid for a new tomb for its founder, Bishop Walter. The visitation of the following year showed much had changed since that of 1587. All the canons, save Mr Wiborne, were orderly and kept to their preaching duties, the services were properly performed, and attended by all but the most severely handicapped of the almsmen; the choristers and scholars were well taught, and all the choir lived charitably and honestly.[93] These improvements may well have come about because the cathedral now had at its head a man free of commitments or aspirations elsewhere. Thomas Blague, dean from 1591 to 1611, was again a royal chaplain and an author, but otherwise less beneficed than any dean but the first. Three short decanates followed. Richard Milborne (1611–15) went on to be Bishop of St David's. Robert Scott (1615–20) died in office. Godfrey Goodman (1621–4) was a royal chaplain, canon of Windsor and Westminster and incumbent of much else besides. He became notorious for his supposedly Romish beliefs and practices while Bishop of Gloucester. The next dean, Walter Balcanquall, was a Scotsman, one of many to have prospered in England after the Stuart accession. Son of a presbyterian minister, and educated at Edinburgh University before Oxford, he became chaplain to James I,

[90] Ac 1, pp. 28, 30. FRb 9.
[91] *CSPD 1581–90*, p. 687. Ar 1/16, ff. 35–36v.
[92] Emf 1. FTb 6.
[93] Thorpe, *Custumale Roffense*, p. 194. Ar 1/16, f. 50v.

who appointed him to Rochester in the last month of his reign. Balcanquall had been dean for less than a year before he was pestering Lord Conway, secretary of state, for the more prestigious deanery of Westminster, perhaps unaware that what Conway had him in mind for was a remote bishopric.[94] The Westminster deanery did not fall vacant, and Balcanquall had to wait until 1639 for promotion, albeit only to the deanery of Durham. The composition of the chapter was almost unchanged throughout Balcanquall's regime, and all seem to have been in sympathy with the move towards better discipline and reverence in worship which is associated with Archbishop William Laud. Improvements had begun when in 1617 the quire was tiled and mats were bought for the communion table and choir stalls; in 1621 thirty yards of yellow and blue calico were made into curtains for the organ.[95] In the first year of his primacy, 1633, Laud received a report from the Bishop of Rochester that the cathedral's glazing was seriously deficient, and that the dean and chapter had impeded his visitation on the rather bogus grounds that their statutes had never been sealed. The King minuted his displeasure.[96] In the next year Laud conducted a metropolitical visitation, and the replies of the cathedral clergy to the articles and subsequent injunctions present a generally healthy picture.[97] The liturgy, chapter meetings, audits, muniments and finances were all in order, and there was no dissension or indiscipline within the cathedral body. Indeed the dean and canons preached more frequently than they were obliged to do, so that there was a sermon every Sunday. The choir was depleted by the absence of three of the ablest (a minor canon and two laymen) in the service of the Chapel Royal, but the dean and chapter promised to make better provision for deputies, if necessary withholding the absentees' stipends. The archbishop recommended that the choirmen should be paid more, but the chapter thought they earned as much as those elsewhere. They were in addition given 20 shillings each at the audit and gratuities at other times, while the canons had for long gone without lease fines and met repair bills from their own resources. At some time between 1576/7 and 1590/1 the number of lay clerks had risen from the statutory six to eight, and by 1613/14 their stipend had been raised to £10. The extra payments which the chapter mentioned are also sometimes recorded: £12, for example, in 1639.[98] The choirmen were said to be content with their rewards. The choristers, though young and 'somewhat rude', were expected to improve. A year later a traveller noted that the boys, though few in number, were orderly and decent, and that the organs were small, but rich and neat.[99] The chapter claimed to have spent £1,000 on the organ and other major repairs, which was their excuse for the still defective glazing: but this too was about to be remedied. The chapter also made a new desk for the quire, presumably the reading desk enjoined by the canons of 1604, and were proud of their new bible and prayer books and rebound choir

---

[94] *CSPD 1625–6*, pp. 143, 145, 147; *1627–8*, p. 41.

[95] FRb 9, 11.

[96] Lambeth Palace MS 943, p. 248, cited in Torr, *Arch. Cant.*, lxxviii, p. 41.

[97] Torr, *Arch. Cant.*, lxxviii, pp. 43–54 for all of what follows, save where otherwise indicated, in connection with the 1634 visitation.

[98] FTb 5, 6, 8. FA 4.

[99] BL Lansdowne MS 213, f. 350v, cited in Torr, *Arch. Cant.*, lxxviii, p. 41.

books. They were ordered to move the communion table to the east of the church, behind rails. This they had already resolved to do, but there was an acoustic problem because of the length of the quire, and they proposed instead to erect a screen and appropriate altar furniture at the point where the table then stood. It is evident from accounts of its desecration just a few years later that a raised, covered and railed-off altar was duly provided. How frequently communion was ministered there we do not know, but in the late 1630s bread and wine was purchased specifically for Christmas, Easter, Low Sunday and October 20 only.[100]

There was a continuing difficulty arising from the contiguity of the town churchyard with that of the cathedral. The chapter felt that a dividing fence, as ordered by the archbishop, would have hindered access between the cathedral and the clerical residences, but they hoped for the co-operation of the mayor and corporation in securing the privacy of the cathedral precincts. The civic authorities were often present in the cathedral, and in 1636 made a gift to the sextons for looking after their seats.[101]

Dean Henry King (1639–42) was the scion of one of the new Anglican clerical dynasties. His father had been Bishop of London, in whose cathedral Henry and his brother were canons, as also they were at Christ Church, Oxford. Henry was a royal chaplain, a poet, and the friend of Donne, Jonson and Walton. His elevation to a bishopric (Chichester) can have occasioned little surprise. His brief spell at Rochester saw the building of a new deanery.[102] Thomas Turner (1642–4) was another ardent royalist, and son-in-law of the secretary of state Sir Francis Windebanke. In December 1643 he was notionally made Dean of Canterbury, but Charles I did not bother with the fiction of naming a new dean for Rochester. Turner had the melancholy duty of attending the King during his imprisonment, but happily survived to take possession of his Canterbury deanery in 1660.

We do not know precisely when and how the Rochester chapter was dispersed at the outset of the Great Rebellion, when the cathedral endured the most desolate stage in its history. In 1641, a year before war broke out, the House of Commons had voted to abolish cathedral chapters. Consideration was subsequently given to the use of cathedral revenues to augment parochial livings, a long cherished puritan aspiration. In those parts of the country which came into the control of Parliamentary forces there was an orgy of vandalism to which the cathedrals were especially vulnerable. Such ornaments of worship as had escaped destruction in the sixteenth century or had been carefully restored in the early part of the seventeenth were once more the targets for puritan iconoclasm or the general mayhem which followed in its wake. At first Rochester seems to have suffered rather less damage than was inflicted at other cathedrals. In August 1642 troops commanded by Colonels Sandys and Smeaton arrived from Canterbury, where they had caused much mischief. At Rochester they did not molest the choir stalls, the tombs or the heraldic emblems, perhaps cautious of irritating local families. They did, however, tear up the prayer

---

[100] FA 4.
[101] Rochester-upon-Medway City Archives, Ro/AC 1.
[102] St John Hope, *Arch. Cant.*, xxiv, p. 81.

books, break down the altar rails and remove the velvet frontal, taking the table itself to the body of the church. During this activity one of the canons, John Lorkin, attempted to reason with the soldiers, and was lucky to escape when a handgun was discharged at him. The dean, whose turn it was to preach on the following Sunday, was ordered by Sandys to dispense with surplice and hood. The dean replied stoutly that he would preach in his customary garb or not at all, and so did. Smeaton contented himself with a contemptuous remark about the organ. Such is the account of the royalist reporter *Mercurius Rusticus*.[103] There are other stories of more extensive desecration in the course of the war and its aftermath: a mob of seamen attacking the glass and the dean's library; the tombs of the ancient bishops pillaged; soldiers using the cathedral as an ale-house, and local carpenters setting up a workshop there. Many decades later an alderman recalled seeing cavalry horses stabled in the choir stalls, and soldiers picking ivory from the walls with their bayonets.[104]

In some of the cathedral churches a puritan ministry was established during the Commonwealth. At York the city fathers showed some respect for the fabric of the Minster of which they were temporarily custodians.[105] At Rochester we hear only of abuse and dereliction. In January 1651 the mayor reported that lead had been stolen from the cathedral, and was ordered by the Council of State to prosecute the culprit. Five years later Peter Pett, the Navy Commissioner at Chatham, began to petition the Admiralty for the College at Rochester, now described as ruinous, to be given to the Chatham Chest, the fund for disabled seamen, and to prevent the theft of such lead as remained. The Admiralty was at first sympathetic: it seems that Pett was interested only in the scrap value of the property, claiming that otherwise £3,000 was needed for the arrears of the chest. But despite repeated requests from Pett and others, nothing was done.[106] The cathedral fell further into decay. Yet some of its treasures were being preserved. Sir Roger Twysden looked after the *Textus Roffensis*.[107] Like many another, the cathedral organ was incongruously but safely housed in a tavern at Greenwich. It would be among the first to be restored to its proper place within months of the return of Charles II.[108]

[103] [Bruno Ryves], *Mercurius Rusticus*, London 1643, repr. 1971, pp. 155–6. Cf. P. Heylin, *Aerius Redivivus*, Oxford 1670, p. 452. But cf. also the account from a different angle cited in A. Everitt, *The Community of Kent and the Great Rebellion, 1640–60*, Leicester 1966, pp. 112–13.

[104] Thorpe, *Custumale Roffense*, pp. 180–1, 222, 228. E. Hasted, *The History and Topographical Survey of the County of Kent*, Canterbury 1797–1801, repr. 1972, iv, pp. 105–6.

[105] *A History of York Minster*, ed. G.E. Aylmer and R. Cant, Oxford 1977, p. 215.

[106] *CSPD 1651*, p. 12; *1656–7*, pp. 430, 431; *1657–8*, pp. 122, 362, 398; *1658–9*, p. 457.

[107] Mackean, *Cathedral Library*, p. 19.

[108] *Historical Manuscripts Commission, Thirteenth Report*, Appendix, pt II (1893), p. 277. *The Diary of Samuel Pepys*, ed. R.C. Latham and W. Matthews, London 1970–83, ii, p. 70 and n. 1.

4

The Reconstituted Chapter, 1660–1820

PATRICK MUSSETT

(1) Introduction

All the English cathedrals suffered more or less from neglect and deliberate damage in the 1640s and 1650s, but Rochester suffered only moderate harm. One report said that the only deliberate damage was the destruction of the communion rail, but a great deal of casual damage must have been caused by the building's use as a 'Tippling House' and a carpenter's workshop. Added to this was the effect of a period of sheer neglect for most of the 1640s and throughout the 1650s.[1] The chapter at the Restoration had virtually no experience of Rochester behind it, for neither the dean nor any of the six prebendaries had been chapter members before the Commonwealth, but they were dealing with business before the end of August 1660 and by the beginning of November they were issuing leases and receiving large fines in return.[2] In September 1662 they reported to Bishop Warner that the deliberate damage to the church had included the defacing of tombs and monuments and that the ironwork of the tombs had been taken down and sold by John Wyld, a Rochester shoemaker. They also reported that they had spent nearly £8,000 on repairs to 'the sad ruines' of the cathedral and the houses in the precinct, and that they needed to spend at least another £5,000, 'which we are not able of ourselves to raise'.[3]

In 1670 Archbishop Sheldon asked all bishops and cathedral chapters to tell him what they had spent since 1660 on fabric repairs, presents to the king, the ransom of Christians enslaved in North Africa and other worthy causes: 'you cannot be ignorant with what an evil eye some men look upon the possessions of the Church, & how much Deans & Chapters are thought to be aimed at, at present more than others of the Clergy'.[4] On 20 October the Rochester chapter replied that it had spent on repairs to buildings alone £9,910 of its own money and about £1,500 bequeathed by Bishop Warner and raised by public subscription.[5] A document of 1670,

---

[1] Hasted, 1st edn, ii, p. 30; Richard Rawlinson, *The History and Antiquities of the Cathedral Church of Rochester*, London 1717, pp. 118–19.
[2] Arb 2, f. 1; Arb 1, f. 9.
[3] Arb 2, f. 23 bis.
[4] Arb 2, f. 38.
[5] Bodleian Library, Tanner MS 147, f. 10.

apparently summarising the total expenditure of a number of chapters, put Rochester at £14,640, which compares well with Bristol at £4,354, Gloucester at £12,094, Norwich at £11,678 and Peterborough at £4,378.[6] This level of spending was not achieved without difficulty; in July 1664 Kenerick Lake the plumber and a number of other men who had been repairing the church were owed in all about £500, and the only way to pay them was for the dean and prebendaries to borrow £400 on their personal security.[7] So chronic was the late payment of the dean's and prebendaries' stipends from about 1670 to 1720 that the Rochester treasurer's books have a special section, 'Insolutes of the Former Year', certainly not found in treasurer's books at Canterbury, Durham, Bristol and Norwich, and possibly not found anywhere else at all.[8]

(2) Estate Administration and Cathedral Finance

At the Restoration the chapter's estates had a rent-roll of £904 a year, of which not quite all could be collected. The sales of cathedral property made during the Commonwealth were deemed under Charles II to be invalid, but the king urged chapters to be gentle with purchasers.[9] Some purchasers of cathedral property had been lessees during Charles I's reign, and they had found themselves in a difficult position under the Commonwealth. The tenant who had bought the freehold of the chapter's property at Monk Wood in Wouldham from the Commonwealth government for £230 did so, not because he approved of that government, but because he felt he had no choice if he was to provide for his family; he asked to be allowed to renew his lease for a reduced fine since he had lost his purchase money.[10] Another tenant with whom the Rochester chapter had to negotiate in the early 1660s was one whose father and grandfather before him had leased the manor of Badmonden but who had not tried to renew the lease under the Commonwealth because he had not wished to deal with the 'robbers'; his failure to renew the lease or buy the freehold had allowed it to be bought by a 'professed & infamous Anabaptist'. The chapter's reply to Archbishop Sheldon's 1670 circular about its spending on worthy causes included the claim that it had made substantial allowances to tenants renewing leases.[11]

Another problem for cathedral landlords in the 1660s was that of records lost, stolen or disorganised during the interregnum. As a result chapters had difficulty in establishing exactly what estates they had owned before the civil wars. At the audit

[6] Tanner MS 141, f. 104v.
[7] Arb 2, f. 27.
[8] The insolutes heading is still present in FTb 60, 1725–6, and as late as 1728–9 the only members of the chapter who are paid their stipends on time are two who have just died; FTb 63. For earlier evidence of financial difficulties see Ac 2/1, p. 45, 1679; Ac 2/6, f. 36, 1682; Ac 4/10, f. 14v, 1696; Ac 5/13, f. 129v, 1715.
[9] Arb 2, f. 38; Ronald Hutton, *The Restoration*, Oxford 1985, p. 141.
[10] Egz 28–9.
[11] Tanner MSS 92, ff. 4–5; 130, f. 66; 147, f. 10.

at Rochester in the autumn of 1678 a list was produced of rents not likely to be collected for the simple reason that the lands and houses from which these rents were due could not be traced.[12] Well into the 1680s there were still a few pieces of property not yet recovered, and the struggle to recover one of these, near Fleet Bridge in London, went on from 1684 to 1787.[13]

The cathedral's estates were the source of almost all its income. They were let, like nearly all ecclesiastical estates up to the 1850s, on long leases at low and static annual rents, with the chapter making up much of the gap between these low rents and the full annual value by taking a fine from each lessee when his lease was renewed. By the late seventeenth century the establishing of the proper level for a fine was in principle a matter of simple routine. The gross annual value of the property was ascertained and the rent deducted to give a net annual value. In fixing the fine allowance was made for the fact that the chapter gained by receiving the fine at the very beginning of the period to which it was related. Thus if the chapter was paid a rent of £10 a year for a property worth £50 a year, then over the period of a 21-year lease it would need £840 (twenty-one times the difference between £50 and £10) to make up the balance; but if the tenant paid £840 at the beginning of the twenty-one years, then the chapter, by investing such part of the £840 as was not needed immediately to make up the first year's rent to the full annual value, would make a profit. And so it was customary to make allowance, at a set interest rate, for this potential investment. A very common interest rate in the later seventeenth century was £11 11s 8¼d per £100 (about 11.6 per cent in modern terminology), and a lessee taking out a new 21-year lease with this interest allowed would pay as his fine just over seven and three-quarter times the difference between his annual rent and the full annual value of the property. If, after seven years of his lease had expired, he followed the usual practice and renewed it, he would pay, if the 11.6 per cent interest rate were again employed, a fine equal to one year's difference between the rent and the full annual value. This may seem a small amount to cover the difference between the rent and the annual value over a period of seven years, but it must be remembered that in renewing his lease the lessee was surrendering a lease with fourteen years left in it and receiving a new 21-year lease in exchange, and so the period to be covered by the fine was only the last seven years of that new period and would not begin until fourteen years after the date of the renewal.

The Rochester chapter in the late seventeeth century used the £11 11s 8¼d per cent interest rate in setting fines for its 21-year leases, which were the majority. The use of this rate, much higher than the prevailing level of interest rates on reasonably safe investments, represented not a conscious decision that such a rate was the most appropriate but rather reflected a custom dating from an earlier period of higher interest rates. Fines were normally expressed in some such words as 'one year's value', this value being the property's net value to the lessee, assuming that he was able to sub-let it for its full value and that he paid the chapter's rent out of that income. Printed tables for the calculation of fines were published, including most notably

[12] Egz 36A.
[13] FTb 19; Ac 3/7, ff. 105–6, 136v; Ac 3/7, f. 60; Ac 8/25, p. 70; Ac 8/27, f. 29v; Ac 8/28, p. 18.

some compiled by George Mabbot of King's College and published in 1686 as the work of Isaac Newton.

This system of leasing had important practical consequences. Every time a lease was renewed three questions had to be answered. What was the property's full annual value? That is, what rent would it fetch if let at the highest rent the market would bear? What rate of interest should be assumed in setting the amount of the fine? What should be done with the income from renewal fines?

The first question was most commonly, most easily and least accurately answered by using a valuation from the past, based on an old survey, or following the valuation used at an earlier renewal. A better way to find out the market value of that large proportion of cathedral property which was sub-let by its lessees was to ask for evidence of the rent paid by the sub-tenant to the lessee. A disadvantage of this method was that a lessee and his sub-tenant could fraudulently agree that part of the rent should be concealed. This trick was being practised about 1760 by the lessee and sub-tenant of the Noah's Ark, a public house in Strood leased to the well-known brewer James Best.[14] Best had formerly sub-let to Mr and Mrs George Boucher, but by 1760 George Boucher had died and Isaac Clarke, having married the widow, had become sub-tenant of the Noah's Ark. When Clarke married Mrs Boucher, James Best raised the sub-tenant's rent from £10 to £14 a year but gave Clarke a receipt for only £10. Thus, so far as the chapter could see, the Noah's Ark was still worth only £10 a year, while Best and Clarke both benefited: Best paid smaller fines at renewals of his lease, and Clarke paid less in parish rates.[15] Sir Thomas Styles, lessee of Wateringbury rectory, as well as practising the same deceit on the chapter as Best, also deliberately allowed the boundary between his chapter leasehold and his adjacent freehold property to become so obscure that the chapter could not establish exactly how much of the Styles estate was chapter property.[16] In the long term the chapter's answer to such problems was to commission professional property surveys: in 1799–1800 it paid Messrs Skinner & Dykes £30 for a survey of Leatherhead rectory estate (a difficult estate to manage because of its distance from Rochester), and by 1811–12 the annual amount spent on property surveys, excluding surveys of woods and of property needing repairs, was as high as £183.[17]

The question of the interest to be assumed in setting renewal fines was answered in the 1660s by custom. It had by then long been usual in the commonest sort of renewal, that of a 21-year lease of which seven years had expired, to charge a fine often called 'one year's clear rent', that is one year's open-market rent less one year's 'reserved' rent to the chapter. A fine of this level effectively allowed the lessee interest of about 11.6 per cent, and in an age when interest on loans was restricted by law to well below this rate many church lessees benefited out of their leaseholds.[18]

[14] Rosemary A. Keen, 'Messrs. Best, Brewers of Chatham', *Archaeologia Cantiana*, lxxii (1958); Victor Salmon, 'James Best, Brewer of Chatham, 1744–1782', *Cantium*, iii, Winter 1971–2, pp. 95–100.
[15] Elr 5; Centre for Kentish Studies, Maidstone, Q/RLv 4/1.
[16] Elr 7.
[17] FTb 131, s.v. Necessary but uncertain expenses; FTb 143.
[18] John Smart, *Tables of Interest, Discount, Annuities, Etc., First Published in the Year 1724*, revised

Plate 3. Four deans of Rochester

(a) Thomas Dampier, 1782-1802.

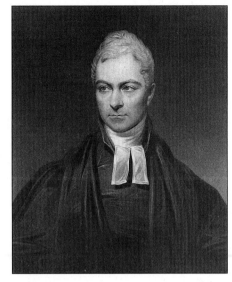

(b) Robert Stevens, 1820-70.

(c) Samuel Reynolds Hole, 1887-1905.

(d) Francis Underhill, 1932-7.

Plate 4(a). The Cathedral Close c.1800.

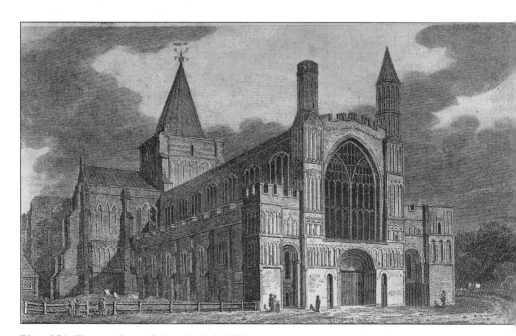

Plate 4(b). The west front of the cathedral, 1806.

As both market forces and an Act of Parliament of 1714 brought interest rates down further still ecclesiastical landlords began to feel that too much of the profit from their estates was going to the lessees and too little to the landlords.[19] At Rochester an explicit table for calculating renewal fines was adopted in 1682. This table allowed lessees who renewed promptly every seven years the traditional rate of 11.6 per cent and discouraged procrastination by allowing lower rates to the less prompt: for instance, a lessee who renewed when eighteen years of his 21-year lease had expired was allowed interest of only about ten per cent.[20] In the summer of 1720, in response to a suggestion from its richer and more influential neighbour, the dean and chapter of Canterbury, the Rochester chapter decided to allow lessees only about nine per cent, which meant an increase of fifty per cent in the fine paid by a lessee renewing a 21-year lease after seven years.[21] The chapter act book reveals some disagreement about the application of this new rate, and in July 1721, on the grounds that both land values as well as interest rates in general had fallen in the past year, a new rate was fixed of about ten per cent; in the language of the period the fine for a renewal of a 21-year lease after seven years was to be one and a quarter years' clear improved rent.[22] On this occasion the chapter explicitly reserved to itself a right which it always felt quite free to exercise, that of 'showing further kindness & favour' to lessees by charging a fine smaller than that dictated by its general policy.

This attempt in 1721 to maintain the financial balance between landlord and lessee produced, after a year's experience, an interesting protest from two of the prebendaries, Edmund Barrell, a member of a local family of lawyers who had had experience as a prebendary of Norwich and had served Rochester cathedral very well, particularly by his handling of its investment in the South Sea Bubble, and Daniel Hill, a conscientious and diligent but also pedantic and pompous man. These two urged the retention of the old rate for calculating renewal fines and argued that to adopt new rates suggested that the chapter members of the 1720s must be wiser or more deserving than their predecessors. 'And we fear our aiming at more will be thought too justly to proceed from the greater Luxury of Some & the greater Covetousness of others of the Clergy of this Age beyond those of the former.' They went on to argue that interest rates in a trading nation fluctuated so quickly that to allow rates of calculating fines to be influenced by market rates of interest would leave lessees not knowing where they were or how to make prudent financial plans. To treat lessees generously, they said, was in the chapter's long-term interest, as it would encourage lessees to maintain, develop and invest in their leaseholds. Finally Barrell and Hill reminded their colleagues that in the dark days of 1640 Bishop John Hacket of Lichfield had told Parliament that deans and chapters did not begrudge

etc. by Charles Brand, London 1780, p. 10n.; David Marcombe, 'Church leaseholders: the decline and fall of a rural elite', *Princes and Paupers in the English Church 1500–1800*, ed. Rosemary O'Day and Felicity Heal, Leicester 1981, pp. 255–75.

[19] 12 Anne st.2c. 16; Edward Hughes, *North Country Life in the Eighteenth Century: The North-East 1700–1750*, London 1952, pp. 310–11.

[20] Ac 2/6, f. 23.

[21] Ac 5/15, pp. 56–7.

[22] Ac 5/15 pp. 75–6; Ac 6/16, f. 5v.

their lessees the profits of their leaseholds six years out of seven, and they urged that in days of prosperity chapters should still follow the line laid down by Hacket.[23]

Dean Pratt, writing from Windsor, where he was detained by his health, drew on his experience as a canon of Windsor and for once in his career poured oil on troubled waters; he decided that the standard fine for renewing a 21-year lease after seven years should be one and a quarter years' clear improved rent, but that this rate should not be imposed simultaneously with the adoption of a new and higher valuation of a property. The dean predicted that no lessee would have his fine increased by more than a quarter at a time. He also ordered that properties worth less than £10 a year should continue to be renewed at the old rates provided that their lessees renewed promptly at the usual intervals.[24]

In the years following the disagreement of 1721–2 and its settlement by Dean Pratt the chapter very commonly exercised its discretion in accepting smaller fines than those it had agreed on as a rule. It was only in 1754, after a decision of chapter based on the response of other cathedrals and of university colleges to depressed interest rates and increased land values, that the method for calculating fines laid down by Dean Pratt thirty years before became the regular practice.[25] A circular letter detailing the new rates was printed in July 1753 and sent to 94 lessees, with another eleven lessees who were due to renew their leases before the new rates came into effect presumably being given the letter in person; the chapter clerk William Gates was given ten guineas for the extra work involved.[26] A further increase in rates for calculating fines was made in June 1804 and contributed to the chapter's increasing prosperity in the first twenty years of the nineteenth century.[27]

A disadvantage of a system under which one of the factors determining a lessee's renewal fine was the open-market value of a property was that lessees could easily have been discouraged from increasing the value by improvements such as building or draining. Like most ecclesiastical landlords the Rochester chapter avoided this problem by deliberately ignoring, at the first renewal of a lease after the lessee had improved his leasehold property, whatever increase in value the improvement had achieved.[28] On a few occasions the chapter actually gave an undertaking not to 'take advantage' of building or some other improvement. In 1686 Charles Smith, an apothecary from Chatham who had just taken out a lease of a piece of ground on which nothing had ever been built, announced his plan for building and asked to be allowed the next three renewals without fines; his petition was granted.[29]

The chapter's dependence on its estates meant that it was necessarily involved with the community around it. A list of the trades and occupations of Rochester chapter lessees would run to over forty items, not counting descriptions of status such as esquire, gentleman, yeoman, widow, and clerk. There was nothing to prevent women from leasing chapter property, and in an age less well provided than our own

[23] Ac 6/16, ff. 31v–33v.
[24] Ac 6/16, f. 35r–v.
[25] Ac 6, *passim*; Ac 7/22, p. 79.
[26] Ac 7/22, pp. 80–87.

[27] Ac 9/34, pp. 35–6.
[28] Ac 6/16, f. 40v.
[29] Ac 5/13, f. 7; Ac 7/22, p. 13; Ac 7/24, pp. 49–50; Ac 3/7, ff. 137v–138.

with safe investments for a woman needing to live on her capital, ecclesiastical leaseholds which could be sub-let at a profit served a useful purpose.[30] Some of the women who leased chapter property were poor widows, to whom the chapter was sometimes kind at its own expense; for instance, Mrs Susanna Melvill of London was allowed to renew a lease in 1693 at half the proper fine.[31] Some were rich widows; Mrs Elizabeth Bouverie, the lessee of Chart Sutton rectory estate towards the end of the eighteenth century, had valuable property, apart from the rectory which was worth over £200 a year.[32]

Much of the chapter's property was agricultural land, but its estates also created links between the cathedral and the industrial and commercial life of west Kent. We have already mentioned the forty trades and professions represented among the chapter's lessees, and while some of these people were leasing for investment purposes or to provide residences for themselves, others were certainly wanting business premises.[33] Of the three adjoining properties in Chatham leased to Jacob Cazenove in 1746 at least one was meant for his distilling business, and the Red Ball, later called the Haunch of Venison, on Ludgate Hill in London, was one of a number of houses, mostly in the Medway towns, leased to the Best family and other brewers.[34] Strood water mill was chapter leasehold, and in 1777 the chapter gave financial encouragement to William Webb to build a new windmill on a piece of its land on the top of Hogg Hill in the parish of Bearsted.[35]

Its ownership of a good deal of land in the Medway valley gave the chapter an interest in the growth of mineral extraction, although the business initiative always came from the lessees. The first lessee to ask permission to extract minerals was Philip Boghurst, who in 1756 suggested mining chalk on his leasehold at Frindsbury, some for sale and some for the improvement of the land, and offered to pay a penny a ton on all the chalk that was sold. The chapter asked Archdeacon Denne to come to an agreement with Boghurst, and soon afterwards this chalk began to make a modest contribution to the cathedral's finances; the £84 received from this source in 1758–9 was more, for instance, than the annual cost of stipends and scholarships for the two grammar-school masters and the twenty scholars.[36] The Frindsbury estate continued to provide an income from its chalk into the nineteenth century, and in the late 1780s George Guy, lessee of the manor and farm lands of Wouldham, followed Philip Boghurst's example and began to pay the chapter small annual amounts for chalk dug on his leasehold.[37] Brick earth and sand were also dug at Frindsbury in the early nineteenth century, and in June 1820 the chapter agreed that

[30] Ac 7/23, p. 40; Ac 7/24, p. 45; Ac 8/28, p. 60.
[31] Ac 3/9, f. 52; cf. ff. 22v, 23v, 70.
[32] Ac 9/30, p. 48; for her other property cf. the index of Hasted, 2nd edn, v.
[33] For example, Ac 6/16, f. 36v; cf. A.J.F. Dulley, 'People and Homes in the Medway Towns 1687–1783', reprinted from *Archaelogia Cantiana*, lxxvii (1962), in *Essays in Kentish History*, eds Margaret Roake and John Whyman, London 1973, pp. 111–12.
[34] Ac 7/21, f. 22v; Ac 6/19, f. 43; Ac 7/21, f. 33v; Ac 7/22, p. 50; Ac 7/23, p. 5; Ac 7/24, pp. 44, 49; Ac 8/25, p. 51; Ac 9/35, p. 69.
[35] Ac 7/23, p. 52; Ac 8/26, p. 44.
[36] Ac 7/23, p. 43; FRb 83; FRb 90.
[37] FRb 134; Ac 8/28, p. 45; FRb 115.

Mr Lomas could excavate brick earth at Denton over the next few months in order to discover whether the venture would be profitable.[38] In 1810 Messrs Joseph & Thomas Brindley, who gave the site for a Methodist chapel at Strood, succeeded Philip Boghurst as lessees of the Frindsbury estate, which by then included a shipyard. Besides an unknown amount needed to buy out Boghurst or his executors, they paid £989 to the chapter to renew the lease, and proceeded to build a lime works and wharves and to extract gravel, ballast and chalk as well as working the remaining agricultural land.[39] The Brindleys became the largest private warship-building firm on the Medway, but in 1826 they went bankrupt.[40]

The estates of the cathedral were mostly leased on 21-year leases, with some urban housing on 40-year leases and only a very few properties leased for three lives. This might suggest some impermanence of tenure. In fact some lessees had a right to renewal written into their leases, and all others found renewals very easily granted provided they did not behave scandalously over repairs or rent payments. Many a chapter property was leased by members of one family for generations: notable examples were Wateringbury rectory, leased to the Styles family from 1682 at the latest until 1808, and Sutton Valence rectory, leased to the Filmers from 1665 at the latest until 1811.[41] This security of tenure encouraged lessees to invest in improvements to their leaseholds, and facilitated sales and mortgages of leaseholds, which on the Rochester estates as elsewhere came to be regarded almost as customary freeholds subject to regular annual and septennial payments to the landlord.[42]

The income from renewal fines at Rochester, as at some other cathedrals, went very largely into the pockets of the dean and prebendaries. Immediately after 1660, following a gap of over a decade during which the chapter had had no legal existence and no leases had been renewed, the income from fines was high: in 1661–2 it was £1,384, but in 1664–5 it was a mere £115, most leases having been renewed within a year or two of the Restoration and not being due for further renewal before 1667.[43] But in the 1660s the condition of the church and its associated houses made very high expenditure unavoidable, and during these years the dean and prebendaries can have taken only a modest share of the fines for themselves. A chapter order of 1673 indicated a return to normality: all fines received were to be divided among the members of chapter as soon as convenient.[44] From then on it was expected that the normal expenses of the cathedral would be met by the income regarded as belonging to it: rents, the proceeds of timber sales (and of minerals sales from the late 1750s) and fees for burials in the church. Sometimes this income proved quite inadequate, and then the dean and prebendaries 'lent', or more often 'subscribed', from the fines

---

[38] FRb 126–7; Ac 10/39, p. 7.

[39] J.M. Preston, *Industrial Medway: an Historical Survey*, Rochester 1977, p. 33; Henry Smetham, *A History of Strood*, Chatham 1899, p. 254; Ac 10/36, pp. 47, 51, 61, 67; Ac 10/37, pp. 54–5; Ac 10/38, pp. 28–9, 38–9, 64.

[40] Preston, *loc. cit.*; Ac 10/39, p. 7; Ac 10/40, p. 54.

[41] Ac 2/6, f. 42; Ac 10/36, p. 9; Arb 1, f. 94; Ac 10/36, p. 65.

[42] Ac 2/2, f. 9; Egz 109; Egz 111A; Ac 2/4A, f. 44v; Ac 3/8, f. 46; Egz 130/24.

[43] FRb 13–14.

[44] Arb 2, f. 52v.

what was necessary, helped out by occasional external loans such as £800 from Thomas Best the brewer in the 1730s and £400 from the chapter clerk and auditor Mr Twopeny in 1801–2.[45] These subscriptions by the dean and prebendaries took place in 1664, 1682, 1778 and then in a series from 1780 into the early nineteenth century, the largest being £3,280 in 1805–6; on most of these occasions the dean, who took twice as much as a prebendary when fines were divided, also subscribed twice as much.[46] Except perhaps in 1682 and 1778, when the record is not specific on the point, all these subscriptions were made necessary by the cost of fabric repairs; twice arrangements were made for the chapter members to be repaid in due course.[47]

The income from renewal fines fluctuated both in the longer term, where the major factors were the improved values of the leased properties (determined partly by general levels of prosperity and rents) and the decisions made by the chapter about the interest rate to be allowed to lessees on their fines, and in the short term, where much depended on precisely which leases were due for renewal and on whether lessees renewed promptly. In the late seventeenth century there are gaps in the financial records, but such figures as are available produce an average of £568 a year, the highest figure in the records being £1,384 in 1661–2 and the lowest £115 in 1664–5.[48] Similar calculations on the complete records for the period 1801 to 1820 show an average annual income from fines of £4,466, with a high point of £7,982 in 1819–20 and a low of £880 in 1809–10.[49] Sympathy for the financial plight of the higher clergy in the early nineteenth century is not fashionable, but these fluctuations must at times have caused problems for domestic budgets: in 1808–9 the dean and prebendaries had a very good year, the dean's total income from the cathedral being £1,273 and each prebendary's £607, but in the following year the dean's income was down to £411 and each prebendary's to £175.

The estates of most cathedrals did not change in extent between 1660 and about 1800; deans and chapters had no power to sell property before the 1790s. The Rochester chapter however owned land in Chatham, where in the late seventeenth and early eighteenth centuries the Navy needed extra space to extend and fortify the dockyard.[50] The chapter was therefore given leave by Act of Parliament to sell property in Chatham to the Navy, at prices to be fixed by commissioners. On these occasions the chapter came out of the negotiations quite well, finishing up, once it had invested the purchase money in new property, with an increased rental.[51]

In its negotiations with the Navy in the early eighteenth century the chapter claimed that it was being badly treated in the valuation of its property and, although

---

[45] Ac 2/6, f. 36; Ac 6/19, ff. 9v, 23; FTb 134, p. 34.

[46] Arb 2, f. 27; Ac 2/6, f. 36; Ac 8/26, pp. 55, 75; Ac 9/33, p. 39; Ac 9/35, pp. 12–13; FTb 137, p. 1.

[47] Arb 2. f. 27; Ac 9/35, pp. 12–13.

[48] Figures calculated from all surviving Treasurer's Books of the period, FTb 13–34, and from FRb 13–16, FRb 29.

[49] FTb 132–151; FR/F 2–3.

[50] F. Cull, 'Chatham Dockyard: Early Leases and Conveyances . . .', Archaeologia Cantiana, lxxiii (1960), pp. 75–95.

[51] Compare FRb 21 with FRb 22, FRb 49 with FRb 50–51.

it eventually persuaded the commissioners to increase the purchase price, the chapter's chief negotiator, prebendary Edmund Barrell, told the dean in January 1715 that he felt there was no chance of getting the £533 which was the difference remaining between what the chapter was being offered and what it felt it had a right to expect. In the end this particular sale to the government turned out very well indeed for the chapter, not because of any generosity on the part of the government but because when the chapter received the purchase money it saw no immediate prospect of being able to invest it in land and therefore put it into stock in the South Sea Company.[52] It was paid £2,664 by the government and in November 1715 bought £2,812 of stock, a total which it soon afterwards increased to £3,000.[53] By late March 1720 it had decided that it ought to sell quickly; on 28 March Edmund Barrell and Archdeacon Sprat were given power to sell all or part of the stock. They discussed selling but hesitated. On 2 May Sprat died, and later in May Barrell, under pressure from his brother Henry the chapter clerk and from Dean Pratt, began selling. The price of South Sea stock was still rising, and Barrell sold the chapter's holding in three blocks at prices between £450 and £510. The total realised was £12,270.[54] So far the chapter's investment had been extremely successful, but as it was obliged to invest the new money in land and there was no land to be bought immediately something had to be done with the £12,270, which was in the usual form of notes drawn on various bankers. Edmund Barrell decided to entrust all these notes to a single banker who would then encash the chapter's notes from other bankers, and he was fortunate to find in Charles Shales of Lombard Street a banker who remained solvent through the many financial collapses caused by the bursting of the South Sea Bubble. Even Shales was not relied on for long. In June 1720 most of the £12,270 was invested in East India Bonds, £500 was lent to a gentleman 'on his private security at 5%', and the rest was held ready for the purchase of land.[55]

The first land to be bought was in Frindsbury; it cost £1,078 in December 1720 and was worth £40 a year in rent, a yield of 3.7 per cent a year. In the next few months other property was bought, at Cliffe and High Halstow, but about half of the total available was used to buy not land but a different type of property which was nevertheless acceptable to the commissioners supervising the chapter's investment of their new capital.[56] Lord Aylesford owned a large number of fee farm rents, some of which he indicated that he would be willing to sell. With the advantage of hindsight it is clear that these rents could not be a good long-term investment; they were fixed for ever at the same monetary value and were incapable of capital growth. As described by Lord Aylesford in 1721 they seemed to offer some advantages over land; they were not 'liable to accidents or repairs' (the chapter supplied rough timber free of charge for property repairs on its estates), and recent legislation had provided

[52] LA1/12; LA1/16; LA1/17; FAs, p. 3; Ac 5/13, f. 132v.
[53] Ac 5/13, f. 137v.
[54] FAs, p. 3
[55] FAs, pp. 3–4.
[56] Egz 67/2: Egz 67/4; FAs, pp. 4–5; FR/Np 1.

an effective remedy in case of non-payment.[57] Furthermore, said Lord Aylesford, what he was offering was 'the flower of the Estate'; the dean and chapter could exclude from the purchase any rents they disliked, and Lord Aylesford offered what sounded like a money-back guarantee if any of the rents turned out bad. So in July 1721 and February 1722 the chapter paid in two instalments a price of £6,054 for rents worth nearly £241 a year, a yield of nearly four per cent.[58]

The chapter's immediate experience with these rents was encouraging, and in 1723 it bought some more of Lord Aylesford's fee farm rents.[59] By 1734 it was quite clear that some of these rents could not be collected. The chapter asked Lord Aylesford to make good his guarantee, but he said that after so many years he did not know which rents the chapter was complaining about.[60] The argument went on for five years and was then taken to court, where in 1746 it was still going on.[61] The expected yield of almost four per cent on this investment, reduced by the rents found to be uncollectable, was made still smaller by the cost of collection. The chapter's first collector, Henry Barrell, charged only five per cent on the amounts he collected, but in 1743 he was succeeded by John Hickman, who charged twice as much.[62] This major investment yielded in practice not quite three and a half per cent, and in course of time the yield became even lower.[63]

The sale of land to the Navy and the investment of the resulting capital increased the cathedral's rental from £904 a year in the 1660s to £1,319 in the 1720s, including what should have been £334 a year in fee farm rents. During the 1750s the income was reduced by about £140 in taxes, bad fee farm rents and the costs of collecting them. Other sources of income were fines for the renewals of leases, already discussed, 'casual receipts', which were mostly from timber sales, quit rents from manors, and income from sales of chalk and other minerals. Casual receipts were very variable, ranging between £20 and £200 a year in the 1750s, sales of chalk were only just beginning and were producing only £30 to £40 a year, and quit rents should have brought in £98 a year.

Quit rents, however, presented an administrative problem. They were small amounts due from a considerable number of properties spread over more than a dozen manors, and they were fixed in amount so that their real value was reduced by inflation. By 1750 therefore the annual 'progress' around all the chapter's manors which the statutes required seemed an unnecessary burden; it was expensive and time-consuming, and the £98 in quit rents was not adequate recompense. Visiting the manors did provide an opportunity for inspecting and reporting on the state of some of the chapter's property, but this was a modest benefit and not easily quantified.[64] The chapter therefore adopted a policy of collecting quit rents only once in six years; in most years no attempt was made to collect, and the whole £98 due from that source was simply added to the list of arrears. In fact at the beginning of the accounting year 1750–1 the arrears of quit rents stood at £2,281, an astonishing

57 LP 22/9; Emp 5A.
58 FAs, p. 5.
59 LP 22/11/2.
60 LP 22/13/1–2, 16.

61 LP 22/17–19, 37.
62 FR/F, f. 2.
63 LP 22/23.
64 Egz 42; Egz 63/1.

enough figure, being over twenty-three times the annual rental, and at the end of that year they had been increased by exactly the £98 9s 0d of the rental.[65] In 1761–2 the chapter held one of its six-yearly collections of quit rents. Its collector brought in £477, reducing the arrears from £2,567 to £2,188, but the cost of holding the courts at which these quit rents were collected was £146, and so an exercise which might in theory have produced an income of £588 (£98 a year for six years) produced £331 net. On over twenty occasions between 1660 and 1820 the chapter considered the problem of quit rents but never solved it.[66] In the 1660s it used a system of collection which seemed promising; it allowed George May, a barrister and the chapter clerk and under-steward of courts, to farm the quit rents, paying the chapter £45 a year and half of the occasional perquisites such as entry fines, and keeping for himself such quit rents as he could collect.[67] There is no evidence to show whether it was the chapter or the farmer who was unwilling to perpetuate this arrangement, but it did not continue after George May's death early in 1673.[68]

Income from sales of chalk and other minerals began only in the accounting year 1758–9, when £84 was received for chalk from Philip Boghurst, the chapter's tenant at Frindsbury. During the next decade this income amounted to £40 or less in most years, but it was destined to become more important after 1800, when Boghurst, and later the Brindleys, as lessees of Frindsbury Manor Farm, undertook mineral extraction on a large scale, producing anything up to £600 a year for the chapter.[69]

To sum up the chapter's financial position in the 1750s, its corporate income was in the region of £1,300 to £1,350 a year. There was also a substantial income, on average £870, from renewal fines, but, since the custom was for this money to be divided among the dean and prebendaries personally, none of it was available to the cathedral save when the chapter saw the need as very pressing. Expenditure was at much the same level as income: in 1751–2 for instance it totalled £1,335, made up of £493 stipends and other payments to the dean and prebendaries, £400 stipends and salaries of minor canons and other staff, including choristers, grammar scholars and bedesmen, £273 routine running expenses, alms, university exhibitions etc., and £172 fabric repairs.[70] The only item of expenditure which varied very greatly from one year to another was fabric repair: in the 1750s it ranged from nothing to £481, averaging £113 a year.

---

[65] FRb 75.

[66] For example, Ac 2/4A, f. 36; Ac 2/6, f. 97v; Ac 3/7, ff. 12, 71, 74, 99; Ac 3/8, f. 73; Ac 6/17, ff. 50, 80r–v; Ac 6/18, f. 46v; Ac 6/19, f. 34v; Ac 7/23, pp. 23, 32, 43. From Michaelmas 1810 some fee farm rents were sold in order to redeem Land Tax: FRb 134.

[67] Arb 2, f. 80.

[68] Arb 2, f. 48.

[69] FRb 137–8; Ac 10/36, pp. 47, 51, 61, 67; Ac 10/37, pp. 12, 54–5. For the quantities of chalk excavated see Preston, op. cit., p. 56.

[70] FTb 83; the figures in the text total £1,338 rather than £1,335, the inaccuracy being caused by rounding off expenditure on individual items to the nearest pound.

(3) Styles of Leadership

The most striking figure among the eighteenth-century deans of Rochester was Samuel Pratt. He was educated at Merchant Taylors' School and went straight into school-teaching without going to university. He became headmaster of Wye School, married and had several children.[71] He wanted to be ordained and was able to find more than one patron willing to give him a living, but Archbishop Sancroft twice refused to ordain him, first because he was too young and the second time because Sancroft felt it his duty to ordain unemployed young graduates rather than the self-educated Pratt.[72] The young man's tenacity eventually won through, and in 1682 he became rector of Kenardington near Ashford. Positions as chaplain to the princess of Denmark and as chaplain and tutor to the duke of Gloucester led to better things, including a prebend of St George's, Windsor.

He was installed as dean on 9 August 1706. Precisely five weeks later the chapter exercised its first patronage since his installation. In accordance with custom the new dean was allowed to nominate to the vacant living, the vicarage of Lamberhurst; he chose his son Samuel.[73] The process of providing for Dean Pratt's sons was to be a long-term one and was not entirely smooth; in April 1722 George was to be moved from the vicarage of Sutton Valence to Boughton Monchelsea, which was vacant because his brother Samuel had died, and the dean wanted his son Daniel to have Sutton Valence. Prebendary Hill objected, very properly, that Daniel was not a member of the cathedral foundation, and ought not to have Sutton Valence as long as minor canon Ralph Clegg was unprovided for.[74] Two years earlier Hill had objected to his colleague Edmund Barrell being given the vicarage of Boxley in addition to that of Sutton-at-Hone while minor canon Charles Birkbeck had no living.[75]

The dean won this little skirmish quite easily, but he had more difficulty later in the year in getting the curacy of Chatham for George. It was prebendary John Robinson's turn to nominate to this vacancy, but he willingly gave up his turn, not wanting the curacy either for himself or for a relative or protégé.[76] Chatham was only a perpetual curacy and so the dean and chapter did not need to present their nominee to the bishop with the formalities appropriate to a rectory or vicarage, but their nominee did need the bishop's licence and they neglected to apply for this. They simply issued to George Pratt the lease of the small tithes of Chatham which provided the curate with his income, but the sealing of this lease was held up for several days by the dissent of prebendaries Barrell and Hill, who afterwards appealed to the bishop as visitor on the grounds that the seal had been affixed in a 'Surreptitious & Clandestine Manner' to a lease not read at a proper chapter meeting and not agreed to by members of chapter.[77] Hill's feelings against the sealing were so strong that he not only objected verbally but also postponed the sealing by refusing to produce the key to the seal-chest which he held as treasurer for the year. Bishop Atterbury

[71] Tanner MS 35, f. 64.
[72] Tanner MS 35, f. 64; 36, f. 114.
[73] Ac 5/13, f. 6v.
[74] Ac 6/16, f. 15v.
[75] Ac 5/15, p. 50.
[76] Ac 6/16, f. 23.
[77] Ac 6/16, ff. 25v, 27r–v.

demanded an explanation, and was angry when he received a reply drafted for signature by the dean and those of the prebendaries present at chapter but in fact signed only by Dean Pratt, with two prebendaries dissenting and a third withdrawing without signing.[78] Atterbury had heard well of George Pratt and wanted someone to serve the 'burdensome cure' of Chatham; he therefore offered to connive at Pratt's officiating there until the matter was settled. Precisely how the matter was settled is obscure, except that it cost the chapter £10 in legal charges,[79] but George Pratt was curate of Chatham, as well as vicar of Boughton Monchelsea, from 1722 until his death in 1747.

Not all of Dean Pratt's sons were ordained. Thomas was in 1718 appointed chapter clerk, auditor and receiver of the quit rents, holding all three posts jointly with prebendary Edmund Barrell's brother Henry, who in practice did all the work.[80]

Pratt's activities were not directed solely to the needs of his family. He took an interest in the cathedral library, presenting to it in June 1712 a large book-case formerly the property of his pupil the duke of Gloucester, and presiding over a chapter meeting which, following the example of some other cathedrals, agreed that in future each new dean or prebendary should give £10 or £5 to the library instead of giving a party to celebrate his installation.[81] Pratt was in general an energetic dean who thought that he possessed considerable power and ought to exercise it. At the first general chapter after his installation new rules were agreed on the dress, attendance and behaviour of the minor canons and lay clerks.[82] Further sessions of the same chapter produced decisions to treat tenants more firmly, by insisting on regular surveys and the prompt renewal of leases for lives, to sell the cathedral's old and useless plate to raise funds for ornamenting the quire, and to raise the number of minor canons to the proper level of six.[83] Some years later, in November 1715, Pratt sent a long letter of complaint to his colleagues, stressing his concern for the restoration of discipline and for better management of the cathedral's affairs and rebuking them for failing to help him. The reply from prebendaries Hill, Grant and Sprat asserted that the cathedral's affairs were managed very well and pointed out that, if Pratt had specified what he saw as wrong in the management, action could have been taken at that audit.[84]

Pratt's high view of the dean's powers occasionally angered his colleagues. July 1716 was a particularly difficult month. On 9 July the dean asked the chapter to consider a request from Francis Barrell, recorder of Rochester and the chapter's under-steward and counsel, for a lease to be changed from twenty-one years to three

[78] Ac 6/16, f. 31.
[79] FTb 60, p. 33.
[80] Ac 5/14, p. 88; the evidence for Thomas's inactivity as chapter clerk is spread through the Act Books until his death in 1756. It is evidence from silence, but references to Henry Barrell until his virtual retirement in 1745 or 1746, and to William Gates, Barrell's successor, from then on are numerous enough to make it clear who did the chapter clerk's work.
[81] Ac 5/13, f. 94v.
[82] ff. 9v–10.
[83] ff. 11r–v, 13r–v.
[84] ff. 129v–130.

lives. The alteration would not have been in the chapter's interest and ought to have been rejected; prebendaries Hill, Grant and Barrell were so annoyed at the dean's putting the question that they walked out, and, when Hill returned and was asked by Pratt to stay, he walked out again and was formally admonished for contumacy. Two days later Hill protested against the dean's action in a typically verbose fashion,[85] accusing Pratt, among other things, of 'ungovern'd passion'. On 10 July Pratt attempted to appoint Jeremy Batley as headmaster of the cathedral grammar school. The four prebendaries present, Hill, Grant, Barrell and the Kent historian John Harris, were willing for Batley to be appointed but were insistent that the appointment be made by the dean and chapter and not by the dean alone; they then left the meeting.[86] On 11 July Pratt argued that according to the statute *De Officio Decani* he was responsible for the church's moveable goods. He proceeded to use the power claimed by calling in all books, papers and other goods not in the hands of the proper officers; in particular he required prebendary Harris to return the cathedral's famous medieval books, the *Textus Roffensis* and the *Custumale Roffense*, to their proper place. The prebendaries present objected to the dean's demand; Harris was in the process of printing his history of Kent, and he had signed for the volumes in the usual way. The dean claimed that Harris had refused to let him use the *Custumale* for one day. Harris claimed that he had offered it to the dean on condition that Pratt promise to return it the next evening, and Pratt had refused to give any such undertaking. The chapter meeting broke up without doing any further business. The session on 12 July was almost wholly taken up by sniping between Pratt and Hill, but at the final session of that general chapter all was orderly once more and business was transacted in an atmosphere which may not have been friendly (the formal record omits such matters) but was at least businesslike.[87]

The dispute between Dean Pratt and some of the prebendaries about George Pratt's nomination to the curacy of Chatham was not the first occasion for expensive resort to lawyers to settle a dispute within the chapter. In March 1679 a dispute had begun between Dean John Castilion and the chapter over a part of the King's Orchard, to the east of the cathedral, which had become in practice a perquisite of the dean.[88] A series of leases to successive deans and relatives of deans in the late sixteenth century was followed by a period in the early seventeenth century when the deans enjoyed the ground without leases but subject to the payment of a rent of £2 10s 0d a year.[89] The precise status of the ground became a more interesting question after the Restoration, since the northern edge of the area had become much more valuable with the building of houses and shops along the line of the High Street. A new agreement negotiated between Dean Hardy and the chapter in the 1660s raised the annual rent paid by the dean to £10, but under Dean Castilion the chapter claimed that the Dean's Orchard, as it was commonly called, was the property of the dean and chapter corporately.[90] After Castilion's death in 1688 the dispute subsided, but during Dean Pratt's time, in 1708, prebendary John Gilman, as vice-dean, and the

[85] Ac 5/14, pp. 9, 13–14.
[86] pp. 10–11.
[87] pp. 15–17.

[88] Ac 2/1, p. 19.
[89] Tanner MS 147, ff. 17–18.
[90] Tanner MS 147, f. 19.

chapter ordered the verger to tell the tenants of the Dean's Orchard not to pay their rents to the dean. Pratt had foreseen this, and before leaving Rochester had made the verger promise not to go on any such errand, but the chapter got James Saunders, the chapter clerk's assistant, to act for it.[91] By 1710 Pratt had taken the business to the Court of Chancery. Feelings ran so high that, when Pratt suggested that he and the prebendaries sign a promise to ensure that the widow of prebendary Gilman (who had died on 17 November 1710) should not suffer whatever the outcome of the case, only the dean and prebendary John Harris signed.[92] In the event Pratt lost the case, and the cost to the church was over £50.[93]

Another matter over which deans of Rochester and the chapter sometimes fell out was St Bartholomew's Hospital in Chatham. Since the Restoration this medieval foundation had been almost the private property of successive deans, who used the rents from its estates to maintain its two brethren, and kept the fines received for renewals of leases for themselves.[94] In Dean Castilion's time the chapter had tried to get some share in the hospital's management.[95] Dean Pratt improved the hospital's effectiveness by increasing its annual income by, as he claimed, fifty per cent, and by, as everyone agreed, adding another beneficiary to the two brethren who were all that anyone could remember.[96] Pratt also rescued the surviving part of the hospital's building from secular uses, repaired it and fitted it with panelling and pews.[97] Nevertheless in his time the £36 a year of the hospital's income that was divided among the three brethren was almost matched by the £35 which on average went to the dean each year.[98] In May 1716 prebendary Hill thought that the intention of the founder of St Bartholomew's had been 'grossly abused', and the other prebendaries said that, as the hospital's management had been the subject of much controversy, the bishop should consider the problem.[99] In 1724 at Bishop Bradford's visitation Hill claimed that for the dean to keep for himself all the renewal fines on the hospital's leases was an abuse, and his colleagues Grant and Barrell supported him. Dean Pratt had died in November 1723, and, although his successor Nicholas Claggett had no intention of sharing the hospital with his colleagues, having granted leases of property belonging to the hospital to two of his relatives without exacting a fine, it needed less courage to criticise him than Pratt.[100]

More skilful and conciliatory than Dean Pratt in his handling of his colleagues was John Newcombe, master of St John's College, Cambridge, who was dean of Rochester from 1744 to 1765. At St John's his reputation after his death was poor,

[91] Ac 5/13, f. 37v.
[92] f. 77v.; Widow Gilman was looked after by being given in June 1712 a completely free renewal of her lease of a house in Rochester; f. 95.
[93] FTb 46, p. 41.
[94] Hasted, 2nd edn, iv, p. 217; Arb 2, f. 169.
[95] Ac 2/1, p. 19.
[96] Arb 2, f. 169.
[97] Hasted, 2nd edn, iv, p. 218; E.J. Greenwood, *The Hospital of St Bartholomew, Rochester*, Rochester 1962, p. 26.
[98] Arb 2, f. 169; Centre for Kentish Studies, Maidstone, Ch 2/18.
[99] Arb 2, ff. 173, 169.
[100] Arb 2, f. 212v; Centre for Kentish Studies, Ch 2/18.

but even there he was known for his 'smooth insinuating manner', and his record at Rochester attests his ability in that respect.[101] Given the quarrels between dean and prebendaries that took place under deans Castilion and Pratt, Newcombe deserves some credit for maintaining the peace. One characteristic of Newcombe's time was the number of members of St John's in need of help or employment who found it at Rochester. In 1746 Thomas Austen, born in Chatham and schooled at Maidstone and Canterbury, became a minor canon of Rochester; he was a graduate of St John's.[102] A long gap followed, but in 1755 the chapter appointed Edward Beadon, a fellow of St John's, as curate of Strood.[103] Two years later the headmaster of the cathedral school, Jonathan Soane, resigned, and Dean Newcombe successfully recommended to the chapter that the new headmaster be Thomas Thompson, a fellow of St John's.[104] In 1762 one of the chapter's two exhibitions at Cambridge fell vacant and was given to a Mr Weatherhead, the son of a Yorkshire clergyman, with no Rochester connection but a graduate at St John's.[105]

Newcombe's delicacy when dealing with appointments was impressive. In 1761 John Toll wanted to resign his position as verger and the dean's coachman wanted a change of work. Newcombe wrote from his London house in Great Marlborough Street in very deferential terms to say how sober, civil, honest and good-natured his coachman Thomas Jolly was and to recommend him for appointment as verger. The chapter accepted the dean's recommendation very willingly but seems not to have written to him on the matter. Two months later, in November, when Newcombe wrote from Cambridge to authorise Archdeacon Denne to act for him at the audit, he expressed the hope that in spite of his own absence and that of prebendary Barrell, who had sprained his back, enough chapter members would appear to enable business to be transacted, and he repeated his polite request for Jolly's appointment.[106] A year earlier Newcombe had been equally delicate in expressing his wish for Samuel Smith to be taken on as a lay clerk, and when at the end of 1762 prebendary Barrell wanted to resign the vicarage of Sutton-at-Hone, so that his grandson could have it, Newcombe was careful to check that prebendary Chardin Musgrave, provost of Oriel College, did not want Sutton for himself.[107] Newcombe's successor as dean, William Markham, gravely offended Musgrave in 1765 by having himself presented to the chapter living of Boxley. Musgrave pointed out angrily that he had been a prebendary for eight years without having a chapter living.[108] One might similarly compare Newcombe's way of easing his nominees into employment

[101] *History of the College of St John . . . Cambridge*, ed. J.E.B. Mayor, part II, Cambridge 1869, p. 1023.
[102] Ac 7/21, f. 22v; Venn, *Alumni Cantabrigienses*.
[103] Ac 7/23, p. 26.
[104] p. 60.
[105] Ac 7/24, p. 35; Venn, *Alumni Cantabrigienses*. For other links with St John's see Ac 7/21, ff. 21, 39; Ac 7/22, p. 16.
[106] Ac 7/24, pp. 24–5, 31.
[107] pp. 17, 41–2.
[108] p. 67.

with Dean Pratt's attempt in 1716 to appoint Jeremy Batley as headmaster without the chapter's approval.[109]

Thomas Dampier (Plate 3a), who became dean in 1782, was the son of an Eton master who ended his career as dean of Durham. When Dampier became dean of Rochester he had already held a prebend of Durham for four years. He kept this prebend until he was translated from the see of Rochester to that of Ely in 1808, and he by no means lost touch with Durham after 1782; in particular he spent some or all of the period of the November audit and general chapter in Durham in ten of his twenty years as dean of Rochester.[110] Under Dampier Rochester Cathedral ran with a smoothness suggestive of the somnolence often attributed to eighteenth-century cathedral closes. The records show very substantial expenditure on the fabric, at £4,670, higher than in any previous twenty-year period, although destined to be dwarfed by the £10,910 spent during the years 1802 to 1820.[111] Close attention to repairs and ornamentation of the fabric was one of Dampier's achievements listed by his colleagues when in 1802 he left the deanery to become bishop of Rochester; the others were an improvement in the service of the quire, wise regulations for securing the constant residence of members of the chapter, and the adoption of prudent methods for the increase of revenue.[112]

The conduct of services is dealt with in another chapter, and residence is discussed elsewhere in this one. The prudent methods for the increase of revenue need a little searching out. The rates for the calculation of renewal fines were not increased, and yet in Dampier's later years the cathedral's income reached new heights. In 1794–5 the income from renewal fines passed £3,000 for the first time, and in the remaining seven years of Dampier's deanery that figure was exceeded four times.[113] The rise in income from fines was partly a reflection of general prosperity and increasing property values, and partly the result of increased strictness in the valuing of property when leases were renewed; in 1788 a new name had appeared in the chapter acts, that of Henry Hogben, who for the next twenty years was to be regularly employed to survey, measure and map many of the cathedral's more important estates.[114] As far as possible fines were assigned to the personal benefit of the dean and prebendaries, but four times in his twenty years Dampier persuaded his colleagues to contribute some of their income from fines towards the cost of fabric repairs.[115] The chapter's grateful recording of Dean Dampier's achievements was unprecedented. Equally unprecedented had been his delivery to the chapter and the entire cathedral foundation of a 'very kind & affectionate address' in which he

[109] Ac 5/14, pp. 10–11; see above, p. 91.

[110] Ac 8/27, ff. 21v, 33; Ac 8/28, pp. 29–30, 53; Ac 9/29, pp. 3, 18; Ac 9/30, pp. 37, 64–5; Ac 9/31, pp. 18–19; Ac 9/32, p. 1.

[111] FTb 114–138.

[112] Ac 9/33, p. 57.

[113] FTb 126–133.

[114] T.S. Ashton, *Economic Fluctuations in England 1700–1800*, Oxford 1959, p. 29; for examples of Hogben's activities see Ac 9/29, p. 7; Ac 9/30, pp. 9, 72; Ac 9/31, p. 22; Ac 9/33, p. 9.

[115] FTb 119, p. 1; FTb 121, p. 1; Ac 9/33, p. 39.

thanked them all for their friendship and kindness to him and gave a particular commendation to Matthew Grain, formerly his butler and since 1785 the verger.[116]

(4) Patronage

The chapter was patron of some twenty-five parishes, nearly all in Kent and mostly within easy reach of Rochester; the most distant chapter livings were Haddenham and Kingsey in Buckinghamshire, Leatherhead in Surrey, and Woodnesborough, near Sandwich. None of the chapter livings was outstandingly wealthy. A number of them were parishes where the great tithes had been appropriated to the monks of Rochester (e.g. Hartlip) or to the canons of Leeds (e.g. West Farleigh, Wateringbury, Stockbury) and had been granted by Henry VIII to his dean and chapter along with most of the other property of those two religious houses. The appropriation of the great tithes left the vicars with the small tithes and a money stipend, an income which was in most cases adequate but not lavish.

To have a number of modestly-endowed benefices not far from Rochester was very useful to the dean and chapter. Like other patrons of their time they usually looked first, in trying to match a priest to a living, to the suitability of the living for the priest's needs rather than to the suitability of the priest's talents to the parish's needs. In particular they used their patronage in order to provide the cathedral's six minor canons, and the headmaster and usher of the cathedral grammar school, with some extra responsibility and increased income. A routine question at episcopal visitations was[117] whether any minor canon had more than one benefice or had a benefice more than 24 miles from Rochester. In 1724 the chapter admitted to Bishop Bradford that although no minor canon had, strictly speaking, two benefices, Caleb Parfect did have the rectory of Cuxton and the perpetual curacy of Strood.[118] It was, however, always able to report that no minor canon had a benefice more than 24 miles away. The chapter was thus enabled by the geographical distribution of its patronage to combine contented minor canons and a contented bishop. In comparison it seems that at Bristol the more dispersed cathedral patronage led to minor canons remaining for significantly shorter periods than those at Rochester.[119]

The early stages of the system of using the cathedral's patronage for the benefit of the minor canons and schoolmasters has left traces in the records. John Crew, who was usher of the grammar school in the 1670s, was not at first given a living. He proved to be a good teacher but not content with his lot, and he threatened to resign. He was therefore presented to the vicarage of Hartlip in 1677, explicitly to encourage and reward him as a teacher, and he promised not to resign the post of usher without also resigning Hartlip. He broke his promise, and kept Hartlip until his death in 1704; there was nothing that the chapter could do about it.[120] By 1684 it was explicit policy

[116] Ac 9/33, pp. 54–6; Ac 8/28, p. 4.
[117] Arb 2, ff. 165v, 206; Arb 3, pp. 23, 126.
[118] Arb 2, f. 209.

[119] Analysis of Bristol Record Office, DC/A/8/1–2.
[120] Ac 2/1, p. 79; Hasted, 2nd edn, vi, p. 24.

to provide minor canons with livings: in September of that year the chapter assumed that it would be impossible to fill a vacancy among the minor canons until a living could be made available, and in December the chapter was still trying to fill this vacancy, pressing the dean to find a suitable man as quickly as possible since the vicarage of Bearsted was vacant and it must present to it before the canon-law rule about filling a vacancy within six months caused it to lose its right to present.[121]

The livings to which the Rochester chapter presented minor canons were only modestly endowed. However there were no means of ensuring that minor canons, and schoolmasters, relinquished such livings when they resigned their positions on the cathedral foundation. In 1753 another usher, Charles Soane, left the school and held on to his two livings of Hartlip and Grain.[122] His successor as usher, John Pratt, a grandson of Dean Pratt, was presented to Halling on condition that if and when he resigned as usher he would resign his vicarage as well.[123] He entered into a bond to forfeit £300 if he resigned as usher and did not resign Halling.[124] But the dean and chapter knew that this was no more than a gentlemen's agreement, which John Pratt could have broken with impunity: the law against simony made any promise made by a priest in order to obtain a living illegal. In the end all the chapter could do in the early nineteenth century, after Henry Thomas Jones and William Bagshaw Harrison had displeased it by resigning their minor canonries and retaining their livings, was to make it very clear to every minor canon presented to a parish that the chapter strongly disapproved of former minor canons who by holding on to chapter livings made it difficult to attract 'respectable clergymen' to minor canonries; this practice was adopted in 1801 and re-stated in 1804 and 1810.[125]

When a chapter living became vacant the first questions to be asked were whether the dean or a prebendary wanted it for himself, or whether it was 'due' to a minor canon or 'proper' for one of the two schoolmasters.[126] When the answers to those questions were negative the choice of presentee was made on the recommendation of a member of the chapter, each taking his turn according to rules which proved very hard to write down unambiguously.[127] A common use of this patronage was to provide for sons. Dean Pratt's son Samuel held in turn the livings of Lamberhurst, Sutton Valence, and Boughton Monchelsea. Prebendaries Hill and Grant objected to his being given Boughton Monchelsea, but he held it until his death in 1722 and was succeeded there by his brother George.[128] When Samuel Pratt moved from Lamberhurst in 1713 he was replaced there by prebendary Grant's son John, who had just taken his MA, having been at Wadham College, Oxford, holding one of the exhibitions the chapter funded.[129] In 1762 prebendary Edmund Barrell resigned the

[121] Ac 3/7, p. 46 and f. 75.

[122] Ac 7/22, p. 87.

[123] p. 88.

[124] KS4.

[125] Ac 9/33, p. 20; Ac 9/34, pp. 48–9; Ac 10/36, p. 41.

[126] Arb 3, p. 45.

[127] Arb 3, pp. 45, 60, 292.

[128] Ac 5/13, ff. 106–7; Ac 5/15, p. 27; Ac 6/16, f. 15v.

[129] Ac 5/13, ff. 106–7, 116v.

Plate 5(a). South-east transept of the cathedral library and chapter house ruins, 1819.

Plate 5(b). The cathedral after the rebuilding of the central tower, 1826.

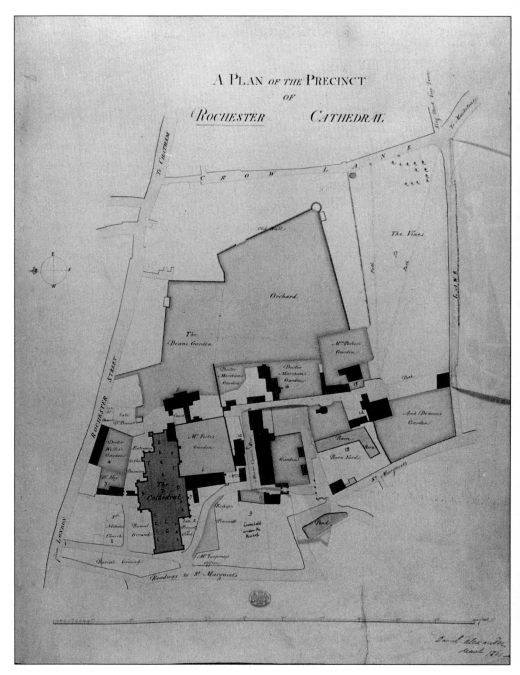

Plate 6. Plan of the cathedral precinct, 1801.

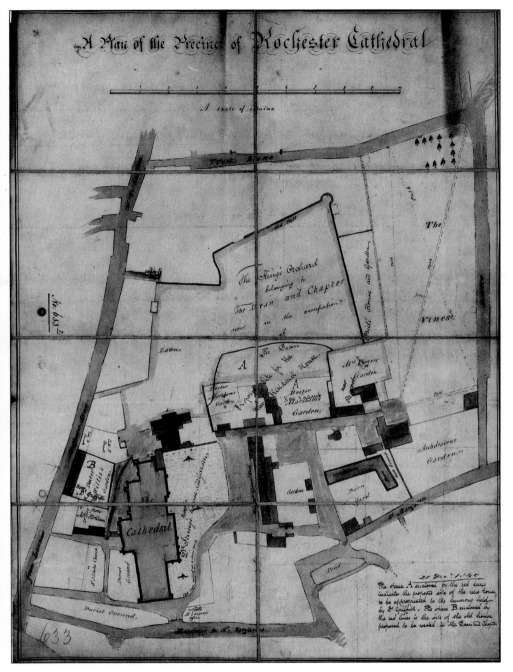

Plate 7. Plan of the cathedral precinct, 1840.

Plate 8. Door of the chapter house from Winkles' *Cathedrals*, 1836.

vicarage of Sutton-at-Hone so that his grandson Edmund Faunce could be presented to it.[130]

The livings which were not normally given to minor canons were the more remote parishes in Buckinghamshire and Surrey, Woodnesborough near Sandwich, and a small number of good livings near Rochester. At Lamberhurst one minor canon, Robert Pickering in 1716, appears in the list of vicars for 1660–1820, along with deans Pratt and Benjamin Newcombe, Samuel Pratt junior, John Grant junior and a sprinkling of prebendaries.[131] James Jones, from 1801 to 1820, was the only minor canon to be allowed the living of Kingsdown, and Boxley was reserved entirely for deans and prebendaries of Rochester and suitable outsiders such as Brownlow North, dean of Canterbury and later bishop of Lichfield and Coventry.[132]

The only serious interference with the chapter's free use of its patronage occurred in August 1685, when John Chadwick, who already held the chapter living of Darenth, brought to Rochester a letter from James II requiring that he be presented to Sutton-at-Hone, a vicarage which prebendary Daniel Hill wanted. A fortnight later the earl of Peterborough, who was to turn overtly Roman Catholic less than two years later, wrote to Dean Castilion with a vague threat of unpleasant consequences if the chapter tried to have the king's letter recalled.[133] The chapter had already by then written to ask Bishop Sprat to explain to the king that Rochester was a poor church and needed to use its patronage to reward its minor canons adequately, and its gloom at Peterborough's letter was deepened by a report from its organist, Daniel Henstridge, that Sir Vere Vane of Mereworth had said that Chadwick preferred the Church of Rome to the Church of England.[134] Daniel Hill, who firmly believed that if the king had all the facts put before him he would withdraw his letter, drafted a petition to the king, but Dean Castilion, who feared that he might suffer immediately and personally from the king's reaction to the petition, refused to have anything to do with it.[135] On 3 December 1685 the chapter ordered Chadwick's presentation to Sutton to be sealed; its only consolation was that he had agreed to resign Darenth if given Sutton, and that he kept his word.[136]

On a later occasion James II's use of his patronage did the chapter no actual harm. When Dean Castilion died on 21 October 1688 it was the king's right to nominate his successor, and accordingly on 25 October letters patent were issued naming Simon Lowth.[137] Early in November Lowth called on Bishop Sprat, showed him the king's letters patent and asked to be formally instituted as dean. The bishop, as he explained in a confidential letter to John Crompe, the Rochester chapter clerk, hesitated at first because the letters patent described Lowth simply as 'clerk'; Sprat thought that the statutes of Westminster Abbey, where he was dean, as well as being bishop of Rochester, required the dean of Westminster to be a Master of Arts, and since Westminster and Rochester had both been refounded by Henry VIII on very

130 Ac 7/24, pp. 39–41; Hasted, 2nd edn, ii, p. 367.
131 C.H. Fielding, *The Records of Rochester*, Dartford 1910, p. 164.
132 *Ibid.*, p. 162; Hasted, 1st edn, ii, p. 136.

133 Ac 3/7, ff. 108v, 112v, 122.
134 ff. 121v–122.
135 ff. 116, 131.
136 ff. 131, 136v.
137 PRO, SP 44/57, p. 215.

similar lines he assumed that the Rochester statutes said the same, so he instituted
Lowth as dean, once he had proved that he was a Master of Arts. Shortly afterwards
Sprat came across a copy of the Rochester statutes and discovered that the dean of
Rochester needed a higher degree. He showed the statutes to Lowth, who said that
he would 'clear the difficulty' before being installed as dean. The bishop's letter
ended by warning that Lowth should not be installed until further notice. On 24
November Lowth again called on Bishop Sprat, explained that he could not take a
higher degree just then because Cambridge University was without a
vice-chancellor, and asked Sprat to allow his institution as dean to stand so that he
could be installed. Sprat replied that Cambridge would soon have a new
vice-chancellor and that he saw no reason to disobey the Rochester statutes. On 27
November Lowth appeared at Rochester and asked to be installed as dean. The
chapter refused, and heard a day or two later that it had the support of both Sprat and
Archbishop Sancroft. By this time the king had greater worries than the deanery of
Rochester; Sprat and the chapter won the fight, and Lowth had to content himself
with his two livings in the diocese of Canterbury, both of which he soon lost as a
non-juror.[138]

(5) Visitation and Residence

The most substantial formal contact between the Rochester chapter and the bishop
was visitation. The bishop was not, as he might have been at an Old Foundation
cathedral, a member of the chapter, and his only patronage in the cathedral was the
archdeaconry, the other prebends being in the gift of the Crown or, after the
annexation in 1714 of a prebend to the provostship of Oriel College, Oxford, of the
fellows of Oriel. By the ordinary rule of canon law visitations should have been
triennial, but the chapter archives record only eleven between 1662 and 1810, with
no bishop conducting more than one visitation.

Ordinary administrative caution and liking for precedent tend to produce a
sameness in visitation records. This is very obvious in the early nineteenth century,
when a copy in the chapter's Red Book of its replies to Bishop Dampier's visitation
articles in 1803 has been altered in pencil at several points, and then used as the
replies to Bishop King's visitation articles in 1819, a process which indicates how
much King's articles of enquiry owed to his predecessor's.[139] Nevertheless the
records of some of the Rochester visitations stand out as showing an interest in
important problems affecting the cathedral's running.

At his visitation in September 1662 Bishop Warner asked a number of questions
which were common to all visitations. Did the dean and prebendaries reside
according to the canons? Did they preach as required by the cathedral statutes? Was
Communion celebrated every month? Were all the places on the foundation filled,

[138] Arb 2, ff. 98v, 100r–v, 101r–v; Hasted, 2nd edn, ix, pp. 20, 41.
[139] Arb 3, pp. 225–30, 279–83.

and filled by suitable people? Were the services sung and said in due order and time? Were the cathedral statutes obeyed? Were the church and other buildings in repair? He also asked some questions which his successors, conducting their visitations with the disturbances of the Interregnum well behind them, felt were not necessary. Did anyone preach false doctrine, or preach against the Prayer Book, or adminster the Sacrament otherwise than as laid down in the Prayer Book? Did anyone who was not ordained celebrate Communion? Did the minor canons who were not preachers have the whole Bible in English and Latin, and did they carefully compare in the two versions at least one chapter (presumably the bishop meant one chapter each week)? Did the dean and prebendaries read the Prayer Book before 24 August 1662 and make public their consent to it? Did the chapter take care to reduce all sectaries resident in the precincts to the obedience and doctrine of the Church? Did anyone keep a private conventicle in the precincts or in his living?[140]

The chapter's replies were in general reassuring. The dean and prebendaries resided and preached as they ought. Communion had not apparently been celebrated every month, but the chapter had only just had the necessary utensils consecrated; Bishop Warner may have felt that it could have been rather quicker about this, but he did not formally say so. All the places on the foundation were filled except those connected with the common table.[141] The services were properly sung and said, and the statutes obeyed. The houses of the chapter members and the minor canons were very well repaired (although six months earlier the deanery and two of the prebendal houses had been still awaiting repair), but the church still needed a great deal of work: nearly £8,000 had been spent on repairs to the church and houses, and the church needed another £5,000. So far as the chapter knew no one preached false doctrine and no one who was not ordained celebrated Communion. Five of the six minor canons were preachers and they had English and Latin Bibles. The dean and prebendaries had obeyed the Act of Parliament and publicly consented to the new Prayer Book. No conventicles were kept in the precincts, and to the question about reducing nonconformists in the precincts to the obedience and doctrine of the Church the answer was that 'This article is fulfilled in every part.'[142] We know that on one occasion, twenty years later, such efforts bore fruit; the chapter act book for 1682 records one Adam Brown's formal renunciation of Roman Catholicism.[143]

After these questions and answers some of Bishop Warner's injunctions are surprising. He asked forty-one questions, and after receiving the chapter's replies he issued only eight injunctions, indicating that on most points he was reasonably satisfied. Yet having been told that the dean and prebendaries resided and preached as they ought, and wore their hoods and surplices at services, he devoted three of his injunctions to specifying penalties to be suffered by the dean or any prebendary if they failed to behave correctly in these respects; perhaps he was carefully

---

[140] Arb 2, ff. 23a–22 bis.
[141] Henry VIII had instructed the minor canons and lay clerks to live a collegiate life and to dine in common, but at Rochester and elsewhere this collegiate life had faded away decades before.
[142] Arb 2, ff. 22 bis – 24; Arb 2, f. 19.
[143] Ac 2/5, p. 74.

Later in the eighteenth century the chapter found it difficult to organise itself so as to have even one prebendary resident, and so in June 1785, under the leadership of Dean Dampier, chapter adopted new rules for residence. These required each prebendary to nominate in November two months of the following year during which he would reside in Rochester; prebendaries chose their months in order of seniority, and anyone failing to keep his chosen period of residence would forfeit 10 shillings a day.[158] The dean was to reside for four months each year, either consecutively or separately. The bishop approved these rules and secured their ratification by the Crown as an addition to the cathedral statutes.[159]

The aim of these rules was modest enough but was sometimes more than the chapter could achieve. Prebendary Charles Coldcall was able to combine his prebend of Chichester and his two parishes in Sussex with his two months' residence in Rochester, attendance at every audit there and the combined responsibilities of vice-dean and treasurer for something over fifteen years, but Henry Courtenay, later bishop of Bristol and then of Exeter, resided for only one month in 1786–7 and for only a week in 1793–4, while William Cooper failed to reside at all for two years of a short career which ended in his removal by Bishop Horsley for adultery with Lady Cadogan.[160] William Busby, dean from 1808 until his death on a tour of Scotland in August 1820, sometimes resided for more than the statutory period and sometimes for much less.[161] Prebendary Thomas Hey performed his residence and other duties so conscientiously for seventeen years that in 1805, when age and infirmity prevented his residence, his colleagues gave him a dispensation for the future and ordered that he be exempt from both residence and fines for non-residence.[162]

(6) Education

Henry VIII's statutes required the chapter to maintain a grammar school with two masters and twenty scholars, who were to be poor boys with some bent towards learning and a modest acquaintance with Latin grammar, to be maintained by the cathedral, and taught for four or at most five years until they had a reasonable knowledge of Latin grammar and could speak and write Latin.[163] The requirement that the scholars be poor boys and without any help from friends had already, at the time of the foundation of Henry's ex-monastic cathedrals in 1541, caused disagreement between Archbishop Cranmer and local gentry who wanted free access to cathedral schools for their own sons,[164] and this was a subject in which Bishop

---

[158] Arb 3, pp. 121–2.
[159] Arb 3, p. 182.
[160] FTb 118; FTb 125; Arb 3, pp. 172–4; *The Times*, 22 August, 28 August, 3 September 1794.
[161] Arb 3, p. 283; FTb 142; FTb 144; FTb 146; FTb 149.
[162] Ac 9/35, p. 8.
[163] *History and Antiquities of the Cathedral Church of Rochester*, London 1717, pp. 89–90.
[164] Peter Clark, *English Provincial Society from the Reformation to the Revolution: Religion, Politics and Society in Kent 1500–1640*, Hassocks 1977, p. 186.

Warner showed interest at his visitation in 1662, when he asked whether the scholars were properly taught, how old they were when admitted, whether at admission they had achieved a proper level in writing and grammar, and whether they were admitted because they were poor or because they had friends and offered money. The chapter's response, that so far as it knew the scholars were admitted according to statute and were properly taught, suggests that its practice at that date was to allow the headmaster, Thomas Yardley, to run the school as he saw fit.[165]

Something of the grammar school's organisation and syllabus is revealed by a list of books belonging to it in March 1683. Assigned to the third class were Virgil's *Eclogues*, Erasmus' *Colloquies* and the Latin New Testament; to the second class a Greek grammar, Dugard's *Rhetorick*,[166] Erasmus' *Colloquies* again and Ovid's *Metamorphoses*; and to the first class Homer's *Iliad*, Juvenal, Isocrates and Valerius Maximus. Available to all were four dictionaries, and all classes seem to have given some attention to the catechism in Latin.[167] This list of books, if they were all used, suggests a mildly ambitious classical curriculum, with Greek taught seriously. Other fragments of evidence confirm that the chapter was more active in the supervision of its school in the 1680s than at any other time: in December 1686 some of the prebendaries visited the school and found several of the boys pretty well improved, and in July 1687 the schoolmaster was ordered to appear before the chapter to give an account of the school and the books belonging to it.[168]

In 1698 the headmaster, Paul Bairstow, warned chapter that the school faced competition: Mr Houghton, assistant curate of Chatham, had set up a grammar school in his parish, and the effect on the cathedral school was already dangerous and was likely to be fatal. A letter to Bishop Sprat produced a promise that he would refuse to issue a schoolmaster's licence to anyone who set up in competition with the cathedral school. Three months later Mr Houghton was still running his school 'in opposition to the laws of the country and manifest contempt of your authority', as the chapter put it in a second appeal for the bishop's help.[169] What further action the bishop took we do not know, but Mr Houghton ceased to be discussed in chapter and the cathedral school went on.

The surviving records do not specify the scholars' places of origin, but it seems likely that in the seventeenth and eighteenth centuries the school was almost entirely filled with boys from the neighbourhood. Moreover the names of the scholars are regularly listed twice a year in the chapter act books, and these names are very commonly those of Rochester families, both townspeople and members of the cathedral foundation. John Pilgrim, a shipbuilder's son from Hampshire who went from the cathedral school to St John's College, Cambridge, in 1749, is the only

[165] Arb 2, ff. 23c, 23 bis.
[166] William Dugard, *Rhetorices Elementa, quaestionibus et responsionibus explicata*, London 1648. There were a number of later editions.
[167] Ac 2/6, f. 45v.
[168] Ac 3/8, ff. 23v, 45. Peter Clark, *op. cit.*, p. 195, argues that probably no Kentish grammar school in this period provided more than rudimentary instruction in Greek.
[169] Ac 4/10, ff. 38, 43v.

example noted of a boy sent a long distance to Rochester for his education.[170] A very few of the cathedral choristers became grammar scholars, but a slightly larger number moved on to be lay clerks and so continued as professional musicians.[171] On occasion members of the foundation provided their children or grandchildren with scholarships, and in the first decades of the eighteenth century it is common to find a son of a minor canon listed among the scholars: in 1705–6 prebendaries John Gilman and Daniel Hill and minor canons Wren and Axe had sons who were scholars, and in 1736 seven of the twenty scholarships were held by three of Dean Pratt's grandsons and the sons of four minor canons.[172]

Throughout the late seventeenth and eighteenth centuries the statutory number of twenty scholars was almost always maintained except for one brief period from 1810 to 1814 when the number of vacancies, although fewer than in the previous decade, exceeded the number of recruits. The reason for this brief failure is obscure. In 1801 Dean Dampier had noted that the headmaster, Evan Rice, although appointed as recently as 1785, was very old; the dean was very keen to have an efficient replacement when the vacancy occurred.[173] Within the year Rice died and was replaced by John Griffiths; for encouragement he was also given the curacy of Strood, and in 1803 the vicarage of St Margaret's, Rochester, instead of Strood. It was roughly in the middle of Griffiths' twenty-four years as headmaster that the poor recruitment of scholars took place.[174]

The grammar school had as well as a headmaster an undermaster or usher. Most of the ushers are now little more than names, but Jeremy Batley, appointed usher in 1706, was later promoted and his promotion created a problem. In 1716 Paul Bairstow, who had been headmaster since 1679, died and Batley was sworn in as his replacement.[175] Bishop Atterbury was at the time conducting a visitation of the cathedral, and Batley applied to him for a licence to run the school, was examined and found to be inadequately qualified.[176] A year later Atterbury examined Batley again, and reported to Dean Pratt that he now translated Greek and Latin better than before but still not well enough for a headmaster; he could retain his post only until the chapter could find someone better qualified.[177] The chapter decided to offer the post to William Dormer, a minor canon, and the bishop approved. So Batley, at the chapter's request, resigned the headmastership and became usher again.[178]

The other educational duty of the chapter, to provide two exhibitions of £5 a year at each of the universities, was performed conscientiously. Although in June 1685

[170] Peter Clark, *op. cit.*, p. 194, citing Egz 18; Ac 7/22, p. 16; *Admissions to the College of St John . . . Cambridge*, ed. R.F. Scott, part III, Cambridge 1903, p. 129.

[171] Ac 2/4A, f. 40; Ac 6/18, f. 10; Ac 7/22, p. 78; Ac 7/23, p. 26; H.G. Cooper, *Choristers of Rochester Cathedral*, London 1956, lists eleven choristers in the period 1660–1820 who became lay clerks.

[172] Ac 5/13, ff. 75, 140; Ac 5/15, p. 14, Ac 6/19, f. 28v; FTb 40, p. 19.

[173] British Library, MS K. Top. XVII, 8–2; Ac 8/28, p. 13.

[174] Ac 9/33, p. 41; Ac 9/34, p. 11.

[175] Ac 2/1, p. 13; Ac 5/14, p. 17.

[176] Arb 2, f. 175.

[177] Ac 5/14, p. 52.

[178] Ac 5/14, pp. 76–7, 82; Ac 5/15, p. 3.

University College, Oxford, sent two of its fellows to the grammar school to elect a scholar there to an exhibition at the college, all other recorded elections to exhibitions were made by the chapter, and an exhibition could be held at any college.[179] We have complete lists of the exhibitioners from the late seventeenth century onwards; only a few were scholars of the grammar school, the remainder presumably being fee-paying pupils of the school.[180] If many of the scholars were poor boys, as required by the statutes, then they would not have been able in the eighteenth century to undertake a university course with an exhibition of only £5 a year as their sole financial support.

(7) Charity

Alms-giving was a duty laid on the chapter by its statutes, which required annual expenditure of £20 on alms and £20 on roads and bridges.[181] In nearly half of the years between 1660 and 1820 it spent more than the required £20 on alms: in the decade 1791–1800 its annual alms-giving averaged nearly £72, in the decade 1801–10 £92, and in the decade 1811–20 nearly £130. A less creditable decade was the 1740s, when alms averaged less than £15 a year. Gaps in the series of treasurer's books in the late seventeenth century make meaningful figures difficult to produce, but the average of the alms recorded in the first ten surviving treasurer's books, spread over the period 1676–94, is nearly £16 a year, with a range from just over £2 to £35.

The chapter's achievement in relation to the statutory requirement for alms-giving can fairly be described as barely adequate until 1750, but steadily improving after that date. Its performance of the requirement for annual expenditure on roads and bridges was more interesting. It did occasionally spend money for this purpose; in 1741–2 it gave the surveyors of the parish of St Margaret's Rochester eight guineas for gravel for the highway, and when the committee for superintending the recent alteration and improvement to the road at Four Elms Hill, Frindsbury, asked for a donation in November 1819, the chapter gave £20.[182] Normally it spent nothing at all on roads, and did this as a result of deliberate and consistent policy, which is first recorded in the replies to Bishop Atterbury's visitation articles in May 1716. Atterbury had been dean of Carlisle, another former monastic cathedral, and had in his time there studied the cathedral statutes very carefully in a search for ammunition to use in his battles against both the chapter and Bishop Nicolson of Carlisle.[183] The Rochester statutes were very similar to the Carlisle ones, and not surprisingly Atterbury's examination of the Rochester chapter was more searching than those of his predecessors had been. One of his questions was whether £40 a year was spent

---

[179] Ac 3/7, f. 97.
[180] Ac 7/22, pp. 16, 42; Ac 7/23, p. 76; Ac 7/24, pp. 35, 39; Ac 9/29, p. 39.
[181] *History and Antiquities of the Cathedral Church of Rochester*, London 1717, p. 106.
[182] FTb 77; Ac 10/38, p. 87.
[183] G.V. Bennett, *The Tory Crisis in Church and State 1688–1730*, Oxford 1975, pp. 89–91.

on relief of the poor and the repair of roads and bridges, and if so how the money was laid out.[184] As to relief of the poor the chapter replied that it gave away unspecified amounts when it held manorial courts, and also gave on average over £15 a year to any deserving people brought to its attention; the treasurer's accounts show this figure to be accurate enough. On highways and bridges the chapter said bluntly that it spent nothing except on paving its own precinct, roads 'being now so provided for by the public that for the Church to contribute towards their repair may make it lyable to a much greater Burden'.[185] At the visitations in 1724, 1733, 1757, and 1776 much the same question was asked, and the answer about roads and bridges was identical in content.[186]

Six cathedral bedesmen, appointed by the Crown, were part of Henry VIII's foundation. The statutes stipulated that they should be sufferers from poverty or war injuries, or physically handicapped, old or otherwise disadvantaged. They were each paid, in the eighteenth century, £6 13s 4d, and in return they were supposed, so far as they were able, to be present at services, to keep the nave and quire clean and to assist the sextons in looking after lights and ringing bells; as a natural corollary to these duties they were required to live near the cathedral. For most of our period there was no shortage of bedesmen. The Signet Office issued patents for bedesmen's places to suitable candidates at a rate generous enough to ensure that no vacancy went unfilled. It was quite common for the recipient of a patent to arrive in Rochester to be told that there was no vacancy. In December 1684 Thomas Wade of Rochester, mariner, appeared in chapter with a patent dated 29 November. He was told that he would be admitted to a place in due course but there were several men ahead of him in the queue. Fifteen years later, in November 1699, he at last joined the list of bedesmen.[187] Thomas Wade's story illustrates another of the practical problems of obtaining a bedesman's place; his wife Margaret came to a chapter meeting in April 1692 with her husband's patent and said that there was now a vacancy caused by the death of Henry Jefferyes. She was told that her husband would be admitted only when the dean and chapter were assured that there was a vacancy and that there were no surviving holders of patents earlier in date than her husband's. Unfortunately for the Wades the rumours of Henry Jefferyes' death proved to be exaggerated.[188]

The chapter's state of uncertainty about whether a bedesman was alive or dead is surprising until one looks at what bedesmen did, as distinct from what the statutes said they should do. Bishop Dolben, at his visitation in 1675, asked whether the cathedral had the full number of almsmen or bedesmen, and whether they frequented the church, lived soberly and received their allowances. The chapter answered carefully, truthfully and economically that there were the full number of bedesmen and that they received their allowances; it then moved on to the next question.[189] In 1716 the dean and chapter admitted frankly at Bishop Atterbury's visitation that the bedesmen never appeared at church nor did any part of their duty except cleaning

184 Arb 2, f. 166.   187 Ac 3/7, f. 73; Ac 4/11, f. 13v.
185 Arb 2, f. 169v.   188 Ac 3/9, ff. 24v, 27.
186 Arb 2, ff. 211, 250v; Arb 3, p. 29.   189 Arb 2, f. 70.

the church, and that not in person but by paying for it to be done.[190] For some bedesmen cleaning the church in person may well have been an impossible task; the statutes, in requiring the bedesmen to do their duty 'so far as their infirmity allows', clearly envisaged that some would be disabled, and John Picket, given a grant of a bedesman's place in 1673, had lost one leg fighting the Turks and the other fighting the Dutch on the ship *Mary*.[191]

At the visitation in 1733 the chapter strengthened its statement about the bedesmen with a little history, saying that the bedesmen never came to church and never had; it did not say whether it had firm evidence for this statement or whether it was just common knowledge. It went on to say that, as the bedesmen were not provided with houses, they lived where they could, often a long way from Rochester, and they cleaned the church by paying for it from their stipends.[192] This admission demonstrates the difficulty of raising standards of behaviour, for in July 1723 the energetic reforming Dean Samuel Pratt had ordered the chapter clerk to write letters to the bedesmen ordering them to attend services in accordance with the statutes.[193] Dean Pratt, who had no objection to firm speech and determined action when he thought them necessary, was presumably planning to rely on the statute *De Corrigendis Excessibus*, which gave the dean alone the power to correct the bedesmen when they misbehaved, and gave the dean, with the consent of the chapter, power to expel any bedesman who remained incorrigible. What the government would have said to Dean Pratt if he had expelled a group of bedesmen some of whom had been given their places as a way of providing them, at no cost to the government, with pensions after naval or military service we do not know, since Dean Pratt was dead within a few months.

The bedesmen continued to draw their stipends without interference. In the late seventeenth century or early eighteenth century some of them sometimes came to the cathedral to sign for their money, but by the 1740s only one bedesman, Lebbeus Ford, still did so, and when he gave up the practice in 1748 direct contact between the cathedral and its bedesmen ceased for many years.[194] Thereafter the chapter had to rely on correspondence for information about bedesmen, and the chapter clerk's files must have contained a number of papers similar to the certificate signed in January 1708 by Dr George Stanhope, vicar of Deptford (and dean of Canterbury), that Gabriel Chapman, a 'pensioner' belonging to Rochester Cathedral, was living in Deptford and was in good bodily health,[195] or the certificate signed by the minister and churchwardens of Poole that John Nickless, almsman of the cathedral, had died on 3 April 1781.[196]

In the 1770s the Crown ceased appointing bedesmen and their number began to fall. Before their revival in the 1850s, the last bedesman recorded as receiving his stipend died in 1803 or 1804,[197] but clerical inertia obscured this fact by including

[190] Arb 2, f. 167.
[191] Arb 2, f. 50.
[192] Arb 2, f. 248.
[193] Ac 6/17, f. 51v.

[194] FTb 27, 28, 34, 36, 39, 56, 67, 77, 80, 81, 82.
[195] Azo 9/1.
[196] FTv 139, part 1.
[197] FTb 135, pp. 20–21.

in the chapter acts an unchanged list of six bedesmen at the call-over at every general chapter for at least the first quarter of the nineteenth century.[198]

There were two main groups who received alms from the chapter. The first can best be described as being any distressed strangers who came to the notice of the dean or a prebendary: in prebendary Daniel Hill's own words at Bishop Atterbury's visitation in 1716, 'poor indigent Foreigners, decay'd Tradesmen, sufferers by Fire … & other poore Travellers'.[199] Most of these categories were represented in 1736–7 for example, when the treasurer's book records gifts of two guineas to a Syrian nobleman, 1 shilling to a farmer who had great losses, 5 shillings to a fisherman who lost his boat, and 2s 6d to a shipwrecked French sailor. A sufferer by fire occurs in the treasurer's book for 1694–5, where there is a payment of 5 shillings to Mr George Bourchier, 'a great sufferer by fire, & by his Father's losses by sea, & his being taken captive by the Turks'.

The second main group of beneficiaries from the chapter's alms-giving were very much local people, poor residents in the precinct and neighbourhood and the families of members of the cathedral foundation. In January 1674 one of the lay clerks, Richard Pearson, died, leaving several children but apparently no widow and clearly very little money. The chapter helped out, paying 2 shillings a week to John Jones for keeping Pearson's son for a few months and 2s 6d a week to Goodwife Waters for nursing one of Pearson's daughters for a few months. Very constructive long-term help was given to Pearson's daughters Elizabeth and Anne by the expenditure of £5 each on putting them out as apprentices.[200] Help could also be given over a longer period: in 1722 John Gamball, the chapter's regular bricklayer and one of the main contractors for the new houses for the minor canons, died, and on 1 July his widow began to receive from the chapter a weekly allowance of 2s 6d, which was augmented in 1726 or 1727 by 7s 6d a quarter for her room hired from Joanna Hawkins, and continued until 1731.[201]

People in debt might also be helped. In 1696–7 John Wood, the bell-founder who in 1694–5 was paid £16 10s 0d for casting the treble and other work in the belfry, was given 6 shillings to relieve him in prison.[202] Thomas Clarke, a lay clerk with a large family, had been unfortunate in the trade which he followed to supplement his lay clerk's salary, and got very badly into debt, owing a total of £112 6s 10d to forty-eight people. In 1726 he appealed to the chapter. It persuaded most of the creditors to accept 5 shillings in the pound, which it covered. In return Clarke was made to enter into a bond binding him to attend services diligently and constantly and not to resign his post without the chapter's consent; it was difficult to get lay clerks with good voices.[203] In 1721 the cathedral organist, John Spayne, got into debt and was rescued in a rather similar fashion.[204]

Occasionally there were distressing occasions for alms-giving. In 1695 2s 6d was given to Jane Solway; the entry in the account is followed by a list of expenses

[198] Ac 9, *passim*; Ac 10, *passim*.
[199] Arb 2, f. 173.
[200] FTb 10.
[201] FTb 56, p. 47; FTb 57–67.
[202] FTb 31.
[203] Azo 12/1–3; Ac 6/17, f. 89v; Arb 2, ff. 171, 209.
[204] Azo 11/1.

totalling £1 19s 4d and revealing that Jane died giving birth in the precincts, that her baby was nursed at the chapter's expense but died when a week old, and that the chapter paid the costs of both the funerals.[205] The chapter learned a lesson from this experience, and two years later it paid the overseers of the poor for St Nicholas' parish, adjoining the precinct, a guinea to take care of a woman who might otherwise have given birth in the cathedral churchyard.[206] Thirty years later it was less successful in warding off this inconvenient occurrence, and an illegitimate child was born in minor canon Beresford's house. Beresford did nothing, and the mother 'had the impudence to lay it at Dr Hill's door, He being then the Church's Treasurer for that year'. The mother then left town in a hurry, leaving the child to be nursed by Mary Marden, at a cost of 5 shillings to the chapter; the episode made Prebendary Hill very angry.[207] In 1751 the chapter moved sufficiently quickly to get John Doggett, a labourer and father of a child born in the precinct to Mary Barber, to indemnify it for the baby's maintenance.[208]

The most financially burdensome orphan whose maintenance the chapter undertook was Charles Birkbeck, son of a minor canon and vicar of Stockbury also called Charles. Birkbeck senior died in March 1725, when his son must have been very small, because it was not until the mid-1730s that he began to cost substantial amounts. In 1736–7 £27 was paid out for two years' board and 'necessary' for Charles, and over £6 for unspecified items relating to his care. Two years later Charles was apprenticed to a Dartford saddler, Joseph Neilde; the apprentice fee was £10 5s 0d and an apron and frock cost 12s 7d. For the next two years Charles continued to be supported partly by the chapter, another £37 being spent on clothes and general maintenance.[209]

In the early eighteenth century the chapter was provided with a new fund which could be used to care for the widows of its staff. A legacy of £1,000 was left to the dean and Mr William Knight as trustees to provide annual pensions for poor widows, to be called Mrs Knight's Poor Widows of St Bartholomew's Hospital in Chatham. In 1716 the executors had not yet paid over the money, but in December 1724 Thomas Pratt, one of the former dean's sons, was appointed receiver of Mrs Knight's Charity, and in December 1725 Dean Claggett put before the chapter some administrative guidelines for the charity, including that all future nominations of recipients be entered in the chapter act book.[210] The two widows nominated in December 1725 seem to have had no formal link with the cathedral, although one of them, Mary Clamp, widow of a King's Lynn doctor, must have had some informal connection or the chapter would not have known of her existence. In November 1727 the widow of minor canon Birkbeck, whose son has already been mentioned, was nominated to benefit from the charity, and in due course the charity often helped the widows of chapter employees; in March 1765, for example, the chapter chose as a Poor Sister on Mrs Knight's foundation the widow of lay clerk Charles Blogg, to succeed Mrs Harwood, widow of a former chapter carpenter and timber agent, and

[205] FTb 31.
[206] FTb 33.
[207] FTb 63, pp. 42–3.

[208] Egz 90.
[209] FTb 72, 74–6.
[210] Arb 2, f. 169; Ac 6/17, ff. 75, 87.

in June 1768 Susannah Hickman, widow of the cathedral porter, replaced Mrs Puckle, widow of a lay clerk.[211]

As time went on the pattern of the cathedral's charity changed a little. The most noticeable developments are the increased sums being spent, and a tendency towards formalising arrangements for relief of those in need. When in June 1796 Elizabeth Rolt, an old woman in poor health whom the chapter supported for a few years, was granted an increased allowance of 5 shillings a week instead of 3s 6d, she was described as 'one of the Paupers of the Church Precinct', as if these paupers were an institution analogous to the thirty Church Widows who were supported by the dean and chapter of Durham from the 1750s onwards.[212] And a few years earlier, in 1789, Francis Saxby's wife asked for the allowance to her husband and herself to be increased, her husband having become too infirm to work at all, in terms which suggest that she regarded the allowance as something permanent to which she and her husband had some sort of right.[213]

In November 1790 the dean and chapter decided that it was 'proper & in the interest of all residents' that the sacrist and verger be *ex officio* overseers of the poor in the precincts; this decision, with other evidence, reveals a close approximation in the extra-parochial area of the precinct to the arrangements for the care of the poor found in ordinary parishes, and was clearly a move in the direction of formality and system.[214] Rather similar is the occasional substantial donation not to an individual but to an organisation, often a parish. The earliest example of this so far noticed was in 1738–9, when twenty-five guineas was given towards the repair of Chatham church.[215] These repairs only postponed a complete rebuilding of that church, to which in June 1786 the dean and chapter agreed to subscribe fifty guineas.[216] In 1779–80 £20 was given to the Society for the Propagation of the Gospel, and in 1812–13 and 1817–18 more was donated for church building: a hundred guineas towards the rebuilding of Strood church and £100 towards the erection of new churches in general.[217]

Towards the end of the eighteenth century those members of the Twopeny family of lawyers, William senior, William junior and Edward, who served as chapter clerks and became increasingly important in the cathedral's administration, took over some of the regular dispensing of charity. Lists survive for four years in the 1780s and 1790s recording their payments of regular allowances to a few individuals who were being maintained by the chapter. The chapter acts for the period do not record any decisions to undertake the maintenance of these people, and so it seems that the chapter clerk not only paid out a substantial part of the chapter's charity but also chose the recipients.[218]

One restriction on its charitable activity which the chapter felt to be necessary was

---

[211] Ac 6/17, f. 87; Ac 6/18, f. 12v; Ac 7/24, p. 66; Ac 8/25, p. 31.
[212] Ac 9/31, p. 31.
[213] Ac 9/29, f. 26.
[214] Ac 9/29, p. 55; F.F. Smith, *A History of Rochester*, London 1928, p. 162.
[215] FTb 74.
[216] Ac 8/28, p. 22.
[217] FTb 111, pp. 38–9; FTb 144, p. 34; FTb 149, p. 38.
[218] FTv 142.

the exclusion, so far as was possible, of paupers from residing in the precinct. In 1696 it ordered that no one come to live in the precinct without leave, and in 1711 it tried to protect the precinct from two problems simultaneously, by ordering that future leases of property there should forbid the lessee to allow anyone to live in the property who either kept an ale-house or might become the chapter's financial responsibility through poverty or for any other reason.[219] One of the motives for pulling down and replacing the minor canons' houses in the 1720s was that the shabby discomfort of the old houses encouraged the minor canons to live elsewhere and to let their official residences to whoever would rent them, mostly the indigent.[220] These houses had been a refuge for the poor since at least 1679, when the chapter, worried by some of their inhabitants and by such people as the poor sick man living in one of the precinct houses leased to Mrs Maplesden, ordered that everyone coming to live in the precinct should give security to save the chapter from having to maintain them if reduced to poverty.[221]

Simply establishing that a new inhabitant in the precinct was able to support himself or herself at the time of moving in might not be sufficient: Elizabeth Heather, a widow who had moved into the precinct as a servant to Thomas Thompson, headmaster of the grammar school, was found in June 1783 to have inadequate means of support and was given an allowance of 2 shillings a week. Only eight months later a similar allowance had to be made to Elizabeth Martin, who had gained her settlement in the precinct by working for Peter Wade, a minor canon, and had been unable to support herself since her master's death in October 1783.[222] An embarrassing pauper resident was Edward Bathurst, son of a minor canon, who, while his father was still serving the cathedral, moved into the precinct with his wife and children; he had been educated at the cathedral grammar school but had been a failure in worldly terms, and in June 1795 the chapter clerk was ordered to take such advice and action as he thought proper about Edward's settlement.[223]

The chapter continued to be cautious about residents in the precinct. In 1806 Matthew Grain, the long-serving verger and sexton who had received special mention from Dean Dampier when he said farewell to the cathedral in 1802, was granted a lease of two tenements in the precinct, but it was made very clear that he must have no sub-tenants or lodgers who were not approved by the chapter.[224] In 1809 the chapter began to hope that it might escape the burden of the poor in the precinct; William Twopeny the chapter clerk was asked to consult the chapter's counsel, Henry Dampier, brother of the former dean, but the chapter acts record no joy at the receipt of Dampier's opinion and the amount spent on charity shows no decline.[225] Eight years later three neighbouring parishes, Strood and the Rochester

---

[219] Ac 4/10, f. 9; Ac 5/13, f. 87.
[220] Arb 2, f. 167v.
[221] Ac 2/1, p. 71. Goodwife Popely was looking after the man in Mrs Maplesden's house and was asking the chapter to pay her 3 shillings a week for the work.
[222] Ac 8/27, ff. 18, 23, 25v.
[223] Ac 8/27, f. 38; Ac 9/31, ff. 11–12.
[224] Ac 9/33, p. 56; Ac 9/35, p. 25.
[225] Ac 10/36, p. 31; FTb 142–151.

parishes of St Nicholas' and St Margaret's, claimed that paupers resident in those parishes ought to be received and maintained in the cathedral precinct as having settlement there. The chapter's counsel Robert Marsham, a son of prebendary Jacob Marsham, advised the chapter to resist this claim and it instructed the chapter clerk accordingly.[226]

(8) Conclusion

The eighteenth-century Rochester prebendaries were not for the most part famous figures in the English church. A number of them served their cathedral and diocese long and meritoriously, for instance Edmund Barrell and archdeacons Denne and Law, but only two are well-known outside Kent. Archdeacon Plume is remembered for his bequest founding a chair of astronomy at Cambridge and, to a lesser extent, for a second bequest founding a library at Maldon, his birthplace; thanks to a combination of good fortune and unusually wise arrangements at its foundation the library survives. Joseph Butler is remembered for his *Analogy of Religion*, completed just before he joined the Rochester chapter, but he was at Rochester for only four years and has not left much trace in the records; it is forceful administrators and difficult people, not theologians and men of prayer, who leave generous traces in the archives. When Dr Pusey in the 1830s compiled a list of important clerical authors whose work was written while they were members of cathedral foundations he named three bishops of Rochester, including in our period Atterbury and Pearce, but no deans or prebendaries.[227] Yet some of the late seventeenth and eighteenth-century deans were very important in their day: Thurlow and Dampier ended their careers as bishops of Durham and Ely respectively, and Lamplugh, Herring and Markham all became archbishops.

Rochester was not one of the largest and richest foundations. At its refoundation Henry VIII had increased its endowment to some extent, but its new secular chapter of seven members, the same size as at Bristol, Chester, Norwich and Peterborough, put it firmly into the second class, overshadowed by the great Henrician refoundations at Canterbury, Durham and Winchester. And in the late seventeenth and early eighteenth centuries it had long-term financial difficulties. The chapter usually managed to pay the staff fairly regularly and promptly, but its own stipends were often badly in arrears.[228] By the middle of the eighteenth century, thanks partly to its splendidly successful investment in the South Sea Company, it had fewer financial worries. Some of the credit for this must be given to its reasonably firm and sensible management of its estates; there is no sign at Rochester, as there is at Norwich, of the chapter often setting a fine for a lease renewal at a proper level and

---

[226] Ac 10/38, pp. 22–3.

[227] E.B. Pusey, *Remarks on the Prospective and Past Benefits of Cathedral Institutions ...*, 2nd edn, London 1833, pp. 172–84.

[228] Ac 2/1, p. 45; Ac 5/13, f. 129v; FTb 63.

then reducing it under pressure from the lessee.[229] The first edition of Hasted's history of Kent, published in 1782, claimed that the cathedral was in danger of collapse, but through the 1770s the chapter had spent on average £182 a year on the fabric, and in the 1780s this figure went up to £190; the second edition of Hasted in 1798 was much more complimentary.[230] The late 1780s saw the introduction of some financial planning, and by the early nineteenth century the chapter was very comfortable, able to spend an average of £676 a year on the fabric in the first decade of the century.[231]

A prominent theme in eighteenth-century Rochester history is therefore the growing prosperity of the cathedral. A second is peace in the chapter; Dean Dampier's touching farewell to everyone on the foundation in 1802 is a pleasant contrast with the spending on legal costs resulting from disputes between dean and prebendaries under deans Castilion and Pratt in the late seventeenth and early eighteenth centuries. A third theme is that of professional administration and a consequent delegation of real responsibility. In the 1660s John Crompe as chapter clerk had very few records in his custody, the dean controlling everything and the chapter as governing body treating Crompe as very much its secretary and servant.[232] By 1820 those members of the able legal family of Twopeny who had in turn been chapter clerks had not only established the chapter clerk's position as one of chief executive, taking decisions on behalf of the chapter rather than taking orders from the chapter, but had persuaded the chapter to welcome the arrangement.[233] Historians certainly may feel grateful for such things as the revealing reports brought back by chapter clerk William Twopeny in 1819 when he was sent to survey the chapter's Buckinghamshire property.[234]

This account has been based on the chapter's archives, but archives, by their silence on matters of no administrative or financial importance, fail to do justice to clergy perhaps more than most groups. Prebendary George Strahan seems from the archival sources to have been a contented pluralist, with the income of two parishes as well as his stall at Rochester.[235] They fail to mention that he was a friend of Samuel Johnson and in 1785 edited Johnson's prayers and meditations.[236]

The eighteenth-century chapter did not record the aims it had in mind in the running of its cathedral, but its actions suggest that it hoped for a quiet and well-run cathedral, with the services reverently conducted by an adequate body of minor canons, lay clerks and choristers; a respectable school; buildings adequately maintained without great expenditure; relations with lessees founded on a tradition

---

[229] Norwich and Norfolk Record Office, Norwich Dean and Chapter Archives, Private Register 1660–1725, e.g. pp. 91–2, 132, 134, 137, 163–4, 211, 305.

[230] Hasted, 1st edn, ii, p. 28; Hasted, 2nd edn, iv, p. 106.

[231] FTb 121; Arb 3, p. 289; FTb 132–141.

[232] Els 2.

[233] Ac 10/38, pp. 28–9, 38–9, 64, 93; Ac 10/39, pp. 10, 13, 22–3, 29.

[234] Ac 10/38, pp. 94–102.

[235] Vicar of Islington 1772–1824; from 1783 to 1824 incumbent in turn of Little Thurrock, Cranham, Sutton-at-Hone, and Kingsdown.

[236] Dr Johnson's Prayers, ed. Elton Trueblood, London 1947, pp. 21–2.

of moderation in the calculation of renewal fines and patience in the collection of rents; the use of the cathedral's patronage and almsgiving to benefit primarily those connected with the cathedral, including the dean and prebendaries, without insistence on residence for much of the year. Since archival sources commonly fail to illuminate an organisation aiming at a steady state but do usually highlight failures, the Rochester archives, full of spectacular detail but very little scandal, suggest that the chapter enjoyed a fair degree of success.

5

The Cathedral since 1820

PAUL A. WELSBY

'The Church as it now stands,' wrote Dr Thomas Arnold in 1832, 'no human power can save'.[1] This used to be a favourite quotation with historians of the Oxford Movement who believed that it was the Tractarians' high doctrine of the church, their emphasis on sacramental worship and their enhancement of the standards of priestly and pastoral work, which rescued the Church of England from the problems and criticisms which beset it in the eighteenth and early nineteenth centuries. Canon Charles Smyth was much nearer the truth, however, when he wrote that 'so far as any human person did save the Church of England, it was saved not by Mr Keble, but by Sir Robert Peel'.[2] Whatever theological, pastoral and spiritual rejuvenation the Church of England received from the Oxford Movement would have been constantly frustrated had not the chaotic, anomalous and occasionally scandalous ecclesiastical administrative structure of the church been reformed. That this reform occurred before it was too late and took the form that it did was due chiefly to Sir Robert Peel who was responsible for the creation of the Ecclesiastical Commission, which proved to be a unique example of partnership between church and state.

It may be difficult today to grasp the intensity of the tide of criticism of the established church which reached its climax in the first quarter of the nineteenth century. Political radicals, religious dissenters, unbelievers, the press and public opinion generally, were united against an institution which they regarded as privileged, corrupt and negligent in the discharge of its duties. The inequitable distribution of the church's wealth, pluralism, non-residence, sinecures, nepotism and idleness were the chief targets of outrage, particularly when the wealth of the 'great clergy' was seen against the poverty of the 'lesser clergy' and when the money and the men were concentrated in established areas while the new towns, with their rapidly growing populations, received negligible spiritual ministrations because money was not available for clergy and for new church buildings.

Rich and affluent deans and chapters were particular targets of criticism because of their supposed idleness, pluralism and non-residence. 'A cathedral,' wrote Frederick Harrison, 'is merely a college where nobody needs study and the Dean is

---

[1] A.P. Stanley, *The Life and Correspondence of Thomas Arnold*, London 1844, i, p. 287.
[2] 'The Church of England in History and Today', *The Genius of the Church of England*, London 1947, p. 47.

its warden in perpetual long vacation'.[3] Rochester Cathedral cannot be exempted from this general criticism. By 1835 normally only one of the canons was resident in Rochester, the day to day administration of chapter business being left in the hands of the chapter clerk, a local solicitor. Dean Robert Stevens (Plate 3b) owed his appointment in 1820 to the fact that he had been chaplain to the Speaker of the House of Commons and, with his deanery, he held a prebend in Lincoln Cathedral and also the vicarage of West Farleigh, near Maidstone. Although the latter was a small parish and he employed a curate, it would appear that he spent a fair amount of his time on his duties there.[4] Ralph Arnold says that 'in 1848 he was a mild-mannered, timid, generous person who, four years later was to be described by the Chapter Clerk as ''an old man oppressed with infirmities''. This description was intended to explain why he preached so infrequently in the Cathedral.' Arnold also describes him as an 'easily led, essentially honest, but rather simple-minded man'.[5] This was the man who for fifty years (1820–1870) presided over the affairs of the cathedral. When he died the *Church Times* reported his death in the following terms: 'The deanery of Rochester has become vacant by the death of the Very Rev. Robert Stevens DD. . . . The deceased had attained the age of 93 years and had held the deanery of Rochester since 1820. For many years before his death the late dean was incapable of performing any clerical duties'[6] – which is an interesting statement in view of the fact that the dean attended a meeting of the chapter six weeks before his death.[7]

Of the six canons,[8] the Hon. Frederick Hotham also held two benefices in East Anglia. He remained a canon for thirty-two years but resided in Bath and for seven years before his death never set foot in Rochester. Dr Matthew Irving held the vicarage of Sturminster Marshall in Dorset and was also perpetual curate of the growing and thriving town of Chatham. The Hon. Jacob Marsham, son of the third Lord Romney, held with his canonry at Rochester a prebend in Wells Cathedral, a canonry at Windsor and two vicarages, one in Yorkshire and one in Kent. Canon John Griffith also held the vicarage of Boxley, then in the diocese of Rochester, and of Thornton Curtis in Lincolnshire, but, although of a somewhat tactless disposition, he had a responsible concern for cathedral affairs. Walker King, who held the stall attached to the archdeaconry of Rochester, owned his appointment to his father, who was bishop of Rochester, and he also held another benefice in the diocese. Finally, there was Dr Edward Hawkins (Plate 9b), Provost of Oriel College, Oxford, to which office a canonry at Rochester had been annexed in 1714. Hawkins lived in Oxford for most of the year, although, unlike most of his colleagues at Rochester, he devoted time and thought to his work at the cathedral. He was also the only member of the

---

[3] *Official Religion*, n.d., pp. 6ff., quoted by David Nicholls in *Church and State in Britain since 1820*, London 1967, p. 102.

[4] See below, p. 145.

[5] Ralph Arnold, *The Whiston Matter*, London 1961, p. 27.

[6] *Church Times*, 12 February 1870.

[7] Ac 14, p. 266.

[8] For the information in this paragraph, cf. *The Registers of the Cathedral Church of Rochester (1657–1837 with Lists of the Prebendaries . . .)*, ed. Thomas Shindler, London 1892, pp. 67ff.; Arnold, *op. cit.*, Chapter 3.

chapter of real distinction, a noted scholar who, although he was a high churchman, became involved in a bitter struggle with the Tractarians at Oxford. His nickname was 'The East Wind' because of his cold and restrained manner, which in fact concealed a warm heart, and also because his rigid truthfulness could produce a frigid atmosphere. In addition to his canonry and his provostship he was incumbent of Lamberhurst between 1831 and 1834. He remained a canon of Rochester until his death in 1882 at the age of ninety-three. J.W. Burgon wrote of him: 'His habit of business and his appetite for work, joined to his lofty integrity and soundness of judgement made him an invaluable member of the Chapter. When he had seen about 80 years of life, he remarked . . . that "in consequence of the age and infirmity of some of his colleagues he was obliged to bestow increased attention on Cathedral business".'[9]

The Ecclesiastical Commission was established in 1835 and in the following year its second report set out plans for the complete overhaul of cathedrals. In April 1836 the Rochester chapter addressed a memorial to the commissioners[10] objecting to the reduction of the number of minor canons to less than three, affirming that the dean should hold a benefice as well as the deanery and should not be expected to reside in the deanery for more than six months of the year. It viewed with great concern the reduction that was proposed in the exercise of patronage and it was opposed to the proposed reduction in the number of prebends, and the formation, out of the revenues from the suppressed prebends, of a common fund for the benefit of the cathedral as a whole. These objections were repeated in a further memorial in December 1836,[11] in which the chapter affirmed that 'no sufficient reasons have been alleged for what must wear the appearance of a violent alteration of our charters'. When it became clear that the commission's proposals were to be embodied in an Act of Parliament, the chapter in May 1838 petitioned the House of Commons against the proposed bill.[12] It expressed its concurrence with the commissioners' desire to promote the efficiency of the established church and it realised 'the urgent necessities of the Parochial system', but its conviction was that 'the principle and leading provisions are dangerous even to the temporal interests of the Country and to the security of property and would be seriously and permanently injurious to the national Church'. Indeed, the result of the proposals 'will be to extinguish the moral influence of our Cathedral Institutions, and to incapacitate them for some of the highest purposes intended by their founders'. Finally, the chapter strongly opposed the entrusting of 'extraordinary powers intimately effecting even spiritual interests' into the hands of 'a Board of Governors who cannot be considered as representative of the Church at Large and of whom the very great majority are both appointed and removable by the Crown'.

All this was of little avail and in 1840 the Deans and Chapters Act received the Royal Assent. Under the act the number of residentiary canons was reduced in

9 J.W. Burgon, *Lives of Twelve Good Men*, London 1888, i, p. 411.
10 Ac 11, pp. 306ff.
11 *Ibid.*, pp. 336ff.
12 *Ibid.*, pp. 386ff.

general to four at each cathedral. Deans were to receive £1,000 per annum and each canon £500 per annum. The money saved by this reform was to be diverted to augment the stipends of poorer clergy and to increase the number of parochial clergy. The patronage of the dean and chapter as a corporate body remained untouched, but the patronage attached to its separate members was transferred to the bishop. In place of non-residentiary prebendaries there were to be honorary canons appointed by the bishop. Under the Pluralities Act of 1838 members of chapters had already been forbidden to hold more than one benefice or to belong to more than one chapter.

At Rochester the number of canonries was reduced from six to four, but the act contained a clause safeguarding the interests of existing office holders. The first canonry to become vacant was to be suspended, the canonry secondly to become vacant was to be filled, and the canonry thirdly to become vacant was to be suspended, although the provisions were not to extend to the canonries attached to the provostship of Oriel College and to the archdeaconry of Rochester. One of the six canonries was immediately suppressed because of the death in the year in which the act was passed of Jacob Marsham. The dean and chapter immediately wrote to the commissioners to express their concern about 'the spiritual condition of the parish of Chatham' and to recommend that the proceeds, or part of them, from the suspended canonry should be used for endowing the chapels of St John and Luton in the parish of Chatham.[13] The second vacant canonry was to be filled, so when the Hon. Frederick Hotham died in 1854 at the age of eighty he was succeeded by Thomas Robinson. The canonry thirdly vacant, on the death of Matthew Irving in 1857 at the age of seventy-eight, was suppressed, and thus the intentions of the Act were accomplished seventeen years after its passing. Under the Act there were to be four minor canons, six lay clerks, eight choristers and four probationers.

In place of prebends, honorary canonries were founded and in October 1841 we find the commissioners asking the chapter for its suggestions for appropriate regulations for the appointment of honorary canons. They enclosed their own suggestions to which the chapter made only three observations of a fairly minor character and the following year it accepted the commissioners' proposals.[14]

The Ecclesiastical Commission was not only concerned with reforming cathedrals. Another of its major tasks was the provision of new dioceses and the reorganisation of existing diocesan boundaries. One of its most extraordinary decisions, under the Established Church Act 1836, was to relieve the diocese of Rochester of all its territory south of the Thames, apart from the city of Rochester with its deanery, which included what were later to become the deaneries of Cobham and Gravesend. Most of the rest of the diocese was incorporated in that of Canterbury. To compensate for this loss Rochester was given the whole of the county of Essex and most of Hertfordshire, formerly in the diocese of London, and a house was provided for the bishop north of the Thames at Danbury, near Chelmsford. It is not surprising that a lot of parishes in Essex and Hertfordshire wondered what

[13] Ac 12, pp. 62ff.
[14] *Ibid.*, pp. 97ff.

possible connection they could have with Rochester![15] This had minor repercussions for Rochester Cathedral which made the arrangements appear even more grotesque. The Act suppressed the archdeaconry of Rochester on the next vacancy, which occurred in 1859, and, for obvious reasons, transferred the archdeaconries of Essex, Colchester and St Albans to the diocese of Rochester. These archdeacons each had a place in the quire of the cathedral, though not in greater chapter unless they held an honorary canonry.[16] In 1863, however, the archdeaconry of Rochester was revived, to be held together with that of St Albans.[17] In 1877 the diocese of St Albans was created and the archdeaconry of St Albans was separated from that of Rochester and, together with the archdeaconries of Essex and Colchester, was transferred to the new diocese of St Albans. In return for the loss of Essex and Hertfordshire the diocese received an area covering much of what is now the diocese of Southwark. In May 1878 the bishop wrote to the dean and chapter pointing out that a new archdeaconry of Southwark had been created and asking if the archdeacon could have a stall in the cathedral. The chapter agreed, 'without prejudice to the precedence of the Archdeacon of Rochester'.[18] The following year it was agreed that a stall should also be assigned to the archdeacon of the newly created archdeaconry of Kingston-upon-Thames.[19]

In November 1865 the dean and chapter agreed to enter into negotiations with the Ecclesiastical Commissioners for the surrender of the capitular estates.[20] These were the estates which were the chapter's corporate properties, the revenues of which provided the cathedral with its main income. In July 1866 the draft of a scheme to be submitted by the Ecclesiastical Commissioners to the crown authorising the substitution of certain money payments in place of revenues from certain lands at present belonging to the dean and chapter was approved by the chapter.[21] Most other chapters entered into similar negotiations and the seal to this transfer was the Ecclesiastical Commissioners Act of 1868, which statutorily confirmed what had by then become the normal procedure. All chapter estates had been transferred to the Commissioners, but certain estates were to be returned to the deans and chapters as their permanent endowment. Between 1869 and 1872 chapter rentals were restricted to property in the Precinct (Plate 7), King's Orchard and the manor of Prior's Hall, Cliffe, which had not been handed over to the Commissioners. It was intended that the dean and chapter should have a permanent endowment which would provide them with an annual income of £9,800, but until the lands which were to comprise this permanent endowment were actually in the hands of the dean and chapter the

[15] Cf. Owen Chadwick, 'The Victorian Diocese of St Albans', *Cathedral and City: St Albans Ancient and Modern*, ed. Robert Runcie, London 1977, pp. 73ff.

[16] Ac 13, p. 771.

[17] At the meeting of the chapter on 27 July 1943 Anthony Grant is described as archdeacon of Rochester and St Albans, *ibid.*, p. 856. Prior to this he is described as archdeacon of St Albans.

[18] Ac 15, p. 652.

[19] Ac 14, p. 92.

[20] Ac 14, p. 92. For details, cf. EC/Le 1–22 (property taken by the Commissioners) and EC/Lr (Estates to be retained).

[21] Ac 14, p. 112.

Ecclesiastical Commissioners would pay them a half-yearly income of £4,930, plus £150 half-yearly for the remuneration of the chapter clerk.[22] Seven years later, in August 1873, the Commissioners re-endowed the dean and chapter with certain lands which were to provide the same income as they had received from the Commissioners, that is £9,860.[23] Unfortunately, by 1880, as a result of the agricultural depression, these estates were yielding less than had been expected, with the result that Rochester, like nearly every other cathedral in the country, was in financial difficulties. More than one unsuccessful attempt was made to induce Parliament to allow the Ecclesiastical Commissioners to give to the cathedrals more of what had once been their own money.

In handling its revenues down the years the chapter may have adhered to the letter of its original statutes, although there is some doubt about this, but it certainly failed to observe their spirit. The chapter was obliged to maintain four 'poor scholars' at the universities of Oxford and Cambridge, each to be paid a stipend of £5 per annum. Similarly the chapter had the statutory obligation to educate at the Cathedral Grammar School twenty 'poor boys', who were to receive free education, free maintenance and a stipend of £2 13s 4d per annum. Thirdly, the chapter was bound by statute to maintain 'six poor men', or bedesmen, each of whom was to receive £6 13s 4d per annum. Since 1790, however, the chapter had paid no stipends to bedesmen for the simple reason that it took no steps to secure their appointment. Moreover, although the revenues of the dean and chapter had increased very significantly since the sixteenth century, no change had been made to the amount of stipend paid to the exhibitioners at the universities or to the scholars at the grammar school, nor did the chapter make the statutory payments for the maintenance of the latter. This meant that money, which ought to have been spent on these matters, became available for other purposes and, indeed, the income of the dean and chapter had increased over the years. Furthermore, for many years it had been the custom to appoint one of the minor canons to the post of under-master at the grammar school. He received the latter's stipend but was not expected to do any teaching. The stipend of the headmaster remained at the figure of £13 6s 8d, as laid down by statute, until the end of the eighteenth century, when it was raised to £33 6s 8d and in addition the headmaster received £2 13s 4d per annum for each grammar boy. The headmaster divided this sum into three parts. Each boy received 19 shillings, £1 3s 6d was paid to his usher, whom he was obliged to employ because the post of under-master had become a sinecure for one of the minor canons, and the rest of the money he kept for himself. This was a clear breach of the statutes, which required the whole sum of £2 13s 4d to be handed to each boy individually. By the end of 1837 there was only one boy in the school – the headmaster's son. It was said of that headmaster, the Reverend D.F. Warner, that 'he had flogged away every boy but one' and in the end he had to be paid to resign. Understandably, there was public criticism that the

[22] Introduction to Estate Papers in Appendix II to Catalogue of Dean and Chapter's Archives: 'Records of the Ecclesiastical Commissioners in connection with the re-endowment of Rochester Cathedral'. Cf. G.F.A. Best, *Temporal Pillars*, London 1964, pp. 459ff.
[23] Ac 14, p. 439.

dean and chapter had allowed a trust for the education of twenty poor boys to lapse. What the dean and chapter clearly needed 'in order to get rid of the taste of Mr Warner and to attract boys to their moribund school', was 'a master with a good local reputation – a clergyman, a gentleman and a scholar, who would be prepared to accept the appointment at the comparatively low stipend they were able to offer'.[24] This they found in the Reverend Robert Whiston.

Whiston, a classical scholar and a Fellow of Trinity College, Cambridge, who had made his reputation in the locality as an able schoolmaster with his own school, known as the Rochester Classical and Mathematical School, was appointed headmaster of the Cathedral School in 1842, with the result that numbers increased and standards improved. Almost immediately, however, Whiston challenged the chapter's interpretation of its statutory obligations. He went further and collected information revealing that many other cathedral chapters were violating their founders' intentions to their own financial advantage. He published these allegations in 1849 in a pamphlet, *Cathedral Trusts and their Fulfilment*, which became a best seller and led to questions in Parliament. For this action Whiston was twice dismissed from his office but he refused to go. Instead he carried on his schoolmastering imperturbably and fought the dean and chapter in the Court of Chancery, then in Queen's Bench, but because of legal technicalities was unable to secure a decision. In the final appeal before the bishop of Rochester in 1852, Whiston was censured for his allegations and for his behaviour, but the dean and chapter were ordered to reinstate him as headmaster. Whiston accepted the decision but, in a letter to the press, he stated that the central question as to whether the chapter had taken to itself a disproportionate share of the cathedral revenues, at the expense of the salaries of the exhibitioners and grammar boys, remained unresolved, and he looked to the support of the press should he decide to re-open his challenge. In a further letter he declared that he was prepared to prove, 'and if necessary in the Court of Chancery', that the scholars were entitled to a proper maintenance, and whether he did this or not would depend on the action of the chapter. Faced with this threat of another chancery action, the chapter, in November 1852, decided 'to increase the stipends of several persons of this Cathedral establishment whose statutable payments and allowances have not been heretofore augmented'. Each bedesman received an additional £8 per annum, each grammar boy an additional £14 per annum and each exhibitioner an additional £25 10s per annum. That was something, but not much and, as Ralph Arnold comments, 'it could hardly be claimed that these concessions established the principle that the Cathedral revenues should be more evenly distributed between the Dean and Canons and the other members of the Cathedral establishment'.[25]

It must have been a cause of deep chagrin to the chapter that its tenacious adversary possessed such a fine reputation as a teacher, for his headmastership marked a turning

[24] Arnold. *op. cit.*, pp. 12–13. Arnold's book on the Whiston matter, on which these paragraphs are based, is the result of research into original material in the Dean and Chapter Archives. This material is now catalogued as LP 34/1/52–183; 34/2/5/1.

[25] Arnold, *op.cit.*, p. 197.

point for the Cathedral Grammar School and under him numbers increased remarkably and the standard of academic achievement greatly improved. He had become a national figure, while the dean and chapter had become a national scandal. When Whiston was in litigation with the chapter, subscription lists to meet his legal costs were opened in London, Manchester, Liverpool, Nottingham, Birmingham, Sheffield, Chesterfield, Worcester, Wigan, Warrington, Bolton and Dover, as well as in the Medway Towns and in Gravesend. The Whiston Matter was one of the two ecclesiastical scandals which provided the plot for Anthony Trollope's *The Warden*, published three years after the Whiston case was concluded, and in which Archdeacon Grantly speaks to the bishop of Barchester of 'the case . . . against the Dean of Rochester' and who at Mr Harding's tea party 'dilated to brother parsons . . . of the damnable heresies of Dr Whiston'.[26]

In some ways it is possible to sympathise with the dean and chapter who were, in their judgement, merely continuing custom and precedent. They were publicly pilloried and held up to ridicule and it was not surprising, therefore, that they wished to get rid of Whiston. In other respects the chapter had treated Whiston well. His salary of £150 per annum on appointment bore little resemblance to the statutory payment of £13 6s 8d and a new schoolroom was built at a cost of £800. What is of greater importance, however, is that the chapter's financial system was considerably more complicated than Whiston and others appreciated. All incoming revenues, with the exception of renewal fines on leases, were paid into the Domus Fund. Out of the Domus were paid all the stipends, all the expenses of repair to the fabric and all the expenses incurred in the maintenance of the cathedral and its services. If, at the end of the year, there was a surplus in the Domus it was never divided among the dean and canons. On the other hand, the renewal fines on leases were kept separate and were divided among the dean and chapter exclusively as soon as they came in. Up until 1820 there had been a surplus in the Domus, which had been expended on extensive repair work to the cathedral. For example, a return was made to Parliament in 1874 which stated that over £14,000 had been spent on repairs to the cathedral between 1827 and 1834. Since 1842, however, the Domus had proved unable to meet all the cathedral's outgoings and the dean and canons had to dip into their own renewal fines to meet cathedral expenses. If the chapter had fulfilled its obligations with regard to the exhibitioners, the grammar school boys and the bedesmen, the money for that would have had to come from the Domus, and the depletion this would have caused to the Domus would have to have been made good from the dean and canons' own dividends from renewal fines, and their individual incomes would have decreased accordingly. This was one of the reasons why the chapter failed in its obligation to the exhibitioners, scholars and bedesmen.[27]

Whiston remained headmaster for another twenty years, finally retiring in 1877, and throughout this time he remained a sharp thorn in the side of the dean and chapter.

[26] Collins Classics Edition, 1955, pp. 84, 119; cf. also p. 27 – 'Dr Grantly . . . is a personal friend of the dignitaries of the Rochester Chapter, and has written letters in the public press on the subject of that turbulent Dr Whiston.' *The Warden* was published in 1855.

[27] For the foregoing, cf. Arnold, *op. cit.*, pp. 176ff.

The chapter minute books bristle with references to disputes in which the headmaster, having failed to get his way with the chapter, appealed constantly to the visitor. He continued to criticise the inadequate provision for the scholars. He accused the chapter of not confining the university exhibition to boys at the Cathedral Grammar School and he complained long and bitterly at the chapter's methods of electing boys to the school, referring to 'crucial examples of the abuses and wrongs which may be inflicted upon the public when scholarships are not decided by competition'. In 1869 he sent a memorial on the subject to the Endowed Schools Commission, signed by the mayor, two members of Parliament, Lord Darnley, representatives of the armed services, the magistrates and the clergy – 190 signatures in all.[28] Whiston appealed in vain to the chapter to provide running water in the school and proper accommodation for the boarders. The chapter refused his repeated requests to partition the schoolroom into separate classrooms, to provide a proper cricket ground, to build a toolshed. And so the struggle proceeded, month after month, year in and year out, until his retirement.[29] He died eighteen years later, on 3 August 1895, on which day, by pure coincidence, the anthem at Evensong in the cathedral was 'O give thanks', by Purcell.[30]

In 1877, under a scheme[31] made as a result of the Endowed Schools Act, the school ceased to be controlled solely by the dean and chapter. A governing body was appointed which included members other than the dean and chapter and which kept a record of its proceedings independently of the chapter. There was a proper provision for scholarship examinations and there was a grant from the Ecclesiastical Commissioners for new buildings to be created on land provided by the dean and chapter.

In discussing the financial background to the Whiston affair we noted that the dean and chapter had been spending considerable sums on the repair and maintenance of the cathedral fabric and, whatever else may have been amiss in its conduct of capitular affairs, the chapter seems always to have taken a responsible attitude towards its obligations for the building. Between 1825 and 1830 considerable work had been done under the supervision of the architect, L.N. Cottingham.[32] The second period of restoration occurred between 1840 and 1850 and in April 1840 the *Maidstone Journal and Kentish Advertiser* told its readers that 'the Dean and Chapter of Rochester are about to commence the renovation of the interior of the Quire of the Cathedral immediately after Easter',[33] and a week later it informed intending cathedral worshippers that the cathedral would be closed for repairs and that services would be held in St Nicholas' Church.[34] By far the greater part of the money for the restoration was found by the chapter itself.[35] A Cathedral

---

[28] Ks 1/4.
[29] Arnold, *op. cit.*, pp. 208ff.; cf., e.g., Ac 13, pp. 75, 584ff., 810ff.; Ac 14, pp. 218ff.
[30] Service sheet for that week.
[31] Ks 1/6.
[32] Cf. J. Myles, *L.N. Cottingham 1787–1847: Architect of the Gothic Revival*, London 1996, pp. 79–83.
[33] *Maidstone Journal*, 21 April 1840.
[34] *Ibid.*, 28 April 1840.
[35] G.H. Palmer, *The Cathedral Church of Rochester*, London 1897, p. 35.

Commission reported in 1854 that the fabric of Rochester Cathedral was in 'a fair state' and that £8,239 1s 4d had been spent on repairs during the previous fourteen years.[36]

A third period of restoration is associated with the architect Sir George Gilbert Scott and commenced in 1871. This depleted the financial resources of the dean and chapter, who by 1874 had spent over £10,000 on the current restoration work, which would have had to cease unless the public contributed the further £17,000 required to complete it. A national appeal was launched which met with such a liberal response, including donations from the archbishop of Canterbury and the Right Hon. W.E. Gladstone, MP, that the restoration was able to continue.[37] The quire, which had been closed for several years, was reopened on 11 June 1875.[38]

In 1856 the novelist Charles Dickens came to live at Gads Hill Place[39] and soon became a well-known figure in Rochester. His last, unfinished, novel, *The Mystery of Edwin Drood*,[40] is set in the cathedral town of Cloisterham, which is a thin disguise for Rochester. Some of the last words that he wrote, on 8 June 1870,[41] were about the cathedral – 'A brilliant morning shines on the old city. Its antiquities and ruins are surpassingly beautiful, with the lusty ivy gleaming in the sun, and the rich trees waving in the balmy air. Changes of glorious light from moving boughs, songs of birds, scents from gardens, woods and fields . . . penetrate into the Cathedral, subdue its earthy odour, and preach the Resurrection and the Life . . . '.[42] Twenty-four hours after writing this Dickens was dead.[43] He was given burial in Westminster Abbey, although it is well known that he himself had wished to be buried at Rochester. What is not so well known is that the dean and chapter had made preparations for his burial in the south transept of the cathedral before the dean of Westminster had offered an Abbey burial. At a chapter meeting on 23 June 1870 it was ordered that 'Messrs. Foord be instructed to forthwith send in their bill for preparation of Grave in St Mary's Chapel originally intended for the late Mr Charles Dickens'.[44] So, instead of a tomb there is merely an unimpressive brass plate now on the east wall of the south quire transept commemorating the novelist and his connections 'with the scenes in which his earliest and his latest years were passed and with the associations of Rochester Cathedral and its neighbourhood which extended over all his life'.

We can obtain some insight into cathedral life in the middle of the nineteenth century from the report of the Cathedrals Commission appointed in 1852.[45] There

[36] *First Report of Her Majesty's Commissioners appointed Nov. 10 1852 to Enquire into the State and Condition of the Cathedrals and Collegiate Churches of England and Wales: Answers from Chapters*, p. 351.

[37] *The Times*, 25 July 1874.

[38] *Ibid.*, 12 June 1875.

[39] John Forster, *The Life of Charles Dickens*, n.d., p. 714.

[40] First published 1870.

[41] Forster, *op. cit.*, p. 943.

[42] *The Mystery of Edwin Drood*, Collins edition, 1956, p. 301.

[43] Forster, *op. cit.*, p. 944.

[44] Ac 14, p. 276.

[45] Owen Chadwick described this as 'a strong Cathedral Commission' which 'made many useful recommendations on which no one acted' – *The Victorian Church*, i, London 1966, p. 523.

were two services on Sundays and on weekdays at 10.30 am and 3 pm, all of which were choral except on Wednesdays and Fridays in Lent. A sermon was preached every Sunday morning and afternoon and on the greater holy days such as Christmas, Good Friday and Ascension Day. Holy Communion was celebrated on the first Sunday in the month and on the greater festivals.[46] The dean was in residence for four months and each of the canons for two months. Residence was understood to mean 'lodging in his own decanal or canonical house, during the time of his residence, besides attending divine service in the church once a day at least during such residences, and a penalty of 10 shillings a day for every default in the performance of such residence'. After twenty-one days of his residence a canon could absent himself one day in each week from cathedral services and from residence in his canonical house.[47] The lay clerks received £50 per annum and were required to attend morning and evening service daily throughout the year, except in Lent, when only one lay clerk was required to attend on Wednesdays and Fridays, the services on those days being said.[48] There were six lay clerks and the precentor and organist had told the commission that the number ought to be increased to twelve on Sundays because, said the organist, 'when the church is full, the affect is very meagre, and the labour to the men very great'.[49] The sum of £84 13s 4d was to be divided among the choristers and the organist received £119 per annum together with a house.[50] The organist was also Master of the Choristers, but there was also another master of the choristers, who was a lay clerk, appointed to instruct the choristers in reading, writing and arithmetic. Finally the report noted that in 1852 the income of the dean and chapter was £10,083 4s 10d and expenditure amounted to £10,556 0s 4d.[51]

On 24 February 1858 the *Rochester and Chatham Journal* reported that 'an application is about to be made to the dean and chapter of the cathedral for the establishment of a Sunday evening service in the nave, similar to that which has been attended with such happy results in Westminster Abbey'. On 18 March *The Times* recorded that the dean and chapter of Rochester had agreed unanimously 'to the Mayor's proposal for the opening of the Cathedral on Sunday evenings. . . . The manner in which the dean and chapter received the application will raise them very high in the estimation of the public. . . . Various clergymen of eminence will be invited to preach the sermons.' In November 1865 it was agreed that evening services in the nave be discontinued, but no reason is given.[52] In some cathedrals the inability to persevere with evening services was blamed on the reluctance of the cathedral personnel to shoulder the burden of extra duty. Hitherto there had been no heating in the cathedral and in 1861 the dean and chapter refused to undertake this necessary task.[53] However, five years later, in March 1866, they changed their minds and in

46 *First Report*, 1854 (cited above, n. 36), p. 350.
47 *Ibid.*, p. 345.
48 *Ibid.*, pp. 349, 351.
49 *Ibid.*, p. 708.
50 *Ibid.*, p. 349.
51 *Ibid.*, p. 30 of 'Analysis to replies'.
52 Ac 14, p. 93.
53 Ac 13, p. 768.

June they accepted a tender for £350 from the London Warming and Ventilating Company for the installation of heating.[54]

Dean Stevens died in 1870 and if his tenure of the deanery was the longest in its history, that of his successor was to be the shortest. Thomas Dale, vicar of St Pancras, London, was appointed in February 1870, was installed on 6 April and died on 14 May. After his death there were reports that Charles Kingsley would succeed him, but in June Dr Robert Scott, the Master of Balliol College, Oxford, was appointed. His name will always be linked with H.G. Liddell, dean of Christ Church, as the co-author of Liddell and Scott's *Greek Lexicon* which had been published in 1843 and which opened a new era in Greek scholarship in England. When Dr Jenkyns died in 1854, Scott had defeated Benjamin Jowett in the election to the Mastership of Balliol and, as a result, for ten years there was tension in the college because Jowett found it impossible to make the changes in the college which he believed to be necessary if Balliol was to flourish.[55] In 1869 Jowett spent two days with W.E. Gladstone at a friend's house and this was followed by a message from Gladstone asking Jowett if there was anything he could do for him. 'I told him', Jowett said, 'I did not intend to leave Oxford and that, therefore, the only thing he could do for me was to make Scott a Dean or a Bishop.' The following year Scott was nominated to the deanery of Rochester and Jowett was elected Master of Balliol.[56] One of his contemporaries remembered Scott as 'a white-haired venerable gentleman, quiet and courteous, and not going out much but spending his time connected with the Cathedral and the school and the hospital'.[57]

It was during Scott's tenure of office that a change was made in the canonry which had been annexed to the provostship of Oriel College, Oxford since 1714.[58] Under the Universities of Oxford and Cambridge Act 1877, the provostship was secularised and provision was made that on its next vacancy the canonry be 'permanently annexed and united to some office or place of theological or ecclesiastical character in or connected with the University of Oxford'. This development coincided with an attempt to establish a new chair of Biblical Exegesis in the university. The upshot was the foundation of the Oriel Professorship of the Interpretation of Holy Scripture, to which was to be annexed the canonry at Rochester when the latter next fell vacant. Provost Hawkins died the following year and the first Oriel Professor, John Wordsworth, became a member of the Rochester chapter.[59] Three years later he became bishop of Salisbury and was succeeded by T.K. Cheyne, an eminent Hebraist, one of the most distinguished biblical scholars of his day and an aggressive and wholehearted exponent of the new biblical critical methods. He had a tendency

[54] Ac 14, p. 111.
[55] Geoffrey Faber, *Jowett*, London 1957, pp. 206–7.
[56] *Ibid.*, p. 348.
[57] Quoted E.N. Dunkley, 'Robert Scott, Dean of Rochester (1870–1887)', *Friends of Rochester Cathedral: Fourth Annual Report*, 1939, p. 28.
[58] Cf. above, pp. 98, 116, 118.
[59] Ernest Nicholson, *Interpreting the Old Testament: A Century of the Oriel Professorship: An Inaugural Lecture*, Oxford 1981, pp. 7, 10. The canonry was separated from the chair in 1950.

to want to shock the more conservative and as time went on he became increasingly eccentric and unbalanced in his judgements.

In 1886 the bishop of Rochester wished to add to the number of the chapter by appointing a Canon Missioner. An Act of 1873 had permitted the re-endowment of canonries in order that a canon might have a specific function, if the stipend was provided by private benefaction and providing that the existing chapter agreed.[60] In this case it did not agree because, it said, diocesan duties would interfere with the proposed canon's residence, because it was proposed that his term would be for a number of years, and because he would 'have no beneficial interest in the corporate property of the Chapter'. It suggested that the bishop should follow the example of St Paul's and, with the assistance of the Ecclesiastical Commissioners, establish a Diocesan Missioner, endowed with such a sum as might be raised for the purpose, with an honorary canonry attached.[61]

In 1812 a Royal Warrant had authorised the foundation of the Royal Engineers Establishment at Chatham to instruct the Royal Military Artificers and junior officers of the Royal Engineers in the duties of sapping and mining and other military field work. In 1869 the title became the School of Military Engineering.[62] From the beginning there was a relationship between the Corps of Royal Engineers and the cathedral, inspired perhaps by the corps' claim that Bishop Gundulf, who could design and build castles for the king and who was represented to be skilled in the art of siege-warfare, was the first Royal Engineer and thus the founding father of the corps. In December 1883 a considerable number of memorials at the west end of the nave were dedicated in memory of members of the corps who had died in the Zulu War of 1879, the first Boer War of 1880–1, the Afghan Campaign of 1878–80 and the Wazire Campaign of 1881. At that time the dean and chapter ordered 'that officers, non-commissioned officers, and sappers of the Royal Engineers shall always have free access to all parts of the Cathedral where their Memorials are or may be'.[63]

Meanwhile the restoration work on the cathedral continued and in 1882 the dean told the Cathedral Commission that £21,750 was being spent on repair work. £10,000 of this came from chapter funds, £2,500 from individual members of the chapter and £4,000 from the former canon, Dr Griffith, and Mrs Griffith, £3,000 of the last donation being earmarked for the restoration of the quire and £1,000 for the organ. The total amount spent on the organ had been £2,550 and stained glass had been inserted in the windows of the cathedral by various gifts amounting to some £4,000.[64]

Dean Scott died in Rochester in 1887 and the *Church Times* reported that Robert Gregory, canon of St Paul's, was most likely to succeed him, and commented that if this happened Rochester would have to be congratulated on having the best possible dean and Lord Salisbury would have earned the gratitude of Catholics for

[60] Cf. Owen Chadwick, *The Victorian Church*, ii, London 1970, p. 389.

[61] Ac 14, p. 948.

[62] Cf. Derek Boyd, *The Royal Engineers*, London 1975, pp. 30 ff.

[63] *Form of Service to be used at the Unveiling of Memorial Windows . . . on Wednesday, 19 December 1883.*

[64] *First Report of Her Majesty's Commissioners for Inquiring into the Condition of Cathedral Churches in England and Wales*, 1882, p. 40.

so excellent an appointment.[65] Once again, however, rumour was not to be trusted
and in December it was announced that the new dean was to be Samuel Reynolds
Hole (Plate 3c), vicar of Caunton near Newark. The appointment none the less gave
the *Church Times* 'great satisfaction',[66] for Hole was a Tractarian, but one who
regretted the excesses of the ritualists. He was, however, probably best known to the
general public as the founder of the National Rose Society in 1877, of which he was
the first president and one of the awards of which is still the Dean Hole Medal. He
also published *A Book About Roses* in 1869, which rapidly became a best seller,
passing through many editions, and in the deanery garden he grew 135 varieties of
roses. Hole had a wide circle of friends, including some of the major literary figures
of his day. He was a keen sportsman, a voluminous correspondent – he always wrote
with a quill pen – and an outstanding preacher, much in demand for conducting
missions to working people.[67]

In announcing Hole's appointment, the *Church Times* had added that ' "sleepy
Rochester" no doubt will be stirred up out of its lethargy by the brilliant oratory of
the new Dean' and he had not been long in office before he began to attract large
congregations, especially to the re-established nave service on Sunday evenings. In
August 1888 the local press reported that 'the Nave of Rochester Cathedral was again
crowded to its utmost limits on Sunday evening (fully 1,000 persons being present)
when Dean Hole continued his series of discourses upon the career of the prodigal
son'.[68] The dean found himself in conflict with Canon Cheyne, whose advocacy of
the new methods of biblical criticism he found obnoxious. We know little of the
controversy apart from the fact that in 1891 the dean complained to the bishop, Dr
Randall Davidson, about one of Cheyne's sermons which the local press had
placarded as 'Sermon on the life of David . . . combat with Goliath a myth'. In his
defence to the bishop Canon Cheyne spoke of Hole 'as an old man, frank, impulsive,
and injudicious (as is well-known to the canons)'. He had been 'brought up from a
country rectory, where he never absorbed any new facts or ideas in theology'. He
accused the dean of acting in a manner 'unbecoming in the head of a Society . . .
sowing strife, where he ought to promote peace and love'. He suspected that the dean
had been stirred into action by another of his colleagues, Canon Jelf, 'whose special
weakness is the desire to make everyone do as he conscientiously thinks everyone
ought to do. From the Minor Canons downwards this is pretty well known in the
Cathedral.' Cheyne then gave a delightful vignette of chapter relationships. Canon
Jelf took offence at a sermon by Cheyne on Psalm 16, in which the Davidic theory
of authorship was not accepted and 'he then proceeded (as the Dean freely admitted)
to stir the Dean up: no, he first of all sat down in the Chapter House with a great
Bible, as I was unrobing after Evensong, and proceeded to catechise me. That having
no result, he stirred up the Dean.' After a letter in which the bishop suggested to

[65] *Church Times*, 16 September 1887.
[66] *Ibid.*, 16 December 1887.
[67] Cf. Betty Massingham, *Turn on the Fountains: A Life of Dean Hole*, London 1974; *The Letters of
Samuel Reynolds Hole, with a Memoir*, ed. G. A. Dewer, London 1907.
[68] *Chatham and Rochester News*, 4 August 1888.

Cheyne that teachers of the new biblical criticism ought not to be surprised or arrogant at an unfavourable response, the matter appears to have been allowed to rest.[69]

In the year that Hole became dean it was estimated that a further £20,000 was required to complete the work of restoration of the cathedral,[70] and the distinguished architect, John Pearson, was called in to advise the dean and chapter. The main concern was for the west front which, in the years that followed, underwent thorough restoration, although, once again, the dean and chapter was obliged to appeal for funds. On 27 October 1892 the Rochester Cathedral Restoration Fund was launched at the Mansion House in the City of London and it was hoped that the appeal would raise between £10,000 and £15,000.[71] The work on the west front took about six years and was dedicated on 25 July 1895 in the presence of the archbishop of Canterbury, the bishop of the diocese and visiting bishops.[72] In the meantime Dean Hole, at the age of seventy-five, undertook a lecture tour in the United States of America and raised £500 for the provision of vestries and for restoration work in the crypt.[73] In his last days Dean Hole was able to see the gradual erection of the new cathedral spire, similar in design to the one erected by Hamo de Hethe in 1343. Two bells were added to the existing six and the clock was restored, all at the expense of Thomas Foord,[74] a member of a well-known Rochester family. The spire was dedicated by the archbishop of Canterbury on 30 November 1904, four months after Dean Hole's death. It was the cathedral's patronal festival in the year marking the 1300th anniversary of its foundation.

Dean Hole's successor was Ernald Lane, a former Fellow of All Souls, Oxford, who was archdeacon of Stoke-on-Trent. He lacked the popular gifts of his predecessor, nor was he a great preacher or organiser, but he was a man of wide sympathies, an antiquary and a lover of country life. At the time of his death the bishop of Rochester spoke of 'the spiritual beauty of his nature' and described him as 'beautiful in presence and in dignity, with the old-world charm which in this hurrying age ever attracts'.[75] A man of prayer, he was deeply concerned for order and decency in the cathedral and its worship. He took pains to improve the quality and dignity of the musical services and it was in his time that the chapter agreed to introduce a daily celebration of Holy Communion.[76]

In 1907/8 the east wall and window of the chapter room were reconstructed and the room itself re-floored in oak at the expense of that generous benefactor, Thomas Foord.[77] In 1909 the chapter bought at auction for £710, out of the proceeds of the sale of Parsonage Farm, the houses in College Yard. It also bought by private treaty,

---

[69] G.K.A. Bell, *Randall Davidson*, London 1938, pp. 214ff.
[70] *Kelly's Directory of Kent, Surrey etc.* . . . , 1938, pp. 214ff.
[71] *The Times*, 28 October 1892.
[72] *Ibid.*, 26 July 1895.
[73] Palmer, *op. cit.*, p. 37; Massingham, *op. cit.*, pp. 194ff.
[74] *Thirteen Centuries of Goodwill*, published by the Friends of Rochester Cathedral, 1982, p. 12; Ac 21, p. 5.
[75] *Chatham, Rochester and Gillingham Observer*, 25 January 1913.
[76] Ac 23, p. 95.
[77] W.H. Mackean, *Rochester Cathedral Library*, Rochester 1953, p. 16.

at a cost of £775, the house at the corner of College Yard and High Street, now No. 60 High Street.[78]

In 1905 the shape of the diocese of Rochester changed once again. The diocese of Southwark was created, the area of the diocese of Rochester, save for Greenwich and Woolwich, being restored to what it had been prior to the upheavals of the previous century, and in the following year the archdeaconry of Tonbridge was established.[79] Eight years later the dean and chapter relinquished its patronage of eleven parishes in the diocese of Canterbury in exchange for ten parishes in the diocese of Rochester which had hitherto been in the gift of the archbishop of Canterbury.[80]

Dean Lane died in January 1913 and his successor was John Storrs, who had as a boy been a Governors' Exhibitioner at King's School in the 1860s. At the time of his appointment he was vicar of St Peter's, Eaton Square, and a prebendary of St Paul's Cathedral. Like Deal Hole he attracted large congregations to the cathedral services, especially to the Sunday evening nave service, for – as the local press reported – 'without being an orator he was an earnest and vigorous preacher, speaking always without notes'. He was greatly interested in sport and was himself a keen golfer and chess player. He was a gifted musician and his love of poetry led him to inaugurate a Poetry Society which met in the deanery. He travelled widely in Japan, Egypt and the Holy Land and on one of these journeys the Patriarch of Jerusalem presented him with a sanctuary lamp from the Church of the Holy Sepulchre, which the dean gave to the cathedral and which now hangs before the high altar.

During Dean Storrs' time the cathedral treasury was re-fitted, the Gundulf Tower was restored and the Lady Chapel was lengthened by taking in the south transept. The south quire aisle and the north and south-east transepts were renovated. By 1930 the total expenditure on repairs, which by that time included the restoration of the cloister and chapter house ruins, the re-leading of the nave and Lady Chapel roofs, together with restoration work on Minor Canon Row, had amounted to £8,024, of which £787 had been contributed by the Freemasons of Kent for Gundulf Tower. An appeal in 1921 had raised £1,866; the remainder came from the fabric fund which, by 1922, had been exhausted. In 1921 the eight cathedral bells were re-tuned and the number increased to ten by the gift of two new bells presented by Alderman and Mrs Charles Willis in memory of their son, Lt George Willis, who had been killed in the Great War of 1914–18.

That war had only a minor effect on the life of the cathedral. When it began the chapter wrote to all its employees encouraging them to join HM Forces and agreeing both to make up their service pay to the amount of their cathedral wages and also to keep their places open until the end of the war. If this were to cause hardship to any individual, the chapter would be happy to consider the situation. If any employee was to be killed, the chapter undertook to augment the government pension to his

[78] Ac 23, p. 119.
[79] Ac 22, p. 17.
[80] Ac 25, pp. 58ff.; *London Gazette*, 23 June 1914.

widow unless she re-married.[81] Because of the lay clerks' war service it became impossible by 1916 to continue with a full choir and week-day services were sung by boys only.[82]

The head verger did three days' work each week at Short Bros as his national service[83] and in 1917 a woman, Miss Verrel, was appointed assistant verger.[84] The crypt was used as an air-raid shelter for people living in the precinct and neighbourhood.[85] In 1917 a war shrine and crucifix was placed in the north transept as a temporary memorial to the fallen[86] and throughout the war a daily intercession service was held in the cathedral.[87] On the day of the armistice in 1918 a service of thanksgiving was held, and just before going to the cathedral to conduct this service Dean Storrs received the news of his son's death.[88]

After the war the duties of the choristers and lay clerks were reviewed and in June 1919 it was agreed that the choristers would sing Matins on Tuesday, Thursday and Saints' Days and that the services on Monday, Wednesday and Saturday would be sung by the lay clerks only.[89] In June the following year choral Matins on weekdays was discontinued except on holy days.[90]

In 1927 the care and maintenance of the precinct roads was taken over by the City Council, although the dean and chapter retained the length of road from the west of the cathedral to Chertsey's Gate, together with the forecourt to the Archdeaconry and Oriel House.[91] The chapter expressed the hope that 'every care would be taken to prevent street cries and itinerant musicians in the Precinct' and it was also agreed that 'no parking place for motor vehicles be allowed in any part of the Precinct'.[92]

Reginald Talbot, who succeeded Dean Storrs in 1928, was described by the bishop of Rochester as being accustomed 'to a dignified ritual within the ambit of Prayer Book loyalty' and so could 'be trusted to continue the services of our Cathedral with stateliness without ritual eccentricities'.[93] In Dean Storrs' time the Sunday morning sermon had been preached at the Sung Eucharist. After his death, Canon D.C. Simpson and Canon W.H. Mackean (Plate 9c) told their colleagues in the chapter that they wished to disassociate themselves from this arrangement and that they also wished that the rule whereby each canon preached on three mornings and three evenings during his month of residence be amended. Presumably this was in order that they should not be obliged to preach at the Sung Eucharist, for they added, that if the sermon was to be preached at Morning Prayer, they would then be very pleased to preach 'the arranged number of times on Sunday mornings'.[94] There is no record for several years of any change in the arrangements. The same two canons also opposed the rule that all the canons should wear vestments at the Eucharist, but Dean

[81] Ac 25, pp. 116ff.
[82] *Ibid.*, p. 280.
[83] Ac 26, p. 44.
[84] Ac 25, p. 263.
[85] Ac 26, pp. 13, 16.
[86] *Ibid.*, p. 13.
[87] Ac 25, p. 201.
[88] *Chatham, Rochester and Gillingham News*, 23 November 1918.

[89] Ac 26, p. 91.
[90] *Ibid.*, p. 176.
[91] Ac 28, p. 26.
[92] *Loc. cit.*
[93] *Rochester Diocesan Chronicle*, May 1928, p. 100.
[94] Ac 28, pp. 39ff., 67.

Talbot would not agree to this and stated that he was the ordinary in all matters pertaining to the services in the cathedral.[95] Ill health, unfortunately, compelled Talbot to retire four years after his appointment.

The next dean was Francis Underhill (Plate 3d), a bachelor and cousin of Evelyn Underhill, the notable retreat conductor. He occupied a prominent place in the Anglo-Catholic movement and, at the time of his appointment to Rochester in 1932, he was warden of Liddon House and priest-in-charge of the Grosvenor Chapel where he had maintained the chapel's tradition of liberal Anglo-Catholicism.[96] In 1918 he had published a book in which he had recommended the use of the rosary, devotions to the Blessed Sacrament and Benediction.[97] On the other hand, when in 1928 the bishop of London prohibited devotions directly connected with the Reserved Sacrament, Underhill was among those who criticised those priests who disobeyed this lawful authority.[98] He was closely involved with the great Anglo-Catholic Congresses held in London and he addressed large audiences at the Albert Hall. Yet, in spite of his Catholic background, it was during his time as dean that the rule for the wearing of vestments, upon which Dean Talbot had taken such a stand, was relaxed, for in January 1934 the chapter agreed that on certain occasions surplice and stole should be worn.[99] Already, since the previous September, the preaching of the Sunday morning sermon had been transferred from the Sung Eucharist to Morning Prayer.[100]

Francis Underhill was greatly concerned with the maintenance of the cathedral fabric and in particular he encouraged interest in the ruins of the priory buildings. His most outstanding work in this field, however, was the inauguration in 1935 of the Friends of Rochester Cathedral.[101] On 9 February that year he addressed a letter to *The Times* announcing the formation of the Friends and appealing for members. By the end of that year 622 Friends had been enrolled from all parts of the British Isles and as far afield as Burma, South Africa and Australia.[102] The duke of Kent accepted an invitation to be the first patron and the Friends' inaugural service was held on 2 November 1935. Dean Underhill had stated that the aim of the Friends was 'not only to hand on to future generations the Cathedral with its beauty unimpaired, but also to bring to light some features long hidden'. Both these aspects were evident in the first group of works undertaken by the Friends. In 1936 they agreed to repair the coping and parapet of the west end gable of the nave and the parapets of the nave aisles, to produce printed notices to be placed against various objects of interest in the cathedral and to open the doorway between the old chapter

---

[95] *Ibid.*, p. 74.
[96] Cf. *Godly Mayfair*, ed. Ann Callender, London 1980, pp. 25ff.
[97] *The Catholic Faith in Practice*, London 1918; cf. Francis Penhale, *Catholics in Crisis*, London 1986, p. 54.
[98] *Ibid.*, p. 55.
[99] Ac 29, p. 26.
[100] *Ibid.*, p. 13.
[101] Cf. Paul A. Welsby, 'The Inauguration of the Friends', *Friends of Rochester Cathedral: Annual Report*, 1985.
[102] *Friends of Rochester Cathedral: First Annual Report*, 1936.

house (now known as 'Palm Court') and the cloisters.[103] The Friends also undertook to give support to the dean and chapter's imaginative decision in connection with the remains of the Norman cloisters. At that time the cloister garth formed the garden of Prebendal House, built a hundred years previously as a residence for one of the canons and occupying the corner between the present South Gate and Minor Canon Row. Prebendal House was to be demolished and the canon's residence transferred to Prior's Gate House, thus fully exposing the south cloister with its thirteenth century doorway and the monks' vaulted *lavatorium*.[104]

In 1936 the dean and chapter was faced with a financial crisis which was the result of the Tithe Act which became law that year. Rochester Cathedral was not alone in this, for the act extinguished tithe rent altogether and, because the compensatory stock produced far less revenue than the tithe rent charge had done, the Church of England generally suffered severely as a result. It is estimated that the Act cost the church some £500,000.[105] It is not surprising, therefore to find that in January 1937 the chapter made proposals for economies.[106] Payments to certain Rochester parishes were to cease, special collections at cathedral services were to be less frequent, the payment of an assistant librarian was to be discontinued, the salary of the chapter clerk was to be reduced by £25 and the emoluments of the organist were to be reconsidered. In addition, the chapter agreed that its investments should be examined by stockbrokers, that the rents of its properties should be increased as and when opportunity occurred and that the Ecclesiastical Commissioners should be consulted about the abolition of the office of bedesmen. Finally, the chapter gave serious consideration to the closure of the choir school. This was not a new thought, for as long ago as 1919[107] the chapter had considered proposals for the amalgamation of the choir school with King's School, but the suggestion had not been proceeded with. Now the matter was revived and it was agreed that the school should be closed at the end of the summer term 1937. The choristers were to be educated free at the King's School, the chapter remaining responsible for their religious education, including their preparation for confirmation.[108]

Later in the year, as part of the financial retrenchment, several of the cathedral staff were given notice,[109] the salaries of the bedesmen were reduced,[110] the organist agreed to a reduction of £25 from his emoluments and the sacrist to a similar reduction in his salary.[111] King's School was informed that the chapter could no longer continue the organ scholarship[112] and it was agreed that King's Orchard should be advertised in the local press for use as allotments.[113]

It is said that Dean Underhill made no secret of his desire to become a bishop[114] and in 1937 that desire was fulfilled when he was appointed bishop of Bath and Wells. One of his last acts at Rochester was to welcome HM Queen Mary to the

[103] *Second Annual Report*, 1937.
[104] Ac 29, pp. 189, 213.
[105] Best, *op. cit.*, p. 479.
[106] Ac 29, pp. 205ff.
[107] Ac 26, pp. 90ff.
[108] Ac 29, pp. 210ff., 216.
[109] *Ibid.*, p. 214.
[110] *Ibid.*, p. 215.
[111] *Ibid.*, p. 217.
[112] *Ibid.*, p. 211.
[113] *Ibid.*, p. 213.
[114] *Chatham, Rochester and Gillingham News*, 19 January 1943.

cathedral for a memorial service to the late King George V. His successor at
Rochester was Ernest Blackie, suffragan bishop of Grimsby and a former minor
canon of Rochester. He was the first person in episcopal orders and the first graduate
of a university other than Oxford or Cambridge to be appointed dean of Rochester.[115]
He was regarded as an eloquent preacher, whose sermons were said to be
characterised 'by an unfailing belief in the fundamental goodness of humanity and
the ultimate triumph of the forces of nobility and righteousness'.[116] He also produced
a considerable amount of unassuming but solid and useful literary work of an
historical nature.[117]

Blackie's tenure of office was overshadowed by the war which began on 3
September 1939, two years after he became dean. The outbreak of war found the
dean and chapter prepared, for at the time of the Munich Agreement in the previous
September proposals for air-raid precautions had been approved and special
arrangements had been made for the choristers in the event of the outbreak of war.[118]
The treasurer, Canon W.H. Mackean, was in charge of war-time arrangements and
between Munich and the outbreak of war a number of steps had been taken to
minimise as far as possible the effects of bombing. In December 1938 a large supply
of sand had been bought and placed in readiness in the deanery stables.[119] In January
1939 it had been agreed that Gundulf's Tower would be the cathedral air-raid shelter
and that the vergers were to undergo training in order to form an ARP unit.[120] Hoses
and shovels had been purchased to deal with fire and the west front of the cathedral
was to be protected. Another proposal, that the roofs of the quire, transepts, ringing
chamber and other areas be covered with fire-resisting paint, had not been proceeded
with after enquiries had been made at Westminster Abbey. Such were the advance
preparations.

The chapter met on 26 September 1939[121] and Canon Mackean reported that on
the outbreak of war the west front had been immediately sand-bagged by previous
arrangement with the City Council and at their expense, and that the Gundulf Tower
had been converted into a public air-raid shelter. The fourteenth century chapter
room doorway had been encased in wood, painted with fire-resisting paint, and the
chief tombs in the cathedral had been protected by non-inflammable hassocks and
cushions. As much inflammable material as possible, including chairs, desks and
wooden kneelers, had been removed from the nave and stored in a warehouse
belonging to Messrs Style and Winch in Five Bells Lane. The most valuable silver,
the *Textus Roffensis* and the *Custumale Roffense* had been sent to the Maidstone

[115] He was a graduate of London University. The new cathedral statutes of 1937 had made possible
the appointment of a non-Oxbridge graduate.

[116] *Chatham, Rochester and Gillingham News*, 12 March 1943.

[117] E.g. in 1924 he edited two works originally published in the sixteenth century – *The Pilgrimage
of Robert Langton* (1522) and *A Most Friendly Farewell to Sir Francis Drake* (1578). He
contributed to a number of learned periodicals and wrote several articles for the *Dictionary of
English Church History*.

[118] Ac 30, pp. 24, 62.

[119] *Ibid.*, pp. 24, 62.

[120] *Ibid.*, pp. 51ff., 56, 58.

[121] *Ibid.*, pp. 84, 89ff., 134ff.

branch of the Westminster Bank. Water and sand had been made available throughout the building and on the roofs. The King's School vestry, off the south transept, had been fitted out as a gas-proof refuge for the cathedral staff and first aid equipment was available in the cathedral. The treasurer and the vergers had been constituted as a unit of ARP Wardens. The major expense of these precautions was borne by the Friends of the Cathedral.

Because of the presence in the Medway Towns of the naval dockyard, a sea-plane factory and various military and naval establishments, Rochester was considered to be a prime target for bombing. At the outbreak of war, therefore, it became part of a residential area which people were not encouraged to visit and from which many of the residents moved to safer areas. King's School was evacuated, first to Lamberhurst and then to Taunton. School house was requisitioned by the Admiralty as a hostel for the WRNS and other buildings for ARP purposes. When the school moved three cathedral choristers went with it, three transferred to the Mathematical School, two to Borden Grammar School and one to Ashby de la Zouche Grammar School.[122] A ladies' choir sang the cathedral services, but by December 1942 the cathedral choir was being re-formed and gradually, as it became more experienced, began to sing regularly.

On the night of 27 August 1940 an incendiary bomb fell on the roof of the nave but through the promptness and efficiency of the fire brigade it was extinguished after only slight damage had been done.[123] In October the chapter engaged a night watchman at 65 shillings a week and a telephone was installed in the cathedral.[124] Later, a wall was built to protect the north door.[125] In January 1941 an appeal was made for volunteers to sleep in the cathedral and, in case the water main should be damaged in a raid, tanks of water were placed in the roof space and elsewhere in the cathedral.[126] A number of windows throughout the building and some of the internal and external stonework were damaged in an air-raid on the morning of 8 April 1941.[127] Under the Emergency Powers (Defence Act) 1939/40 the chapter was ordered in September 1941 to remove the railings round the cathedral and its churchyard so that the metal could be used for war purposes.[128] The chapter appealed against this wholesale destruction and in the end it gave up the railings enclosing the churchyard on the north side of the cathedral but retained those on the south side on the grounds that they were necessary for the safety of the public. It also retained the iron gates immediately in front of the west door.[129]

Dean Blackie died suddenly in March 1943 while waiting on Rochester station for a train to London[130] and it was left to his successor, Thomas Crick, to lead the cathedral through the final years of the war and the period of reconstruction that followed. With his naval background Crick was no stranger to the Medway Towns and in his earlier years he had been senior chaplain to the Royal Dockyard and the

---

122 *Ibid.*, p. 92.
123 *Ibid.*, p. 131.
124 *Ibid.*, p. 137.
125 *Ibid.*, pp. 141, 145.
126 *Ibid.*, p. 150.

127 *Ibid.*, p. 156.
128 *Ibid.*, p. 172.
129 *Ibid.*, p. 190.
130 *Chatham, Rochester and Gillingham News*,
     12 March 1943.

Royal Marines barracks at Chatham. By 1943 he had served in the chaplains' department of the Royal Navy for thirty-two years, during the last five of which he had been Chaplain of the Fleet and Archdeacon of the Royal Navy. Thus his appointment to Rochester was an appropriate choice in a community which still retained naval connections, and while he held office he did much to establish closer relations between the cathedral and the naval establishments at Chatham. He must greatly have regretted the disbandment in May 1950 of the Chatham Division of the Royal Marines after 250 years in the district. At a service on 28 May their colours were laid up in the cathedral and a book of memory placed under them in the north quire aisle.

Dean Crick made no claim to be a great preacher; it was in the realm of personal friendship and guidance that he left his most characteristic and enduring mark. His friendly contacts and genial approach made people much more aware of the significance of the cathedral in the local community and many more local organisations came to look to the cathedral as the place for their annual services. Dean Crick regarded the 6.30 pm nave service as very much the dean's service and in 1957 he recruited a voluntary choir to lead the singing. Known then as the Special Choir, its name was later changed to the Precinct Choir and finally to the Rochester Cathedral Auxiliary Choir. For nearly forty years it played an important part in the life of the cathedral and, because of the very high standard of its singing, it not only led the 6.30 pm worship every Sunday, but was also competent to maintain the full round of cathedral-type services on Sundays when the cathedral choir was on holiday.

In 1953 the dean and chapter launched an appeal for £60,000 to 'preserve, improve and maintain' the cathedral, parts of which were suffering from the effects of dry rot, deathwatch beetle and erosion. The roof timbers were renovated, repairs to the spire were undertaken and new lighting was installed. In 1954 the vestries in the crypt, which had been built in Dean Hole's time, were removed and the space used as a chapel. In the same year the diocese of Rochester celebrated the 1350th anniversary of its foundation and a great service in the cathedral was attended by the Queen Mother and the archbishop of Canterbury.

Thomas Crick retired as dean in 1959 and was succeeded by William Stannard, suffragan bishop of Woolwich. The most significant event during his tenure of office was the establishment of a theological college closely associated with the cathedral. The inspiration for this came from the bishop of Rochester, Dr Christopher Chavasse, and when the old deanery was pronounced unsuitable as the residence of the dean, the bishop seized the opportunity to make use of it as a college for the training of ordinands. Dean Stannard was appointed as its first (part-time) Warden and the college opened for the Advent term 1959 with thirteen students. By 1965 the number had increased to forty-eight. The college specialised in training older students who came from a rich variety of backgrounds and who did a two-year course. The first full-time warden was Canon Stuart Blanch who was appointed in 1960 and, on his nomination as bishop of Liverpool in 1966 (he became archbishop of York in 1975), he was succeeded by Canon Stanley Allen. Both wardens occupied the stall formerly associated with the Oriel Canonry. The presence of so many theological students added a much valued dimension to the worshipping and social life of the cathedral and precinct. The college shared in the morning worship of the cathedral and it used the Trinity Chapel in the crypt as its college chapel. Some of the members of the chapter were involved in teaching in the college and the students lived either in the old deanery or in houses or flats in or near the precinct. From 1967 onwards, however, the college suffered from the general decline in the number of ordinands and it closed in June 1970.

On Maundy Thursday 1961 HM the Queen visited the cathedral for the distribution of the Royal Maundy. In the 1960s the custom began of holding three 'Cathedral Lectures' each autumn, delivered by leading figures in church or state and which were attended by church people from all over the diocese in such numbers that for the first few years the nave was usually full to capacity. The highlight of these lectures occurred in 1973 when three archbishops – Ramsey of Canterbury, Coggan of York and Simms of Armagh – were the lecturers.

By this time the dean was Stanley Betts who had been installed in 1966. Prior to his appointment he had been suffragan bishop of Maidstone and bishop to HM Forces. His simple and direct preaching, his goodness and his friendliness attracted many people to the Cathedral and it was during his period of office that one saw the genesis of the cathedral as a place which people, over the coming years, would visit in even greater numbers, and as a centre suitable for music, drama, exhibitions and other large events. The usefulness of the cathedral in this last respect was greatly enhanced in 1968 by the building of the new nave footpace or platform, incorporating the former steep steps from nave to quire – a construction which, incidentally, led to the discovery of the remains of the Saxon cathedral which lie beneath the present nave. In 1973 the Cathedral Flower Guild combined with thirty flower clubs from the whole of Kent to promote a great flower festival, which attracted vast numbers to the cathedral. This event was repeated, with equal success, in 1981.

As the twentieth century nears its end, the life and work of the cathedral can be described in terms of four concentric and ever-widening circles. The smallest and inner circle is the Cathedral Foundation (the dean and chapter, the honorary canons, the choir and organist, the vergers, the King's School), the inhabitants of the precinct and the members of the cathedral congregation, who come mostly from the Medway Towns and their vicinity. It is this group which, in various ways, sustains the ordered round of worship and prayer in the cathedral. In the last twenty years the cathedral congregation has come to be regarded as a much more important part of cathedral life than it appears to have been in the past. Quite apart from its personal contribution to the worshipping and social life of the cathedral, it is from among its members that the cathedral largely depends for the volunteers (some two hundred in number) who are involved in its daily life. In order to recognise the importance of the congregation, in 1977 the Cathedral Council was inaugurated. It consists of the dean and the chapter, some *ex officio* members, representatives of cathedral organisations, such as the Flower Guild, and – most importantly – representatives of the cathedral congregation, elected at an annual meeting of the congregation. Because legal responsibility for the cathedral must lie with the dean and chapter, the Cathedral Council cannot be other than an advisory and consultative body, but it does enable the chapter to discuss and share ideas and proposals with representatives of the congregation and also to receive from them their suggestions and criticisms.

Moving outwards, the second circle is the relationship of the cathedral with the immediate neighbourhood of the Medway Towns. The annual civic service is held in the cathedral and services associated with the various organisations based in the Medway Towns – Men of Kent, Royal Engineers, Royal British Legion, Battle of Britain, etc. – take place there. Schools use the cathedral for their carol services and school-leavers' services and the Rochester Choral Society holds its concerts in the nave.

In yet another and wider circle the cathedral is the mother church of the diocese of Rochester and in this capacity it is the place where services particularly associated with the bishop and the diocese are held. These include the ordination services twice a year and other great diocesan services such as choir, Sunday school, church school and Mothers' Union festivals. Diocesan youth events and pilgrimages centre on the cathedral and parish parties and groups from all over the diocese are welcomed to see, or hear about the cathedral, to offer their own worship or to join in cathedral worship.

The widest circle of all is the cathedral as a centre of pilgrimage to which, particularly in more recent years, is drawn an ever-increasing number of coach parties, school parties and individuals from a wide area, including many from overseas as visitors, tourists and pilgrims. This faces the cathedral authorities with special tasks and special responsibilities. To meet these they have provided, in the summer months, welcomers and guides and also chaplains who come from all parts of the diocese to offer 'a day of ministry' in the cathedral. Some years ago a gift stall was established near the south door and in 1979 the St Andrew's Centre for Visitors was opened in part of the old deanery. There is also an educational unit which provides special facilities for school children.

Rochester Cathedral, far from being a Barchester backwater or simply a focus and support of ecclesiastical life, now finds itself on the frontier of much mission activity and evangelistic opportunity. It seeks to be a centre of mission, a house of welcome and a place of prayer. It is the latter which is fundamental to its being and the cathedral remains – and ever will remain – essentially a centre of worship, which continues day in and day out throughout the year. In the words of the report of the 1924 Cathedrals Commission, 'the first supreme aim of a Cathedral is, by its own beauty and by the religious services held within it, to give continous witness to the things unseen and eternal, and to offer continuous and reverent worship to Almighty God'.

6

Worship in the Cathedral, 1540–1870

NIGEL YATES

It is clear that the Anglican reformers of the sixteenth century always intended that worship in the cathedral churches they had deliberately retained, and indeed increased in number, should be more elaborate and frequent than in ordinary parish churches. In Cranmer's first Prayer Book of 1549 it is assumed that there would be a daily communion so that it would only be necessary to read the exhortation on its proper reception once a month.[1] The celebrant was directed to wear a 'vestment', that is a chasuble, or a cope, and the assistant ministers to wear tunicles, over their albs.[2] In the explanatory notes on ceremonial it was enjoined that 'in all Cathedral churches and Colledges, tharchdeacons, Deanes, Prouestes, Maisters, Prebendaryes, and fellowes, being Graduates, may use in the quiere, beside theyr Surplesses, such hoodes as pertaineth to their several degrees'.[3] In Cranmer's second book of 1552, the use of any vestment apart from the surplice was prohibited, even in cathedrals.[4] However it was assumed that in cathedrals there would still be frequent Communion services and that in them, 'where be many Priestes and Deacons, they shall al receyue the Communion wyth the minister every Sunday at the least, excepte they have a reasonable cause to the contrary'.[5] It was also intended that services in cathedrals should be choral. In the injunctions published by Elizabeth I in 1559 it was laid down that plainsong should be used for all sung parts of the service, except before and after Mattins and Evensong when a hymn 'or such like song' in figured music might be sung provided the meaning of the words was not obscured.[6]

This was the origin of the anthem, which was finally enshrined in the rubrics of the Prayer Book of 1662, when after the third collect of both offices there was inserted a note to the effect that 'in Quires and Places where they sing, here followeth the Anthem'.[7]

In 1560 the bishops agreed that the cope should be worn at all celebrations of Holy Communion in both cathedrals and parish churches, but there was considerable

---

[1] *The First and Second Prayer Books of Edward VI*, ed. E.C.S. Gibson, London 1910, p. 216.
[2] *Ibid.*, p. 212.
[3] *Ibid.*, p. 288.
[4] *Ibid.*, p. 347.
[5] *Ibid.*, p. 392.
[6] *Liturgy and Worship*, ed. W.K.L Clarke, London 1932, p. 183.
[7] *Ibid.*, p. 276.

opposition on the part of those clergy with Puritan sympathies, and in 1566 this
provision was modified in Archbishop Parker's *Advertisements* so that only 'in the
ministration of the Holy Communion in collegiate and cathedral churches, the
principal minister shall use a cope with gospeller and epistoler agreeably'.[8] A similar
provision was enacted in the Canons of 1604.[9]

What is not clear is how far cathedrals carried out in practice the liturgical ideals
required of them. At Rochester the fact that the first dean, Walter Phillips, who
survived until 1570, had been the last cathedral prior before the dissolution of the
former monastic cathedral, may have ensured a high degree of continuity in the
proper celebration of the divine office and frequent communion. However at
Canterbury in the early years of Elizabeth's reign, though the ante-communion was
celebrated each day, the officiating minister only wore a surplice and the full
communion service was only celebrated once a month. On that occasion, however,
the three ministers, celebrant, gospeller and epistoler, were all vested in copes.[10] A
major increase in cathedral ceremonial began to take place in the early seventeenth
century with the appointment of advanced high churchmen to occupy the stalls of
dignitaries and prebendaries. At Rochester both Godfrey Goodman, dean 1621–4,
and Walter Balcanquall, dean 1625–39, were high churchmen. Goodman, as bishop
of Gloucester, was openly accused of having secretly become a Roman Catholic.[11]
A visitor to Rochester in 1635 commented:

> The Cathedral . . . be but small and plaine, yet it is very lightsome and pleasant:
> her quire is neatly adorn'd with many small pillers of marble; her organs, though
> small, yet are they rich and neat; her quiristers though but few, yet orderly and
> decent.

The total establishment then consisted of the dean, vice-dean and five other
prebendaries, sixteen singing men, six petty canons and eight boys.[12] Thomas
Turner, dean 1642–4, another high churchman, insisted upon wearing his surplice
and hood at all services much to the disapproval of the Puritan reformers, who also
denounced the organ as 'bag-pipes' and broke down the altar rails.[13] The Puritans
were contemptuous of cathedral worship which they saw as little short of outright
popery:

> The Pettie Canons, and Singingmen there, sing their Cathedral Service in
> Prick-Song after the Romish fashion, chanting the Lord's Prayer, and other
> Prayers in an unfit manner, in the chancell, or Quire of that Cathedrall; at the
> East end whereof they have placed an Altar (as they call it) dressed after the

[8]   *Ibid.*, pp. 184–5.
[9]   *Ibid.*, p. 854.
[10] G.W.O. Addleshaw and F. Etchells, *The Architectural Setting of Anglican Worship*, London 1948,
      p. 32.
[11] See H.R. Trevor-Roper, *Archbishop Laud*, 2nd edn, London 1962, pp. 392–3.
[12] W.B. Rye, 'Visits to Rochester and Chatham', *Archaeologia Cantiana*, vi (1866), p. 63.
[13] P.C. Moore, 'The Development and Organisation of Cathedral Worship in England', Oxford
      D.Phil. thesis 1954, p. 79.

Romish fashion, with Candlesticks, and Tapers, for which Altar they have lately provided a most Idolatrous costly Glory-Cloth or Back-Cloth; towards which Altar they crouch, and duck three times at their going up to it, and reade there part of their Service apart from the Assembly.[14]

At Canterbury, to which this description applied, though it could have been used of several other cathedrals, the altar was also furnished with an almsdish, cushions for the service books and a silver gilt canister for the wafers. Some cathedrals had on their altars an incense pot and a knife to cut the sacramental bread.[15]

With the victory of the Puritan party after 1645 there was a general desire to close or demolish cathedrals. Some were divided for use by separate congregations as the larger Scottish churches had been since the Reformation. At Rochester parts of the cathedral were used as a stable for horses and a carpenters' workshop.[16]

With the re-establishment of the Church of England after 1660 there seems to have been a speedy return to the standard of cathedral worship abandoned fifteen years earlier. In 1662–3 prebendary Ralph Cooke presented the cathedral with new communion vessels, to replace plate lost or destroyed during the years of religious chaos. The earliest surviving cathedral inventory, of about 1670, lists this as two chalices and covers, two patens, two flagons, an almsdish and two candlesticks. To those were added in 1701, by the gift of Sir Joseph Williamson, two chalices and covers, two flagons, two standing patens with covers, an almsdish and two candlesticks. All, apart from the candlesticks, had been made in 1653–4 for James, Duke of Lennox and Richmond. In addition to the rich gifts of plate the cathedral altar had a dossal formed by two pieces of tapestry, a frontal and two cushions of purple velvet for the service books. The pulpit had a hanging and cushion of purple velvet. The seats of the dignitaries and prebendaries, as also those for their wives and for the Corporation of Rochester, were likewise fitted with hangings and cushions.[17] The Laudian ceremonial, of which the Puritans had complained, was also mostly restored. The ante-communion was usually sung, but not the full communion service, generally celebrated monthly.[18] At Canterbury, however, there was weekly communion throughout most of the eighteenth century, but it was abandoned for a monthly service in about 1790.[19]

In some cathedrals the litany was sung by lay clerks but at Rochester it was sung by two minor canons following a rule made in 1706.[20] The lessons were read from an eagle lectern at Canterbury Cathedral until this was given up at the same time as

---

[14] R. Culmer, *Cathedral Newes from Canterbury*, London 1644, p. 2. Copy in Centre for Kentish Studies, Maidstone, U235 Z1.

[15] Moore, *op. cit.*, pp. 59–60.

[16] *Ibid.*, p. 84; cf. *supra*, pp. 76ff.

[17] Elf 1; W.A.S. Robertson, 'Church Plate in Kent', *Archaeologia Cantiana*, xvi (1886), p. 391; F.F. Smith, *History of Rochester*, London 1928, pp. 292–4.

[18] Moore, *op. cit.*, p. 121.

[19] C.E. Woodruff and W. Danks, *Memorials of Canterbury Cathedral*, London 1912, p. 343.

[20] Moore, *op. cit.*, p. 130.

the weekly communion service, in about 1790.[21] An eagle lectern for the bible was recorded in the Rochester Cathedral inventory of c.1670.[22]

There is, however, little evidence for the continued use of copes by cathedral clergy beyond the early eighteenth century. In 1737 it was noted that they were only used at Durham Cathedral and Westminster Abbey, and their use at Durham was discontinued in 1760 when they were described as 'those raggs of popery'. Candles were used and were lighted at York Minster in 1769, but at most other cathedrals it appears that, though used as altar ornaments, they were not lighted.[23] There was a greater emphasis on the singing of anthems after 1660. The Rochester Chapter ordered in 1741 that the the anthem was to be 'named to the congregation by the Chantor, or his Deputy'.[24] At the enthronement by proxy of Bishop Thomas Sprat in 1684 the minor canons, lay clerks and choristers sang an anthem in procession.[25]

Nevertheless, despite generally high standards of cathedral worship, deans and chapters had to be watchful of the other members of the cathedral establishment who, in their frequent absences, carried out most of the liturgical functions in the cathedral. At Rochester the chapter resolved on 25 November 1706 that:

> Whereas complaint has been made to the Dean and Chapter that severall persons in holy orders belonging to this Cathedrall Church have usually appeared in their night gownes in the Church aforesaid. Therefore it is ordered that no person in holy orders belonging to this church do hereafter presume at any time to enter the said church otherwise habited than as priests and deacons ought to appear in publique. And it is hereby further ordered that no person presume to officiate in Divine Service in this church but in a surplice. Likewise that the lay clerks whose course it is to attend at early morning prayers do never hereafter neglect the said duty. Ordered that from this time the office of the litany shall not be performed by any lay clerke but always by priests or deacons in this Cathedral Church. And that upon Wednesdays and Fridays it be performed by two minor canons (vizt) the minor canon whose course it is to officiate and the minor canon whose course it was to read prayers the preceding week. As likewise upon Sundays whenever it shall so fall out that two minor canons are present. And if there shall be any minor canon belonging to ye Church that shall not have any cure of souls such minor canon shall be obliged constantly on Sundays to assist at the Littany and the Communion Table and every defaulting minor canon shall be mulct.[26]

On 6 July 1708 it was 'ordered that the lay clerks do diligently and frequently attend the organist at such times in the quire as he shall appoint in order to improve themselves in the knowlege and practice of church musick'. Defaulters were to be reported to the dean or vice-dean.[27] On 6 October 1709 the chapter noted with concern the continuing absences from divine service of some lay clerks and resolved to secure their attendance in future. By 19 January 1710 it was clear that the 'gentle

21 Woodruff and Danks, *op. cit.*, p. 350.
22 Elf 1.
23 Moore, *op. cit.*, pp. 133–5.
24 *Ibid.*, pp. 139–40.
25 *Ibid.*, p. 163.
26 Ac 5, f. 13/9v.
27 f. 13/47v.

method of admonishing' was insufficient and it was agreed that future indiscipline would have to be treated with fines.[28]

Even the minor canons were found in 1712 going out during divine service and were to be asked to give reasons for this if it occurred in future.[29] On 6 July 1754 the chapter made new regulations for the 'service and discipline' of the choir as a result of recent 'neglects and irregularities'.

All members of the cathedral establishment were to come into quire 'before the first *Gloria Patri* in surplices and the hoods agreeable to their respective degrees'. Minor canons and lay clerks were to be 'constantly and regularly at Prayers in the quire, morning and evening', and to be fined for non-attendance unless excused. The chanter was not to be absent without appointing a deputy and was to be responsible for maintaining a register of attendance. The organist was not to be absent without leave and was to teach the choristers and maintain discipline; the lay clerks were to report to him for music practice on Tuesdays and Thursdays.[30] The standard of music, however, was far from wholly satisfactory. Ralph Banks, organist from 1790 until his death in 1841, noted that 'when I came from Durham . . . only one Lay Clerk attended during each week. The daily service was chanted. Two services (Aldrich in G and Rogers in D) and seven Anthems had been in rotation on Sundays for twelve years.'[31]

Throughout the eighteenth century the dean and chapter maintained the cathedral in good repair and added to its furnishings and ornaments. In 1706 the bishop gave the chapter a 'piece of rich silk and silver brocade' which it resolved should 'be applyed to ye making an altar piece'.[32] This was contracted for in 1707.[33] In 1709 a new altar carpet was purchased and the cushions repaired.[34] In 1713 the treasurer was ordered to provide new books for the quire and the organist to transcribe in them six of the best services, twelve verse anthems and six full anthems.[35]

The 1725 inventory noted a new altar carpet of 'crimson velvet and purple silk brocaded with gold and silver, two cushions one side being of the said purple silk lined with red silk' in addition to other altar carpets of purple velvet and black baize.[36] This crimson carpet had been replaced by a new purple one by c.1740.[37] In 1752 it was 'agreed that the Dean do return the thanks of this chapter to the most Reverend his Grace the Lord Archbishop of Canterbury for his late benefaction to this Church towards finishing and ornamenting its altar piece'.[38] In 1743 the quire was refitted with new stalls and pews and 'very handsomely new paved'; a new organ over the quire screen was erected in 1791 to replace what was described as 'but a very

---

[28] ff. 13/63, 67.
[29] f. 13/92.
[30] Ac 7, ff. 23/7–9.
[31] Quoted in *The Oxford Companion to Music*, ed. P.A. Scholes, 10th edn, Oxford 1970, p. 162.
[32] Ac 5, f13/13.
[33] f. 13/22; Emf13/1–2.
[34] Ac 5, f. 13/60.
[35] f. 13/106.
[36] EIf 7/1–2.
[37] EIf 9/1–2.
[38] Ac 7, f. 22/57. The Archbishop was Thomas Herring, previously dean of Rochester.

indifferent instrument'.[39] Nathaniel Smith, Member of Parliament for Rochester, subscribed £100 towards this new organ, the bishop £50, the dean £10 and each prebendary £5. It was resolved to raise the rest of the money by selling some surplus communion plate and this sale realised a further £74 16s.[40] This new organ was enlarged in 1842 at a cost of £2,500 paid by one of the prebendaries, John Griffith (1827–72), and further alterations made in 1864 and 1872. It was entirely rebuilt in 1875 as part of Sir George Gilbert Scott's restoration of the Cathedral. This rebuilding was not, however, entirely satisfactory and the organ had to be rebuilt again in 1904–5.[41]

The regular round of daily worship in the cathedral was conscientiously maintained. In 1711 it was:

> ordered that prayers begin in the morning throughout the whole year exactly when ye clock strikes a quarter past 10 in the morning and in ye afternoon from All Hallows Tide to Candlemas when it strikes a quarter past 3 and from Candlemas to All Hallows Tide when it strikes a quarter past 4.[42]

Until the late eighteenth century early prayers were read in the Lady Chapel but that practice was discontinued when it was taken over for use by the bishop as his Consistory Court.[43] In 1707 the chapter resolved that no less than six quarts of wine should be purchased for the communion service and in 1708 that a sermon on Good Friday should be established in perpetuity.[44]

Cathedral chapters were not at the forefront of the reform movement within the Church of England in the early nineteenth century. The vast, and largely empty, cathedral churches, of which usually only the quires were fitted up for worship, with their relatively small resident establishments, must have closely resembled the decaying monasteries of the later Middle Ages. At Rochester Cathedral services in 1835 had changed barely at all from what they had been a century, or even two centuries, earlier. The chapter return to the Commission on Ecclesiastical Duties and Revenues noted:

> Morning and Evening Prayer on every day throughout the year and a sermon on every Sunday morning, and also Christmas Day, Good Friday, 5th of November, King's Accession and King Charles's Martyrdom. The Sacrament of the Lord's Supper administered the first Sunday in every month and on Christmas Day, Whitsunday and Easter Sunday. The Dean or the prebendary in residence always preaches and reads the Communion Service and occasionally reads other parts of the Church Service.[45]

[39] E. Hasted, *History and Topographical Survey of the County of Kent*, 2nd edn, Canterbury 1798, iv, p. 102.

[40] Ac 9, ff. 31, 38, 48, 60, 79.

[41] *Ex inf.* Paul Hale, Assistant Cathedral Organist.

[42] Ac 5, f. 13/91.

[43] Hasted, *loc. cit.*

[44] Ac 5, ff. 13/36, 54.

[45] Ac 11, f. 263.

The greater observance of the 'state' as opposed to the 'religious' festivals in the calendar was consistent with practice elsewhere at this time. There was still some evidence of neglect. On 18 July 1834 it was recorded that 'divine service having been several times recently omitted in consequence of the non-attendance of a minor canon: the Dean and Chapter deem it their duty to inform the minor canons that should a similar neglect occur again they will find it incumbent upon them to make some new regulation to prevent the like omission'.[46] It is clear that the main burden of liturgical provision fell on the minor canons and not on the prebendaries, though both were likely to hold other preferment the duties of which they had either to discharge themselves or supply through the appointment of a deputy.

An examination of the senior members of the Rochester Chapter in the early nineteenth century shows that all were pluralists and that most held their cathedral stalls for long periods. It was, therefore, not surprising that cathedral establishments were extremely conservative. Even among the deans Samuel Goodenough (1802–8) was also incumbent of Boxley, and both William Beaumont Busby (1808–20) and Robert Stevens (1820–70) held the living of West Farleigh. Stevens was a major obstacle to reform at Rochester.[47] Although West Farleigh was a small parish and he employed a curate it clearly took up a good deal of his time. He signs the register frequently up to 1856[48] and was present at about half the vestry meetings up to 1846.[49] It was only after 1860 that the prebendaries of Rochester ceased to be pluralists and that the chapter ceased to use its own livings as an additional source of income for its senior personnel.

Before 1860 there was little thought on the part of chapters that cathedrals ought to fulfil a function in the diocese. Outside service times most cathedrals were kept locked.[50] Many did not even attract substantial congregations to their Sunday services. At Rochester the religious census of 30 March 1851 showed a cathedral congregation of 210 in the morning and 312 in the afternoon, in each case somewhat down on the estimated average Sunday attendance. These figures were substantially lower than those returned for the two parish churches of St Margaret and St Nicholas, and about the same as that returned for Strood where the incumbent had commented 'I think it right to state that the Parish of Strood has been subjected to many years of spiritual neglect.'[51] To some extent the size of the cathedral congregations was determined by the inadequacy of the seating arrangements. Although the cathedral pew-openers had been instructed by the chapter in 1839 'to accommodate as well as they are able strangers with seats, always observing towards them the utmost civility and attention, and never accepting any gift towards such accommodation',[52] sufficient spare seats were simply not available. Most were allocated to members of

[46] f. 234.
[47] C.H. Fielding, *Records of Rochester*, Dartford 1910, pp. 353, 412, 539; cf. *supra*, pp. 116–17.
[48] Centre for Kentish Studies, Maidstone, P143/1/3.
[49] P143/8/1–2.
[50] Moore, *op. cit.*, p. 167.
[51] W.N. Yates, 'The Major Kentish Towns in the Religious Census of 1851', *Archaeologia Cantiana*, c (1984), p. 420.
[52] Ac 12, ff. 17–18.

the foundation and their families or guests and the few remaining seats had been rented out on a very unsatisfactory basis. On 29 June 1840 the chapter noted that:

> The principal subsacrist or verger having hitherto received payments from persons accommodated with pews and seats in the cathedral, resolved that he be, and he is hereby, prohibited from receiving any such payments in future, and that no person or persons, permitted to occupy pews or seats in the Cathedral, be subject to any charge whatsoever for such occupation.[53]

The following day the chapter clerk sent a letter to all those who had been paying pew rents:

> The Dean and Chapter having learnt that you have paid a fixed sum annually for the seat which you occupy in the Cathedral have directed me to inform you that they desire to put an end to this practice and that they have instructed their verger not to demand any such payment.[54]

The income from such pew rents had been very modest, totalling £38 4s 6d annually. Those renting their pews included the mayor and corporation of Rochester.[55] The chapter then re-allocated the pews. The surviving plan (Plate 9a) shows that only a few seats on the north side of the choir remained unallocated and therefore available to 'strangers'.[56] Of the total seating accommodation of about 450 some two-thirds of the seats were allocated to cathedral personnel so that hardly more than a hundred could be allocated to others who wished to worship in the cathedral. Seats had to be applied for in writing and there was a considerable scramble for any that became vacant through the death or removal of the occupants. The arrangement was unpopular with local people. One worshipper wrote in 1847 complaining about the difficulty of getting a seat in the cathedral and advocated a return to the system of pew rents, since otherwise pews were allocated but not always occupied. Unless the situation improved he would be forced to worship elsewhere, since families had to be broken up to sit in the few unallocated seats.[57] No improvements, however, took place until 1867 when the old pews (Plate 10) were removed and the quire and transepts refitted with chairs and benches (Plate 11).[58]

The pressure for the reform of cathedrals, both as corporate bodies and as places of worship, was enormous.[59] What, however, could not be denied was that, whatever their other shortcomings, cathedrals had maintained and fostered over three centuries a tradition of choral worship in the Church of England which from about 1830 some churchmen, such as W.F. Hook, endeavoured to transplant, with varying degrees of success, to the larger urban parish churches.[60] In 1852 every English cathedral, with the exception of Chester and Ripon, had two fully choral services every day.[61]

[53] f. 36.
[54] AZz 6/11.
[55] AZz 6/15.
[56] AZz 6/1.
[57] AZz 6/22.
[58] Smith, op. cit., p. 286; Ac14, p. 140.

[59] See W.O. Chadwick, The Victorian Church, London 1966–70, i, pp. 126–41, 523–6; ii, pp. 366–92
[60] Addleshaw and Etchells, op. cit., pp. 209–22.
[61] Moore, op. cit., p. 338.

At Rochester some cautious moves to improve the quantity and quality of cathedral services began with the resolution of the chapter on 1 December 1838 'that a sermon shall be preached in the Cathedral every Sunday afternoon throughout the year'.[62]

In 1840 £538 was expended on a new pulpit, episcopal throne and altar rails, though of this Bishop Murray contributed £100 towards the cost of the throne. The chapter gave the redundant pulpit to the new church at Luton in Chatham.[63] In 1847 it was laid down that the minor canons must be present at both Sunday services, at services on all festivals, on Ash Wednesday, every day in Holy Week, on the Mondays and Tuesdays in Easter and Whitsun weeks, and on all special occasions. They had to be present for all the services during their duty periods, two weeks in every six, and preach as required.[64] However, an attempt by some of the minor canons to bring the cathedral more in line with advanced liturgical thinking for that period was strongly resisted by the chapter. In a note dated 13 July 1849 a list was drawn up of discrepancies between liturgical practices in Rochester Cathedral and those directed in the rubrics of the Book of Common Prayer, the chief purport of which was to show that at Rochester intoning was restricted to the lay clerks and ordained members of the foundation were only permitted to read parts of the service.[65] The chapter conceded on 9 November that in future the litany might be sung by the minister as well as the lay clerks as far as the Lord's Prayer.[66] A further submission by the sacrist and precentor requested the chapter to permit more of the service to be choral but the chapter was not prepared to move any further.[67] In a letter dated 1 December the sacrist and precentor asserted that chanting was the rule in other cathedrals and enjoined by the statutes at Rochester which directed that the performance of divine service there should be 'secundum ritum et morem aliarum ecclesiarum cathedralium'.[68] On 4 January 1850 the chapter reconsidered its previous decisions and agreed that the Apostles' Creed could be intoned,[69] that the versicles could be chanted by both ministers and clerks, as could the first portion of the litany, but that the other prayers could not be intoned.[70] The sacrist and precentor were still not satisfied but the chapter declined to 'assent to any further alterations'.[71] After further dispute the chapter declared itself willing to abide by the judgement of the bishop in respect of choral services. In its draft submission it pointed out that only two of the four minor canons were opposed to the existing practices, that minor canons knew at their appointment that they would not be obliged to intone prayers, and had, to this end, only been tested for reading and not for chanting.[72]

The Holy Communion had been celebrated at Rochester Cathedral on the first Sunday of each month and on the major festivals since at least 1795, and probably throughout most of the eighteenth century. From August 1855 the number of celebrations was doubled to one a fortnight, and weekly communion was introduced

[62] Ac 11, f. 413.
[63] Ac 12, ff. 49, 54–5.
[64] f. 240.
[65] CCZ 22.
[66] Ac 12, f. 379.
[67] f. 381.
[68] ff. 383–4.
[69] ff. 390–1.
[70] f. 392.
[71] ff. 415–16.
[72] CCZ 22.

from January 1868.[73] An additional service, on Fridays in Lent, was introduced in 1856, and in 1858 an evening service in the nave was permitted on Sundays between the beginning of May and the end of September.[74] But the chapter was unwilling to take other steps to popularise the cathedral services. On 28 November 1860 it declined to appropriate seats in the cathedral 'except to the inhabitants of the precincts, [its] own members and those employed in the cathedral establishment'.[75] On 27 November 1861 the chapter resolved that it was 'not prepared to undertake the warming of the cathedral', and deferred consideration of this topic again in 1863.[76] It would appear that there had even been some falling away from the earlier practice of daily choral services since, at his primary visitation in 1867, Bishop Claughton recommended that they be resumed, except during Holy Week, that weekly communion be instituted and that the practice of closing the cathedral for services during the annual cleaning should be discontinued.[77] Claughton presented a brass lectern to the cathedral in 1868, and in 1872 prebendary John Griffith, on his retirement from the stall he had occupied since 1827, offered the sum of £3,000 towards the decoration and fittings of the quire, expressing a hope that a handsome stone reredos might be erected.[78] This reredos was designed by Sir George Gilbert Scott and completed in 1873.

In modern times cathedrals have tended to reflect, and indeed to set the pattern for, the norms in Anglican worship. This, however, is a comparatively recent development. As this survey of worship in the cathedral at Rochester has shown, there was a substantial gulf between cathedral and parochial worship in earlier years. In the seventeenth and eighteenth centuries the standards of worship in cathedrals tended to be considerably in advance of those in parish churchs, and Rochester was no exception to this general rule. By the nineteenth century cathedrals had become bastions of entrenched conservatism, and were well behind parish churches in adapting to the new liturgical ideas that had begun to be introduced by both Evangelicals and the radical high churchmen who allied themselves, to a greater or lesser extent, with the leaders of the Oxford Movement. No cathedrals had fully committed themselves to liturgical reform and the popularisation of their services until the 1850s at the earliest. Rochester, where this development was delayed until well after 1870, was among the later group of cathedrals to appreciate that it was not just the survival of an ancient corporation, but that it had the potential to become the liturgical and spiritual focus, the true mother church, of the whole diocese.

[73] S4.
[74] Ac 13, ff. 597, 659, 714.
[75] f. 733.

[76] ff. 768, 855.
[77] Ac 14, pp. 162–3.
[78] pp. 183, 383.

7

The Medieval Fabric

J. PHILIP McALEER

Not surprisingly, the standing fabric of Rochester Cathedral is the product of the two late medieval periods, the Romanesque and the Gothic, although it is not quite equally divided between them. Of the Romanesque, the lesser part, the remains represent the early and mature phases of that style: part of a crypt which must be counted among the earliest of surviving Romanesque works in England; and most of a nave and west front which constitute one of the primary examples of mature Romanesque with its emphasis on lavish displays of richly varied ornamental motifs and arcading. The several Gothic styles are less broadly represented, as the major alteration of the Romanesque structure was executed almost entirely within the Early English style, even if its erection was not exactly confined to that period. That work consists of a long presbytery, a minor (east) transept, a quire and side aisles, and a major (east) transept and crossing. The Decorated style is present only in the form of four vaults: those of the arms of the major transept and the quire aisles (of which one is of wood and a second is really a ceiling). Perpendicular work, with one significant exception, is primarily confined to the alteration and enlargement of windows. That exception, never completed, constitutes the last major structure added to the cathedral, probably in the early sixteenth century, and, consequently, one of the last works executed in the Perpendicular style in the country: it is the so-called Lady Chapel.[1]

It is nearly one hundred years since a comprehensive history of the cathedral fabric was last attempted. That history was written by W.H. St John Hope (1854–1919) and published in two successive volumes of *Archaeologia Cantiana* and then separately in one volume.[2] Many of Hope's conclusions regarding the original form

---

[1] Owing to the necessary constraints on the size of this volume and the consequent limits on the extent of each chapter, the focus of this contribution is on the standing medieval fabric. Thus vanished or destroyed structures will be considered little or not at all, the latter in the case of the Saxon cathedral. Following the traditions of the *Victoria County History*, emphasis is placed on a description of the visible fabric; conclusions concerning the chronology of the building sequence are based upon evidence and arguments fully presented in a longer comprehensive reassessment of the medieval building history which, it is hoped, will appear as a monograph in the near future.

[2] W.H. St John Hope, 'The Architectural History of the Cathedral and Monastery of St Andrew at Rochester', *Arch. Cant.*, xxiii (1898), pp. 194–328, and xxiv (1900), pp. 1–85; published

of the destroyed parts of the Romanesque fabric and the dating of both the Romanesque and, especially, parts of the Gothic fabric can no longer be accepted. This is due in part to the fact that, in some respects, Hope relied heavily on the observations and, most importantly, on the interpretation of those observations, made by J.T. Irvine in the course of the restoration work he carried out under the supervision of Sir George Gilbert Scott (1811–78) between 1871 and 1878.[3] Hope himself was writing nearly twenty years later and therefore he had not seen the physical evidence forming the basis for many of his judgements. In other aspects, Hope relied heavily on the meagre surviving documentary evidence for the chronology of the building and not at all on a comparative stylistic analysis with other monuments of the evolving Romanesque and Gothic styles. The following study thus departs in many respects from the chronology which, since Hope's work appeared, has been generally accepted, and, as well, suggests alternatives to some of Hope's hypotheses.

I. The Romanesque Church

(1) *The late eleventh-century building*

William of Malmesbury, writing sixty years or so after the event, described the church at Rochester at the time of the death of its last Anglo-Saxon bishop, Siward (1058–75), as 'derelicta ecclesia miserabili et vacua, omnium rerum indigentia intus et extra'.[4] The *Textus Roffensis* informs us that during his long episcopate, the second Norman bishop appointed by Archbishop Lanfranc (1070–89) of Canterbury, Gundulf (1076/7–1108), formerly of Bec, 'ecclesiam Sancti Andreae, pene vetustate

---

separately, London 1900 (subsequent references are to this edition, cited as Hope [1900]). About the same time, and reflecting Hope's work, G.H. Palmer, *The Cathedral Church of Rochester: A Description of its Fabric and a Brief History of the Episcopal See*, 2nd edn, London 1899, appeared. Hope also published two preliminary studies: 'Notes on the Architectural History of Rochester Cathedral Church', *Transactions of St Paul's Ecclesiological Society*, i (1881–5), pp. 217–30 (hereafter cited as Hope [1881–5]), and 'Gundulf's Tower at Rochester, and the First Norman Cathedral Church There', *Archaeologia*, xlix (1886), pp. 322–34 (hereafter cited as Hope [1886]); a brief summary, 'Rochester Cathedral Church', appeared in *The Builder*, lxi, no. 2539 (3 October 1891), pp. 259–61.

3   The papers of James Thomas Irvine, relating to his role as clerk of the works, are now on deposit in the Medway Studies Centre, see specifically Emf 77/1–135.

4   *Willelmi Malmesbiriensis Monachi de Gestis Pontificum Anglorum libri quinque*, ed. N.E.S.A. Hamilton (Rolls Series 52), London 1870, p. 136.

The *Vita Gundulfi Episcopi Roffensis* (British Library, Cotton MS Nero A.VIII), ff. 55[52]r–v (*Anglia Sacra*, ed. Henry Wharton, 2 vols, London 1691 [hereafter Wharton, *Anglia Sacra*], ii, p. 280; *The Life of the Venerable Man, Gundulf, Bishop of Rochester*, trans. the nuns of Malling Abbey, West Malling 1968, p. 25; *The Life of Gundulf, Bishop of Rochester*, ed. R. Thomson, Toronto 1977, p. 40; and exerpt in O. Lehmann-Brockhaus, *Lateinischen Schriftquellen zur Kunst in England, Wales und Schottland, vom Jahr 901 bis zum Jahre 1307*, 5 vols, Munich 1955–60, ii [1956], p. 390, no. 3710) states the old church had been destroyed.

dirutam, novam ex integro, ut hodie apparet, aedificavit'.[5] Construction of the new cathedral, however, may not have begun until as late as 1082/3,[6] at which time Lanfranc introduced monks in place of the secular canons.[7] Although the archbishop had been able to regain most of the property alienated from the see in 1076, and the next year returned some of the income to Rochester in order to re-establish its fortunes, other property regained in 1076 was not returned until 1083, at which time he – Lanfranc – made additional gifts of land he had newly purchased; Gundulf also apparently acquired property between 1077 and 1083.[8]

Of the early Romanesque church erected under Gundulf, the only part that has survived later reconstruction is its crypt, and it is not complete. Still visible are the two western bays of a crypt which once extended at least one bay farther east. They are divided into a nave and aisles by thick walls, with plain arched openings allowing lateral communication. The nave retains six bays of original groin vaulting supported on two slender monolithic round piers and coursed, half-column wall responds. On each side at the east, the capital only of one more wall respond can be seen embedded in the later Gothic masonry, implying there was at least one more free-standing row of round piers to the east. The profile of the base mouldings consists of a torus above a quarter curve; the capitals are neither conventional volute nor scallop-cushion, but are a more primitive cushion type with a straight-sided abacus above. In the aisles,

5 R1, f. 172 (*Textus Roffensis*, ed. Thomas Hearne, London 1720 [hereafter Hearne, *Textus*], p. 143. Facsimile edition: *Early English Manuscripts in Facsimile*, vols 7 and 11: *The Textus Roffensis*, ed. P. Sawyer, Part I, Copenhagen 1957, Part II, Copenhagen 1962). See also R.W. Southern, 'Aspects of the European Tradition of Historical Writing: 4. The Sense of the Past', *Transactions of the Royal Historical Society*, 5th Ser., xiii (1973), p. 253. According to a number of sources, Lanfranc was generous in his support of the new construction: *Vita Gundulfi*, ff. 55[52]r–v; *Eadmeri Historia Novorum in Anglia*, ed. M. Rule (Rolls Series 81), London 1884, p. 15; and *Gervasii Monachi Cantuariensis [actus pontificum Cantuariensis ecclesiae]* in *The Historical Works of Gervase of Canterbury*, ed. W. Stubbs (Rolls Series 73), 2 vols, London 1879 and 1880, ii, p. 368 (Lehmann-Brockhaus, *op. cit.*, p. 390, no. 3712). In the *Mortilogium Ecclesiae Christi Cantuariae* (Lambeth Palace Library, MS 20; c.1520), f. 190 (cited by Hope [1900], 7), the construction of the new cathedral is credited entirely to Lanfranc.
   On Gundulf, see R.A.L. Smith, 'The Place of Gundulf in the Anglo-Norman church', *English Historical Review*, lviii (1943), pp. 257–72.
6 Hope (1886), 324–5, and (1900), 5. Cf. R. Gem, 'The Origins of the Early Romanesque Architecture of England', Cambridge Ph.D., 1974, p. 545: church begun shortly after 1077; advanced far enough by 1083 to receive the monks. It should be noted that the translation of the relics of Bishop Paulinus (625–644) did not take place until c.1088 (*Vita Gundulfi*, f. 56[53]r [Wharton, *Anglia Sacra*, ii, p. 280; Lehmann-Brockhaus, *op. cit.*, p. 391, no. 3715] and Cotton MS Vespasian A.XXII, f. 86[88]r [*Registrum Temporalium Ecclesie et Episcopatus Roffensis* (*Registrum Roffense*, ed. J. Thorpe, London 1769 [hereafter Thorpe, *Registrum*]), p. 120; Lehmann Brockhaus, p. 390, no. 3713]): if the quire was complete in 1083, one would expect the translation to have been about the same date, especially if the relics were placed in the crypt.
7 R.C. Fowler, 'Cathedral Priory of St Andrew, Rochester', in *VCH, Kent*, ii, London 1926, p. 121; A.M. Oakley, 'The Cathedral Priory of St Andrew, Rochester', *Arch. Cant.*, xci (1975), p. 48. For the pre-Lanfranc secular history of Rochester see R.A.L. Smith, 'The Early Community of St Andrew at Rochester', *The English Historical Review*, lx (1945), pp. 289–99.
8 Hope (1886), p. 325, and (1900), p. 7. For a summary of the financial history between 1066 and 1083 see Oakley, *op. cit.*, pp. 48–50.

also groin vaulted, the responds are flat pilasters with quirked and chamfered imposts.

Entrance to the crypt was by stairways at the west end of the original quire aisles: a blocked doorway at the end of the north aisle of the crypt is still visible (Plate 13). Two windows, later altered, remain on the north, one – later enlarged to a doorway – on the south; the east edge of an external flat pilaster buttress is also visible on the south, to the west of the former window.

The supposed eastern limit of the crypt, in the form of 'foundations of a huge rubble wall . . . upwards of eight feet thick', reportedly was found by boring in 1853,[9] at a distance far enough east of the surviving portion of the crypt to suggest a total original length of four bays. In 1881 Hope conducted further investigations and claimed to have discovered a projecting rectangular chapel, nine feet wide by six feet six inches long, at the east; he also confirmed the wall earlier discovered by A. Ashpitel, but determined it had extended across the aisles as well.[10] Despite Hope's repeated claims that he carefully traced the outline of the chapel himself, his attribution of these purported foundations to the late eleventh-century building may be questioned. The exact nature and extent of Hope's excavations is not at all clear and, unfortunately, his investigations were not documented by plans or sections, let alone by photography.[11]

Until proper excavations are carried out, the possibility that the east end of the first post-Conquest church consisted of a small crypt terminating in three apses must be considered. A crypt of this conventional plan can be more easily reconciled with the only other remains of the church, the solid side walls of the quire now incorporated in the later Gothic remodelling. Hope's reconstruction of a seven bay, straight-ended quire over a crypt nearly as large, both with a tiny projecting oblong eastern chapel,[12] in the light of subsequent developments, not only in Early English Gothic architecture, but especially at Rochester, appears both implausible and inexplicably precocious.[13] A building with a quire of more modest length, with solid side walls, and apses terminating quire and aisles, fits more comfortably into the late

[9] A. Ashpitel, 'Rochester Cathedral', *Journal of the British Archaeological Association*, ix (1854), p. 275.

[10] Hope (1881–5), pp. 219–20, and (1886), p. 329.

[11] The only contemporary document known to me is a letter of 20 October 1881, Emf 77/81 with a brief one–line description.

[12] Hope (1881–5), p. 220, (1886), p. 331, and (1900), pp. 15, 16; he stated a length of six bays but his plan shows seven.

[13] Admittedly, this plan has been generally accepted: e.g., F. Bond, *An Introduction to English Church Architecture*, 2 vols, London 1913, ii, pp. 134, 136; or more recently, as possible for the late Eleventh century, by Gem, *op. cit.*, pp. 545–8, and *idem*, 'The Significance of the eleventh-century Rebuilding of Christ Church and St Augustine's, Canterbury, in the Development of Romanesque Architecture', *Medieval Art and Architecture at Canterbury before 1220*, eds N. Coldstream and P. Draper, London 1982, p. 11 and fig. 5. For the type see M.F. Hearn, 'The Rectangular Ambulatory in English Medieval Architecture', *Journal of the Society of Architectural Historians*, xxx (1971), pp. 187–208; he accepted Rochester as possibly the earliest example, but preferred a date of 1115–25 (the time of Bishop Ernulf).

eleventh century, and, especially, the ambience of Lanfranc's cathedral with its short apsidal quire and crypt below.[14]

Hope's reconstruction of other aspects of Gundulf's church most probably should also be rejected, in favour of less unusual, less eccentric solutions. A church with a normal crossing and transept is more likely than the plan advanced by Hope consisting of a building with projecting narrow 'wings' in place of a transept and a small tower 'balancing' the larger mass of the earlier northern tower (now familiarly referred to as 'Gundulf's Tower') on the east side of the south 'wing'.[15] Of the nave of this building, little can be said except that like its successor it was aisled and eight bays in length.

The underpinnning of the existing west front in 1888 is notable for having revealed an earlier Romanesque one.[16] It was a simple west wall, with pilaster buttresses at the angles and in the line of the nave arcades, and a central portal of three orders. In other words, the facade was of the common sectional type, and did not anticipate in any particular way the unique aspects of the later (existing) one belonging to the beginning of the third quarter of the twelfth century. Thus, the transept, nave, and, especially, the west front, all appear to have been 'standard', except for the apparent lack of projecting chapels in the transept arms.[17]

(2) Alterations and rebuilding in the twelfth century

The nave and the west front now form the most obvious and conspicuous remains of the Romanesque period. They clearly date from the twelfth century, not the eleventh, from a later rebuilding which replaced the nave of the structure begun and finished by Gundulf.[18] Because they still exist, it might be thought they present fewer problems of interpretation than does the largely destroyed eleventh-century building.

---

[14] H.J.A. Strik, 'Remains of the Lanfranc Building in the Great Central Tower and the North-west Choir/Transept Area', Coldstream and Draper, op. cit., p. 25 and figs 3, 5.

[15] Hope (1881–5), p. 220, (1886), pp. 325, 332, 333, and (1900), p. 10, 17–18, and pl. I (plan). The tower itself has been omitted from this study for the reasons cited in n. 1. I am inclined to believe it predates Gundulf, but see T. Tatton-Brown, ' "Gundulf's" Tower', Friends of Rochester Cathedral: Report for 1990/91 (1991), pp. 7–12, who favours a date of c.1150.

[16] G.M. Livett, 'Foundations of the Saxon Cathedral Church at Rochester', Arch. Cant., xviii (1889), pp. 269–76, pl. II, nos 3, 5. Documents relating to the restoration under the direction of the Gothic Revival architect, John Loughborough Pearson (1817–97), are found in Emf 65/9–30, 34, 42, 43, 45, 48, of which perhaps the most interesting with respect to the west front are 9, 16, 17, and 48. Tracings from a notebook of John Thompson of Peterborough, the contractor for the work, were later made by Irvine: see Emf 77/90–91.

[17] Transept chapels were probably also lacking at the nunnery church of West Malling: F.H. Fairweather, 'The Abbey of St Mary, Malling, Kent', Archaeological Journal, lxxxviii (1931), plan between pp. 174–5, F.C. Elliston-Erwood, 'The Plan of the Abbey Church of the Benedictine Nunnery of Saint Mary, West Malling, Kent', Antiquaries Journal, xxxiv (1954), plan, pl. X between pp. 56–7.

[18] Despite the fact that the inside of the first facade was plastered right down to its footing, Livett, op. cit., p. 276, and after him Hope (1881–5), p. 221, and (1900), pp. 18, 23–4, maintained that the first church was never completed, mainly because, in the first bay of the north aisle, the so-called 'Early Norman' walling, of which two unplastered courses remained, was succeeded by 'at least and inch of mould' before a Later-Norman course of tufa took its place.

Such, however, is not the case for, although some attention has been focused on them, there has been, historically, little agreement about the precise date of their construction. And there is evidence that the initial intentions were altered in the course of construction, even if the exact sequence of events is not always easy to determine; the reasons for the changes are seldom apparent.

The nave design most obviously is not complete. The Romanesque clerestory and roof were replaced in the Perpendicular period (fifteenth century) and the easternmost bays were lost owing to an aborted project to rebuild the entire nave begun in the mid thirteenth century. In the aisles, all the Romanesque windows have been replaced, and the eastern three bays on the south were mostly removed by the construction, c.1500, of a large structure (now generally identified as the Lady Chapel) opening off the west side of the south transept arm.

Less conspicuous is the loss of much of the fabric of the aisle walls, especially as the interior surfaces of the walls are heavily plastered. The remaining bays of the south aisle wall, west of the Perpendicular addition up to the south-west stair-tower, are largely the result of necessary conservation work carried out in the second half of the seventeenth century.[19] About the same time, the north aisle was rebuilt from the buttress to the west of the third bay from the east (the joint is on the east side of the buttress) to the seventh bay, above the inserted Perpendicular door and window (the buttress to the west was rebuilt in 1802).[20] It appears the Gothic windows were reset during the seventeenth-century rebuilding, as only that in the fifth bay has been entirely renewed.

The Romanesque fabric of the north aisle wall therefore consists of the remains of two buttresses and three bays of a decorated string-course at the east end of the aisle, as well as a length of decorated string-course in the western bay (Plate 14a). The buttresses, of the shallow pilaster type, are executed in ashlar: the eastern one rises to, or near, its original height; the western has been truncated at the string-course. The west section of string-course, which is carved with lozenges decorated with pellets, has been reset, no doubt when the north-west angle

---

[19] Hope (1900), p. 89, cited the date 1664 for the south aisle wall, the basis for which is a stone embedded in the wall under the remaining eastmost window bearing the letters 'C/IG' under the date '1664'.

[20] Hope (1900), p. 89, gave 1670 for the rebuilding of the north aisle wall. According to S. Denne, 'Memorials of the Cathedral Church of Rochester', *Custumale Roffense, from the original manuscript in the archives of the Dean and Chapter of Rochester*, ed. J. Thorpe, London 1788 (hereafter Thorpe, *Custumale*), p. 182, in 1670, a Robert Cable was to take down forty feet of the north wall and rebuild it. Emf 5/2, 'A Survey of the Bricklayers and Masons and Plasterers Worke of necessary renovations of Cathedral church', 14 August 1660, from Thomas Flight and John Nellis, includes references to the 'repairing' of both the north and south aisles without specifying the extent of the work required. If the north wall was rebuilt in the 1660s, it was not done very well as in 1760 this wall is described by Henry Keene, in Emf 34, as considerably bulged or thrust out in the middle. Forty years later, Daniel Alexander, in his 'Report on a General Survey of Rochester Cathedral', November 1799, Emf 38, noted that the north aisle wall was in a bad state, and in a subsequent survey, Emf 47/1, 'Report on the State and Condition of the North Wall of the West Nave of the Cathedral', 9 September 1802, he described the whole wall as leaning outwards, eleven inches at the west end and three inches at the east.

stair-tower was rebuilt in 1888, at a higher level than the section remaining *in situ* at the east end of the same wall.[21]

The south wall was perhaps only refaced rather than rebuilt, but as the inner face of the wall is completely plastered, it is impossible to know how much, if any, may be original work. It is worthy of note that the responds have a much stronger projection than those of the north aisle. Nothing original is visible on the exterior of the south aisle except the (restored) lower courses of four buttresses.[22] The top three to four feet of this wall were rebuilt in 1801 but are of a (deliberately) different character from work at the same level on the north side, carried out in 1802 (Plate 14b).[23]

Of the exterior design of the Romanesque clerestory, only a hint remains. On the south side adjacent to the stair-tower at the west end of the nave arcade, there is an angle-shaft which is best explained as the terminal shaft of bays of blind arcading which would have flanked the clerestory windows (Plate 15).

In the interior, original details consist of only the two eastern buttress-like responds of the north aisle, accompanied by a stretch of decorated string-course extending over three bays (Plate 16), and a section of decorated string in the west bay of the south aisle. The form of the responds up to the string-course is that of a shallow pilaster (like the exterior buttresses); above that level, for an equal height, they gain slender angle-shafts; a third section is again a plain pilaster, shallower than the lower part. The string-course at the east end of the north aisle is carved with a kind of double or overlapping zigzag with rosettes in the resulting lozenge-shaped centres; the pattern on the string-course at the west end of the south aisle is quite different, as it is a type of double scale pattern with raised edges and small circles at the junction of the scallops.

Of the nave arcade, five pairs of piers plus the west responds remain, along with the second-storey arches (Plate 12). Together they constitute one of the more unusual and curious nave designs in twelfth-century architecture. Three features in particular are remarkable. Each pair of piers is of a different design; there is neither vault nor floor separating the two stages in the aisles; and a passageway runs through the thickness of the second-storey arcade wall. Other features of interest are the half-shafts which once rose up the wall from the level of the nave pier abaci to the clerestory, but which now stop at the floor of the second stage, and the diaper patterns applied to all the tympana in the second storey.

From east to west, the pier designs are: a square core with a large half-shaft on each face;[24] a quatrefoil shape created by round columns at the angles with half-shafts

[21] Palmer, *op cit.*, pp. 36–7; also see above, n. 16.

[22] The remnants of the buttresses were probably restored by Scott. They had been preserved, despite the seventeenth century refacing of the wall above them, because the ground level around the cathedral was not lowered to near its original level until the early nineteenth century: see the report of Robert Smirke, Emf 52/1, 'Remarks on the State of Rochester Cathedral at a Survey made on March 11, 1825', pp. 1–2.

[23] See Emf 40, 'Specification of Repairs to be made at the Cathedral, Rochester', March 1801, and Emf 42, 'Specification of Sundry Work to be done to Rochester Cathedral', May 1802.

[24] In his plan, Gem, *Medieval Art*, p. 12, fig. 5, shows them as part of Gundulf's work. Yet these

in between on each face;[25] a cruciform core with two half-shafts on the north and south faces, three on the east and west faces, and re-entrant shafts; an oblong core with a half-round pier on the wider east and west faces flanked by shafts, and a large half-shaft to north and south; and, finally, an elongated octagon (long axis east-west).[26] The west responds consist of two half-shafts engaged to a broad pilaster flanked by angle-shafts.[27] The west face of the partially rebuilt pier at the east retains a large half-shaft against a rectangular(?) core, but there is no trace of a similar shaft on the aisle or nave faces.

These florid designs rise from bases which are square and simply chamfered – the four western ones of the north arcade bearing spurs (Plate 17).[28] It may be noted that the south-eastern half-Romanesque/half-Gothic pier, which has a more elaborate base consisting of two thin rolls above a narrow quarter-hollow, like the corresponding (rebuilt, Gothic) pier in the north arcade, sits on an octagonal plinth (the easternmost pair of Gothic piers do not have a single large plinth of a simple geometric shape but, instead, one that anticipates the outline of the heavily moulded Purbeck bases of their pier shafts). Chamfered plinths were also found under the aisle responds: they remain under the first, fourth, fifth, and sixth (counting from the east) responds of the north wall.

The abaci are all uniform with a roll inserted between the straight and hollow chamfered sections. The inner or lower order of each arcade is unmoulded (those on the south are plastered over), while each outer order bears a chevron design, identical on north and south; the label received a large nailhead motif. Finally, a string-course consisting of a broad fillet and a roll runs under the second stage. Above the capitals,

---

piers stand on simple, large, square, chamfered bases like all the others. The nature of their coursing also corresponds to that of the other piers to the west: the coursing on all piers is somewhat variable and not uniformly consistent in height.

[25] The second pair were compared by B. Cherry, 'Romanesque Architecture in Eastern England', *Journal of the British Archaeological Association*, cxxxi (1978), p. 23, to Great Paxton, and accepted by E. Fernie, 'The Romanesque Church at Waltham Abbey', *Journal of the British Archaeological Association*, cxxxviii (1985), p. 72, 'as an example of the revival of interest in Anglo-Saxon architectural forms in Anglo-Norman England'.

[26] These piers are somewhat larger than the others: their increased size has been taken as an indication of an intention to construct two west towers. Additional evidence was found during the underpinning of the north aisle in 1875 and of the west front in 1888 in the form of large tufa blocks: see Emf 77/77 (letter of Irvine), and 77/39 (tiny sketch of location of foundations); also Hope (1881–5), p. 221; Livett, *op. cit.*, p. 278; Hope (1900), p. 28.

[27] The plans of the piers and west respond were recorded in Thorpe, *Custumale*, pl. XXXIV.

M.J. Swanton, 'A Mural Palimpsest from Rochester Cathedral', *Archaeological Journal*, cxxxvi (1979), pp. 125–35, and 'The Decoration of Ernulf's Nave', *Friends of Rochester Cathedral: Report for 1989/90*, pp. 11–18, has detected incised graffiti on the nave piers which he has interpreted as various religious figures and scenes. Whatever they represent, it is most unlikely, as he suggests (134/17), that the Romanesque piers were originally frescoed and covered by a figurative programme.

[28] N. Pevsner and P. Metcalf, *The Cathedrals of England: Southern England*, Harmondsworth 1985, p. 238: 'Some of the pier bases are of brown local marble'; why it is said 'some' and not 'all' is not clear, as all are of the same stone. That stone is limestone which at some time, presumably in the nineteenth century, has been varnished thus giving it a Purbeck-like appearance: I have been enlightened on this point by T. Tatton-Brown to whom I am indebted.

a single shaft formerly rose up the elevation in each bay. The pier designs are so eccentric and complex that in no case could these shafts be coordinated with a similar element of the pier, except in the case of the easternmost remaining pair, which is the simplest and most conventional in design.

In a similar but less conspicuous fashion the diaper patterns of the tympana of the second storey are also subject to variation rather than strict repetition (Plate 19a). Although the designs are similar, all are individual arrangements which are not disposed in pairs; generally those on the south are somewhat simpler. The medallions of the four north-east bays are the most similar of any; the tympana of the second, fourth, and fifth (east to west) bays on the south are the most neatly arranged. Hope thought the diapering was a later insertion, and that the space between the upper and lower arches was originally open, as in the eastern nave bays at Romsey Abbey, because of irregularities in the coursing of the pattern, 'many of them being chopped up to fit them in'.[29] The irregularities, however, seem the result of carelessness because they occur in the lower courses, above the double arches, not at the outer circumference where they would be expected if the space was filled in later. In contrast to the variety displayed in the tympana, the mouldings and decoration of the gallery arches like those of the main arcade are more uniform and consistent, including also the use of multiscallop capitals. The chamfered labels are decorated with a scallop pattern.

Within the decorative details, there are indications of the sequence of the work, if one accepts a general tendency towards more complex forms as a line of development. Thus, all the capitals on the north main arcade have more numerous scallops than those on the south, and became progressively richer from east to west. The four west piers on that side also are the only ones to bear spurs – in a leaf design – on their base plinths,[30] although it is the spandrels above the westernmost pier on the south which received a pair of sunk roundels with chevroned frames.

The design bears evidence of several changes of intentions.[31] The rough or uneven surface of the spandrels around the arches on the north aisle side suggest there was once preparation for, or at least the intention to erect, vaults over the aisle at this level (Plate 18).[32] The spandrels on the south are smoother, more finished, and suggest that the idea of vaulting the aisles was given up before this arcade was constructed. The aisle side of the south arcade also lacks the chevron decorated order and label with a radial zigzag found on the north, while there is a chamfered string

[29] Hope (1881–5), p. 221, and Hope (1900), p. 27. For Romsey see M.F. Hearn, 'A Note on the Chronology of Romsey Abbey', *Journal of the British Archaeological Association*, 3rd Ser., xxxii (1969), esp. pp. 35–8 for the east bay of the nave arcade (c.1140/5–50).

[30] Mary R. Covert brought to my attention a small griffe on the base of the shaft at the south-west angle of the third pier from the west in the south arcade. Beak-shaped spurs occur on the bases of the shafts to the chapter house doorway, c.1140, a work roughly contemporary with the nave.

[31] These are spelled out in detail in J.P. McAleer, 'Some Observations on the Building Sequence of the Nave of Rochester Cathedral', *Arch. Cant.*, cii (1985), pp. 158–66.

[32] Also noted by Gem, Ph.D. thesis, pp. 552–53, but attributed to the earlier building (Gundulf's), the form of the intended vaults groin; he observed the evidence is stronger in the *north* aisle, which no one else except Ashpitel, *op. cit.*, p. 274, has suggested is of Gundulf's period.

under the gallery sill. On both sides, however, pilasters rise from the arcade capitals into the gallery level.

Judging from the height and width of the arches, if the existing design can be taken as a reflection of the original intentions, a type of gallery was anticipated – the arcades opening into the area above the aisle vaults and under the sloping roof covering them. It would have been either a false gallery, if there was neither exterior wall nor windows (hence, a low dark space lighted only from the nave), or a low gallery (as at Durham), if there was a low exterior wall (i.e. one not equal in height to the arcade) and external windows. Other subdivided gallery arches of similar proportions are found at Christchurch Priory, Chichester and Hereford cathedrals.[33] The decision to abandon vaulting certainly affected the design of the second storey in one respect. As a result of the elimination of the aisle vaults, a passageway through the second-storey piers was included in the construction of the 'pseudo-gallery'.[34] It also became necessary to carry up the aisle walls higher than was first planned. As actually executed, the second-storey arcade displays the same uniformity in design as the nave arcade, since the tympana patterns, despite their variety, do not show any significantly richer effects at the west than the east. The only progression revealed is the appearance of a few varied leaf capitals replacing the multi-scallop type in the last three bays on the south and last two on the north.

The nave was attributed to Bishop Ernulf (1114–24), Gundulf's successor, as a rebuilding of the latter's, by Hope,[35] despite the lack of any documentary evidence, and his dating has been perpetuated in the subsequent literature. However, the style of the nave makes it evident that it could not have been built before 1124 and more likely that the rebuilding of the nave was a consequence of the fire of 1137 which is said to have ravaged Rochester city, cathedral and monastery.[36] The building of the nave should then be placed in the 1140s, extending possibly into the early 1150s. Whether or not it was preceded by any extensive work at the east end which might account for the supposed foundations of a (enlarged) straight-ended east end 'revealed' in the nineteenth century by Hope, again must remain only a hypothetical possibility until excavations are carried out.

The existing west front (Plate 4b) was not built with the aisle walls and nave arcades. There is a pair of vertical joints visible at the end of each arcade: the coursing

---

[33] Cherry, *op. cit.*, p. 8, n. 21.

[34] A.W. Clapham, *English Romanesque Architecture*, II. *After the Conquest*, Oxford 1934, p. 55, n. 2, dated the removal of the aisle vault to 1137 – following the fire – when 'a triforum passage [was] contrived in the thickness of the main wall, between the triforum openings'. Regardless of date, this is incorrect, as the passageway was definitely *built* with the arcade and was not cut through at a later date.

  Hope (1881–5), p. 221, and (1900), p. 27, stressed that the arches of the wall 'passage' throughout are *pointed*, not round. This, too, is incorrect, as many are either semicircular or ambiguous in shape; there is no sequence to the varied forms.

[35] Hope (1881–5), pp. 221–2, and (1900), pp. 24, 25.

[36] Stubbs, *op. cit.*, i, p. 100. Also BL, Cotton MS Vespasian A.XXII, f. 29[28]v. BL, Cotton MS Nero D.II, f. 112[111]v, gives the date as 1138: Wharton, *Anglia Sacra*, i, p. 343. The damage to the monastic buildings was great enough to make it necessary for the monks to seek temporary refuge elsewhere: Fowler, *op. cit.*, p. 122.

is not continuous across the responds and the west wall.[37] This suggests that the arcades were built while the first facade was still standing, and that it was only replaced as the last phase of work. The enlarged scale of the western piers further suggests there had been some thought of erecting a pair of west towers. This implication appears to have been confirmed during the underpinning of the north aisle wall in 1875–6, and later, in 1888, of the west front, when large blocks of (reused?) tufa were found. They were interpreted as the beginning of foundations for a west tower.[38]

The interior design of the west wall at Rochester has been gravely affected by the insertion of the Perpendicular west window; although traces of the original arrangement remain, they are not fully revealing of all its particulars.[39] The central portal is flanked by two registers of three arcades equivalent to the nave arcade in height. Preserved at the sides of the west window are the first bays of two additional registers, the lower one of which only roughly corresponds to the height of the second storey of the nave. It would seem the lower arcade was originally open.[40] There is no evidence for the size or shape of the Romanesque west window, although it has been suggested it may have been round.[41]

The unseen internal arrangements of the facade are perhaps as interesting as the visible ones of its wall faces. The spacious, generously proportioned newel-stairs of the angle stair-towers lead up to a passageway in the thickness of the wall which crosses the front below the sills of the upper aisle-end windows, and which corresponded to the (lost) register of arcading immediately above the central portal's arch.[42] This wall passage also gave access to the passageways through the second-stage arcades.[43] At the junction with the nave arcades, narrow newel-stairs lead to higher levels: to the original clerestory, to a passageway across the level of the gable, and to the nave roof eaves; the well-formed exits from the newel-stairs are preserved at all levels on both sides.[44] At clerestory level, there is also evidence of a second passageway across the west front. It would have been behind the uppermost level of internal arcading, and must have been supported above the lower passageway by means of a series of small vaults.

Despite the fact the west front is modest in scale and in its basic architectural form,

---

[37] The west bays of the nave arcades and the west front had been identified as a separate build, one attributed to Ernulf, by Ashpitel, *op. cit.*, p. 274.

[38] Livett, *op. cit.*, p. 278; Hope (1900), p. 28: unfortunately, no precise plan (or description) of these blocks was given. Irvine's papers include only one tiny sketch, Emf 77/39; see also a brief reference in Emf 77/77 (undated letter from Irvine, probably to Hope).

[39] For full discussion see J.P. McAleer, 'The West Front of Rochester Cathedral: the Interior Design', *Arch. Cant.*, ciii (1986), pp. 27–43.

[40] Hope (1900), p. 30, specified 'an arcade of seven Norman arches alternately blind and open'.

[41] Hope (1900), p. 30: 'large circular or other window, or pair of windows'. For fuller particulars see McAleer, *op. cit.*, p. 35 and nn. 18, 19.

[42] The base of the north-west angle stair-tower is solid up to this level, presumably as a result of its rebuilding, first in the 1760s (see below n. 48) and again in 1888 (see below n. 47); there is no evidence as to whether it originally had a newel-stair from the ground up.

[43] The passages were blocked up c.1875, during the restoration directed by Scott, at which time iron tie rods were inserted: see Emf 65/3.

[44] See McAleer, *op. cit.*, pp. 27–31, for full description of the circulation system.

it is not without impact due to its richly arcaded and decorated exterior surfaces (Plate 19b). Nor is the fundamental form without interest with respect to the history of facade design in this century, as it is neither of the two standard types – the sectional facade and the twin-tower facade – that predominated, although it is closer to the former than the latter.[45] Rather it represents the beginnings of a new type, the screen facade, which will climax in the next century, as at Salisbury Cathedral.

The Romanesque design of the facade now appears complete, except for the obvious destruction wrought by the intrusion of the great west window. It was, however, subjected to considerable deconstruction and restoration during the eighteenth and nineteenth centuries.[46] Only at the end of the last century was it returned more or less accurately to its late medieval appearance.[47] Much of this work of subtraction and addition affected the four turrets, one of the facade's most conspicuous features. Actually, the angle turrets are small stair-towers because they contain unusually ample newel-stairs within. Only the turret in the line of the south arcade is original, for the north one had been rebuilt in the Perpendicular period. It was replaced with a copy of the south one during the restoration begun in 1888. Of the angle stair-towers, only the lower two registers of the southern one are original: its upper stages were removed between 1772 and 1816 and rebuilt during the restoration of 1888. The north angle tower has been twice rebuilt from the ground up. In the 1760s, it was torn down and then rebuilt only to a height equal to the north aisle.[48] During the restoration of 1888 that work was completely taken down and the tower rebuilt: its reconstruction and the octagonal stages of the southern one were based on early engraved views. Finally, with respect to the aisle end walls, the arrangement of graduated arcades, which reflected the original slope of the roofs over the aisles, had survived only on the south side where it had been incorporated under a horizontal parapet which was the result of the flatter roof placed over the aisle in the course of the Perpendicular alterations. On the north side, the graduated arcade disappeared during the 1760s rebuilding of the north angle stair-tower; it was

---

[45] See J.P. McAleer, 'The Significance of the West Front of Rochester Cathedral', *Arch. Cant.*, xcix (1983), pp. 139–58.

[46] The small vignette of the cathedral in the (lower left) margin of the large engraving, 'View of the City of Rochester' (T. Pradeslade, Delin., J. Harris, sculpt.) from J. Harris, *The History of Kent*, London 1719, between pp. 250–1, depicts the west front before the modern alterations.

[47] Palmer, *op. cit.*, pp. 26, 30, 36–7. Also see above n. 16.

[48] See Emf 32, 'Report of Repairs Absolutely Wanting to be Done', 15 July 1760, and Emf 34, 'A Survey of the State and Condition of the Buildings of the Cathedral Church of Rochester', 11 October 1760, prepared by Henry Keene. According to Denne, *op. cit.*, in Thorpe, *Custumale*, p. 183, the north-west tower was taken down in 1763 and rebuilt, probably with money left for the repair of the fabric in the will of Dean John Newcombe (d.1765). By June 1769, the north-west stair-tower was nearing completion: Emf 35/2–3, estimates from plumbers and carpenters for roofing the 'New tower', 30 June 1769.

Two engravings of 1772 show the result of the rebuilding of the north angle stair-tower: *Gentleman's Magazine*, xlii (December 1772), facing p. 576 (B. Cole, Sculp.); and [?Denne and Shrubsole,] *The History and Antiquities of Rochester and its Environs*, London 1772, facing p. 57 (F. Baker del.). Crenellations were added to the stair-tower and the aisle end walls at the same time.

replaced by an arcade of three tall bays, the centre one with an ogee arch. The original design was restored in 1888.[49]

The facade is characterized by the clear and emphatic articulation of its five components: the two large stair-towers at the angles of the aisles, the terminal walls of the aisles, and the end wall of the nave (Plate 19b). The articulation is achieved by setting back the walls of the aisle, thus throwing the nave end and the stair-towers into prominent relief. Rather unusually, no buttresses are used. Originally, there was only one west portal, the central one (the north aisle portal is a later, probably late thirteenth-century, insertion) which is flanked by shallow arched recesses. Taller shallow recesses were placed in the aisle facades, high enough to rise over the windows at the end of the aisles.

The surfaces are decorated with registers of arcading which were not continuous in design or level, but which were symmetrically disposed on the five planes. Three registers above a plain dado are on the nave end: the archivolts of the central portal interrupt the lowest; the later Perpendicular window has displaced most of the two upper ones. An additional three registers of arcading, again above a plain dado, are found on the turrets which rise out of the angles of the nave end and which originally flanked a steeply pitched gable. And, as noted, on each aisle end, a band of arcades gradated in height corresponded to the original slope of the aisle roof. Each angle stair-tower received four registers of arcading different in height and detail from those of the nave end.

The decorative motifs of the nave end are rich and varied, and include notable features such as small carved tympana under the second register of arcading (Plate 20). As to the portal proper, in addition to the notable presence of figurative sculpture in the form of two column figures, unusual for England, and a carved lintel and tympanum, there are a number of distinctive features. The shafts of the three outer orders employ shaft-rings which were not simple mouldings but were carved with various motifs, all now badly eroded.[50] The capitals of the shafts are also richly carved: in most cases their underlying form is that of the cushion type. The five orders of the portal are also all richly carved with deeply undercut motifs of similar but varying patterns. But it is the figure sculpture, rather than the architecture, which has been the main focus of scholarly attention.

The date of the west front, as calculated in the past, has usually been influenced

[49] The engraving by John Coney for J. Caley, H. Ellis and B. Bandinel, *Dugdale's Monasticon Anglicanum*, i (1817), between pp. 152–3, shows the west front after all the eighteenth-century alterations. Also see two drawings by L.N. Cottingham, 'West Front and Tower of Rochester Cathedral as it appeared previous to the repairs in 1825', and 'Restoration of the West Front of Rochester Cathedral with the Ashlering of &c to the Tower when finished': the latter shows the facade according to Cottingham's proposed restorations which were not carried out. See also Plate 4b.

[50] According to T.W.T. Tatton-Brown, 'Building Stone in Canterbury c.1070–1525', *Stone: Quarrying and Building in England, AD 43–1525*, ed. D. Parsons, Chichester 1990, pp. 74, 75, the material of the outer shaft on the north is onyx – a material which appears slightly earlier on the cloister facade of the dorter undercroft and which was also used in contemporary work of Prior Wibert at Canterbury such as the vestiarum and infirmary cloister, dated c.1155–60 by D. Kahn, *Canterbury Cathedral and Its Romanesque Sculpture*, London and Austin 1991, pp. 107, 111.

by that assigned to the column figures of its west portal.[51] These figures, once thought to be insertions of c.1180, then considered originals of c.1160,[52] could just as well be products of the early 1150s, at a time when construction of the nave was drawing to a close and plans were being made for the erection of a new facade with greater pretensions than the old one. The style of the column figures has been seen as closely dependent on certain figures of the Royal Portal at Chartres Cathedral, of c.1145,[53] so much so that a date for the Rochester figures of c.1160 seems rather unnecessarily late. There is no stylistic redirection between nave and facade, only an intensification of the enthusiasm for a wide variety of decorative motifs. A date in the 1150s, for both the facade and the west portal sculpture, therefore, seems more likely and most plausible.[54]

II. The Early Gothic Rebuilding

The new work at the east end completely replaced all the Romanesque structure east of the nave proper, except for the supposed solid side walls of its quire and the two western bays of the late eleventh-century crypt. It represents a very considerable enlargement and includes a greatly expanded crypt. The work consists of an aisleless presbytery of two double bays with a straight east wall, an aisled minor east transept extending two bays on either side of the crossing, quire aisles of four bays, a new clerestory and vaults over the quire, and a major east transept – the arms projecting more boldly than the minor ones – with a towered crossing.

Stylistically, but not necessarily chronologically, this work breaks down into five, if not six, phases: presbytery and minor transepts; quire; north and south quire aisles; north arm of major transept; south arm of major transept. Chronologically, it is possible that the quire aisles were being worked on at the same time as the quire; it is also possible that they were constructed separately from each other, as well as from the quire. Work on the crossing relates to the units around it, the quire, the aisles, the transept arms, and reflects their various phases.

---

[51] E.g., Clapham, *op. cit.*, p. 143 and pl. 28 (1160–70).

[52] E.S. Prior and A. Gardner, *An Account of Medieval Figure Sculpture in England*, Cambridge 1912, pp. 194, 201–2. G. Zarnecki, *Later English Romanesque Sculpture, 1140–1210*, London 1953, p. 39, also considered the column figures to be insertions, but dated them c.1175; later he, in 'The Transition from Romanesque to Gothic in English Sculpture', *Studies in Western Art, 1. Romanesque and Gothic Art*, Princeton 1963, p. 155, accepted the column figures as original but retained a date of c.1175; this date was eventually revised by him to c.1160, see 'A Twelfth Century Column Figure of the Standing Virgin and Child from Minster-in-Sheppey, Kent', *Kunsthistorische Forschungen Otto Pächt zu seinen (Ehren) 70 Geburtstag*, eds A. Rosenauer and G. Weber, Salzburg 1972, p. 212 nn. 20, 21.

[53] See especially D. Kahn, 'The West Doorway at Rochester Cathedral', *Romanesque and Gothic: Essays for George Zarnecki*, ed. N. Stratford, 2 vols, Woodbridge 1987, p. 131 n. 24.

[54] In McAleer, *op. cit*, pp. 165–6, I argued for a date of the 1140s and 1150s for the nave (in this respect, coming back to the date proposed by Clapham, *op. cit.*, pl. 22). But the mistaken attribution continues: see Swanton, *op. cit.*

(1) *Presbytery and minor transept: exterior*

The presbytery is characterized by massive turret-like buttresses at its eastern angles which, however, do not contain newel-stairs in their lower half, and by strongly projecting buttresses placed in the middle of the side walls, quite unlike any others used in the construction of the east end because of their four-sided (demi-hexagonal) form. Externally, the new work is extremely plain; the walls are of flint rubble with ashlar used for such elements as angle quoins, string-courses, and a belt at the level of the windows (Plate 21).[55] Each elevation consists of three tiers of windows corresponding to the crypt, main ('ground') floor and clerestory. Ashlar masonry occurs in bands equal to the level of the crypt window arches (spandrels), and the full height of the lower windows, but is not used at the level of the upper windows. It also appears in the crypt level of the eastern turrets, in all of the polygonal buttresses up to the level of the apex of the lower window arches – above which it is used only for the diagonal faces, and for all of the buttresses between the transept chapels.

The crypt windows are of two orders, both of a hollow chamfer, with a double chamfer label, and lack any decorative motifs. The windows of the lower level have a nook-shaft and continuous dog-tooth, while the upper level (clerestory) has a double surround of dog-tooth. It appears that all the windows, including those of the crypt, have been completely restored except for the lower part of the outer, dog-tooth decorated order of the four lower windows of the presbytery north wall.[56]

There are six string-courses above the crypt: at floor level, sill and impost levels of the lower windows, sill and impost levels of the upper windows (the last not continued over the buttresses), and below the parapet; they are each composed of a scotia under a downturned roll, and are undecorated.[57] The turrets and buttresses have bases for angle shafts which were abandoned by the time the level of the first string-course was reached.[58]

The eastern aisles of the minor transept, which internally form two chapels in each arm, have smaller flat-faced buttresses with chamfered angles between the bays, and – on the north arm only – a miniature turret-like buttress at the angle. The chapel blocks terminate in east-facing gables. The chapel windows, like the lower windows of the east front, have been restored with a nook-shaft between rows of dog-tooth.

---

[55] According to G.M. Livett, 'Early-Norman Churches in and near the Medway Valley', *Arch. Cant.*, xx (1893), pp. 153–4, 'the Early English choir and transepts' are built of 'firestone' from quarries at Godstone near Reigate (cf. G.M. Livett, 'Medieval Rochester', *Arch. Cant.*, xxi [1895], pp. 30–1). According to Tatton-Brown, *op. cit.* (n. 50), pp. 76–7, the use of Reigate or Merstham stone began about 1200 in Canterbury.

[56] Before the restoration by Scott, the east clerestory-level window was a nine-light Perpendicular one; the gable was pierced by a single quatrefoil. Its appearance was recorded in a watercolour of 1805 by J.C. Buckler: Dean and Chapter Library, Rochester; see also a pencil drawing in the British Library, Add. MS 36, 368 ('Buckler Architectural Drawings', XIII), f. 83r (1804). Scott's drawings for the restoration, formerly in Dean and Chapter Library, Rochester, are now in the Medway Studies Centre.

[57] According to J. Newman, *The Buildings of England: West Kent and the Weald*, Harmondsworth 1969, p. 458, Scott added the upper two.

[58] Hope (1881–5), p. 224; this change of design is still very evident.

(The south elevation of the presbytery and the lower part of the east face of the south arm of the minor transept are obscured by the structure now serving as the chapter house and library. The presbytery's south elevation is visible from a small court between it and the library.)

The north arm of the minor transept is also characterized by large turrets at its exterior angles which, in this case, each contain newel-stairs beginning at ground level. There are no balancing turrets at the exterior angles of the south arm, no doubt owing to the claustral buildings which once adjoined. The facade of the north arm between the angle turrets is divided into four registers by string-courses continued from the turrets. The lowest contains two windows of the crypt, and, in the westernmost bay, a portal. (The present condition does not allow a judgment as to whether the western bay was originally a window.) The second level was originally blank but a pair of small (restored) two-light windows with Geometric tracery, associated with the tomb recess of Bishop Walter de Merton (1274–7), has been pierced through the middle,[59] as well as a small cusped lancet to the west. The third and fourth registers each have three lancets; three lancets have also been placed in the (restored) gable.

The exterior face of the south minor transept arm, completely refaced by L.N. Cottingham (1787–1847) during restoration work he carried out from 1825 to 1830, was divided into three nearly equal registers by two string-courses.[60] Before restoration, the lowest register retained traces of five arches (abbba), the central three pierced by windows to the crypt; the heavy wall piers of the arcade now take the form of a strongly projecting triangle of three shafts engaged against a pilaster with chamfered jambs.[61] The second level has three windows, the wider central one with a nearly semicircular arch, a large dog-tooth on the jambs, and a continuous label. They are flanked by narrow, equally tall bays with keyhole-shaped arches. Traces of two more similar blind bays were once visible on either side of the three-light window, with elaborate Decorated tracery, inserted in the south wall of the chapel.[62] The third tier possesses only three windows, the middle one tallest and widest, although again decorated with a dog-tooth pattern. A small oculus is now placed in the (restored) gable, again with a continuous label.[63]

[59] See Palmer, op. cit., pp. 97–8.
[60] Hope (1900), pp. 92, 167. The condition of the facade before Cottingham's work is recorded in Thorpe, Custumale, pl. XXXIII, fig. 1 (opp. p. 151); and J. Storer, History and Antiquities of the Cathedral Churches of Great Britain, 4 vols, London 1814–19, iv, [Rochester] pl. 5. For the attempts to deal with the structural problems presented by the south arm in the eighteenth century see Denne, op. cit., in Thorpe, Custumale, p. 169.
[61] Old prints (see above, n. 60) show a doorway with a flat lintel in the east bay. Pearson is said to have re-exposed the old work, which 'Cottingham had covered on the exterior with a copy', and converted it into a window; Hope seemed to regard the doorway as original: (1900), p. 167, and fig. 34 (on p. 91).
[62] According to Hope (1900), p. 167, this Decorated window was replaced by Cottingham and later 'beautified' by Pearson, who apparently replicated the original pattern (based on Storer, op. cit., iv, [Rochester] pl. 5).
[63] The gable was taken down about 1760: its removal was recommended in Emf 32, an unsigned 'Report of Repairs Absolutely Wanting to be done, 15 July 1760'. It was rebuilt to a high pitch by Scott, but the roof has never been raised: Hope (1900), pp. 91, 92.

(2) *Presbytery and minor transept: interior*

The crypt extends under all of the new minor transept, its chapels and the presbytery. The major spaces, corresponding to transept and presbytery, are subdivided into three equal aisles by slender monolithic columns supporting ribbed vaults. Massive rectangular piers mark the position of the eastern crossing piers above, and smaller ones (in terms of north-south thickness) mark the division between the transept chapels, and form support for three arches across the entrance to the eastern arm.[64] Half-shafts, also monoliths, are engaged on the walls and sides of the piers as responds. The crypt was well lighted by three windows in each terminal wall, four in each side wall of the section under the presbytery, with additional ones in the transept chapels. Altogether, there was provision for seven altars: two in each transept arm, and three at the east wall of the east ('presbytery') arm. Small piscinas appear in the north and south-eastern chapels, and the south-east chapel of the north arm: two have trefoil arches and one a semicircular arch (that in the south wall of the south chapel at the east).

The columns are round and octagonal. They alternate in the section under the presbytery; in the section under the transept, the west row is all round but in the east row only those in the line of the crossing are round (thus o, r, o, o, r, o).[65] The capitals are of the moulded bell type, with two rolls at the top separated by a chamfered moulding. The bases are characterized by double rolls separated by a small hollow. There is one aberrant capital and one aberrant base in the 'crossing' area, on different shafts: they each have an unusually large roll. The ribs all have a simple hollow chamfer profile; the diagonal ribs – except in the window recesses – are semicircular. Wall ribs are used in the east arm, and in the chapel bays.

The walls erected above the crypt are anything but thin and their substantial thickness is everywhere revealed in the interior elevation of the presbytery which is divided into two unequal storeys (Plate 22).[66] The lower two-thirds of the wall are treated as a tall continuous arcade, with a single order of Purbeck shafts, forming a deep recess around each window which in addition has an order of limestone shafts.[67] Triple or single shafts are placed between the window arcades corresponding to the major or minor divisions of the main sexpartite vault. There are four windows in the long side walls, two tiers of three on the east wall (the lower east windows have two orders of non-Purbeck shafts and capitals).[68] In addition to shafts, Purbeck is used

---

[64] These two piers partly occupy the site – as identified by Hope (1900), pl. III – of the purported projecting east chapel of the earlier crypt.

[65] See L. Hoey, 'Pier Alternation in Early English Gothic Architecture', *Journal of the British Archaeological Association*, cxix (1986), p. 52.

[66] Newman, *op. cit.*, p. 52, '. . . structurally Rochester, with its thick walls and vast clasping buttresses, reverts to Norman traditions'.

[67] Hope (1900), p. 50, suggested the presbytery wall recesses may have been intended for tombs; three are now so occupied: north side, second bay, Purbeck tomb attributed to Bishop St Martin (ob. 1274); third bay, Purbeck tomb attributed to Bishop Gilbert Glanville (ob. 1214); south side, second bay, Purbeck effigy attributed to Bishop Ingoldsthorpe (ob. 1291).

[68] The three upper windows are Scott's design, in place of the nine-light Perpendicular window. There are a number of views of the interior before Scott: a drawing by G. Gunning, c.1840, formerly

everywhere, for bases, shafts, shaft-rings, strings, and most capitals.[69] The capitals are of the moulded bell type; the arches are moulded in thin rolls and hollows with an outer label carved with billet. In front of each window of the clerestory, which includes a wall passage, there is a triplet of stepped arches decorated with dog-tooth rising from thin Purbeck shafts. Lintels of Purbeck, extending from the capitals straight back into the wall, form supports for a series of pointed barrel vaults.[70] The main vault, consisting of two sexpartite bays, springs from about halfway up the height of the clerestory.

The minor transept elevation continues the basic two-storey division of the presbytery. On the east side, where the arcades form the openings of the chapels, the sides of the jambs are treated as flat sections of walling with two orders of shafts at the entrance; three arcades continue across both the end walls and on to the west walls. Continuous string-courses are found at the base of the window sills, at the level of the imposts, and below the sill of the clerestory passageway; they are continued over the shafts to form shaft-rings. The lower windows have two orders of limestone shafts; otherwise Purbeck, as in the presbytery, is everywhere used for shafts. Limestone is also used for the capitals of the wall arcades, again as in the presbytery.

There are no clerestory windows on the east side; instead, there is only an arcaded passageway fronted by a series of equal-sized arches with single shafts continued from the west bay of the presbytery. There is one small asymmetry between the outer bays of each arm: the south-east bay has three arches, the north-east bay, four. The lack of clerestory windows on this side of the transept is explained by a large room built over each block of chapels: their windows are at clerestory level on the exterior. The interior wall of each towards the presbytery bears two large bays of blind arcading: otherwise the rooms are bare.[71] The outer bays of the west clerestory have a triple arcade, while the inner ones have a triple arcade plus two lower arches. Each clerestory window on the north and south has a triplet of arches of equal height –

in Dean and Chapter Library, Rochester (Palmer, *op. cit.*, p. 87); an unattributed and undated photograph, formerly in Dean and Chapter Library, Rochester; and an anonymous watercolour, Dean and Chapter Library, Rochester.

69 For the Purbeck industry see J. Blair, 'Purbeck Marble', *English Medieval Industries*, eds J. Blair and N. Ramsay, London 1991, pp. 41–56, esp. 47–9, and R. Leach, *An Investigation into the Use of Purbeck Marble in Medieval England*, 2nd edn, Crediton 1978, p. 13.

70 L. Grant, 'The Choir of St.-Étienne at Caen', *Medieval Architecture and its Intellectual Context: Studies in Honour of Peter Kidson*, eds E. Fernie and P. Crossley, London and Ronceverte 1990, p. 122, noted the use of a small buttressing strut between the capital and back wall of the passage in the 'west transept' (however, the minor *east* transept – and quire – must have been meant) at Rochester. She advanced such parallels as the east wall of the Chichester retrochoir and St Hugh's quire at Lincoln, the source being found in the west wall of the minor transept at Canterbury.

71 The room on the south was mostly rebuilt by Cottingham as a result of the extensive work necessary to stabilize the south wall of the minor transept in 1825–30. There is evidence of there having been a pitched roof, as exists over the north room since Scott's restoration, against its west and northern walls. These rooms are generally referred to as the 'Treasury' (north) and as the 'Indulgence Chamber': e.g. see Palmer, *op. cit.*, p. 87, and Ashpitel, *op. cit.*, p. 282. The north one has recently been converted into a 'lapidarium': see A. Arnold, 'The Lapidarium', *Friends of Rochester Cathedral: Report for 1990/91* (1991), pp. 21–2.

the lateral arches absurdly narrow – in front of it. As in the presbytery, the lower wall arches have billet-decorated labels, while dog-tooth is used on the clerestory arcades.

In the south wall of the south arm, there are two semicircular archways, the east one leading to a stair vice ascending to the room located above the east aisle chapels, the west to descending steps which exited, not into the crypt, but into a room which was constructed at this time opening off the south aisle of the eleventh-century crypt; it is located under the stairs now linking the minor transept arm to the lower level of the south quire aisle.[72] Both stairways are now blocked. Two stair vices are found in the north arm: one is reached through a door in the north wall of the north-east chapel; the second opened directly off the main space in the north-west corner (the doorway is now blocked).

The new work was entirely vaulted, although, in the north arm of the minor transept, a change in wall plane, marked by a horizontal chamfer high up within the area of the vault lunettes on east and west, suggests a vault may not have been intended at first. The projecting bays of the presbytery received two bays of sexpartite vaulting, with a regular quadripartite vault constructed over the narrower western bay in the line of the transept chapels; the latter also received (square) quadripartite vaults. A large, quadripartite vault is found over the nearly square crossing, enriched by a boss consisting totally of deeply undercut foliage (now gilded). The minor transept arms are covered by sexpartite vaults with the intermediate transverse rib in each one deflected to meet the apeces of the diagonal ribs.[73] There are no heavy arches defining the crossing; instead, there are only thin ribs: as a result, the vaulting bay of each arm extends to include the thickness of the crossing piers, thereby enlarging the vault bay from a rectangle to a square. Thus, the vertical division in the elevation, on the east between the chapels, on the west between the quire aisles and the projecting bay, no longer corresponds to the axis of the vault bay. If the vault area had been made rectangular, two more or less equal divisions would have resulted and this would have allowed the intermediate rib to transverse the arm on a straight (unbroken) line.

(3) *Presbytery and minor transept: suggested chronology*

There is no documentation regarding the start of this considerable enlargement of the east end of the cathedral. It has been dated c.1195/1200,[74] following hard on the extensive restoration of the hypothetical (Gundulf's) straight-ended quire,

---

[72] Ashpitel, *op. cit.*, p. 282, identified this room (on what authority?) as, 'the dreaded penance chamber', describing it as 'a small, groined cell, perfectly dark, and receiving air from above by a small suit of flue; it is approached from the church by a stair in the thickness of the wall'.

[73] Hope (1900), p. 75, accepted the observation of Livett that, owing to the outward settlement of the south front, 'the entire reconstruction of [the transept's] vault and of parts of the upper works as well' was necessary 'not much more than a century after its building'. However, I could see no stylistic evidence of any such rebuilding which, if done, was remarkably unsuccessful, as the continued outward lean of the transept front led to its rebuilding in the early nineteenth century.

[74] Bond, *op. cit.*, pp. 113, 652; E.S. Prior, *A History of Gothic Art in England*, London 1900, p. 32; J. Harvey, *The English Cathedrals*, 2nd edn, London 1956, p. 167; G. Webb, *Architecture in*

presumably damaged by a fire in 1179, reportedly as severe in its consequences as the one forty years before.[75] Stylistically, however, and practically, there is no reason not to accept the existing presbytery and minor transept, and the crypt extension under them, as the immediate consequence of the fire of 1179. The work shows great stylistic and constructional unity and was clearly pushed forward in one continuous campaign. Traditionally, it is thought to have been complete by the death of Bishop Gilbert Glanville who was supposedly buried on the south side of the presbytery in 1214.[76] Work, nonetheless, if begun as early as c.1180, could have been completed well before that date.

(4) *Exterior of the quire*

On the exterior of the quire, the north clerestory windows are all restored: they differ from those of the west face of the north minor transept arm only in the lack of a label, as is also true of the east windows of the major transept's north arm. The uppermost string-course is at the same level on the west face of the minor arm and the quire; yet, although of the same design, it is placed at a higher level on the east face of the major arm. The quire's south clerestory windows are also lancets with unmoulded and undecorated frames, lacking any string-course or label.

The exterior elevation of the north quire aisle is mostly hidden by the north ('Gundulf's') tower. A massive, strongly projecting, flat-faced buttress now divides it into two sections; it was constructed when the aisle was remodelled in the fourteenth century (it is 'balanced' by one against the south face of the south quire wall).[77] There is evidence of an earlier, original buttress having been partly ripped away between bays three and four. Otherwise, no work of the Early Gothic period is visible on the exterior of the aisle.

(5) *Interior of the quire*

In the quire, instead of the usual arcade and some type of gallery, there is a solid wall on each side supporting the clerestory level. These walls are generally considered to be the remains of the solid side walls of the earliest Romanesque ('Gundulfian') church, refaced (Plate 23).[78] Above a dado left bare to accommodate

Britain: The Middle Ages, Harmondsworth 1956, p. 79. T.S.R. Boase, *English Art, 1100–1216*, Oxford 1953, p. 256, *c.*1210. It therefore followed upon the Chichester retrochoir (1187–99) and was contemporary with the great transept at Lincoln (c.1200–20), the retrochoir of Winchester (1202–c.1235), and the quire and retrochoir of Southwark (c.1208–35).

[75] Stubbs, *op. cit.*, i, p. 292; BL, Cotton MS Vespasian A.XXII, ff. 30v–31r[29v–30r]. BL, Cotton MS Nero D.II, f. 118 [117], gives the year as 1177: Wharton, *Anglia Sacra*, i, p. 345.

[76] BL, Cotton MS Nero D.II, f. 128[127]v: Wharton, *Anglia Sacra*, i, p. 347. For his tomb, see above n. 67.

[77] See plan, Hope (1900), pl. II, and F.H. Fairweather, 'Gundulf's Cathedral and Priory Church of St Andrew, Rochester: Some Critical Remarks on the hitherto Accepted Plan', *Archaeological Journal*, lxxxvi (1929), fig. 1 and p. 208.

[78] The eleventh-century date of the walls has never actually been ascertained by an examination of the core masonry. There are, however, no known examples of solid quire walls constructed in the late twelfth or early thirteenth century, in the Early English phase of Gothic, so an early date for

the choir stalls, the wall is decorated with bays of blind arcading,[79] on a pattern of two per section of vaulting above, with the symmetry failing at the east end, next to the minor transept, where an increased thickness of wall eliminates one bay of the blind arcade. These projecting sections are actually the ends of the west walls of the minor transept's arms: a vertical joint, masked in part by a nook-shaft, marks the eastern limit of the surviving eleventh-century solid quire walls. Details of the arcading are similar to those found in the minor transept and presbytery: Purbeck shafts, moulded capitals, and billet-decorated labels. Decoration, of a type not found in the work to the east, takes the form of lobed (stiff-leaf) foliage found at the ends of the long tapering corbels to the wall shafts and over the central shafts of each pair of blind arches.[80] Carved heads are included on one corbel on the south (the easternmost), two on the north (the western and eastern ones, the head on the latter female), and the south-east crossing shafts (accompanied by foliage); three descending animals are found on the middle corbel on the north side; the richest foliage is found under the east crossing shafts.

Each of the four clerestory windows on each side is fronted by a stepped triple arcade, on the arches of which dog-tooth appears. In contrast to the presbytery, the clerestory windows rise much higher into the lunette area under the vaults. As in the presbytery, Purbeck lintels spanning the passageway, from shaft capitals to window wall, support transverse pointed barrel vaults. Purbeck shafts, corresponding to the ribs, rise up the elevation singly or in triplets from corbels. String-courses at the level of the blind arcading's imposts and the clerestory sill cross the vaulting shafts as rings.

Sexpartite vaults, which spring from a level well above the clerestory sill, were extended into the quire in two unequal bays. Transverse ribs are decorated with a bold dog-tooth and there are two bosses following on from the earlier one in the east crossing, making the quire vaulting the richest in the eastern arm. The bosses each have a tyre-like frame, the eastern one decorated with dog-tooth, surrounding a rosette of four lobed leaves in a '+' plan; in the more complex western one, there is a swirl of long stemmed lobed foliage deeply undercut, somewhat similar in form to that of the western quire boss.[81]

---

the walls seems quite appropriate. Fairweather, *op. cit.*, pp. 202–3, 210, proposed they were *extended* in the course of the rebuilding which he postulated (p. 205) followed the 1137 fire; according to him, the south wall was actually mostly rebuilt at that time; he provided no archaeological evidence, however.

[79] The area of the dado between the top of the stalls and the string-course below the arcading is covered by a fourteenth-century painted diaper pattern restored by Scott in 1867: Smith, *op. cit.*, p. 286.

[80] S. Gardner, *English Gothic Foliage Sculpture*, Cambridge 1927, pl. 89 (the corbel at the east end of the south wall, dated c.1220).

[81] According to C.J.P. Cave, *Roof Bosses in Medieval Churches. An Aspect of Gothic Sculpture*, Cambridge 1948, p. 207, the bosses in the quire are modern, 'except perhaps the eastern one'. But T. Tatton-Brown informs me that this is not the case, as was confirmed during the recent cleaning: the bosses are all original.

(6) *Date of the quire proper*

The quire is said to have been entered in 1227,[82] but it is difficult to accept that work in the quire proper was not completed before that date. The remodelling of the quire is a natural extension of the enlarged east end and is stylistically closely related to that campaign. Its use may have been delayed by construction then following in the quire aisles.

What is most remarkable at a time in the early thirteenth century is the decision to retain the archaic feature of the solid side walls from the late eleventh century building and not to replace them by an arcade. Compared to the work in the presbytery and minor transept, the quire is somewhat, and appropriately, more decorative with stiff-leaf and figurative carving making an appearance in the corbels relating to the shafts of the blind arcading and vaults. The upper levels of the quire, the clerestory and vaults, continue the sobriety of the work to the east, in the preference for moulded capitals, continued use of billet and dog-tooth. Only two large bosses, as also grace the eastern crossing, and the appearance of a giant dog-tooth distinguishes the vault from the earlier work.

(7) *The north quire aisle*

Both the quire aisles have been extensively altered since first built – the south more so than the north.[83] Because of the proximity of the north tower, the north aisle must have been initially rather dark. Owing most probably to later structural problems, the windows were blocked up, the exterior of the wall refaced – and possibly thickened – with a new heavy buttress built against it, and a series of clerestory-like windows inserted at the top of the wall, along with a new vault (Plate 24).[84] The latter has transverse and longitudinal ridge ribs and bosses. The initial early Gothic construction included single wall shafts which, rising from a stepped bench at the base of the wall, divide the length of the aisle into four bays. The inside of the exterior wall bears traces of the jamb of a single lancet window in the west bay, while the jambs of two lancets, and segments of depressed (pointed) arches, are exposed in the east bay.[85] This suggests that, initially, the two middle bays may have been blind, since windows in them would have been directly opposite the north tower, so little

---

[82] BL, Cotton MS Nero D.II ('Annales ecclesiae Roffensis, ex historia ecclesiastica Edmundi de Hadenham monachi Roffensis'), f. 134[133]r: Wharton, *Anglia Sacra*, i, p. 347; Lehmann-Brockhaus, *op. cit.*, ii (1956), p. 398, no. 3755.

[83] Gem, *op. cit.*, p. 546, and n. 39 (p. 568) identified the aisle faces of the 'inner' (quire) walls as original, stating that the thirteenth-century shafts simply had been inserted and, in the north aisle, the wall surface cut back to accommodate the thirteenth-century vault wall rib. The latter wall is really only cut back at the east and west ends (more at the east than at the west) where the *fourteenth*-century corbels were inserted in order to support the ribs of the new vault.

[84] For Hope's very different reading of this aisle wall see Hope (1900), pp. 35, 59–60, 85. For the area between the quire north aisle wall and Gundulf's Tower see also Fairweather, *op. cit.*, pp. 208–10, fig. 1, and pl. II. Neither Hope nor Fairweather recognized the extent of the fourteenth-century repairs.

[85] These traces were uncovered when the aisle was refurbished by the cathedral architect, C. Hodgson Fowler, in 1910: Emf 77/148, and 71/8.

light would have reached them. The pair of windows in the east bay is opposite the wide space between the tower and (new) minor transept north arm, hence taking advantage of the brighter location; the single window in the west bay corresponded to the narrower gap between the tower and the north arm of the (still standing?) Romanesque transept or of the later Gothic major transept (in the latter case, the gap partially closed by its shallow east chapel).

(8) *The south quire aisle*

The south quire aisle presents a very irregular appearance consisting as it now does of one space equal to the full length of the minor transept arm for the entire distance between the transept arms, major and minor (Plate 25). It has undergone more than one alteration, but its original form can still be discerned: it did not duplicate the north aisle. Unlike the Romanesque arrangement, an entrance to the (enlarged) crypt was retained only on the south side. It was therefore necessary to widen the eastern section of the aisle to allow for the placement of the enlarged descending stairs, their increased width equal to one half of the projection of the minor transept south arm, and for a parallel set of ascending stairs, occupying the outer half of the arm, leading to a landing at the level of the transept floor. Thus, after one bay from the major transept south arm, the normal narrow aisle was to widen out to double its width in order to accommodate the two parallel flights of stairs. The descending one was now provided with a rich portal forming the crypt entrance; two orders of Purbeck shafts rise from a base of two rolls on a circular plinth; the arch is almost straight-sided, with moulded capitals, and an inner order of Purbeck shafts.

Vaulting shafts on the west face of the west wall of the south arm of the minor transept and two large arches with jambs of two orders all indicate the west face never was an external wall.[86] These arches, along with a single shaft on the south face of the south quire wall, suggest that the space to its west, over the stairs, was intended to receive vaults in four bays which do not appear to have been ever carried out. Such a vault would have required a central column. There is, however, no trace of its implacement which would have fallen on the stepped bench between the two flights of stairs, although wall ribs for the vault do remain above the (later) wooden ceiling, against the south face of the south quire wall. They can be seen from the doorways opening into the roof space from the quire clerestory passageway: at the east, there are two wall ribs, the east one decorated with billet, the west one interrupted by the massive buttress later placed against the south quire wall; at the west, corresponding to the narrow section of the aisle, the lunette face can be seen but the wall rib has been ripped out.

---

[86] According to Hope (1900), p. 75, the vaulting shaft in the middle of the west face, conspicuously *not* in Purbeck marble, was a result of later repairs to this arm necessitated by its sinking.

The small doorway now inserted in the south arch was formerly in the archway to the aisle from the major south arm: see [H. and B. Winkles,] *Winkles's Architectural and Picturesque Illustrations of the Cathedral Churches of England and Wales*, 3 vols, London 1838–42, i, pl. 42, facing p. 120. It was moved to its present location by Cottingham, c.1825: Palmer, *op. cit.*, p. 115; Hope (1900), pp. 75, 92.

The south wall of the quire aisle is now a tantalizing mess. When the aisle wall of the wider, eastern section was initially built, it seems to have incorporated an earlier wall as its lower half, for at its eastern end, next to the stairs leading up to the minor transept south arm, there are traces of two adjacent arches, each of a single unmoulded order and a slightly flattened curve. Above (in the section over the stairs) is a window with Purbeck shafts to its jambs which clearly belongs to the new work. The south wall was eventually continued westwards, still over an earlier wall, judging from what appears to be the arch of a former portal above the arch of the existing doorway (which would then be a later replacement), presently giving access to the site of the cloisters: the outline of a segmental arch of two orders of similar span is visible. On the exterior, the south wall retains evidence of a cloister roof in the form of corbels for the roof plate, below a plain string.[87] Inside and out, the original (thirteenth-century) build of the upper eastern section of the south aisle wall ends just west of the lancet window: the vertical joint is marked on the exterior by the change from ashlar (around the window) to rubble construction, and inside (where the wall is plastered), by the abrupt ending of the Purbeck string-course.

It appears, then, that a wall of the late twelfth century, probably associated with work in the cloister carried out under Bishop Gilbert Glanville (1185–1214),[88] existed here before the construction of the minor south arm and the south quire aisle. On its north face were the three unmoulded arches, already mentioned, of which the western may have belonged to a portal. At its west end, this wall abutted the north-east angle of the pre-existing structure forming the west range of the cloister,[89] as the line of (restored) quoins – with a continuous, vertical joint to the east – above the west jamb of the (later) cloister portal attests: this wall became part of the south wall of the wide section of the aisle.[90] Two lancet windows – the western shorter than the eastern one – with unshafted jambs were inserted in the extended (upper) section. What is not at all clear is why this section of wall (between the east lancet window of the aisle and the line of quoins) is not of the same build and date as the east window and the other early features of the aisle.

At a later date, but still in the thirteenth century, the south wall of the narrow western section of the aisle was removed – if, indeed, it had ever been erected – and

---

[87] Hope (1900), p. 167, claimed the lower part of the exterior of the wall showed traces of two large blocked openings with depressed pointed heads: I could not confirm this. Scott, Emf 77/65/3, remarked only: 'The south wall of the South aisle of the Choir or St. Edmund's chapel, has been also restored. This wall contains externally interesting evidence of the arches of the ancient cloister and internally evidence of arched recesses before invisible'.

[88] Thorpe, *Registrum*, p. 633, 'fecit claustrum nostrum perfici lapideum'.

[89] For the west range see J.P. McAleer, 'Rochester Cathedral: the West Range of the Cloister', *Friends of Rochester Cathedral: Report for 1992–93* (1993), pp. 13–25.

[90] According to Hope (1900), pp. 71–2, the south tower, which he theorized Gundulf had built as a pendant to the tower on the north, was torn down c.1322. The quoins were considered as the only remnant of the south tower, marking the 'section' of its east side: Hope (1886), p. 332, (1900), p. 17. They were uncovered by Irvine: see Emf 77/133, Notebook No. 2, p. 5 (Emf 77/135, p. 4), where he reveals the 'old quoins as far as could be done were preserved and *some others placed so as to preserve this curious bit of historical information* (italics added)'. Irvine thought the 'south' tower had been removed 'at a period prior to the erection of Glanville's stone cloister', that is before c.1185/1214.

the arch that separated it from the wider east half was taken down, leaving only its north respond against the south face of the quire wall (Plate 26). The respond is in the form of a cluster of five shafts plus a corbel head, retaining shaft-rings and moulded capitals, all in limestone. The details correspond in type and level to the responds of the arch between the aisle and the major transept's south arm. It may have been the removal of this arch that necessitated the construction of the strongly projecting buttress against the south face of the south quire wall that now partially blocks access to the stairs descending to the crypt. This buttress has chamfered angles and, on its south face near the top, a blind arch with Purbeck shafts and abaci, moulded stone capitals, and Purbeck upper string.[91] With the removal of the south wall of the narrow section of the aisle, the west part of the aisle became equal in width to the east section. A trefoiled arched recess is now found in the wall at the foot of the stairs. Its austere details suggest it is a slightly later insertion: the arch is chamfered, not moulded, and the chamfered label lacks stops. About this time, or slightly later in the thirteenth century, a new portal, with a pointed arch (the existing one giving access to the cloister walk), replaced the late twelfth-century one.

(9) *Date of quire aisles*

The style of the north quire aisle and the initial phase of the south quire aisle show no strong departure from the work of the presbytery, minor transept, or quire, except for the diminishing use of Purbeck and the absence of stiff-leaf. For these reasons it is difficult to determine the building sequence, for there is little indication of whether their construction preceded, accompanied, or succeeded that of the quire. In any of these possibilities, it is impossible to account for the failure to complete the south aisle according to plan, a decision which aborted what would have been one of the more interesting spaces in early Gothic architecture, or to date the final arrival of the aisle at its existing formless form. The extraordinary wooden ceiling with its numerous (fourteen) carved bosses and its grotesque corbels has been dated to the early fourteenth century, but the style of the carving indicates that an even later date, c.1350, is possible.[92]

(10) *The major transept: exterior of the north arm*

The major transept arms had strongly projecting, flat-faced buttresses with three setbacks placed at right angles at each exterior angle. Owing to the north tower's location, an unusually shallow chapel, with a slender north-facing lancet, opened off the north arm. There is no similar balancing chapel in the south arm, an asymmetry again perhaps owing to the adjoining cloister.

The exterior details of the major transept are less plain than on those parts to the

---

[91] Hope (1900), p. 54, considered it part of the original construction, to buttress the thrust of the quire walls. But this is not the case, as it interrupts the wall rib of the north-west compartment of the unexecuted vault of the wide section of the aisle.

[92] Hope (1900), p. 74 (and figs 28, 29) paid no attention to this extraordinary 'ribbed' ceiling, and certainly does not seem to have examined the bosses.

east. The north front is divided into three stages by string-courses.[93] In the lowest, at the west end, there is a heavily restored portal of two orders (plus moulded inner jambs) with jamb-shafts ('water-holding' bases, squat bell capitals), moulded arches, and (restored) head-stops to the moulded label. On the second stage, there are three lancet windows with blind bays in between and flanking them, forming a continuous arcade of seven bays with detached shafts (abcdcba). The three windows of the upper (clerestory) level are also set in a continuous arcade of seven stepped bays. The east face of the arm is effectively invisible owing to the proximity of the north tower; only the clerestory can be seen. The west face, also of three stages, has two lancet windows in the second stage, flanked and separated by blind arches in the north bay, while each of the clerestory-level bays has two lancets with a blind arch between and (restored) Purbeck shafts.

(11) *The major transept: interior of the north arm*

In contrast to the presbytery and minor transept, the elevation of the north arm of the major transept was conceived of as three stories, with the exception of the arches leading to the quire or nave aisles and the arched opening to its eastern chapel. Another conspicuous difference from the earlier work is the use of corbels and label-stops carved with human heads, in wide and animated variety.

On the east side in the north arm, the wall is divided into two halves by a group of three Purbeck vaulting shafts (Plate 28). The chapel arch fills the north half; on the south, the narrow section of wall between the tall aisle arch and the vaulting shafts is filled by two arches, one above the other, the lower forming a shallow recess, the narrower upper one enframing a small (blocked) window.[94] Because of the free-standing tower to the north, there was no space for the transept arm to have an eastern aisle for chapels as in the minor transept. Instead, there is a single shallow oblong chapel lighted only by a slender lancet in its narrow north wall.[95] The jamb

---

[93] According to Hope (1900), p. 64, almost all of the external ashlar was renewed by Scott who, at the same time, restored the high pitch of the roof and the gable based on evidence from early views: R. Dodsworth and W. Dugdale, *Monasticon Anglicanum*, London 1655, pl. facing p. 28; a view of the cathedral from the north-east by J. Buckler, 1804, BL, Add. MS 36, 368 ('Buckler Architectural Drawings', XIII), ff. 81v–82r; John Buckler view, 1810; John Chessell Buckler, *Views of the Cathedral Churches of England and Wales with Descriptions*, London 1822 (no pl. nos). Scott also gratuitously added the pinnacles which did not appear in any earlier views before the roof was lowered (between 1788 and 1816). See also Palmer, *op. cit.*, p. 51.

[94] As Fairweather, *op. cit.*, p. 209, has pointed out, the exterior jambs of this window are still visible.

[95] Such shallow chapels were rare in England: at Horton Kirby, there are two shallow non-projecting chapel-niches in each east wall, and a piscina on the adjoining north or south end wall, with the wall pierced by a lancet: see J. Russell Larkby, 'Some Churches in the Darant Valley, I. St Mary's, Horton Kirby, Kent', *The Reliquary and Illustrated Archaeologist*, New Ser., xi (1905), pp. 166–9; and Newman, *op. cit.*, pp. 335–6 (dated to c.1190). Also for French examples see E. Lefèvre-Pontalis, 'Les niches d'autel du XIIe siècle dans le Soissonnais', *Congrès archéologique*, lxxviii, 2 vols (Reims 1911), ii, pp. 138–45, esp. 140 for examples in transepts. In France, non-projecting ones are also found at St.-Germer-de-Fly (J. Henriet, 'Un édifice de la première génération gothique: l'abbatiale de Saint-Germer-de-Fly', *Bulletin monumental*, cxliii [1985], pp. 131–2), and La Trinité, Fécamp (J. Vallery-Radot, *L'église de la Trinité de Fécamp*, Paris 1928, p. 34).

shafts of this window bear the only capitals carved with stiff-leaf foliage in the entire building.[96]

The lower two stages on north and west are each of about the same height and are filled by three bays of arcading, the ground storey ones blind, the upper ones forming a continuous arcade over deeply splayed windows. The west bay of the north wall is occupied by a portal: the Purbeck shafts of its tall inner jamb support a broad, almost straight-sided, pointed arch. The bases and shafts of the lower window zone are of Purbeck, the moulded capitals of limestone; in the blind arcades below, the capitals are Purbeck. The upper level – on all three sides – is a clerestory with a wall passage: as further east, it is fronted by a triple arcade, except across the north wall where the gradated units (4/3/4), with Purbeck shafts and capitals, read continuously, only separated by thin piers formed at the junction of the units. Dog-tooth appears in the clerestory where, rather distinctively, the centre arch in each bay of triplets on the east and west sides is straight sided.

The arch to the north nave aisle is curious for it projects up into the clerestory level; that is, it is much taller than the nave arcades and aisle were to be. To correspond to the actual height of the nave arcade and aisle, an arch was inserted under it – with capitals and arch mouldings of the same profile as the upper arch. It is doubtful that there could ever have been the intention of making the nave arcade or aisles as high as this arch. It seems designed to reflect the tall quire aisle arch rising to the clerestory sill on the east side – in itself unusually tall because of the uniform level of the vaults maintained above the aisle stairs. The springing point of this aisle arch is coordinated with the window arches, but being so much wider, its arch rose much higher, thus breaking into the clerestory sill.

The construction of the supports for the vaults over the clerestory passage-way – which are effectively pointed barrel vaults – differs considerably and significantly from that used in the quire and presbytery. In the north arm, lintels of Purbeck extend from the compound piers between the windows to the exterior wall. An arch springs from their inner end, its other end rising from head corbels placed next to the splayed jamb of the window opening; this arch thus crosses the passage-way diagonally. Consequently, a small pocket of vaulting is created between it, the wall, and the lintel.

(12) *Date of north arm of major transept*

In the approach to its all-over design, as well as in its details, the north arm represents a significant departure from the work of the east end as a whole. Yet, despite the new or different organization of the walls, and the appearance of head corbels and label stops, other features are sympathetic to the style of the work to the east: the continued use of Purbeck marble, of shaft-rings, and, especially, of moulded capitals, that is, the continued avoidance of stiff-leaf. For all its differences, then, it is in

---

[96] This, despite the appearance of elaborate, fully developed stiff-leaf foliage in the quire corbels; Newman, *op. cit.*, p. 54, noted that foliage capitals 'petered out' in Kent after the 1180s, and stiff-leaf proper was rare.

harmony with the earlier work, and it does not seem likely that too many years separated them. The traditional date of 1240–55 appears impossibly late.[97]

If 1227 has any significance, and can be taken as marking the completion of work in the quire and its aisles (the south aisle left in a temporary state?), the construction of the north arm of the major transept should have followed as a work of the 1230s. Even so, one wonders, because of its style, if it was not already in progress earlier, because that style is, in its sobriety, perhaps closer to the work at Salisbury Cathedral, begun in 1220, rather than to the more exuberant work of the east end (presbytery and quire) of Worcester Cathedral, c.1224–31, or the nave at Lincoln Cathedral, begun c.1225.

(13) The major transept: exterior of the south arm

The south facade of the major transept is a simple design, again of three registers. The lowest is bare; the second is mostly filled by the three equally broad two-light windows ('Y' tracery) with two orders of jamb shafts; the third is occupied by the similarly designed frames of five lancets stepped in height. The gable is dominated by an inlaid cross executed in flint checker work placed above a horizontal band, also of checker pattern, bearing three shields.[98] The lower part of the east face was originally overlapped by the west range of the cloister; at clerestory level there is a flat pilaster buttress between each bay (Plate 27a). The east clerestory windows are now filled by simple two-light (restored) Geometric tracery: the lights have but one pair of cusps and support a pointed quatrefoil. The west face below its clerestory has been altered by the addition of the structure now known as the Lady Chapel; at the upper level, a single deep buttress is placed only in the line of the nave aisle wall. The window tracery on this side is very different from that on the east. A shaft-like mullion, with base and capital, divides each clerestory window into two-lights; the pointed arches lack cusping, while the otherwise solid spandrel between them is pierced by an oculus with a quatrefoil within.

(14) The major transept: interior of the south arm

The interior south arm of the transept does not match that of the north arm, nor did it before the later alterations as a result of the addition of the so-called Lady Chapel on its west side. The original interior elevation of the south major transept arm continued the design of the presbytery and minor transept: tall bays of arcading nearly filled the wall below the clerestory (Plate 29). On the east side, the arch to the south quire aisle

[97] This late date was assigned by Hope (1900), pp. 65–6, on the basis of BL, Cotton MS Vespasian A.XXII, f. 91[92]v (Thorpe, *Registrum*, p. 125; Lehmann-Brockhaus, *op. cit.*, ii [1956], p. 398, no. 3757), 'Richardus de Eastgate monachus, et sacrista Roffensis, incepit alam borialem novi operis versus portam beati Willelmi, quam frater Thomas de Mepeham fere consummavit.'
[98] The gable on this facade also was removed (by Cottingham?) in the early nineteenth century and replaced by one of a lower pitch. That in turn was removed by Scott who based the design of the existing one on the old design as depicted in Thorpe, *Custumale*, pl. XXXIX (facing p. 165); Hope (1900), pp. 70–1. The original gable had been reported as 'secure', and the roof still of a steep pitch, by D. Alexander in November 1799: Emf 38, sec. 6.

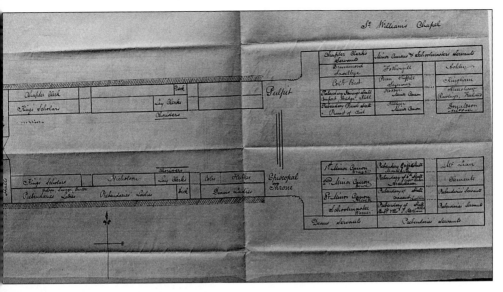

Plate 9(a). Seating plan of the quire, c.1840.

Plate 9(b). Edward Hawkins, Provost of Oriel College, Oxford 1828-74 and prebendary of Rochester, 1828-82.

Plate 9(c). William Herbert Mackean, Canon Librarian, 1925-58.

Plate 10. Interior of the quire, 1842.

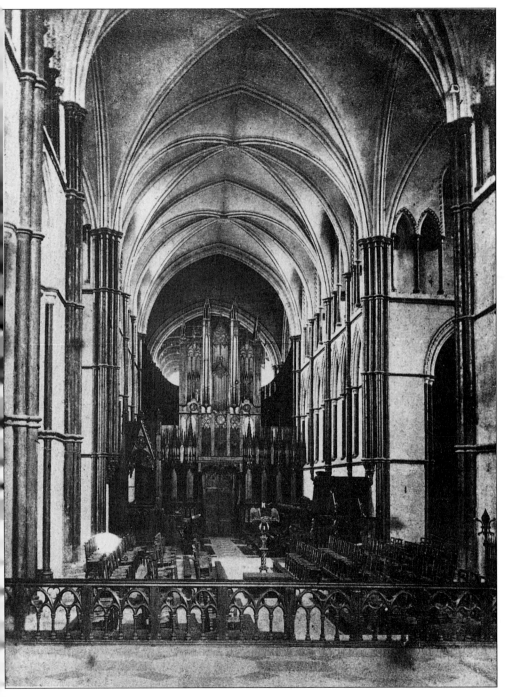

Plate 11. Interior of the quire, 1870.

Plate 12. Water-colour of the interior of the nave by J. Buckler, 1804.

Plate 13. Crypt, north aisle, view to west and original entrance.

Plate 14(a). North aisle wall, exterior, second bay from east.

Plate 14(b). South aisle wall, exterior, five west bays.

Plate 15. Nave, south clerestory, exterior, remains of Romanesque arcade (shaft) against south-west facade turret.

Plate 16. North aisle wall, interior, view towards west.

Plate 17. Nave, north arcade, fourth pier from east or west.

Plate 18. North aisle, view to west.

Plate 19(a). Nave, north gallery, bays two and three from west.

Plate 19(b). West facade, indicating, within line, original Romanesque fabric.

Plate 20. West front, detail of arcading on north side, second and third registers.

Plate 21. View of east facade before restoration, from a water-colour by J. Buckler, 1804.

Plate 22. Interior of presbytery, north elevation.

Plate 23. Interior of quire, detail of north elevation, east bay.

Plate 24. North quire aisle, interior, view to east.

Plate 25. South quire aisle, interior, view to east.

Plate 26. South quire aisle, interior, view to west.

Plate 27(a). Major transept, south arm exterior, east clerestory.

Plate 27(b). Major transept, south arm interior, arch to Lady Chapel and west clerestory.

Plate 28. Major transept, north arm interior, east elevation.

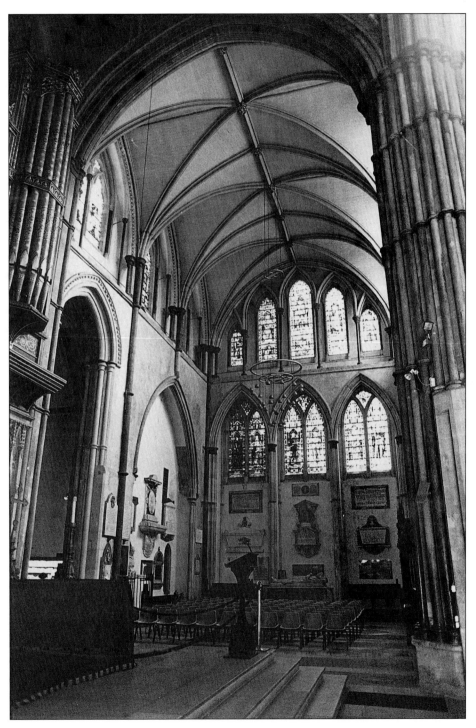

Plate 29. Major transept, south arm interior, east and south elevations and vault.

Plate 30. Major transept, north arm interior, north-west crossing pier and eastern two bays of north nave arcade.

Plate 31. Nave, two eastern bays of north arcade viewed from aisle.

Plate 32. Major transept, north arm interior, north and east elevation and vault.

was originally followed by two narrow arches; three similar arches rising over windows are on the south wall, and two more were on the west wall plus the arch to the south nave aisle. At some time, the two original tall blind arches of its east elevation were converted into a single wide arch like that opening into the shallow chapel in the north arm. Whether this alteration was made in the course of construction or shortly after the transept arm was completed is difficult to determine because the new arch is uniform in style with the other elements of the transept arm.

The three lower windows of the south wall (under the arcades) are broad lancets subdivided by 'Y' tracery: the central mullions and jambs all bear shafts – bases, shafts, capitals, and arch mouldings all being of limestone.[99] The clerestory design on the east side, continuing the wall passage, has a triple arcade on the interior with a very wide central bay, still with dog-tooth on the outer arch moulding forming a kind of label. The windows are now filled with (restored) late geometric tracery consisting of two pointed and cusped lights, with a pointed quatrefoil above.[100] The south clerestory has five graduated lancets and an internal arcade of five arches: the spandrels are not pierced. The western clerestory alters the design by introducing a single wide window of two lights with a quatrefoil above, and an inner 'screen' that repeats the design: a centre shaft supports a kite-shaped spandrel pierced with a quatrefoil (Plate 27b).[101] The window jambs and central mullions are only chamfered, not moulded, with the curious detail of labels over the windows supported on stops formed by either foliage or human heads. The free-standing shafts of the screening arcade have rings, a feature lacking on the south and west sides. In the south arm, only the vaulting shafts – as well as their bases, shaft-rings, and capitals – are of Purbeck, which is also used for the bases, shafts, and capitals of the clerestory arcade.

(15) *Date of south arm of major transept*

Although the treatment of the wall below the clerestory as a single zone of tall arcading can be seen as a return to the dominant organizational aesthetic of the early work at Rochester, after the 'aberration' of the tripartite elevation of the north arm, the south arm continues other features of the north arm such as the use of head corbels; it also remains loyal to the moulded capital and shaft-rings, as well as Purbeck marble.

The most significant aspect of its design is, however, the appearance of early tracery forms in its windows: 'Y' tracery in the lower south windows (and perhaps

---

[99] The 'Y' tracery appears in pre-restoration engravings: Storer, *op. cit.*, iv (1819), [Rochester] pl. I ('Rochester Cathedral from the Canon's Gate').

[100] According to Hope (1900), p. 72, the tracery was all restored by Scott, 'copied from the remains of the old'. But a view of the church from the south-east, by William Alexander, c.1801 (BL, MS Add. 15, 966), and a later engraving in Storer, *op. cit.*, iv, [Rochester] pl. 6, show the north window blocked up, the middle one with a dividing vertical mullion only and no tracery, and the third walled up and pierced by a narrow lancet.

[101] Willis (Cambridge University Library, Add. MS 5128, f. 7), drew a small rough sketch of the west clerestory and part of the south wall, which seems to confirm that the patterns pre-date Scott's restoration.

originally in the east clerestory), and the twin-light windows (and inner arcade) with pierced spandrels of the west clerestory (if accurately restored by Scott) which may be among the earliest appearances of tracery in England, with parallels at the Consistory Court at Lincoln Cathedral, c.1240/5.[102] A date of construction with completion no later than in the early 1240s seems more probable than one of c.1280 as has been suggested.[103]

(16) *The crossing*

The area of the crossing is a confusing one, not least of all because its present condition is misleading and partly unintelligible. The shafts of the east responds flanking the entrance to the quire appear to be of a curious almost lilac-coloured stone, with a darker stone more like Purbeck used for shaft-rings, capitals and abaci. On the west side of the crossing, the piers have shafts of a more conventional Purbeck colour, although tending towards an orange tone. These odd, if not absolutely alarming colours, are due to the fact that the shafts have been repaired in modern times, those on the east side of the crossing by giving them a thin coat of cement resulting in the strange lilac tone; those on the west side have received a different, if undetermined, 'treatment'. The bases of the north respond of the north quire aisle arch and some of the bases of the east crossing responds on both the north and south also have been patched and/or painted in imitation of Purbeck.[104] Despite these deceptions, a reliable guide to the constructional sequence may be found in other details.

As built, the middle order of the north, south, and west crossing arches was a large roll with a wide fillet, in contrast to the east (or quire) crossing arch in which the middle order was decorated with a giant dog-tooth. The arch to the north nave aisle has shafts of limestone, on both its north and south responds, like the arch to the north quire aisle. The bases of the responds for this arch, that is, its north respond and the opposing respond against the west crossing pier, are also of limestone,

---

[102] For Lincoln see gen. ed. P. Lasko, *Courtauld Institute Illustration Archive: Archive I. Cathedrals and Monastic Buildings in the British Isles, Pt 5. Lincoln: Gothic West Front, Nave and Chapter House*, ed. P. Kidson, London 1978, p. iii and illus. 1/5/2–6, and, specifically, G. Russell, 'The Thirteenth-century West Window of Lincoln Cathedral', *Medieval Art and Architecture at Lincoln Cathedral*, eds T.A. Heslop and V.A. Sekules, London 1986, pp. 85 and 89 n. 6. She describes the gable tracery as plate; the central shafts lack capitals, and the spandrels are solid and decorated. Plate tracery forms had appeared earlier at Salisbury, after 1220, and at the Hereford Lady Chapel, c.1200–25.

[103] Bond, *op. cit.*, pp. 122, 652; Harvey, *op. cit.*, p. 167, thus putting it contemporary with the beginning of Exeter Cathedral Lady chapel and retrochoir, c.1275/80, for instance. According to BL, Cotton MS Vespasian A.XXII, f. 91[92v] (Thorpe, *Registrum*, p. 125; Lehmann-Brockhaus, *op. cit.*, ii [1956], p. 398, no. 3758), 'Ricardus de Waldene monachus et sacrista, alam australem versus curiam', but there are no recorded dates for Richard of Walden. Hope (1900), pp. 66–70, placed the work *after* the beginning of the nave which had followed upon the completion – except for the vault – of the north arm.

[104] Just when these 'repairs' to the shafts and bases were done is not clear; I have found no mention of them in the documents relating to either of the major nineteenth-century restorations (those of Cottingham and Scott). I am greatly indebted to T. Tatton-Brown for helping me to see and understand what has happened to them.

suggesting this arch belongs with the erection of the north quire aisle arch and preceded the construction of the north arm of the major transept wherein the use of Purbeck reappeared. As the pier element corresponding to the middle or axial order of the eastern arch with the giant dog-tooth, as well as the axial element of the east responds, are shaped like a pilaster with chamfered sides, it is clear that the chamfered pilaster forming the middle order of the north-west pier's east-facing respond was also intended to correspond to an arch order decorated with giant dog-tooth, like that in the quire arch. The similar middle order of the east-facing respond of the south-west pier was likewise also designed for an arch order of giant dog-tooth. Yet, in the event, both the north and south arches, like the western crossing arch, lack the giant dog-tooth and have, instead, a large filleted roll.[105]

The opposed faces of the west crossing piers are not symmetrical. The *south* face of the north-west pier was also designed for a middle arch order of giant dog-tooth, for it has the axial chamfered form, but the *north* face of the south-west pier was not because it has an axial shaft. Somewhat confusingly, the respond of the south face of the south-west pier was designed for an aisle arch with a middle order of giant dog-tooth, but the opposed south aisle respond was not, for it has an axial shaft. The arch into the south nave aisle also eliminated the use of the giant dog-tooth in favour of the filleted roll. For the first time, the use of hollow chamfers on the angles between the shafts appears; they are found on the south respond only. The bases of this respond are, significantly, Purbeck towards the transept, but limestone facing into the aisle.

Thus, it would seem the west crossing piers were begun at the same time as the east responds but that they were not carried up uniformly. The aisle wall and pier responds – with limestone shafts – of the north nave aisle arch were first (the respond carried up in advance of the rest of the pier) followed by the east faces of the north-west and south-west piers and the south face of the north-west pier – all with Purbeck shafts; lastly, the north face of the south-west pier and the aisle wall respond of the south nave aisle arch were carried up with a changed design to the middle order, while generally continuing the use of Purbeck for shafts. That the west piers were not immediately carried up to their full height along with the east side of the crossing is indicated by the fact that the first set of shaft-rings on both piers correspond in design to those of the north arm, not to those of the north and south quire aisles or east responds. Their capitals also match those of the north arm's vaulting shafts. Consequently, it is quite clear that the crossing was not raised as a unit to provide abutment for the quire vaults, and to serve a similar function successively for each transept arm. Rather, the piers were raised in piece-meal fashion, with the north, west, and south arches constructed to one design as a final phase to allow the raising of the tower and the building of the transept roofs. This

---

[105] Hope (1900), p. 60, attributed the western bases of the north and south arches of the projected central tower (and perhaps those of its western arch), together with those of the north and south responds of the arch into the north aisle of the nave and the north respond of that into the south aisle, to the architect of the north quire aisle. He noted that, although these bases are all limestone, 'some are painted to imitate marble', but did not identify the culprit.

raises the possibility that the Romanesque crossing piers were retained, to be gradually recased as work proceeded.

Once completed, the crossing was not vaulted. Since the diagonal faces of the piers are composed of five shafts, it is possible the axial shaft initially was intended to correspond to a diagonal vault rib. In the final form, each of these shafts corresponds to a pair of departing labels for the adjacent crossing arches. These labels project far enough to suggest a vault was not finally precluded, but its rib pattern could not have had any visual coordination with the shafts.

(17) *The nave*

It is apparent that it was intended to replace the Romanesque nave as well, although work never progressed beyond the first two bays. The opposing faces of the west crossing piers now consist of much restored but regularly coarsed masonry in their lower part, forming a tall polygonal 'plinth' for the taller upper part, presumably evidence that a screen had been constructed between them in order to separate the monastic and parochial parts of the church (Plate 30). The upper portion of the piers bears the normal shafting, complete with bases placed well above floor level.

The new Gothic arcade was to be taller than the Romanesque arcade, the arches rising into the level of the old pseudo-gallery openings, but falling well short of equalling the height of the two storeys of the Romanesque elevation. Only the first pier on each side of the nave arcade was completed – the first examples of true Gothic pier design in the building.[106] They have a lozenge-shaped core with eight attached shafts of Purbeck marble.[107] The axial shaft towards the nave lacks a capital: there is just a continuation of the abacus forming a shaft-ring as if it were intended ultimately to relate to vaulting.[108]

On the north side, the second pier – of the same plan – was rebuilt up to the springing of the third (Romanesque) arch. The east face relates to the new tall arcade, the west face to the lower Romanesque arch, with moulded capitals appearing in place of the original scalloped ones. The south pier was only partially rebuilt, for the east half is Gothic, the west still Romanesque in its lowest courses, although its capital, decorated with Gothic oak leaf, is obviously a replacement. In contrast to the first pair of Gothic piers, the shafts of the second ones are in coursed limestone. The arch profile of the few nave arcades completed, featuring rolls with fillets, corresponds to the crossing arches – north, south, west – and the arch from the south transept arm to the aisle.

---

[106] Hope (1900), p. 67, described these piers as 'essentially decorated'. He attributed them to a new architect, his fifth, who was responsible for the south transept, which he thought followed after the (aborted) work in the nave.

[107] The shafts have been treated or patched in a manner similar to those of the west crossing piers, especially the north one, so that what seems to have been basically a light brown Purbeck has acquired its odd orangy colouration.

[108] L. Hoey, 'Piers versus Vault Shafts in Early English Gothic Architecture', *Journal of the Society of Architectural Historians*, xlvi (1987), p. 263, n. 106, pointed out that the inclusion of a shaft apparently meant to rise to the nave vaults from the floor was consistent with the attitude towards vertical articulation shown in the eastern parts of the building, even if it was rare at the time.

The aisles retain indications of the intention to cover them with ribbed vaults: the springers of the projected ribs are found on both the north and south piers, and at the arch between the south aisle and the transept arm (Plate 31).

＊

III Later Gothic Work: Completions and Alterations

(1) *The vaulting of the major transept and the raising of the crossing tower*

The vaults eventually constructed over the major transept arms are not symmetrically designed. The north arm is covered by two broadly oblong sexpartite units (Plate 32), the south arm by three narrow oblong quadripartite units (Plate 29); in both arms, wall ribs, which were not generally used in the work to the east (they occur only in the chapels under the presbytery in the crypt and in the minor transept east chapels) and longitudinal ridge ribs appear. A large boss marks each intersection of the transverse or diagonal ribs with the ridge rib.[109] The bosses are similar in style and motifs: they are plump roundels of oak leaf-like foliage with, in all cases but two, human or animal heads at the centre.[110] A stone vault was never constructed over the south arm. Rather, a wooden vault was put up; the stone springers for the vault ribs are in evidence nonetheless. This vault also received carved bosses very similar in style to those of the stone vault of the north arm.[111] The nature of the foliage which appears in the bosses of both the stone and wooden vaults indicates that neither vault is contemporary with the structure beneath it. The foliage is of the so-called cabbage-leaf or seaweed type revealing a date of erection for the vaults only after 1300 – probably well after – rather than an expected date of c.1240. This permits the suggestion that the vaults were completed at the time that the central tower was raised above the level of the adjoining roofs, that is, in the 1340s.

(2) *The crossing tower*

The medieval crossing tower has been twice replaced. The tower and spire were in alarming condition in 1679, but only modest temporary repairs were carried out in 1680. In 1749, the spire was finally rebuilt.[112] This work was removed by Cottingham during the restoration he carried out from 1825 to 1830, and the lower storey recased and a new upper stage built, without a spire (Plate 5b).[113] Cottingham's tower was

---

[109] For photographs of the transept bosses by C.J.P. Cave, see National Monuments Record, neg. nos. AA52/6515–18 (north), and AA52/6519–23 (south).

[110] In the north vault, reading from the crossing out, the subjects are: (1) two rather flat trilobed leaves, (2) a bovine head with branches of oak leaves and acorns coming out of its mouth, (3) a human face surrounded by oak leaves and acorns, (4) one large oak leaf in the centre surrounded by four smaller ones, (5) foliage.

[111] In the south vault, reading from the crossing out, the subjects are: (1) foliage, (2) a human face surrounded by leaves, branches coming out of its mouth, (3) four small human faces and leaves, (4) a dragon (on east half) and foliage, (5) bare branches forming a central square within a circle of foliage, (6) a dog's head (on west half) and foliage.

[112] Denne, *op. cit.*, in Thorpe, *Custumale Roffense*, p. 183; Palmer, *op. cit.*, p. 30.

[113] Hope (1900), pp. 90, 92; Palmer, *op. cit.*, pp. 39–40.

replaced in 1904 with one by C. Hodgson Fowler,[114] his design – the existing one – loosely based on the 'original'. Thus the Gothic tower is known only from engraved views prior to 1830.[115] They show the stage corresponding to the steeply-pitched roofs to have been decorated with bays of tall, shallow, trefoil-headed arcading, characterized by a lack of capitals or imposts as well as shafts. There were flat buttresses at the angles, with one slight set-back.

In 1343, Bishop Hamo de Hethe is reported to have had a belfry stage and spire added to the central tower: 'Anno xviii regni Edwardi III [Christi MCCCXLIII]. Episcopus [tunc] Campanile *novum* ecclesiae Roffensis petris atque lignis altius fecit levare et illud plumbo cooperire, necnon et quatuor campanas novas in eodem ponere, quarum [sic] nomina sunt haec, Dunstanus, Paulinus, Itamarus, atque Lanfrancus.'[116] The tower raised by Bishop Hamo was not elaborate; indeed, it appears to have been merely functional – a bell chamber.[117] Above the stage abutted by the quire and transept roofs, he added a rather low stage with pilaster buttresses at the angles and a single rather modest opening in each side; the parapet was straight, the spire probably octagonal. There was no architectual detailing except for a striped effect created by the use of stone and brick in alternating bands.

Rather curiously, neither transept arm was provided with newel-stairs: their clerestories could have been gained only via those of the Romanesque nave for they do not connect with those of the quire. The central tower, therefore, was reached from an approach over the quire (as at present) or transept – or nave? – vaults, for which purpose a pointed arched doorway was placed in the middle of each side.[118]

(3) *The nave clerestory and west window*

During the fifteenth century, the Romanesque clerestory of the nave was completely replaced (Plate 12). The new design eliminated the passage-way.[119] The new

---

[114] For the rebuilding in 1904, see F.F. Smith, *A History of Rochester*, London 1928, pp. 289–91, also pls 29, 30, 31.

[115] Probably the most accurate and informative view is that by John Buckler published in 1810 (cf. J.C. Buckler, *op. cit.*, unnumbered plate, 'Rochester Cathedral, N.W.', dated 1818). The 1816 view by John Coney (for the new edition of Dodsworth and Dugdale's *Monasticon, op. cit.*) is less complete and precise.

[116] BL, Cotton MS Faustina B.V. (*Willelmi de Dene [Notarii Publici] Historia Roffensis ab anno MCCCXIV ad annum MCCCL*), f. 90[89]v: Wharton, *Anglica Sacra*, i, p. 375.

Four bells are mentioned as being placed 'in majori turri' at various times before c.1300: two by Prior Reginald (1155–60); one named Thalebot after the sacrist, late twelfth century; and one named Bretun, in the time of Ralph de Ros, sacrist (before 1193–1203/8); see Hope (1886), p. 326; (1900), pp. 8–10, where the *majoris turris* is identified as Gundulf's Tower. In the mid-sixteenth century, the north tower was seemingly identified as the three-bell steeple, the central tower as the six-bell steeple (lease of 1545: Hope [1886], p. 327).

[117] See above n. 115; also Cottingham's watercolour of the west elevation prior to its restoration (formerly in Dean and Chapter Library, Rochester).

[118] The present crossing roof was built by Cottingham in 1840. It replaced an earlier one of his own design, constructed when he built the central tower, which in turn replaced an eighteenth-century wooden vault: Palmer, *op. cit.*, pp. 29, 33, 73.

[119] Willis in Hope (1900), pp. 85–6, described the windows as work 'of the plainest and meanest character . . . awkwardly arranged, so that no one window stands above the centre of a pier arch,

clerestory is twenty-one feet high, only two feet less than the Romanesque nave arcade (from the present floor to the string-course under the gallery arches).[120] It is unlikely the Romanesque clerestory was as tall. The low-pitched roof apparently was introduced at this time. The great eight-light west window belongs to the same general period but it is impossible to say if all this work represented one campaign.

These renovations may have been instigated by the removal of the parish altar to a separate new church (St Nicholas, built 1418–23) in 1423. In the mid-fifteenth century, two bishops willed money for the repair of the nave. Bishop John Langdon, in a will dated 2 March 1433/4, left £20 'ad reparacionem tecti navis ecclesie nostre Roffensis', and former Bishop Thomas Brouns (1435–6), in a will dated 28 October 1445, also left £20 'ad fabricam navis ecclesie cathedralis Roffensis . . . Proviso quod opere fabrice hujusmodi aliquod memoriale fiat per sculpturas armorum meorum et nominus mei'.[121] If his money was used for this purpose, his stipulation was ignored, as neither his name or arms are present in the nave.

(4) *The Lady Chapel*

The last sizable addition to the building before the Dissolution was a large structure built against the three east bays of the south wall of the nave aisle, and opening off the south transept arm (Plate 27b). It is usually identified as a Lady chapel,[122] but strictly speaking, it was meant as the nave to a chapel which had been created in the south transept arm, perhaps in the fourteenth century, when an altar to the Virgin was apparently established there.[123] The new addition was of three bays with tall

each being more or less to the west of it'. Harvey, *op. cit.*, p. 167, dated the clerestory twenty years (c.1490) later than the west window (c.1470).

[120] Carden & Godfrey, Architects, 130/3 (23 December 1953).

[121] Hope (1900), p. 86: London, Lambeth Palace Library, Registrum Chichele, I, f. 462v (*The Register of Henry Chichele, Archbishop of Canterbury, 1414–1443*, ed. E.F. Jacob, 4 vols, Oxford 1937–47, ii, pp. 556–8]), and Registrum Stafford, f. 132, respectively. I am grateful to Victoria Peters, Assistant Archivist, for the correct date of the will of Bishop Brouns (*not* 28 October 1455 as given by Hope [1900], p. 86).

[122] Ashpitel, *op. cit.*, p. 284, 'a chapel called by tradition St. Mary's chapel'; Hope (1881–5), p. 226, 'It is also equally certain that the Perpendicular extension was never called the Lady Chapel until modern times.' Palmer, *op. cit.*, p. 70, 'The so-called Lady Chapel was really built as a choir [*sic*] to the Lady Chapel proper in the south transept.'

[123] The first reference to an altar of the Virgin Mary is in the early fourteenth century (c.1305?): Thorpe, *Custumale Roffensis*, p. 13: 'Lucas de Honeberwe vi d. de terra de Monekedone ad altare beate Marie in novo opere'. This does not specify its location, but the south major transept arm would have been the most recent work at the time, although hardly new, unless the alterations in its east wall were the 'novo opere' referred to.

Two later references to an altar or a chapel 'de novo constructa' are sixty years apart. One is a grant in 1322 for a lamp to be placed at the altar, recorded in the chapter records (Thorpe, *Registrum Roffense*, p. 546 [Cartae Elyanorac Coman]); the second dates from 1389, the will of Bishop Thomas Brinton (Registrum Courtney, f. 231a), who desired to be buried in the chapel. If the altar existed as early as c.1305, it is difficult to understand how the same altar or chapel could be considered 'de novo constructa' in 1322 or, especially, in 1389. There was an altar dedicated to the Virgin in the Infirmary chapel from 1240: Ashpitel, *op. cit.*, p. 281.

Hope (1900), pp. 102–4, cited many other references to a chapel of St. Mary, primarily in wills of the fifteenth century – usually requesting burial. None, however, specifies its location.

windows of three lights, and a transom. The tracery pattern in the heads is particularly worthy of note. Three large window-like arches without tracery were inserted in the aisle wall. The extension (presumably) was meant to be fan vaulted in six compartments, but the vaulting was never carried out.[124] The use of bell-type bases, the tiny capitals, and four-centred arches suggest a date in the fifteenth-century at the earliest. Indeed, it may be even later, as Hope was no doubt correct to associate the 'western annex to the south transept' with a payment recorded in 1512–13 to one John Birch, carver, in the accounts of Prior William Fressell.[125]

It appears to have replaced an earlier chapel which was slightly narrower. The axis of the existing chapel is not lined up with that of the large arch in the west wall of the transept, as is very evident from the west: the corbel between the north and south wall ribs is considerably to the south of the apex of the arch. The entrance arch is more or less centred on the space of the two arcades of the east face of the transept west wall which it replaced (Plate 27b).[126] The style of the arch is completely different in its massive heavy forms from the details of the space into which it now opens. The combination of a double-ogee moulding with a three-quarter attached shaft is typically Perpendicular, and can be found as early as the 1380s, in the nave of Christ Church, Canterbury,[127] while the base mouldings are of a type that appear at Rochester, on the portal attributed to Bishop Hamo (d.1352), and at Canterbury, with variations from c.1360.[128]

With this construction, the history of the medieval fabric of the cathedral is brought to a close.

[124] Hope (1900), pp. 87–8.
[125] Society of Antiquaries, Dr Thorpe's Collection, MS 178.7, f. 147. See J. Harvey, *English Medieval Architects: A Biographical Dictionary down to 1550*, rev. edn, London 1984, p. 25; idem, *English Cathedrals*, p. 167, c.1500–12.
[126] This arch may relate to the chapel 'de novo constructa' mentioned in the will of Bishop Brinton (see above n. 123).
[127] I am most grateful to Richard K. Morris for looking at my crude profile sketches and confirming my suspicions as to the relative dates of the entrance arch versus the 'chapel' proper, and for suggesting parallels.
[128] See F. Woodman, *Architectural History of Canterbury Cathedral*, London 1981, fig. 124.

8

Repair and Restoration of the Fabric since 1540

DIANA HOLBROOK

(1) 1540–1660

The religious changes of the mid-sixteenth century appear to have had relatively little impact on the fabric of Rochester Cathedral. The three shrines of Saints William, Paulinus and Ithamar 'were probably destroyed in 1538', and the rood loft and idolatrous monuments during the reign of Edward VI.[1] The precincts, however, after the dissolution 'seemed to be a scene of devastation and confusion, the buildings huge, irregular and ruinous', according to Hasted.

The first major incident recorded after the Reformation was in 1591 when 'a great part of the Chancel of the Cathedral Church was lately burned and is now re-edified'. A bond of £400 was secured for the repairs and £300 repaid by the chapter that same year, it having been 'deeply charged in respect of their several and small livings'.[2] At the end of the century, in 1598, the defaced monument of Bishop Merton was replaced.

At a metropolitical visitation in 1607 it was stated that the cathedral 'though requiring weekly repair from its antiquity, was as a whole in reasonable condition'; yet thirty years later, it was reported at a subsequent visitation that a large programme of repairs had been undertaken. In addition to the ordinary annual expenditure on the fabric, the dean and chapter had expended more than £1,000 on repairs and new organs. Their report was accepted by the archbishop, who only added that the glazing they had delayed doing should be done immediately.[3] A visitor to the building in 1635 commented that the monuments were 'dismembered, defac'd and abus'd', but thought the cathedral otherwise to be 'neat and its organs pretty'.[4]

The Civil War and resulting Puritan campaign against 'popery' saw the instigation by Parliament in 1641 of a Defacing and Demolition Commission which toured the country to devastating effect; however, a surprisingly limited amount of damage was

[1] W.H. St John Hope, 'The Architectural History of the Cathedral and Monastery of St Andrew at Rochester', *Archaeologia Cantiana*, xxiii (1898), p. 281.
[2] Emf 1.
[3] G.H. Palmer, *The Cathedral Church of Rochester*, London 1897, p. 22.
[4] *Ibid.*, p. 23.

done to Rochester Cathedral during this period, or during the subsequent interregnum. A raid by Cromwellian soldiers appears to have resulted in little other than removing the altar to another position and breaking the altar rails. A commentator of the day observed that 'the Monuments of the dead, which elsewhere they brake up and violated, stood untouched – the seats of the Stalls of the Quire escaped breaking down'.[5] It was however alleged that 'a gang of seamen battered down the images and glass of Rochester Cathedral and destroyed the cherished library accumulated by the poet Dean Henry King',[6] and a certain John Wyld, shoemaker of Rochester, is said to have taken down and sold iron and brass work from some of the tombs. The quire was used as a stable by Fairfax's troops, whose horses' heads were turned into the stalls. Further depredations were at the hands of Rochester people when local carpenters, taking advantage of the large space of the nave, assembled timber house frames above saw pits which they had dug into the pavement.[7]

(2) 1660–1760

It was not until the 1660s that the first major post-Reformation restoration got under way. Some workmen's estimates survive[8] and reveal the cathedral now to be in need of a great deal of work; repair was needed to the spire, quire and east end roofs and arches, north nave aisle wall, and the pavement of the whole church. By 1662 the dean and chapter reported to the bishop that the then enormous sum of £8,000 had been spent, but that defects still remaining would cost a further £5,000. The nave had been paved by a benefactor, and Bishop Merton's tomb, again having been 'deformed by rabid fanatics', was renewed by Merton College.[9] The south wall of the nave was partially rebuilt,[10] but the bulging north nave aisle was left shored up until further funds were available.[11]

A legacy of £2,000 left to the cathedral in 1666 by Bishop Warner enabled sums still owing for repairs to be paid and further work to be done.[12] A survey was undertaken in 1667 by Capt. Richard Rider and Joseph Marshall. Rider was the architect of Bromley College, founded by Bishop Warner for orthodox clergymen's widows; Joseph Marshall was the sculptor of the Warner Monument. Their survey dealt mainly with the state of the roofs, which they considered would require a further £600, but included the cost of £90 for the demolition and rebuilding of the shored north wall of the nave north aisle.[13]

By 1670 the two main items of concern to the dean and chapter were the spire, and the leaning north nave aisle wall.[14] The spire was surveyed by Mr Guy of Strood,

5   *Ibid.*, p. 26.
6   C.V. Wedgwood, *The King's War*, London 1958, p. 124.
7   Palmer, *op. cit.*, p. 26.
8   Emf 5/1, 2, 3.
9   Palmer, *op. cit.*, pp. 26–7.
10 Arb 2.
11 Emf 7/127.
12 Arb 2a.
13 Emf 7/127.
14 Arb 3.

and Mr Fry, carpenter of the City of Westminster. It was recommended that the insertion of a mid bressumer at the lower third end on the east side could save it,[15] and the chapter ordered in June 1670 that this should be done immediately. At the same time they agreed that forty feet of the bulging north nave aisle wall should be taken down and rebuilt from the ground to the battlements, finishing within and without for £21.[16]

However, by 1679, despite its earlier repairs, the spire was again causing concern. Mr Guy reported to the dean and chapter that he found it in a very ruinous condition, 'ready to sink down into ye Church and to carry all below it by reason of ye rottenness of ye plates and the great Gurders are rotted quite through so that a stick may be safely thrust through ye same, and yet all ye lead is so thinn that there is no mending of it. The three corners of ye stone worke of ye Tower west of it all are soft and crooked and must be taken down.' He recommended taking down the old spire, putting up a new one, and repairing the stonework of the tower, at a cost of about £1,600.[17] At the same time Mr Fry also had been asked to investigate its condition, and the cathedral's carpenters travelled to London to give sworn evidence on its state.[18] From the quantities of timber and lead subsequently purchased, and the painting of the vane, one can only assume that Mr Fry again recommended repair, and that this was accepted.[19] Also a sum in 1680 of £1 10s, paid to 'Henry Fry who survey ye Repayres of the Steeple' tends to confirm this.

In 1681 the old Consistory Court, for the trial of 'civil causes', and which had been located 'in the west quarter of the palace precincts', was moved into the cathedral's south aisle near the great west door, where it was partitioned off and later reported to contain 'most of the wainscott of the Church and other ornaments'.[20] It remained here until its removal to the Lady Chapel in 1743. Other work at this time consisted of newly paving the Lady Chapel with Dutch tiles (brought to Rochester by boat),[21] and a great deal of work on the bells. An agreement was made in 1683 with Christopher Hodson 'to take down out of the Steeple the tenor and fouarth bells, both of them Crack'd, to new cast and make the same Strong and Substantiall . . . and shall make another Treble to the said ring of Bells, to make a tuneable Ring of six . . . .' The work was not completed until 1695, by which time the casting of the treble had been undertaken by another bellfounder, John Wood of Chancery Lane.[22] The old organ was repaired and a new choir organ acquired.

In 1687 the chapter house, 'that is now fallen down' was surveyed. The cost 'in the opinion of the workmen' would be £35, but receipted bills 'for the rebuilding of ye Chapter House by me', H. Turner carpenter and J. Gamball bricklayer, show it was done for £25. The carpenter's bill for 'flouwering the flour . . . usuant of ould timber from the ArchDekens ould house'[23] was not presented until 1701; the 'ould house' had been demolished in 1699. It seems for some time that the chapter house

[15] Ac 2/4, 8a.
[16] Ac 2/4; Arb 3.
[17] Ac 2/3, 14a.
[18] FTb 18.
[19] FTb 16, 17.

[20] FTb 17.
[21] FTb 17, 18; FTv 12.
[22] Emf 55; FTv 230/7; FTb 19.
[23] FTv 17, 33.

was in a state of unfinished restoration, as work on the chimney and windows is recorded in November 1700. The time taken over the work may have been due to the diversion of the cathedral's workmen to other more urgent work, such as the repeated repairs to adjacent prebendal properties, damaged by falling stones from the cathedral, and a crack in the arcade of the nave requiring immediate attention, all clearly indicating the deteriorating state of the cathedral's fabric.[24] A generous benefactor, Sir Henry Solby, donated his annual salary in 1694 'due to great need of expending great sums of money in Repairs of the Cathedral for good and necessary work'.[25]

The time taken over completing the chapter house was probably caused also by the decision in 1698 to rebuild the petty canons' houses: 'for £405 a year each Minor Canon consented to the demolition of their old and ruinous buildings in Petticanon Row and erection of new ones'.[26] These and the archdeacon's old house were all demolished in the following year.[27] Over the year funds were raised by the sale of timber and lead, and 16,000 tiles salvaged from the demolitions were stored in the crypt.[28] In 1700 the bishop signed 'an instrument' for the rebuilding of the minor canons' houses to proceed.[29]

A violent storm in 1703 greatly accelerated the decaying state of the cathedral;[30] the building was so badly damaged that the programme commenced was to last several years; repairing pantile roofs and leadwork, glazing windows, and the use of 8,000 bricks is recorded as used in the 'stipell and other plaices'.[31] However, somewhat surprisingly, the timberwork of the further weakened spire was again only repaired, possibly by the insertion of a sixteen foot girder purchased at this time,[32] and strengthened with '8 cramps for Stepell for to key ye stone worke waying 20 pounds'. The opportunity was taken, whilst the scaffolding was up, for the timberwork and lead repairs, to place a new weather vane and spindle on top of the steeple. Whilst all this work was in progress it was ordered that the bells should not by rung 'in peace on any occasion until the work settled and there is no danger of the steple'.[33]

The next major work undertaken was in 1705, when the nave roof was completely re-covered with 25 tons of new lead at 8 pounds to the square foot,[34] the final bill amounting to £378 4s 10d. The names of the workmen, bishop, dean, prebendaries and verger were thereon inscribed for posterity. A large programme of repair of the windows is also revealed in the glazier's bill for 1707 which showed over 2,500 quarries had been replaced that year, and 2,250 in 1709. Some houses to the south-east of the cathedral were ordered to be investigated in 1708; their close proximity was causing damage to the walls of the cathedral, and they were

24 Ac 3/9.   30 FTb 37; Ac 4/12.
25 *Loc. cit.*   31 FTb 37; FTv 230/153.
26 Egz 50.   32 FTv 37, 46.
27 FTb 33.   33 Ac 4/12.
28 Ac 4/11.   34 Emf 12/1.
29 FTb 34.

demolished in 1709.[35] An imposing stone fireplace was erected in the chapter house in 1708, a further improvement.[36]

The weakened state of the spire and tower appears to have been underrated, as again a great deal of work is recorded on it in 1711, eight years after the repairs following the storm. Bills record the bricklayer requesting payment for 'worke and stouff don at the Stipell' and from the smith for 'ironwork for steepel', 'barrs' and 'ten large holdfasts for the stonework of the steeple, and 'flatt headed nayles and eighteen large Holdfast for Mr. Gamball to use upon the stonework of the Stepell'.[37]

In 1716 the chapter minute book records: 'Injunction given by Francis Bishop of Rochester during primary visitation; observed that the Cathedral Church is now very much out of repair and having ratified a view to be taken of the said Church and an estimate made by an appointed Surveyor of the charges requisite to put the said Church into due sufficient repair which shall amount to £1161 7s . . . and being satisfied that the sum of about one hundred pounds yearly . . . will scarce preserve the old church from falling into a worse than now ruinous condition and being willing to provide such a remedy as may in the time bring the aforementioned church into fit and convenient repair without lessening the yearly income, the Bishop doth decree: that annual sums reserved for individual repairs should go to repair of the fabric and that the school house be put into convenient repair.' The costed survey to which the minute refers, and which survives, had been provided by a Mr Dickinson,[38] about whom nothing is known; he may have been a local surveyor or builder. His survey listed repairs necessary to groined ribs, underpinning, extensive roof repairs including removal of pantiles from the south nave aisle roof, alteration of its profile to enable lead to be laid, and so accord with that of the north nave aisle. He also made a recommendation that the bell ringing gallery, which at that time was over the steps to the quire, and approached from Gundulf's Tower, should be removed, and the bells rung from a newly boarded ringing chamber above the crossing. This proposal was eventually carried out, but not until fifteen years later.

The nave south aisle roof was altered and leaded in 1717,[39] and the following year the Lady Chapel roof was new leaded and its timbers strengthened with additional timber and bolts;[40] but little other major work appears to have been done, although the usual ongoing minor repairs are recorded. However a graphic description, which survives, was made in 1719 by the plumber, John Proby, of the leaking roofs all over the cathedral, revealing the need for a great deal of expense.[41] At this time Henry Turner, carpenter of long service, was 'dismissed at the same time he was paid from ever working for the church more, on account of his very unfair dealing by it'.[42] That a decision had been made to start a major repair programme is revealed in a letter from one John Hales of Rochester, offering to supervise the work. Having retired after thirty years in the building trade and with time to spare, he wrote 'judging it a

35 Ac 5/13; FTv 43.
36 FTv 230/58.
37 FTv 44–5.
38 Red Book p. 174; Emf 14.
39 FTv 50.

40 FTv 52.
41 Emf 18/2.
42 Ac 5/15; FTb 53; Turner was mayor of Rochester in 1710.

matter of no little difficulty as well as thing not commonplace for any of the Gentlemen belonging to the Church to ascend a Scaffold or Battlement, and likewise the leads, to see the Workmen don't triffle away their time, and also which is absolutely necessary to avoid all imposition that may be done by often times taking and removing good timber and putting bad in the lieu there of likewise with lead'. The chapter would have been aware of these risks from its recent experience with Henry Turner, but whether or not it accepted Mr Hales' offer is unknown.

A need to raise funds urgently is recorded in the minutes of the dean and chapter in September 1719: 'Repairs of ye Cathedrall in the timberwork therof being very Great, . . . treated and agreed for sale of 250 elm trees now standing on the Manor of Frindsbury (ye forest being at its full growth at ye best they would ever be) . . . Mr. Phillips to pay half at Christmas, balance at Lady Day for ye price of twenty six shillings ye load.'[43] The re-building of Minor Canon Row completed in 1723, at a cost of £1,699,[44] would suggest that they successfully raised the necessary finances for this, as well as for repairs to the cathedral. A visitor to the cathedral in 1723 recorded that after 'a cursory view . . . that ancient building . . . now looks very poorly and desolate. I think every one of the brass plates are taken off the gravestones but there are two or three old monuments still remaining. The oldest as I remember is Bishop Lowes' enclosed in a pew on the S. side of the Choir, it is built with stone, altarwise, and a modern one very remarkable on Dr. Caesar, a physician formerly of this place on the left hand as you enter into the church at the S. gate'.[45]

However Bishop Bradford, at his primary visitation in 1724, was assured by the dean and chapter that 'we know of no defects in the walls of the Cathedral Church of any moment – windows are kept in good repair as far as tithe payments will admit, and three quarters of the whole roof hath been new leaded within these twenty years',[46] although four years after this reassuring account, the crumbling masonry of the north west tower had to be strengthened with the insertion of iron ties.[47] The nave north aisle roof was re-leaded, the timbers strengthened with iron bolts, and small works generally, including leadwork continued to be done as usual; in 1727 three sash windows were inserted into the south face of the chapter room, replacing the small high casements.[48] The strict enforcement was requested of an order made in 1679 to prevent the passage of wagons and carriages through the cathedral, to protect the pavement from unnecessary damage.[49] In 1730 Mr Dickinson's proposals of 1716 for the re-location of the bell ringers was at last put in hand. The bells were taken down, a new bell frame and truss made and the bells rehung. The belfry floor was boarded and soundproofed with two boat loads of cockle shells to protect the ringers from the noise.[50] These changes led to London architect John James being asked to design a classical scheme for the new ceiling under the crossing – the 'cupulo under the Steeple . . . we intend it to be an ornament to the Fabrick'.[51] Dean

43 Ac 5/15.
44 Arb 2.
45 V.J. Torr, 'A Canterbury Pilgrimage 1723', Archaeologia Cantiana, lvii (1944), p. 63.
46 Arb 2.
47 FTv 70.
48 FTv 71; Ac 6/18.
49 Ac 6/16.
50 FTv 74.
51 Emf 19.

Nicholas Claggett was closely involved in its design and decoration, and his correspondence with the architect reveals ideas of taste at the time; the dean accepted the advice of Mr James that the carving by Richard Chicheley of a pendant, flowers and oakleaves should not be gilded too much,[52] as it would 'render it more rich than any part of the Ceiling of the Choir which I think should not be'. However taste changes, and every succeeding generation of architects at Rochester was to pour harsh criticism on the efforts of their predecessors! The first, Daniel Alexander, commenting on the crossing seventy years later whilst doing his survey in 1799, recorded: 'the Cieling of the central part under the Tower has been coloured as the rest of the cross Aisles (the intersection of the Mullions bordered by black stripes on each side) and the central ornament round the bell hole . . . made in the grecian stile of Architecture is peculiarly disgusting . . .'[53] Whilst the crossing was being altered in 1731 it was agreed also that 'Mr. Harwood be employed to wainscott that part of the organ loft fronting ye Body of the Church with plain and raised wainscott like that of the Altar piece'.

Although during the ensuing decade the attention of the dean and chapter continued to be focused primarily on the appearance of the interior of the cathedral, a house for the organist was added to Minor Canon Row in 1735.[54] A decision to beautify the quire was taken in 1741, and a plan and estimate by Charles Sloane for its paving with Portland and Bremen stone was accepted. Proposals included new seats next to the walls from the prebendaries' stalls to the pulpit, wainscotting the walls, new paving the cross aisle, and new fronts and seats to the prebendaries' stalls to which a 'collonade of Ionick Columns and arched Intablature' were to be added; the ribs and columns of the ceiling were to be painted. A new bishop's throne was designed by Sloane. Also the whole of the interior of the west end of the cathedral was to be repaired and whitewashed.[55] At this time the consistory court, which had been located near the west end of the south nave aisle since 1681, was moved to the Lady Chapel. The drawings by Sloane for the new benches and desks survive. Sloane informed the archdeacon that he had shown them to 'my Lord of Bangor, which he approves of, but desires it may be placed in the first quarter on the right hand of St Marie's Chapel; my Lord's reason for it is that it will be screen'd from the North winds that comes in at the north door, and be much warmer in the winter season.'[56]

The south-west end of the cathedral, the ancient gateway entrance to the precinct and the Porter's Lodge, and other adjacent buildings, were becoming extremely decayed and a source of concern; the college gatehouse was surveyed by a workman from Rochester Bridge in 1740, and in 1743 the south wall of the south nave aisle was reported to be 'injured in its foundations by the continued rains that have course off from the Church . . . and that the opinion of Judicious workmen should be sought to secure and amend'. In July 1744 the chapter ordered 'that the Old Gate House and porters Lodge adjoyning being both very Ruinous and Dangerous be taken down and that the Provost's House be made Good at West End thereof by a Strong and

[52] Acd 15; Emf 20/2, 3.
[53] Emf 38.
[54] Emf 26.
[55] Ac 6/27; Emf 26, 27.
[56] Emf 27.

Substantiall Wall and that the Area thereof be Paved and the Limetts of the Precincts there be marked out and preserved with Posts'.[57] Bills were submitted in the following months for underpinning, presumably of the south wall, and demolition of the gatehouse only; evidence of a three storied structure remaining is revealed in an etching by Schnebbelie, published in 1788; this is probably the Porter's Lodge, later referred to in bills for minor repairs, but which, by 1810, an illustration by Buckler shows to have disappeared.

Once again the attention of the dean and chapter was now drawn to the condition of the spire; it was considered so dangerous that the advice of three surveyors was sought.[58] Of these only Mr Ransome's detailed report of 1747 survives, revealing the timbers to be extremely decayed; he reported that the walls of the tower 'for want of proper security of Timber work and irons were forced out considerable from their original Perpendicular, and the floor on which the Bells hang is greatly overloaded and lay proping against ye sides of ye walls and must in time force them out, and the floor of the Belfrey was too weak being chiefly kept up by two very old beams much too slender for such a purpose'.[59] Plans and sections of his proposals for repair or rebuilding which he estimated would cost £564 also survive. However it was to John Sloane's design that the new spire was built in 1748; his model of its structure remained in the crypt late into the nineteenth century. The final bill, including repairs to the tower, after the deductions for sale of old lead and timber, came to £419.[60]

In the 1750s the leaning south face of the south-east transept, which had also caused concern for some years, began to require urgent attention. These walls were not buttressed as were those on the north side, probably because the cloister and other conventual buildings originally had supported and sheltered them. The cloisters were now long gone and several of the houses demolished recently, so removing support. Previous efforts to restrain the roof from pushing out the wall had been made by tying the roof truss with bolted timbers. Under the direction of Mr Sloane two great brick buttresses were raised against the south face,[61] one of which required major repair seven years later. It appears that his 'Report of several needfull Repairs to be don at the Cathedral Church', dated December 1754, was the date on which it was presented for payment, much of the work recommended in it apparently having been done in the previous year or two. Included in the survey is: 'One of the windows in the S. Isle of the Steeple Cross, is fell down, being worn out with age, and quite rotton; as also the stone work of the other two, therefore am of opinion it may be best (as it will help to succor the wall) to brick it up; and perhaps it will be best to brick up the two others . . .'[62] These instructions, judging by subsequent surveys, involved the replacement of decayed stone window jambs, mouldings and mullions with brickwork, rather than the modern interpretation which would be to completely fill the opening with brickwork.

At the east end of the cathedral Sloane discovered that 'the heavy rafters in several places seem to push very hard on the walls, as appears by several rents in the vaulting;

[57] Ac 6/20.   [60] FTv 99.
[58] Ac 7/21.   [61] FTv 104.
[59] FTv 97, 99.   [62] FTv 110.

seems necessary to tye the Roof in over the vaulting with some Timber works to resist that great push and prevent the bad consequence that may attend the same'. His survey of the west end of the cathedral started with the nave roof leadwork, done fifty years previously, and his comments were scathing – the too broad leads were not very workmanlike and the great deal of soldering repairs done were bad husbandry, being dear work and going but little way in curing the evil; he advised that all future cracked sheets should be taken up and re-cast and soldering avoided. At the west end of the nave he observed that a large beam and corbel post on the north side was rotten and decayed, and ordered the insertion of a new oak corner post and the girder to be trussed. On the exterior of the west end he observed a large rent in the wall of the north-west tower below the iron ties inserted some years earlier, but felt careful observation would suffice for the time being. He also considered that several of the greatly decayed parapet walls should be lowered at least a foot to lessen expense, and bills record that certainly those on the north side, where stones were loose, were lowered in 1757.[63]

(3) 1760–1820

In 1760, despite Sloane's repairs and only six years after his report, a further two surveys were done, the first by George Younger. He described a cathedral in greatly decayed condition – he found the north-west tower 'in a very bad and rotten state, the iron strapps and stayes that have heretofore been made use of have not bin any service to the same, but very much otherwise . . . the sooner released from the Gable end of the Church the better'. He considered that the top should be demolished as low as the gallery and covered with a temporary roof. He found the roofs of the east end in need of speedy repair, and the south-east transept roof 'is realey in danger of some parts falling down', and suggested that the gable end be taken down to the wall plates to relieve the weight on the leaning wall, covering it with slate instead of 'that weighty affair ye lead'. He concluded his recommendations with the comment that the want of proper gutters 'has occasioned great damage to the whole of this fine old Church . . . I must say I ham very sorry to see the same Hath been so much neglected which its two plaine has been the Case.'[64]

The second, more detailed and educated, report was provided by Henry Keene.[65] His recommendations were radical to say the least, and included the demolition and rebuilding of the south quire aisle wall which he found to be greatly out of perpendicular, and the demolition of Gundulf's Tower, its masonry to be used for future repairs, so answering two purposes – of saving money in the purchase of new materials, and the removal of 'this unnecessary and unsightly ruin'. He noted that the north nave aisle wall was again considerably bulged, and suggested that it should be restrained by three buttresses between the windows rising to the top of the wall

[63] FTv 112.
[64] Emf 33.
[65] Emf 34.

from which arches could be sprung against the north wall of the nave. He considered the north-west tower now to be incapable of repair and in need of taking down and rebuilding, and also recommended demolition of the decayed octagonal section of the south-west tower which he thought should be rebuilt to the same height as the north west tower with the removal of the parapet between the towers. He also wanted the north middle turret to be rebuilt to the same appearance as that on the south. The rest of the west end was 'in tolerable good condition', but he found the nave roof to be racked and in need of strengthening with ties and braces.

Keene recommended the removal of several of the houses and buildings which were 'home to the south west cross', as he considered that they harboured the damp, and the run off from their roofs was increasing the decay of the walls of the cathedral. The south-east transept he found to be in a very dangerous and irreparable state, nearly three feet out of perpendicular and the inside drawn away with it also, taking the two first arches and their columns. Fresh cracks had occurred and old ones re-opened since the building of the brick buttresses nine years previously. These he considered had been 'injudiciously performed, . . . they do not answer the intended purpose' and he recommended 'not only as a point of Prudence, but absolutely necessary . . . the erection of a Truss Buttress against the said End to secure it until a convenient time to demolish it and rebuild'. Keene's survey gives a graphic description of the state of the tower – 'decaying multering stones plaistered over, bricks used for patching the decay'd places, altogether providing a most shabby appearance with a motley face of brick, stone and plaister'.

Fortunately for the cathedral, lack of funds probably prevented the implementation of some of his most energetic recommendations; however, over the next few years the west front underwent a radical change in its appearance. Initially a further attempt was made in 1760 to save the north-west tower with the insertion of more iron ties and brickwork, but this failed to make it secure, and three years later it had to be demolished, together with the upper part of the north aisle beside it.[66] By 1766, it had been rebuilt from the ground, at a cost of £374, using Portland and Purbeck stone; prior to its demolition a carved figure, considered at the time to be that of the Virgin Mary, was removed, cleaned and re-set on the north side in the new structure.[67] It was not finally roofed and coped until 1769,[68] when sufficient funds became available. According to Thorpe, the author of *Custumale Roffense*, the pinnacle of the south-west turret was taken down at this time also, and crenellated parapets added to the west end of the nave aisle roofs. At the instigation of Bishop Pearce the registrar's building was erected in 1760 in the gaoler's old garden. In 1767 George Silverside, the dean's surveyor, became involved in the cathedral's efforts to stabilise the leaning south wall of the south-east transept. There is no evidence amongst the bills that the timber strutting to support the wall, suggested by Henry Keene, was ever constructed, but this is not necessarily an indication that it was not done. It had obviously continued to deteriorate, and in 1768 the gable was demolished to reduce the load on the wall and the roof hipped back.[69]

[66] FTv 117.
[67] FTb 94; Ac 7/24.
[68] Emf 35/3; Ac 8/25; FTv 124.
[69] FTv 126.

Throughout the 1770s there was great expenditure on draining and paving the precinct. Inside the cathedral the groins of the quire were whitewashed, side walls scraped and cleaned, the pillars polished and repaired with plaster of Paris, and a great deal of gilding done.[70] The Early English north-west transept gable was taken down in 1776 and rebuilt, and faced with new ragstone[71] – 'in a low commonplace manner' according to a nineteenth-century commentator.[72]

In 1776 Robert Mylne was paid for a survey of the cathedral; he studied in particular the leaning face of the south-east transept and made recommendations and drawings, none of which survives. At his instigation the wall was 'secured' by building solid brick and stone work under several of the arches in the undercross and a firm and solid base made to the outer wall by filling up with brickwork the staircase and the two arches leading to the chapter house; also at last 'struts were placed to prevent the wall from Bursting'. By 1778 Mylne was able to report that the 'defective front was thoroughly secured', and the shores removed. However, three years later the arches inside had to be shored up; the arch over the chapter house doorway was repaired with firestone and Portland, and the small columns in the gallery repaired and re-set on a new Portland curb.[73]

Contemporary commentators reveal that by the 1780s the cathedral was probably at its most decayed and vulnerable state for centuries. Hasted took an extremely gloomy view of its condition: 'the whole bears venerable marks of its antiquity, but time has so far impaired the strength of the materials with which it is built that, in all likelihood the care and attention of the Present Chapter towards the support of it will not be sufficient to prevent the fall of a great part of it, even in their time'.[74] In December 1780 the chapter recorded that 'large and necessary expenses . . . and many and absolutely necessary Repairs are recommended by its Surveyors to be forthwith done . . . agreed . . . Repairs to be made as are represented . . . to be so expedient as cannot be postponed without imminent danger to the building'.[75]

Despite this the aesthetics of Sloane's forty-year-old spire was the subject of discussion between Dean Cust and Mr James Lawford of Dartford. The dean wanted it demolished as he so disliked it. Mr Lawford presented a drawing which 'he thought might please better . . . but as you say, you have no Money to pull it down'. Lawford attempted to influence the chapter against any cosmetic work: 'when I was at your Audit I Discouraged every alteration which would be expensive for I saw enough to do that was Necessary Repair. So large a Building and Ancient cannot be supported at a small expence.' He expressed the hope that the absolutely necessary repairs to the parapets would not be done with red brick and coped with Portland stone.[76]

The state of the cathedral's rainwater disposal was the subject of a detailed investigation in September 1785 by John Oldfield. He found the gutters and parapets to be in such a bad condition that 'from these several causes the water penetrates into the roof to the prejudice of the timbers as well as the walls and vaulted ceilings,

[70] FTv 129.
[71] FTv 132.
[72] Palmer, op. cit., p. 51.
[73] FTv 136, 138, 140.

[74] Hasted, 2nd edn, iv, p. 101.
[75] Ac 8/26
[76] Emf 36/3.

and must if not timely prevented prove destructive', and some of the parapets were 'so very ruinous . . . [they] should be taken down now to prevent their falling'.

Eventually, by 1788, a great deal of work was in hand, both on the inside and outside of the cathedral. The spire leadwork was repaired, the arches of the chancel were strengthened with Portland stone repairs and the insertion of iron bars. Externally the decayed pinnacles were taken down and 'worked up' with 2600 hard clinker burnt bricks, the gable heads pointed up and garretted. The main east gable was taken down and rebuilt, the chancel window removed and a new Portland stone 'gothic' window inserted. At the north cross aisle the east turret was considered to be in a dangerous state, and the top taken down to gutter level, capped with a parapet and flat roofed. Its failing quoins were replaced with hard clinker burnt bricks. In 1790 the great tower was new faced on its south and east sides with 8500 bricks and 9½ loads of headed stone, costing £90, and a new Portland stone string inserted.[77]

The sale of battered church plate in 1790 enabled the chapter to purchase a new organ for 600 guineas.[78] At its installation in 1792 'the old stalls were demolished', the organ loft floor was shored up with joists, new trimmers inserted and the old partitions beneath secured. The 1730 classical front of the organ was replaced by one of Gothic design. The old floors and joists of the choir stalls were replaced and new stalls fixed. These were then painted with burnt umber and stone ochre. New Portland stone was laid to make good the pavement in the new stalls.[79] Hasted recorded that 'notwithstanding earlier restorations, time has so corroded and weakened every part of this building that its future existence for any length of time has been much feared, but this Church has lately had every endeavour used, great repairs made which it is hoped will secure it from the fatal ruin which has threatened it . . . its inside beautified and kept exceeding clean, it makes at this time a very pleasing appearance'.[80]

In 1799 Daniel Alexander, the architect of Maidstone and Dartmoor Prisons, produced the most comprehensive costed survey to survive and possibly the most detailed ever before undertaken at the cathedral.[81] He calculated that £600 a year over an eight year period totalling £5,317 would be required. His description of the interior of the cathedral gives a clear idea of its appearance at the close of the eighteenth century. The pavement of all parts west of the quire consisted of shabby red tiles; the four main piers of the tower were painted marble: 'real marble itself would perhaps not be the best coloured stone for this purpose – the resemblance is still worse'. The nave he considered 'admits of little improvement with regard the appearance – walls were not many out of the perpendicular and the settlement of very ancient date. The roofs all chestnut chiefly and oak beams, not painted or coloured, and walls are simply whitewashed – including the little Pillars' which he thought should be restored to their original colour – whitewashing having impoverished their effect. The columns he thought appeared to be Kentish stone ashlar, which would bear scraping to resume its bluish grey colour. He recommended

[77] FTv 139 (I); FTv 153; Emf 37.
[78] Ac 9/29; FTv 145.
[79] FTv 145, 146.

[80] Hasted, 2nd edn, iv, p. 106.
[81] Emf 38.

a lath and plaster ceiling to the nave to help keep it warm, but if that was considered too expensive, painting the principal beams 'a half tint between the cream coloured walls below and the darker oak colour of the rafters . . . to divide the space and prepare the eye for the sudden transition from the light coloured walls below them and the darker oak colour of the rafters'. He described the decoration of the cross aisles of the western transepts, where the regular panels in the arched ceiling, formed by the intersection of the mullions, were bordered by black stripes on each side, which produced a harsh appearance, especially when contrasted with the white of the panels, making the mullions into nothing more than even flat white stripes and not appearing as projecting mouldings. His description of the ceiling of the crossing has already been referred to earlier, and he recommended '. . . it had better give place to a proper junction of the several Mullions in the Gothic way which must be formed anew'.

As regards the state of the fabric, he found the settlement of the south-east transept virtually stabilised, but the oak ties in the hipped roof which had been introduced to prevent it spreading had decayed, and he recommended their replacement with iron. The steeple he described 'as ugly as can well be conceived', but its timber and lead, although very good, would hardly pay for its demolition or the 'four turrets at the four corners which it would be adviseable there to erect'. Most of his proposals concerned repairs of roofs, gutters, parapets and walls, but the south nave aisle wall battlements were found to be dangerous and requiring rebuilding. His report concluded with the comment that the cathedral would still need annual repair, and that his recommendations contained in the survey were for matters requiring immediate attention. Future works should include new stone mullions to a great many of the windows 'as they will only last out the present leaded glass work . . . these have been in a gradually perishing state for centuries and would in the end drop entirely out if not renewed with stone that will not moulder, and pavements will require attention with better materials than red tiles'.

'So immediately close to the Fabric of the Cathedral as to be detrimental thereto' were several houses (Plate 4a), which Alexander recommended should be demolished; he suggested also the non-renewal of the lease of one of them in order that it could be demolished eventually, provided 'the doing shall not be detrimental to the fifth prebendal house'; this prebendal dwelling was attached to the provostship of Oriel College, and was 'the ancient almonry of the Priory . . . which stood in the angle formed by the south wall of the nave and that of the Chapel of St Mary, with which it communicated by a stair . . . passing through one of the chapel windows. It was the apartment where, of old, the alms of the convent were distributed and stood as was the custom . . . close to Gate House.' It is not clear precisely when it was demolished; there are receipts recording the sale of materials from demolished houses and from another about to be taken down in 1805.[82]

In December 1800 the dean and chapter in accepting Alexander's report of 'the great and extensive Repairs therein declared to be necessary . . . resolve forthwith

[82] FTb 136.

to enter upon the same'. The chapter however had 'no Funds particularly appropriated to the Purpose of Repairs; and had to devise 'a least burthensome and most effectual Plan for defraying this extraordinary Expense'. The plan agreed required subscriptions from individual members of the chapter, sale of estates under the Land Tax Redemption Act and the payments for chalk and brick earth from the tenant Boghurst, all to be used exclusively for repairs, 'and the particular Repairs to be undertaken in each year to be determined at the St Catherine's Audit preceding'.[83]

Work stated in 1801 on the south nave aisle wall. Alexander's specification gives a detailed insight into building techniques and materials of this period; a note written at the top of the document however says 'underwritten contains only Repairs to be had to the external parts of the south side aisle and Bishop's Court, as no more is intended now to be done'. Included in the specification is replacement of brick strings and patches of brickwork with Kentish stone in rubbled courses, replacement of the openings of two old chimneys and their brick shafts, cutting out stone mullions left in the wall of the blocked window behind the Henniker tomb 'to fill in same with rough stone to answer the appearance of the other walling' and to 'match the old work as nearly as possible so as when the pointing shall be done no difference whatever shall appear'. The parapets were to be dismantled from the south-west turret 'home to angle of the Bishop's Court', rebuilt to the same height as previously, with Kentish rag rubble masonry with embrasures of the same openings 'as at present over every window now there and one between and over each', coped with Portland stone. The builder has added 'done' at the bottom noting that the stone chimney frames which Alexander had ordered should not be disturbed were in fact taken down. The windows were glazed in eight by six inch square crown glass ground on one face.[84] The specification calls for repair and increased falls of the sunken flat roof of the south nave aisle, but at the bottom the builder notes 'all omitted in consequence of new roof'.[85]

The work specified to the west end of the Lady Chapel (referred to always as the Bishop's Court) reveals it to have had a high gable, presumably intended to take a high roof over the never completed groined ceiling; Alexander ordered this to be demolished to the level of the bottom cornice 'and to be rebuilt from this level to its present height of the top of the angular coping eighteen inches in Rag masonry, and coped in Portland'. The builder noted that this was done but rebuilt about fourteen inches lower than requested. The appearance of this face, as well as having a high gable, was different from now in that the lower half of the southern window had a door, which connected it originally to the old almonry building; the doorway was ordered to be removed and the window repaired with 'an old piece of mullion stone' (new used), and all the compartments of the window to be newly stuccoed. The lower half of the northern window (as too were all those on the south side) was blocked

---

[83] Emf 39/1. A survey of the cathedral precincts drawn up by Alexander in 1801, and annotated by Dean Dampier with comments on the order of work and state of the properties survives, British Library Map Room K-xvii-8-2 (Plate 6).

[84] FTv 157; Emf 41.

[85] Emf 41.

and stuccoed. Alexander ordered that it should be newly done 'with Bayley cement made up with coal ashes instead of sand, so as to give the windows the appearance of being glazed at a distance'; common plaster was noted as used. Under this window 'a hole that had been excavated' was ordered to be filled up. The top half of this window was to have two new Portland stone mullions (sketched in the specification), with the gothic heads re-worked 'as before', but the builder notes 'executed different; head taken out'. The stuccoing of these windows may have been for privacy and security for sittings of the Bishop's Court. The access mentioned earlier of the staircase from the almonry into the Bishop's Court is not mentioned, although a great deal of eighteenth-century brickwork was found in this area during repairs in the 1980s.

The brick parapet on the south side was to be rebuilt in stone and coped in Portland. Alexander added that the Kentish rag could 'be procured either new from Quarries up the Medway or by pulling down parts of the Keep going into the Deanery'. The brick arches over the three Gothic windows on this side of the Bishop's Court were to be replaced with Kentish rubble face work over the stone moulding, and the most eastern and most western windows 'to be formed anew by taking down the Mullions of the whole opening with the enriched work above the springing of the arch' and filled with plain Portland stone uprights. The middle window,[86] 'having had new mullions does only require new saddle bars . . . and new stucco the three compartments formerly glazed'. The upper halves of all three windows were fitted with purple and yellow stained glass.[87] Alexander favoured the use of small flint gallets placed in green mortar whilst walls were pointed, 'which is usual all over the sourthern parts of the County'.[88] At the same time the Bishop's Court roof was repaired, with the insertion of some new oak joists and iron ties; the lead was re-laid and new lead rainwater pipes with large moulded cistern heads installed.

The nave north triforium arcade suddenly appeared to require urgent attention. In 1801, the Clerk of Works, John Smith of Maidstone, in the absence of Alexander, ordered the masons 'to secure the Saxon arches'.[89] His prompt action met with Alexander's approval. He commented that 'the small collars of iron round the little pillars had been very properly introduced'. Alexander, when examining the nave arcade the following year (when work on the roof had started) described its construction in an analysis of its problems. He noted that it was 'constructed of Massive Saxon Columns, turned over with two tiers of semi-circular arches and small double arches on little double insulated pillars under the middle of the upper ones; 'tis at this point, and above, that the Evil exists in this wall; for the work having been originally a mere casing of two fronts of stone, filled in the interior with unbounded rubble, has yielded to the incumbent weight; and being already divided lengthwise by the little double pillars, and by the alley formed by said arches, has naturally followed the principle of this mode of Structure, and as it is divided below, has slit itself above . . . [This] has been the case for many years, and the workmen in boring through the same, to fix the iron work of the new Roof (which ought to

[86] Emf 141.
[87] Emf 157.
[88] Emf 40.
[89] FTv 57.

connect itself with, as well as tie together these walls) have of necessity disturbed it, so that in three places it has shown faint signs of additional settlement'.[90] At this time the great west window also was strengthened with a 'large broad Bar with large brackets dovetailed in' weighing over two hundredweight.[91]

Whilst investigating the nave arcade Alexander also looked at the north wall of the nave north aisle. His report dated 9 September 1802[92] notes that 'whole of this side of Fabric has now for many years leant out of perpendicular towards north. . . . having been, before the repairs of this year began, 11″ at the west end and 3″ at the east end out of the upright, and the west of the Nave following it, though not in so great a degree. The said N. wall is found to go down only 6′ below the surface, and is there built on Chalk and other loose uncemented Rubble, on a stratum of loose ground . . . to prevent further settlement . . . at its eleven inch end, a Buttress has been thrown up at the commencement of this year's work, whose foundation is carried down to the Solid Native Loam.' He added that he considered this a prudent precaution even though from observation of the interior of the cathedral the walls 'of late years have not sensibly moved'.

In 1802 a piece of timber falling from the nave roof led to its inspection by Alexander. He found that it had fallen from a row of ornamental plates, 'from which if all were down, no injury to the Roof would arise'. The exterior he found to be 'strait without Bumps or Hollows, apparently as good as when the Lead thereof was laid in 1705', and the boarding to be good.[93] He had several large parts of the lead and boarding lifted, found the ends of many of the principal timbers rotten and defective 'so that in some places the same are supported by little knees (sketched) which may be seen from the bottom of the Church, placed under every intersecting beam, and which is the peculiar foresuing characteristic of the Carpentry of that Age, when the ends which were the original support are rotten . . .' He instructed Smith to uncase and inspect each beam by means of a lifting cradle. The roof was found by Smith to be much worse than expected, 'the whole of the Plates being entirely Rotten from end to end on both sides of the Roof . . . These plates while they remained sound form the Chief support of the walls by preserving their perpendicularity and keeping them from spreading . . . if the plates had been sound the other defects of the Roof might have been repaired by Splicing Sound pieces of Timber to several Decayed Parts . . . of opinion such a partial mode of repair would be of no real utility, as the plates are the only connecting medium to the two walls . . . be utterly impracticable to insert new plates without taking up beams and principal rafters . . . nothing short of a New Roof will be of essential benefit.' Alexander then investigated the roof himself: 'have examined and probed almost every Timber in the Roof'. He thought the main beams generally to be of chestnut and the smaller ones oak, although 'when old they are difficult to be distinguished'; he found them without exception 'rotten independent of bad ends and hollow insides as to be irreparable . . . as timber it may be said its substance is gone'. He recommended that a new roof should be 'begun and finished in one season even tho' the whole Expence could not

[90] Emf 47.   [92] Emf 47.
[91] FTv 157.   [93] Emf 45, 47.

immediately be cleared'. He instructed Smith to take levels and other measurements to enable him to report further to the chapter.[94] Plans and a specification by Alexander dated 25 June 1803[95] were presented to the chapter – the specification survives. The cost, allowing for old lead, was estimated at £511; he recommended that the oakwork was the necessary work to be done that year, consisting of 'two lengths of plates (to be under the tie beams), 32 counter braces, 80 sleepers, 10 queen posts, for which it is necessary to make working plans to give to the Carpenter to Set out the same, from timber fallen in the Spring of last year, that it may be properly seasoned by the time it is put up in its place. It will be proper to sell the old timber now laying in the S. Aisle to be sold by auction to the highest bidder.'[96] It went for £13.[97] On 29 June 1803 the chapter ordered 'that Mr Alexander do acquaint Mr Baker (carpenter) as to the Oak Timber to be used in the Roof of the Church'.[98] At the end of 1803 the chapter repaid a loan at 5% to Mr Twopeny for £420 borrowed for repairs.[99] The roof appears to have been rebuilt the following year, the carpenter's bill from 23 June – 10 November 1804 for £1,512 14s 10d was certified as completed by Clerk of Works J. Whiting and Surveyor J. Wilson on 5 October 1805.[100] In 1809 the sale of further old oak timber and fir raised £89.[101] Alexander's recommendation that the tower should be repaired and repointed, estimated at £150,[102] prior to the completion of the new nave roof, appears to have been done.[103]

There is no evidence of further work authorised by Daniel Alexander after this time; by 1805 the surveyor John Wilson appears to be in control of the cathedral's repairs and alterations, and was paid £150 for a survey.[104] He put an account to the November Audit for work 'compleating the buttresses, parapet walls, etc. to N. end of Cathedral . . . to be finished with Portland ashler like unto those already done . . .' It is possible that these buttresses were to the north nave aisle wall, recommended to be erected by Keene in 1760,[105] not mentioned as necessary in Alexander's 1799 survey, but possibly started by him before Wilson took over. Wilson details Portland and Yorkshire stone for the copings in this area, and 'the centre part between the buttresses which is already taken down to be made good with Kentish ragstone.'[106] It may be around this time that the demolition of the top of Gundulf's Tower occurred, since an illustration of 1804 shows it still to be intact, but by 1817 the second edition of *History of the Antiquities of Rochester* records '. . . that a part of this ancient tower has lately been taken down to supply materials for the repairs of the church'. Later the dean and chapter were reproached for their despoilation of 'one of the most curious and interesting pieces of architecture remaining in England.'[107]

The difficulty, often, of interpreting the precise location and nature of work undertaken is revealed in a bill of November 1805 for £183 submitted by John

94 Emf 43.
95 Emf 46, 48/1.
96 Ac 9/34.
97 FTb 135.
98 Ac 9/34.
99 FTb 134.
100 FTv 161.

101 FTv 167.
102 Emf 48/1.
103 FTb 135; FTv 159.
104 FTb 136, Emf 49.
105 Emf 34.
106 Emf 38, 39.
107 Palmer, *op. cit.*, p. 54.

Wilson 'to cut down the remains of the old building lined with the other wall in front' and 'the whole to be made good with Kentish rag stone, and the whole front to be raked, jointed and galloted', and 'the stonework of the windows reinstated, glass taken out and thoroughly repaired'.[108] This most probably refers to the old conventual building adjacent to the south-east corner of the south-west transept and the transept's south face, on which Alexander had commented in 1799:[109] '. . . south parapet wall is dangerous . . . must be rebuilt. Work of wall below is composed of rough material and the window [lying behind Dr Eveleigh's house] is of Brick Mullions to which nothing can be done but hereafter to rebuild the window with stone; it is disgraceful, though not much out of repair in its present condition . . .' (probably the brickwork jambs and mullions recommended by Sloane in 1754). It is likely that it was during this period that the south-west transept gable also was altered; at its restoration by Scott in the 1870s, it was found to have been constructed of upright timber beams surrounded by a thin coating of stone, about three inches thick. This is confirmed in an illustration of 1816 by Storer, who commented that 'the old gable was taken down in the early part of the century and replaced by a lower one of debased classical character, flanked by pedestals on the tops of the buttresses'.[110]

Sums spent by the chapter on repairs to the fabric in 1806 of £4,241 may refer to final payments for work done in previous years, as was frequently the practice, or they could be for work done of which no records survive.[111] The precinct had been extensively paved and surrounded by iron railings. In 1808 the chapter received a 'statement by Dr Willis regarding the need for the erection of a new prebendal house upon a different site and at which time he be allowed to pull down the present . . . cost invested with various provisos regarding delapidations to be £745'. This probably refers to the house erected in the south-west corner of the garth.

The roofs at the east end of the cathedral had now become a source of great anxiety, those of the quire in particular. In June 1810 the chapter ordered[112] that 'part of the roof of the Choir be repaired according to the plan and estimate . . . by Mr John Wilson' (the architect).[113] His instructions to the carpenter[114] were 'to take down old timber. To frame all the principal Rafters and re-frame the smaller with the sound part of old timber making good with as much new as shall be found wanting, same to wall plates', and loose boarding 'to let the air through. That part in immediate danger is shown on Plan and so much only of the present Roof may now be rescued leaving the Remainder . . . till a future time.' The carpenter Siddon was later paid 'for shoreing and repairing the roof'.[115] The roofs of the east end transepts were repaired at the same time.

---

[108] Emf 49.

[109] T. Tatton Brown considers that it is, most probably, the south-west transept; adjoining buildings in the west range of the cloister (depicted in a drawing in the British Library of c.1799) were demolished in the very early nineteenth century.

[110] Emf 135; J. Storer, *History and Antiquities of Cathedral Churches*, London 1819.

[111] FTb 137.   [114] Emf 50.

[112] Ac 10/36.   [115] FTb 141.

[113] FTv 165.

(4) 1820–1860

A great gale in 1820 required the immediate repair of leadwork on the spire and nave and replacement of windows, including fixing 'all the twelve purple squares and fourteen orange'.[116] However, the spire leadwork had to be totally relaid in 1822.[117] In 1824, the foreman of works of Canterbury Cathedral was asked to visit Rochester at the request of Dean Stevens, and his views were reported to the chapter. His advice was considered and on 1 December the chapter resolved 'that the Cathedral be repaired and that a Mr Cottingham, Architect (well skilled in Gothic architecture)[118] should be sent for to survey the Building . . . and that a sum not exceeding £1,500 be sold out . . . for purpose of defraying expence of improvements'. The beautifying of the interior of the quire was the immediate intention for inviting Lewis Cottingham, but on surveying the fabric, he found the quire roof and transepts (repaired only in 1810) to be so infected with dry rot 'that the roof was in danger of falling in'. The idea of restoring the interior was abandoned, the chapter considering it its first duty to look to the fabric. During his survey Cottingham discovered the hidden monument of Bishop Sheppey between the quire and north-east transept.[119] In 1825 work on the quire roof and its parapets began and the roofs of its transepts were substantially repaired and new leaded; the east end was underpinned, and the flying buttress and the stonework round the great east window repaired. In the meantime the chapter had commissioned Robert Smirke to survey the cathedral to confirm its decision to abandon alterations to the interior for the more urgent structural work. His detailed survey survives.[120] He reported the spire, erected in 1748, to be already in a decaying state, the timbers apparently having been wet for a considerable time, and he thought it should be taken down. The construction of the tower and its piers would not allow, he thought, much additional weight. The walls above the belfry were patched with brickwork and the quoins bulging, requiring rebuilding with stone.

Unfortunately none of Cottingham's reports or specifications has survived, although many workmen's bills have. These list labour and materials only and rarely the nature or location of the work in question. However, the major work done is listed in various minutes and notes, the most significant being the alteration of the appearance of the cathedral with the demolition of the spire, substantial raising of the tower and its re-facing with Bath stone, and battlements with pinnacles erected in each corner.[121] His work in the tower involved taking out the thirteen beams of the belfry floor, which were totally decayed and whose ends '12 or 14 inches square went quite through the whole of the walls, occupying fully one third of the bearing part of the Tower'. These spaces were filled with Portland stone. The new floor was

---

[116] FTv 176.
[117] FTv 177.
[118] Acz 1; for Cottingham's work at Rochester see Janet Myles, *L.N. Cottingham 1787–1847: Architect of the Gothic Revival*, London 1996, pp. 74–5, 7982, 107–8.
[119] Emf 135; FTv 180.
[120] Emf 135.
[121] FTv 181.

supported by four trusses, the ends supported on iron sockets let into the masonry to avoid future decay, and the tower was tied together with the insertion of double chain bolts passing through the angles of the tower to an iron strap on the outside; the trusses of the roof and more iron chains within it further tied the structure together. The strength of the tower was also equalised by the filling in of the apertures in the triforium behind the two eastern piers, the western ones having been done by earlier builders, probably in the 1790s when the tower was 'new faced' with brickwork and stone and a carpenter's bill in 1793 refers to 'making centers for bricklayers under Galililay ledg'. James Savage later considered Cottingham's measures, although perhaps not absolutely necessary, still 'judicious as a precautionary measure and fully justified'. Despite Cottingham's endeavours, the final appearance of the tower was not considered a success by later commentators (Plate 5b).[122]

During Cottingham's work on the tower, apprehension by local people was expressed that his raising of it was overloading the piers. The chapter appointed James Savage to give a second opinion. His investigation (which survives)[123] found 'the four piers upon which the Tower stands . . . to be perfectly sound from top to bottom, and without any crack or fissure or bulge or anything to denote weakness from lateral strain or perpendicular pressure . . . upon plumbing them . . . little deviation from the perpendicular viz:- from half an inch to two inches . . . doubtless in the original construction . . . not material to the stability . . . piers, having been cut into two places prove to be built internally with rubble work and flint and mortar of extraordinary excellence . . . the foundation of the south west pier . . . of same construction, viz:- rubble work as hard as rock itself. The base of this pier appears to be spread in the most ample manner . . . general soil of neighbourhood being chalk rock (than which there can be no better) the foundation of the building is unquestionable . . .'. He concluded: 'I am perfectly satisfied that the piers are fully equal to bear the weight . . . and additional weight that is now upon them . . . so decided is my conviction . . . should not hesitate to raise the Tower fifty feet higher upon the same piers if required'. Although Cottingham was vindicated he complained that, by yielding to pressure from the local builders, his work was spoiled.[124] He was presented later by the chapter with a hundred guineas 'in testimony of the high sense . . . of the distinguished ability which he has shewn in planning the restoration of their Cathedral . . . his unwearied zeal and fidelity in arranging the same into effect'.[125]

Other work included in this first major restoration of the cathedral was the removal of the great perpendicular west window, reported to have been in a very dangerous state and incapable of repair; an entirely new one with a battlement above was erected. The great east window, also found incapable of repair, was replaced with entirely new work, with the exception of some tracery. A large fracture in the north wall at the east end was 'effectually stopped up'. The roofs of the nave, Lady Chapel and quire aisles were repaired. The ceiling of St Edmund's Chapel, 'which was in a

[122] Emf 65/47, 20v.   [124] Palmer, *op. cit.*, p. 40.
[123] Emf 135.   [125] Ac 11, p. 23.

very bad state has been entirely renewed with the exception of the curious woodwork, which has been restored and brought clearly into view with all its grotesque figures'.[126] Entrance to this chapel from the nave was created for the first time by the removal of part of the stone screen which separated them, and was re-erected in the southernmost arch of the south-east transept. In the crypt two stopped-up windows at the east end were unblocked, and the arches and many of the columns repaired. The wall over the gateway to St William's Chapel, which 'had interrupted the view of the range of arches', was removed. In the quire the Grecian cornice and panelling was taken down, revealing an undistinguished seventeenth-century painting. Many monuments fixed against the piers and buttresses of the nave were dismantled and set up on adjoining walls, the holes left by their removal filled with solid masonry, and the piers made firm and secure.[127] In all a total of £6,107 was spent in 1825.

The other major work for which Cottingham is remembered, and which continued until 1829, is his restoration of the south-east transept. In order to stabilise it he put in an entirely new front 'built up all around it', concealing and supporting its leaning face. Its design was a reinterpretation in the Gothic style of its original appearance, faced like the tower in Bath stone, (so fashionable at the time that difficulties arose in its continued supply). Inside this transept, the early fourteenth-century chapter room doorway was 'recarved' according to the records (Plate 8). This appears to refer to the new carved heads fixed to the damaged headless sculptures, and later discovered to be quite incorrectly interpreted. The windows to the right and left of it were restored, and the brickwork placed there in the eighteenth century to strengthen the wall, and in the arches, for the same purpose, was removed. A new font, bishop's throne and pulpit were installed. Cottingham's long period as cathedral architect enabled him to review some of his earlier work, and the groined ceiling at the crossing,[128] which he had removed in 1826 and replaced with large timber beams, was decorated in 1840 with the addition of large plaster bosses of grotesque faces, brightly painted. During the work of clearing masonry from the arch east of the north-west transept doorway, a large figure in distemper of St Christopher, bearing the Infant Christ, was uncovered; its condition, however, was so fragile that as it became exposed to the air it quickly faded. A drawing of it by Dean Stevens' daughter is in the British Museum. At this time also figures in fresco could, despite whitewash, still be traced on the lower part of the south-west transept end wall.

Cottingham was succeeded in 1844 by Lewis Vulliamy, whose survey has not survived.[129] He had apparently already worked for the cathedral, as drawings exist by him of a new prebendal house, built in 1841. One of his first instructions from the dean and chapter was to estimate the expense of paving the nave, west transept and chapels and aisles on the south side; on receipt of his costings it was resolved that Purbeck stone should be used. Contemporary comment in the *Ecclesiologist* noted that 'every day increased our knowledge of ancient pavements and Rochester contains several exquisite specimens'. The writer expressed disgust at their

[126] Emf 135.   [128] FTv 195.
[127] *Loc. cit.*   [129] FTv 206.

replacement by 'street flagging'. *The Times*, however, thought the stone paving an improvement on 'the old red tiles, which were so great a disfigurement'. In 1845 Vulliamy was commissioned to restore the nave aisle roofs and construct their false ceilings.[130] This having been done they and the nave were stained, with 'asphalte'. *The Times* commented that 'the increased darkness of the roof (the effect of staining) will throw out to a greater degree than formerly the magnificent Norman architecture'. In 1844 the chapter had decided that seats in the cathedral should be provided for the grammar school boys who were not on the foundation, to be placed on the floor of the quire 'on both sides between the entrance and the Throne and Pulpit'. *The Times* considered 'the choir too . . . undergoing great improvements; fronts of the pews, as far up as the pulpit and bishops throne, which were formerly stained deal, and quite plain, having been removed and handsomely carved Gothic panelling introduced in their stead. Four additional pews erected . . . Dean and Chapter, far from laying themselves open to censure, entitled to great credit for the improvements they are now making'. Vulliamy also designed the new font. In 1848 Bishop Walter de Merton's tomb was opened. This had been done two hundred years earlier, when a chalice was found and taken by Merton College. This time 'much of the vestments still adhered to the feet and legs, but in black clotted masses . . . skeleton of a man six foot in height. The forehead was low and the eye sockets near one another'. A new stone was placed over the coffin.[131] Otherwise Vulliamy's twenty years as cathedral architect appear to have been spent dealing mainly with small works and repairs, although he designed and supervised the building of the grammar school in 1843. In 1854 the dean and chapter, in a letter to the Home Secretary, had agreed that the burial ground ajoining the cathedral was overcrowded, 'but it is not so with the Nave, Aisles and Side Chapels . . . only twenty burials in the Cathedral during last forty years . . . every coffin enclosed in lead, and the Vault or Grave in which it is deposited . . . arched over and the floor re-paved, and no Vault or Grave made within six feet of any wall or pillar of the Church . . . also a fee of fifty pounds for internment of any person who is not a Member of the Cathedral or one of his family'. The dean and chapter trusted that this information would persuade the Home Secretary to reconsider the absolute prohibition of burials within the cathedral itself. Following an Order in Council, the ancient overfilled graveyard was finally closed, and a new one created in the adjacent glebe land formerly belonging to St Margaret's church; it was consecrated in 1855.[132]

(5) 1860–1900

In 1866 the second great restoration of the century got under way. George Gilbert Scott was invited to give his opinion on the state of the fabric. His report of June 1867 survives,[133] but unfortunately little detailed information of the subsequent

---

[130] Ac 12.
[131] FTv 200; Ac 12; Emf 135; *The Times*, 16 September 1845.
[132] FTb 174; Ac 13; Egz 134.
[133] Ac 14; Emf 136.

restoration has survived in workmen's bills, estimates or other documents. He found '. . . the Cathedral, especially its exterior . . . has undergone such serious mutilation and disfigurement and suffered so seriously from decay . . . limit operations in first instance to portion . . . used for divine service . . . at the E. end; in fact every ancient feature more or less perished or demeaned . . .' In a letter to the chapter in 1871 he explained his intentions and philosophy: '. . . the eastern portions of the Cathedral . . . are throughout of fine Early pointed architecture, and though sadly mutilated and decayed, their design is in the main intelligible . . . I propose therefore that these parts shall be completely restored retaining all old work which is sufficiently sound, following the old design in every detail which remains, and using one's best judgement in restoring those parts which are hopelessly lost . . . I would propose to use for the restorations the Chilmark stone . . . durable and sufficiently harmonizes in colour with the old stone in the Cathedral.'[134]

Scott's work was later highly criticised, in particular the restoration of the east end: 'his worst mistake was to yield to the pressure of the Dean of Rochester and restore the east end perpendicular window to lancets'.[135] However, the situation he found is recorded in his *Recollections*.[136] He recalls how a perpendicular window had been inserted and the lower range of lancets filled in with tracery of later date: 'These parts had been renewed some forty years back and the questions arose whether it would not be best, as the old design was evident, to bring it back to its original form. The great argument in favour . . . was the extreme ugliness of the great perpendicular window, which was very offensive to the Dean and others. This course was determined on and carried out.'

Scott's restoration started in 1871. In 1873 the cathedral launched an appeal to the public for further funds.[137] In it Scott claimed that, apart from Cottingham's restoration, 'the entire exterior had come down to our own time in a state of decay or disfigurement from ill advised repairs, architectural stone work having for most part perished, replaced with ordinary bricks or stone work of the most heterogeneous character . . .' He lists work already undertaken: '. . . restored to the ancient state the East End, the exterior of the north side of Presbytery and Choir and the two North Transepts, and some portions of the southern side; put into sound repair the Clerestory of the Nave. The Eastern and North Eastern parts may (with one exception) be now considered complete, and present a perfect and harmonious appearance, studiously exact to the ancient forms.' The exception he mentioned was the roofs 'which have not been restored to their ancient pitch, except on the North West Transept; but the gables have been carried up to their proper height' awaiting further funds 'to back them up with the roofs which they are designed to terminate'. In the interior of the cathedral 'the fittings of the Choir are to be restored . . . following as far as possible ancient remains, including new Reredos advanced one

---

[134] Emf 65/1.

[135] P. Johnson, *Cathedrals of England, Scotland and Wales*, London 1990, p. 178.

[136] *Personal and Professional Recollections of the late Sir G.G. Scott*, ed. G.G. Scott, London 1877, p. 349.

[137] Emf 64/5/2.

bay from the eastern wall in agreement with position of Sedilia and levels of ancient floor. Provision made for a new Pulpit in the Choir, the old removed to the Nave. The pavement of the Choir renewed, the ancient Choir Screen restored; the old colouring (of great beauty) discovered behind the stalls will be reproduced.' The chapter's appeal then lists the extensive work still to be done, which included the pressing need to restore the exterior of the south-west transept and the entire restoration of the interior of both western transepts and crossing, 'one of the most elegant portions of the ancient structure', as well as interior and exterior repairs to the nave, and many other major items: '. . . the exterior of the south transept has been spoilt by modern alterations . . . an old drawing will afford great assistance in supplying the features which have been destroyed . . . south wall giving way outwardly, requires extensive underpinning . . . and high pitched roof must be restored. The vaulting of this Transept has oak ribs much decayed and threatening to fall . . . spaces between them, formerly boarded, are now of lath and plaster.'

By the end of 1875 the quire fittings, pavement and decoration were mainly completed; the screen had been restored and the central organ case divided and placed to each side, so enabling the east end to be seen from the nave. The south quire aisle's south wall had been restored and buttressed, and inside the ancient arched recesses exposed. The south-west transept too had been completely restored with a high pitched roof erected, and the timber groining and interior of the clerestory cleaned and repaired. Whilst underpinning this transept, Mr Irvine, Scott's Clerk of Works, records the finding of a 'dry well or cesspool, connected with the old Prebendal house, of considerable width, which had been sunk to 14 feet below the very bottom of Gundulph's foundation; this reckless excavation was emptied and filled with concrete.' A buttress was added to the south-east angle. The nave triforium,[138] in which 'signs of weakness had become so threatening . . . adviseable no longer to delay remedial measures', was strengthened by 'building up solidly the passages passing through the main piers and rebuilding the Aisle side of the tympana of the great arches of the N. Triforium. Iron ties inserted through the main piers and others binding together the coupled columns of the smaller arches.' The north nave aisle wall was underpinned, during which Irvine revealed the point in the original construction of the wall at which Gundulf's builders had stopped at the third bay from the east, and to which the later builders had not joined up precisely, the remainder being erected on a lightly impacted ditch, so explaining the reason for the wall's constant settlement and movement over the ensuing centuries.[139] Underpinning was also done on the south side of the cathedral, where the same phenomenon was revealed in the last bays to the west end; during this work on the south nave aisle wall, Irvine exposed the remains of an ancient apsidal building.[140] Irvine noted that the whole of the outer face of the nave south wall had been rebuilt, 'seemingly from certain initials and dates about 1664. The rebuilding appears to have been with the old materials and if so seems to prove that Gundulph's work had

[138] Emf 65/3.
[139] Emf 135; Emf 77/77.
[140] Emf 77/76; Irvine's detailed reports on the excavations will be found in Emf 135.

been mostly rebuilt when the late Norman work of the nave was executed, as the many Norman fragments used as walling stone in it seems to prove . . . little doubt that this wall contains so much of its old ornamented dressings used as wall stones that if ever it was taken down from any cause, probably an entire recovery of the old design might be made'.

The next survey of the cathedral was by William Butterfield in 1882, though it has not survived,[141] but the third and penultimate restoration of the nineteenth century was presaged by a report by J.L. Pearson in March 1888.[142] He had been asked to investigate the state of the west front. In view of the great criticism of his final restoration by, amongst others, the Society for the Protection of Ancient Buildings, it is worth repeating parts of his report and his attitude to the work. He found the west front (Plate 4b) 'in so sad a state of dilapidation that unless its restoration be taken in hand some of its most interesting and unique features will be lost and its South West Tower will . . . become a ruin . . . first necessary to undertake underpinning . . . in restoring the Norman work it will be necessary to take out and reset all masonry which has separated and bulged out from the core of the walls and to replace with new stone only such stones as are entirely perished, but in every case each new stone must be of the same size as the old it replaces and be an exact imitation of it . . . doubtless will be necessary to introduce new to some extent but as the general effect of the old work is so beautiful my desire is to retain every stone which may by any contrivance be kept in its place . . .' Estimates from Thompsons of Peterborough were accepted for complete restoration of the west front, underpinning, protecting the west window, taking down and restoring the south-west tower and the upper part of the north-west tower, the upper part of the west end of the nave aisles and new central doors, and new work to the north turret amounted to £11,700.[143] Of Cottingham's tower Pearson 'regretted it was necessary to rebuild the upper part at the time when mediaeval architecture was only beginning to be studied, and judging by the work of the period so very little understood . . . present state miserably poor and mean and so much so as to lower the character of the whole building to that of a very unimportant Parish Church . . . especially when seen from a little distance . . . trust may be possible to reform its external appearance . . . to make it somewhat worthy of the noble Church it surmounts'.

In 1889 controversy raged over the proposal to erect a memorial to Dean Scott by removing the ancient quire screen and building a new one. The Kent Archaeological Society[144] and the Society of Antiquaries[145] were outraged at the idea, but Dean Hole wrote to them 'you will be as delighted to read as I am disappointed to write . . . scheme has been rejected by a majority of Chapter'. A further scheme, which entailed decorating the plain screen with carved figures under canopies, was then presented. A special chapter met to consider this proposal, and decided to 'respectfully suggest' a possible alternative in the form of stained glass inserted in the windows of the Lady Chapel. However, the will of the joint subscribers prevailed, and the chapter 'in

[141] FTb 213.
[142] Emf 142.
[143] Emf 64/5/3.

[144] Emf 64/5/5.
[145] Emf 64/5/4.

deference to the wishes of the Committee . . . decided to give their consent . . .',[146] and the screen, decorated with the figures of bishops of Rochester, under canopies, designed by Pearson and sculpted by Nathaniel Hitch, was unveiled as the Scott Memorial in October 1890. Another important alteration to the interior of the cathedral related to access to the Lady Chapel; in 1889 a doorway from the south aisle was formed in the most western bay of the separating stone screen.

By 1891 Thompsons' men had practically completed the first stages of work ordered to the west front, but Pearson wrote that 'the condition of this Front is so precarious that I should be very glad if Chapter were in a position to go on . . . next stage most delapidated condition . . . must become rapidly worse unless something can be done'.[147] An appeal to the public was launched by the Restoration Committee explaining that nearly £20,000 had been spent over the last twenty years, and a further £5,000 was needed, giving priority to the west front and the raising of the east end roofs.[148] Work proceeded, but in 1892 great debate arose as to whether the north-west turret should be restored or rebuilt. The Society for the Protection of Ancient Buildings was active in the debate, one suggestion being made that cracks should be filled with plaster of Paris to preserve the turret. Pearson replied that it could be 'made fairly substantial and might possibly be retained if it possessed any feature of interest to render its retention desirable, but as in any case the outside surface must be almost wholly new . . . all that could be retained would be some portions of inside core . . . adhere to my Report of 1888 that better to take down and rebuild',[149] and in May the Restoration Committee resolved by twelve votes to four that 'the whole of Mr Pearson's design for the W. Front be adopted . . .' In 1896 a benefactor enabled the sculpture on the chapter room doorway to be restored.[150] It had been discovered that the bishop figure replaced at the time of Cottingham's restoration should in fact have been a woman, to represent the church; there were other inaccuracies also; Nathaniel Hitch sculpted the replacements.[151]

The closing years of the century saw the appointment in 1898 of a new architect, Charles Hodgson Fowler.[152] His survey survives. In addition to other recommendations are proposals for the improvement of the tower, signalling the final major changes to the external appearance of the cathedral. His analysis of the structure of the tower concluded that

> . . . it is generally stated to have been all built by Cottingham in 1827 and its exterior is certainly all his work, but main body of walls and inner facing up to the height of 33' above the ringing chamber floor are mediaeval work, I venture to think, of the same date as the E. arch of the crossing underneath. It is stated in some accounts that although the great arches of the crossing were completed in 1255, yet the tower was not raised above the roofs until the Episcopate of Hamo de Hythe. Cannot help thinking it was carried up to ridge level of the then high pitched roofs, when the arches were completed, and that Hamo de Hythe

[146] Ac 15.
[147] Emf 65/24, 25.
[148] Emf 47/2.
[149] Emf 142.

[150] Emf 69/3; Ac 17.
[151] Emf 69/16.
[152] Ac 18.

only added the upper storey and the lead covered spire. If that is so, the body of the walls is Early English. Cottingham took down Hamo's work and lead spire then existing, refaced the lower (the E.E. work) and added the upper part as we see it now, painful in its smoothness and shallowness of moulding, and with its four dreadfully disproportionate pinnacles . . . I therefore suggest the entire removal of his work and its replacement by new facing to the lower part and an entirely new storey above, with a short spire of wood and lead reproducing in its main outline something of Hamo's work which is shown on several engravings . . . all agree in showing certain features. Engravings also show arcading on the lower part of the tower . . . has entirely disappeared . . . probably E.E. . . . if Cottingham's facing is removed some traces of it may remain which would settle its date.

Fowler enclosed his designs with this survey and explained that 'I have not endeavoured to keep exactly to his work . . . but one which while in keeping with the old design is adapted to the altered conditions of today. One of the main features of the original belfry was somewhat small single window in each face . . . I have put two of rather larger size as consider four small openings would not be sufficient to give free vent to the sound of the bells. In Bishop Hamo's time there were but three bells, and they would not be rung, while now there is a peal of six'.

Fowler's intention to raise the height of the tower was constrained by difficulties concerning dead weight. He thought Cottingham's tower had stood very well and considered that, if he kept to the same weight there should be no danger of crushing the four main piers which carried it; increasing the weight might affect them as he did not (unlike Savage in 1826) think they appeared to be specially well built. However, he later saw Savage's report and 'found his examination of the piers extremely helpful – it shows that clearly there has been no movement or settlement in the piers since Mr. Cottingham raised the Tower, and as weight of proposed new work will be less than the present, there can be no danger in raising the spire'.[153]

(6) 1900–1940

The early part of the twentieth century saw Hodgson Fowler's major transformation of the external appearance of the cathedral, which has remained virtually unaltered to the present time. The reconstructed tower and a spire were made possible by the benefaction of Thomas Hellyer Foord. After further research into ancient drawings and prints, Hodgson Fowler had concluded that they 'all show an arcade round lower storey of the Tower . . . and fairly well the general character of the work; . . . seems to have been Early English of some date as east arch of Tower over present organ, and agrees with the lancet window still remaining in three sides . . . behind the oak framing that supports bell chamber floor . . . therefore I have shown Early English arcade with trefoil headed arches as indicated in one of clearest of engravings . . .

[153] Emf 144.

belfry stage much as I first designed but with extra richness in the window mouldings and carvings of cornice . . . spire . . . would be nearly twenty feet higher than that of Hamo de Hythe . . .' He had submitted his revised designs for the approval of Mr Foord as well as the chapter, and in October 1903 they were agreed.[154] Mr Foord, however, was bitterly disappointed when he first saw the new spire: 'I could have stamped my foot.' Fowler was not surprised: 'I know all along he has wanted a high spire and the comparatively short one covered with lead would not meet his ideas, one has to remember that the old tower piers were not built for a high heavy spire.'[155] The archbishop of Canterbury attended the dedication of the tower and spire work in November 1904.[156] Whilst work on the tower had progressed, further provision of funds by Mr Foord had enabled two bells to be added to increase the peal to eight; the bell framework was strengthened, and four of the old bells recast.

The chapter room underwent alteration and restoration in 1906; the eastern timber window was replaced by a stone oriel, designed by Hodgson Fowler; the window and all dressed stonework was built from 'old Bath stone from the Tower lying at Mr Foord's Acorn Wharf'; all the new stone was best St Aldhelm brand of Bath stone. He also supervised the installation of a new floor. The restoration of the north quire aisle, again as the result of munificence by Mr Foord, enabled a built-up doorway in its north face to be re-opened, three new oak doors installed, and the roof lowered over the staircase.[157] However, in December 1910, before the work was completed, Hodgson Fowler died and his partner in Durham, W.H. Wood, supervised the project.

Before his death Hodgson Fowler had been designing proposals for the Lady Chapel to revert to its fifteenth-century arrangement, with an oak screen across the south-west transept, as a memorial to Canon Pollock;[158] this proposal was finally abandoned in 1926.[159] Temple Moore was appointed successor to Hodgson Fowler in 1911[160] and presented his survey of the cathedral in 1914; however the outbreak of World War I precluded major work and the crypt was used as an air raid shelter. On resumption of normality in 1919 Temple Moore was asked to update his survey on the nave roof which was becoming a source of concern. His recommendation that it should be rebuilt entirely was accepted by the chapter and a public meeting convened to raise funds. However a group of powerful individuals was hastily co-opted to the executive of the Restoration Committee, and their strong criticism led to the abandonment of this proposal. Temple Moore's relationship with the chapter seemed not to be quite harmonious, with a defensive reply to an enquiry as to the state of his health,[161] and little work on the cathedral is recorded as being done by him. He died suddenly in July 1920 and was replaced as consultant architect by Professor Lethaby, to be assisted by the Rochester based architect, E.F. Cobb.

With sums from the Foord Bequest, set up on the death of T.H. Foord, the restoration of the south quire aisle began in 1921. Modern whitewash was removed,

[154] Ac 20.   [158] Emf 139.
[155] Emf 143.   [159] Ac 27.
[156] Ac 21.   [160] Ac 24.
[157] Emf 148.   [161] Ac 26.

and over the monument of Bishop John de Bradfield the extensive surface of a very simple medieval decoration in good condition was found, consisting of red outlines representing masonry, on a creamy white ground. On its west wall, on the south side of the arch leading into the transept a large figure of St Andrew was revealed, holding his cross. The old layers of limewash were difficult to remove and the plaster was in bad condition.[162] The bequest also enabled work on the north transept to be done in 1924; marble shafts, which had been covered with paint and distemper were cleaned and repolished, several loose lengths of shafting made fast, and missing stay irons replaced; the vaulting was cleaned with methylated spirit and coated with a wax preparation, specified by Professor Lethaby, to preserve the colour and bind flaking surfaces,[163] which, during restoration in the 1970s, was to prove extremely difficult to remove.

Gundulf's Tower was restored in 1925, for which great approbation was received from the Kent Archaeological Society.[164] In 1927 Professor Lethaby resigned; he indicated the work which he thought most urgently needed attention and, in 1928, W.A. Forsyth was appointed as his successor. His survey indicated the necessity of re-casting the nave roof lead and covering the south aisle roof with copper, in his view a more urgent exercise than heating or lighting improvements, and in November 1928 the chapter gave instructions for repairs to proceed, at an estimated cost of £10,000. The design of the proposed Dean Storrs memorial screen to the south transept was approved by the Council for the Care of Churches, who considered it 'faithful to principles of wood architecture'.[165]

The 1930s was a decade of great economic difficulty, both nationally and for the chapter; work on the preservation of mural paintings in the south aisle and crypt was deferred owing to lack of funds, as was the improvement of the Lady Chapel. The deteriorating condition of the medieval wall paintings was greatly worrying; Mr Forsyth offered a reward of £100 for suggestions on their preservation, particularly those in the crypt, executed in the early years of the fourteenth century. However, apart from spire leadwork repairs and other small work, Forsyth reported the structure of the cathedral to be in good condition, and the chapter congratulated Mr Cobb on its care. The Friends of the Cathedral paid for the excavation and restoration of the old dormitory in the cloisters,[166] and in 1937 they undertook responsibility for the complete upkeep of Cloister Garth, and the subsequent demolition of the prebendal house in the south-west corner enabled the layout to be greatly improved.

[162] Ac 27.
[163] Council for the Care of Churches: correspondence stored in its library.
[164] Ac 27.
[165] Ac 28.
[166] Ac 29.

(7) Since 1945

With the end of the war the blast wall which had been erected in front of the west doorway was dismantled, railings reinstated, and air raid shelters in the crypt and Gundulf's tower taken out. However, the extreme shortage of building materials, and the licensing system which, of necessity, gave a low priority to ecclesiastical buildings, meant great delay in repairing the damage suffered to vaults and windows. Fortunately the structural state of the cathedral was reported by Mr Forsyth, just before his death in 1951, to be generally good, with all roof slates in sound condition.[167] Emil Godfrey was appointed as Surveyor of the Fabric in 1952, with J.S. Baldwin, the cathedral's house surveyor, as his assistant. An extremely comprehensive survey was immediately undertaken, during which dry rot was found in some roof timbers at the east end, and death watch beetle in the south quire aisle, which had partly reduced one timber boss to powder. Amongst Godfrey's numerous proposals for repair was 'removal of the ugly strap work pointing' with which the exterior of the cathedral was covered, to be done in a programmed manner.[168] War damage to the Lady Chapel vaults and windows was not repaired until 1958, when finance from the War Damage Commission was made available.[169]

In 1957 the steeplekeeper reported movement in the bell frame. Tightening of the long bolts, which ran vertically through the frame, produced no improvement, and excessive movement was observed when the bells were rung together. Following inspection from the bell-founders, the replacement of the old timber frame was advised with a 'massive cast iron frame of low-side type; this frame to be carried on steel girders, fixed transversely beneath, and anchored into the masonry', to rest on concrete pads. In 1959 the bells were removed and the new frame installed by Kentish Church Builders, Taylors Bellfounders and Webbs (the local firm of builders) at a total cost of £3,366. Re-hanging of the ten bells cost a further £2,741.[170]

The cathedral's finances were extremely limited, but a programme of cleaning the interior and limewashing was started, commencing at the east end, and the marble columns were polished with beeswax; the crypt too was decorated and furnished with an altar. A new lighting scheme for the nave designed by Godfrey was approved. He was, however, keen to persuade the chapter of the merits of washing the complete exterior of the cathedral, not only to improve its appearance, which at that time was black and stained with the grime of centuries, but by so doing to enable necessary repair to be identified, and suitable stonework repair inserted. The west front was the only part which it was agreed should be cleaned initially. Despite problems with fungal growth and some immoveable stains, it was a great success.

Godfrey's reiteration, in his 1963 survey, of his 'wish that the whole of the exterior of the cathedral should be washed', resulted in approval being finally received, no doubt the chapter having appreciated the improvement at the west end, and a programme of cleaning and repair started at the east end; this was to continue slowly round the whole structure over the next twenty years. Recorded also in this survey

---

[167] Medway Studies Centre, Strood, DE 209.
[168] *Loc. cit.*

[169] DE 209/IA(c).
[170] DE 209(R).

was the installation of a new heating system, and the repair and decoration of the interior of the nave. Also in 1963 the unique space of the crypt was greatly enhanced by the removal of a wall between two columns, situated directly below the original location of a heavy high altar in the presbytery. With careful support to the structure, the wall was removed, revealing the columns to be coloured from a fire and the capitals badly cracked, confirming the need for the strengthening support of the wall. The capitals and column shafts were repaired and the groin strengthened. The greatly improved space enabled a new chapel to be provided.[171]

Cracks in the south jamb of the chapter room doorway in 1967 revealed, following use of a metal detector, numerous iron cramps in the stone frame, quite possibly inserted when the east wall of the south-east transept was restored in 1781. The possibility of dismantling the doorway and removing the rusting ironwork was considered, but the damage likely to be caused in doing so was thought likely to exceed that done by leaving the cramps *in situ*. The Victoria and Albert Museum was consulted on methods of stone cleaning and conservation. British Museum tests revealed no evidence of earlier preservation, but that the surface was altered by sulphur dioxide. The damaged stonework was repaired and in 1977 the whole poulticed with Sepiolite.[172]

In 1972 the Cathedrals Advisory Committee approved the architect's proposals to go through the medieval stone bench on the west wall of the north-west transept, to form a doorway to a new underground chair store. They considered the stone arch proposed by Godfrey to be 'immensely suitable'. Work on restoration of the transept's interior started, continuing alongside the work on the chair store. A painting conservator's report on the vaults revealed recent plaster patched between the webs, the whole coated with dark tone beeswax, requiring removal before limewashing. This proved impossible and it was decided to paint over it with Sandtex. The carved heads were cleaned with Sepiolite, and chalk replacements to spalled blocks inserted in the vaulting.[173]

In 1973 a contribution of £6,000 from the Friends enabled restoration of the interior of the south-west transept to be undertaken. An extensive area of medieval wall painting on the east wall was cleaned and conserved. The previously plain oak vaults were cleaned and varnished, and 23 carat gold leaf applied to the timber ribs, and colour and gilded highlights added to the six roof bosses. The walls were limewashed and all completed in 1975.[174] During Evensong one day in 1975 'three separate loud cracks were heard, and tiles in the transept blew up scattering the chairs'. At first it was feared that the foundations of the whole building were giving way, and the architect and structural engineer were sent for post haste. They concluded that the building was in no danger, and that the cause was the expansion of the tiles due to abnormal heat in the crypt below caused by lighting for a television programme. Substantial movement had resulted causing rupture and tilting of the presbytery stone step. At an estimated cost of £3,800 the existing undamaged tiles were salvaged, and tiles as near matching as possible replaced those shattered. Whilst

171 DE 209/IV.   173 DE 209/VII.
172 DE 209/V; FTv 139(1).   174 DE 209/VIII; IX(1).

experienced tilers were on site, the opportunity was taken to clean and re-lay the ancient mosaic in St John's chapel. The spire required constant attention, with frequent leaks being reported; no funds being available for a major programme of replacement, emergency leadwork patching was resorted to.

The washing programme had, by 1979, reached the north wall of the north nave aisle. As in Scott's restoration of this wall, Chilmark stone was used (this time from a supply rejected by Westminster Abbey) for infill repair: 'Scott used this stone for his renewals for the same reasons as mine . . . because compatible in appearance and texture with greensand stone and rag of original build'. During the work a crack was revealed beneath the parapet, where rusting iron ties to the roof were located. Shortage of funds brought the stonework repair to an immediate halt, and finances were diverted to the insertion of stainless steel ties. Rejigging funds from other programmes enabled the stonework repairs eventually to be completed.[175]

A design for an entrance porch to the south quire aisle was approved by the Cathedrals Advisory Committee, but in 1982 Emil Godfrey was killed in a car crash, and its building was supervised by his partners. His thirty years as architect to the cathedral had wrought a transformation to the external appearance of the building, and many improvements to the interior, but chronic shortage of funds had frustrated many of his other proposals, amongst which were re-leading the spire and cleaning the crossing and reopening the people's door on the north nave aisle wall. His successor, Martin Caröe, appointed in 1983,[176] was able to undertake a major restoration as funds eventually became available.

[175] DE 209/X.
[176] Chapter Minute Book held in Cathedral Comptroller's Office.

Appendix A
The Cathedral Library

Study and reading formed as much part of the Benedictine Rule as did prayer and manual work. 'From Easter till 14 September, they should be set out in the morning and work at whatever is necessary from the first hour till about the fourth. From the fourth hour until about the sixth they should be engaged in reading . . . From 14 September until the beginning of Lent they should be free for reading till the end of the second hour.'[1] Consequently, every Benedictine house possessed its collection of books and the beginning of Rochester Cathedral Library therefore dates from the establishment of the Benedictine priory in 1082.[2] The Precentor was the Librarian, responsible for the care and maintenance of the books and for the provision of the necessary materials for copyists, illuminators and authors. There was no separate library building and the usual place for storing the books was in cupboards against the wall in the north-east part of the cloister. It has been suggested that in Rochester there was a 'recess beneath the vestry [which] might very well have formed the *armarium* or closet in which were kept such books as were used in the cloister by the monks at reading times'.[3] The traditional place where the monks read and wrote was along the north wall of the cloister.

The *Textus Roffensis*[4] contains a catalogue of the Priory Library compiled in 1123[5] and is the oldest catalogue known to exist of a considerable number of books from an English library. It numbers ninety-three volumes and includes the celebrated Gundulf Bible[6] and the first part of the *Textus* itself. There is a considerable number of biblical commentaries and various theological treatises by the Fathers. Among the latter the works of St Augustine are particularly well represented, including his *City of God* and his *Confessions*. Historical works include two volumes of Josephus's *History of the Jews* and a copy of Bede's *Ecclesiastical History of the English People*. There are lives of the saints and books relating to the monastic life, such as the life of St Anthony, the founder of Christian monasticism, and the Rule of St

---

[1] *The Rule of St Benedict*, Chapter XLVIII, trans. David Parry, London 1984, p. 75.
[2] For this chapter I acknowledge a considerable debt to the late W.H. Mackean for the information in his booklet, *Rochester Cathedral Library: Its Fortunes and Adventures through Nine Centuries*, Rochester 1953. On the early history of the library, cf. Katharine Waller, 'Rochester Cathedral Library: An English Book Collection Based on Norman Models', *Colloques Internationaux du Centre National de la Recherche Scientifique*, 1984, pp. 238ff.
[3] W.H. St John Hope, *The Architectural History of the Cathedral Church and Monastery of St Andrew at Rochester*, London 1900, p.168.
[4] Cf. below, pp. 220–1.
[5] N.R. Ker, *English Manuscripts in the Century after the Norman Conquest*, London 1960, p. 31.
[6] Waller, *op. cit.*, p. 240.

Benedict. There is a copy of Archbishop Anselm's classic treatise *Cur Deus Homo* (1098). The library reflected the powerful influence of Lanfranc on the life of the priory and St Andrew's was one of the very few monastic houses to have possessed a copy of his *Constitutions*, which he had drawn up for the reform of monastic life. The library also had copies of his *De Corpore et Sanguine Domini* (c.1070), in which he defended the doctrine of transubstantiation against the eucharistic teaching of Berengar of Tours. All these books were in Latin, but in Old English there were the first part of the *Textus*, two volumes of sermons and King Alfred's translation of St Gregory's *Liber Regulae Pastoralis* (591), which became the pastoral textbook of the medieval episcopate.

During the nineteenth century a later catalogue of books in the Rochester library was discovered.[7] It was found on two vellum leaves at the beginning of a copy of St Augustine's *De Doctrina Christiana*, which had originally been in the library at Rochester but was then in the British Museum (and still is in the British Library). The catalogue had been compiled in 1202 by Alexander, the precentor and librarian, and listed some three hundred volumes. There were considerably more biblical commentaries and among the lives of the saints were those of Paulinus and Ithamar, bishops of Rochester. There were more volumes of sermons and the number of books on canon law had increased. These included Gratian's classic *Decretum* (c.1139), a collection of nearly four thousand patristic texts, conciliar decrees and papal pronouncements touching on all aspects of church discipline, which quickly became the basic canon law text. There were copies of the popular *Etymologies* by Isidore of Seville and among more recent writings was Peter Lombard's *Book of Sentences* (c.1156). The number of historical works had increased and they included a copy of William of Malmesbury's *History* (1120 and 1125) and there was also a copy of John of Salisbury's *Policraticus*, sketching an ideal state. There was a collection of medical works and books on grammar, rhetoric, dialectic, philosophy, arithmetic and music. Perhaps the most notable addition consisted of the Latin classics – works by Cicero, Sallust, Terence, Virgil, Horace and Ovid. The library is not known to have suffered in the fires of the twelfth century, but when King John besieged Rochester Castle in 1215 it is stated that manuscripts belonging to the cathedral were destroyed and in 1264 many charters and other records were lost as a result of the activities of the troops of Simon de Montfort. The Rochester books in the British Library,[8] however, show that many were added in the following centuries. These included a number on the scriptures, a variety of medieval works and several volumes of the Code of Justinian, which was the authoritative and ordered statement of Roman law. Often the names of the donors were inscribed; some books were given by the prior and various monks and from time to time the bishop of Rochester encouraged the studies of the monks by presenting books to the library.

At the dissolution of the priory in 1540 the books and manuscripts of Rochester were subjected, but on a larger scale, to the kind of treatment meted out to most other

---

[7] Cf. W.B. Rye, 'Catalogue of the Library of the Priory of St Andrew, Rochester, AD.1202', *Archaelogia Cantiana*, iii, pp. 47ff.

[8] Cf. below, p. 219.

dissolved houses and were either confiscated or sold. John Leland, the king's librarian, who had received a commission under the great seal to search for records, manuscripts and books in all the cathedrals, colleges, and religious houses in England, collected these items for the library of Henry VIII at Westminster and ninety-nine volumes from Rochester found their way there. They are now in the King's Library at the British Library and most of them bear at the foot of the first page the inscription, 'Liber de claustro Roffensi.' Forty-one other books have been traced (in addition to seven which have remained at Rochester) as follows:[9]

Baltimore: Walters Art Gallery		1
Berlin: State Library		1
Brussels: Royal Library		1
Cambridge: University Library		2
Corpus Christi College		6
St John's College		2
Trinity College		3
Dublin: Trinity College		1
Edinburgh: National Library of Scotland		3
Eton College		1
London:	BL Cotton Collection	4
	BL Harley Collection	3
	Lambeth Palace Library	1
Oxford:	Bodleian Library	7
	All Souls College	1
	St John's College	1
	Worcester College	1
Rome:	Vatican	1
San Marino (USA): Huntington Library		1

The main question, however, must remain unanswered. Why were so many more books taken from Rochester Library than from any other monastery, even those with larger libraries? It may be that the fact that the monastic buildings were converted into a royal residence facilitated the transfer of books,[10] but that is pure guess-work. The most serious single loss sustained by the library was that of the famous Gundulf Bible, a manuscript of the eleventh century which contains the Old and New Testaments in Latin in two folio volumes, beautifully written in double columns, the initial letter of each book coloured vermilion. Although it has long been assumed that this had been the gift of Gundulf to the Priory, the Bible is linked to him only by a later, thirteenth century, entry on the fly-leaf of each volume. A long description of it, without any reference to Gundulf, appears in the catalogue of the library in the *Textus*. It is also assumed that it remained in the cathedral until the dissolution,

[9] N.R. Ker, *Medieval Libraries of Great Britain*, 2nd edn, London 1964, pp. 160ff.
[10] Mackean, *op. cit.*, p. 12.

though this cannot be proved conclusively. Around 1611 it was listed in the catalogue of Lord Lumley's collection as 'Biblia vetusta quondam Gundolphi episcope Roffensis.'[11] In 1734 it appeared in Amsterdam in a sale of books of Herman van de Wall and for a number of years thereafter it continued to turn up at sales in the Netherlands – at Malines in 1763, at Louvain where it was sold for two thousand florins, and at Antwerp in 1823. After this it appears to have fallen into the hands of the Revd Theodore Williams who had it bound in blue morocco, with his monogram, crest and motto on each volume and at whose sale of books in 1827 it was bought by Sir Thomas Phillipps. On the latter's death in 1872 it passed to his son-in-law, the Revd J.E.A. Fenwick. In 1924 it was purchased by Mr Henry Huntington and is now in the Huntington Library at San Marino, California. In view of its travels there is a certain irony that on the first leaf of each volume those who carry away the book are threatened with excommunication.

Of the few volumes from the monastic library which remain at Rochester by far the most important is the *Textus Roffensis*. This is a beautiful twelfth-century manuscript with some later additions. It existed originally in two or three parts which were brought together under one cover before 1400. It consists of 234 leaves of vellum and is written partly in Old English and partly in Latin. The initial letters are illuminated in green and red and at the beginning of the section dealing with Rochester there is a large 'R', composed of an angel and a winged dragon coloured in blue, crimson and green (Plate 1). The *Textus* is of considerable importance for our knowledge of Anglo-Saxon laws and institutions. The first half consists of a collection of legal texts, lists of emperors, popes, archbishops and royal genealogies. The second half contains a cartulary of the priory, listing all the important charters from Aethelberht I to Henry I. Finally, there is the catalogue of the books in the monastic library to which reference has already been made.

The *Textus* contains an account of the ceremonies of the ordeal for testing the innocence or guilt of a suspected felon by the use of red-hot irons, boiling water and immersion in cold water. This took place in the nave of the cathedral to the accompaniment of an appropriate religious ritual. One of the best known passages of the manuscript is the excommunication or curse, under which the wrong-doer is cursed by the Holy Trinity, the Mother of our Saviour, angels and archangels, patriarchs and prophets, apostles and evangelists, martyrs, virgins and all the saints; he is cursed at home out of doors or in church, living or dying, eating and drinking, hungry and thirsty, sleeping, walking and standing, working and resting, inwardly and outwardly. His hair, brain, ears, eyes, mouth, arms, hands, fingers, stomach, legs, toe nails, and indeed every part of his body are cursed; and it ends with 'Amen. So be it. So be it. Amen'.[12]

The *Textus* has had its adventures. In 1630 it was taken to London for the purposes of research and an arrangement was made for John Lorkin, one of the canons of the cathedral, to bring it back to Rochester. Unfortunately, he left it at his lodgings in

---

[11] Mary P. Richards, *Texts and Their Traditions in the Medieval Library of Rochester Cathedral*, London 1988, p. 68.

[12] This curse is quoted in Laurence Sterne, *Tristram Shandy*, Vol. ii, ch. xi.

Fleet Street while he was absent and it was removed by Thomas Leonard, a physician who was staying in the same house. Leonard refused to return it and after two years of unavailing effort to regain possession the dean and chapter were compelled to institute legal proceedings for its recovery and it finally returned to the cathedral in 1633. In 1712 Dr John Harris, another canon of the cathedral, was writing a history of Kent and wanted to consult the *Textus* in London. It was taken both ways by boat along the Thames and on the return journey bad weather resulted in the volume being submerged in the river for some hours. Fortunately it was recovered with only slight damage, although signs of its submersion can still be seen on its pages.[13]

The second most valuable manuscript from the monastic library which remained at Rochester is the *Custumale Roffense*, written in Latin in c.1300 by John de Westerham, a Rochester monk who later became prior. It supplies considerable information about lands owned by the priory and the income accruing from them and considerable detail is given of the domestic arrangements of the house and of the duties and wages of the priory officials and servants. It also throws light on the services in the cathedral church.[14]

There are five other volumes from the priory library which have remained at Rochester:

1. *De consensu Evangelistarum* with other works of St Augustine, dating from the first half of the twelfth century.

2. *The Book of Sentences* by Peter Lombard, dating from the latter part of the thirteenth century.

3. *A Commentary on the Psalms* by Ludolphus of Saxony, published in Paris in 1506. It contains the signature of 'John Noble, monk of the Sanctuary of St Andrew' and we know that John Noble was Precentor in 1510, Sacrist in 1521 and that he had died by 1526. The volume disappeared at the Dissolution but was purchased by the Dean and Chapter in the 1980s.

4. In 1921 a fragment of a fifteenth century Psalter and Kalendar was presented to the cathedral. Because of references to St Ithamar, St Paulinus and Romanus, all of whom were bishops of Rochester, it is believed to be part of a volume prepared for use by the priory.

5. A Bible Commentary, c.1320, probably compiled by John de Westerham. There is an entry on the second page showing that he gave this book to the priory when he was prior.

There are four other pre-Reformation volumes but, as there is no evidence that they belonged to the library of the priory, they were presumably acquired by the later dean and chapter. They are as follows:

1. A Latin Bible, 1478, which is an extremely beautiful example of early printing.

---

[13] A facsimile of part of the *Textus*, edited by Peter Sawyer, was published in 1957.
[14] A printed edition, edited by J. Thorpe was published in 1788.

2. Early Theological Tracts, fourteenth century. After brief sentences for use in moments of need and a prayer written at a later date, the tracts proper follow with a title page bearing the heading, *Tractatus qui vocatur ymago vite*.

3. A Sarum Missal, published in Paris in 1534, in double columns of black and red letter.

4. An MS Book of Hours of the fifteenth century.

After the dissolution of the priory, which involved the destruction of the medieval chapter house (Plate 5a), the newly-established dean and chapter designated the former monastic vestry, where the vestments had been kept, as the chapter room where official meetings of the capitular body were held. This room, approached through the magnificently carved fourteenth-century doorway in the south-east corner of the quire (Plate 8), became also the Cathedral Library and has remained so until the present day. Presumably in the beginning the only contents were the few volumes left at the cathedral at the time of the dissolution, but as early as 1545 there is a reference in the treasurer's accounts to the expenditure of £21 – a large sum at that time – 'to buy books for our new Library'.[15] Nevertheless the number of books remained comparatively small and a number of these were removed or lost during the Civil War period. It was not until the eighteenth century that the library began to grow significantly and a regulation was made that new deans and canons should give a sum of money, or books to that value, in place of the entertainments which had hitherto been given on their admission,[16] and the amount became established at £10 for the Dean and £5 for a canon.[17] From time to time books have been presented by numerous donors and many have been purchased from the general funds of the chapter, which nowadays budgets annually a sum for the maintenance of the library.

The library contains a considerable number of volumes printed before 1540, including works by Bishop Fisher. It has a large section on the Old and New Testaments and the reason for this is that when in 1950 the Oriel Professorship of the Interpretation of Holy Scripture was severed from the cathedral canonry,[18] a library belonging to the successive holders of that office, and which had been housed for many years in the chapter room, became part of the cathedral library, which also contains a very large collection of bibles from every century and representing most published editions. There are a number of books written by members of the chapter, the most widely known being *The Analogy of Religion* (1736) by Joseph Butler (canon 1736–1740) and the famous Liddell and Scott (Robert Scott, Dean 1870–1887) *Greek Lexicon* (1843). The present contents of the library are very much a reflection of the interests of individual members of the chapter through the ages.

[15] Quoted Mackean, *op. cit.*, p. 14. This statement cannot be verified, there being no extant treasurer's account for the year stated.

[16] Ac 5/13, 94a.

[17] Ac 6/16–17, 83.

[18] Cf. above, p. 126.

The most important post-Reformation volumes possessed by the library are as follows:

1. *The Complutensian Polyglot Bible,* in six large folio volumes, prepared by Cardinal Ximénes and printed at Alcalá in Spain (anciently known as Complutum) in 1514–17, though not issued until 1522. The Greek and Latin texts, with the Hebrew of the Old Testament, are printed side by side.

2. *Coverdale's Bible,* 1535. This was the first printed edition of the whole bible in English, of which only fifty copies are known to exist. The Rochester copy is bound between the *Book of Common Prayer* and the *Book of Psalms,* the whole volume being dated 1629.

3. *The Great Bible,* 1539. This was the first bible ordered by royal authority to be set up in cathedrals and parish churches. This copy was given to the cathedral in 1745 by Edmund Barrell, canon and treasurer of the cathedral.

4. *The Bishops' Bible,* 1568. This superseded the Great Bible for official use in churches.

5. The 'Sealed' *Book of Common Prayer,* 1662. Only about thirty-five copies were issued, certified by commissioners as true and perfect copies and sealed under the Great Seal of England, and every cathedral was ordered to obtain one. The letters patent, complete with the portrait of Charles II and the seal, are well preserved and are a fine example of the craftman's art.

The library also possesses a valuable copy of Speed's *Maps,* published in 1676.

Paul A. Welsby

Appendix B

The Cathedral Archives

The archives of the cathedral were deposited in the Kent Archives Office (now the Centre for Kentish Studies) at Maidstone in 1959 and transferred to the newly established Medway Archives Office (now the Medway Studies Centre) at Strood, with the consent of the dean and chapter, in 1992. Whilst at Maidstone the archives were catalogued by Anne Oakley.[1] The archives have been arranged in two groups, those of the cathedral priory before 1540, and those of the dean and chapter after 1540.

(1) *The Archives of the Cathedral Priory*

The great strength of the priory archives is the magnificent collection of deeds and charters beginning in the late eleventh century. There are a total of twenty-six royal, papal, archiepiscopal and episcopal charters (T47–68) between then and the early sixteenth century.[2] The title deeds and leases (T69–664) are arranged by the parishes in which the individual priory properties were located with separate sections for Leeds priory, the church of St Mary at Chatham, the chapel of St Augustine at Chatham, and Strood hospital. This arrangement is archivally perverse since some of these medieval records belong to institutions whose property was not acquired until the secular dean and chapter were set up in 1540. Even more perverse was the cataloguing of the episcopal registers as part of the archives of the cathedral priory, but this error has since been rectified and the registers recatalogued as part of the diocesan archives still deposited at the Centre for Kentish Studies in Maidstone.

The other records of the cathedral priory are by comparison extremely thin. There are a few late mediaeval rentals, surveys and manorial accounts (F1–8). Compared with the fine series of financial records at some other monastic cathedrals, notably Canterbury and Durham, there is very little at Rochester (F9–17).[3] There is a solitary fifteenth-century survey and rental, and a cellarer's account roll of 1390–1, for Leeds priory (F18–19). The manorial records of Strood hospital are somewhat fuller (F20–43). The hospital, however, has only one surviving account roll, for 1347–8 (F44). There are three fifteenth-century account rolls for St Bartholomew's hospital

1   A summary of this catalogue is published in *Guide to the Kent County Archives Office: First Supplement 1957–1968*, ed. F. Hull, Maidstone 1971, pp. 78–89 and *Second Supplement 1969–1980*, ed. E. Melling, Maidstone 1983, pp. 77–8.
2   The numbers T1–46 were never allocated in the cataloguing process.
3   See R.A.L. Smith, 'The Financial System of Rochester Cathedral Priory', *Collected Papers* (1947), pp. 42–53, and A. Brown, 'The Financial System of Rochester Cathedral Priory: A Reconsideration', *Bulletin of the Institute of Historical Research*, 1 (1977), pp. 115–20.

at Rochester (F45–7) and a fifteenth-century rental of manors in Upchurch belonging to Boxley Abbey (F48). The legal papers are also fragmentary. They are arranged in separate groups for the cathedral priory itself (L1–21), Leeds priory (L22–34) and Strood hospital (L35–9). Among a small group of miscellaneous records (Z1–34) the most interesting surviving item is part of a twelfth-century list of books in the library of the cathedral priory, cut up to line seal bags, and from their surviving shape known as the 'butterfly fragments'.

There remain in the archives of the cathedral priory three documents of exceptional interest and importance. The prior's book (E1b1) is a combined cartulary and letter book covering the period 1478–1504 but incorporating copies of some earlier documents. The volume known as the *Textus Roffensis* (R1) which dates from the first quarter of the twelfth century, contains an earlier cartulary, together with legal material, lists of popes, bishops of Jerusalem and the archbishops and bishops of the English dioceses. Although now kept as part of the archives it has tended in the past, because of its importance as an illuminated manuscript, to be regarded as part of the cathedral library, as has the fourteenth-century custumal attributed to Prior John de Westerham (R2).[4]

(2) *The Archives of the Dean and Chapter*

As might be expected, the archives of the dean and chapter after 1540 are considerably more extensive than those of the cathedral priory. They are divided into eight main groups: administrative records; estate records; financial records; legal records; charity records; King's School records; sacrists' records; and chapter clerks' papers.

The administrative records begin with the donation charter of 1541 (Ad1) and letters patent of 1671 (Ad2) constituting the new non-monastic chapter and its endowments. There are three copies of the cathedral statutes (As1–3). The Red Book in three volumes (Arb1–3) initially recorded both the granting of leases and the minutes of chapter meetings. With the increase in chapter business, a separate series of lease and minute books was started, and the Red Book used for the registering of official documents. Apart from one earlier volume of chapter minutes covering the period 1571–84 (Ac1), the main series of chapter minute books does not begin until 1678, but they are complete thereafter, those up to 1968 being deposited in the archives (Ac2–32). Useful material relating to the management of the chapter estates is contained in the audit bundles covering the period 1746–1831 (Aa1–39). The other administrative records include those relating to the election and enthronement of successive bishops from Henry Holbeach in 1544 (Abe 1–25), the installation of deans, archdeacons and prebendaries (Aod1–13, Aok1–11, Aop1–30), the appointment of chapter clerks and other officials (Aoc1–11, Aos1–3, Aoa1–5, Aoh1–11), and the appointment and resignation of minor canons, lay clerks, choirmasters, organists and vergers (Aom1–29, Aol1–54, Aoo1–13, Aov1–23).

---

[4] Both the *Textus Roffensis* and the *Custumale Roffense* are described in more detail above, pp. 220–1.

There are also records of the appointment of bedesmen over a long period (Aob1–131), of honorary canons from 1881 (Azh1–115) and of presentations to chapter livings (A1p1–191).

The key estate document is the parliamentary survey of 1649 (Esp1). The lease books cover parts of the period 1541–1640 and are complete from 1673 (Elb1–32). The individual leases are organised on a parish and property basis (E1e1–289). Complete schedules of chapter leases from the mid-fourteenth century are brought together in four composite volumes (E1s1–4). The cathedral inventories covering the two centuries between 1670 and 1870 (EIf1–10) are a valuable guide to the furnishings, books and plate. As well as a general survey of the chapter estates compiled in 1623 (Est1A) there are terriers of individual properties arranged by parish (Est1–27), surveys of the estates between 1770 and 1812 (Es1–3), returns of timber (Et1–175) and other materials (Eb1–50), and a large group of miscellaneous papers relating to the management of the estates (Egz1–198). A separate group of records relates to the fabric of the cathedral (Emf1–154) and the other chapter properties (Emp1–77). The former are particularly detailed for the major restorations that took place in the last quarter of the nineteenth century. The last group in the estate records is a small group of plans for various chapter properties, mostly for the nineteenth century (EP1–38). These plans are supplemented by others transferred to the Ecclesiastical Commissioners in 1861. These records, together with other estate material transferred at the same time, have also been deposited at Strood.[5]

The core of the financial records are the receivers' books, which begin in 1542 and are complete from 1698 (FRb1–164, 173). These are supplemented by a few sixteenth and early seventeenth century bailiffs' accounts (FR/B1–2), arrears books between 1670 and 1731 (FR/Ab1–15), fine books between 1677 and 1841 (FR/F1–6), and seal books between 1666 and 1919 (FR/S1–6). The court rolls and rentals (FRm1–24) are arranged by manor, supplemented by other general court books (FRm25–38) and collecting books (FRm39–52). There are bundles of stewards' vouchers for the period 1670–1846 (FR/Sv1–77). The quitrent records include books (FR/Qb1–6), accounts (FR/Qa1–7, FR/Qr1–10) and vouchers (FR/Qv1–69).

These are all records emanating from the office of the receiver-general. The chapter's second financial officer was the treasurer, whose office produced another large group of records. The treasurers' books begin in 1548 and are complete from 1672 (FTb1–265). These are supplemented by bills and vouchers which again are remarkably complete from the 1670s (FTv1–62). The chapter's third financial officer was the auditor, whose office produced relatively few documents, the most significant of which are the record of the investments made by the chapter in the South Sea Company (FAs, FAv1–7) and the account of the value of the deanery between 1768 and 1802 (FD1). The legal records include papers relating to the fortification and enlargement of Chatham dockyard in 1709–15 (LA1), the enclosure of the chapter's property at Haddenham (LA2), the compulsory purchase of land in Frindsbury and Strood by the Thames and Medway Canal Company in 1810 (LA3),

5   Hull, *op. cit.*, pp. 90–1; Melling, *op. cit.*, pp. 78–9.

the disputes over the dean's orchard (LP19), Goudhurst tithes (LP20), Aylesford fee farm rents (LP22), Guy's Hospital fee farm rents (LP30), the rectories of Cuddington, Haddenham and Kingsey in 1711–13 (LP31), Chatham parsonage (LP32), Lady Clerke's Charity at Cliffe (LP3), Shorne Vicarage (LP41) and property in the cathedral precinct (LP42).[6] A considerable archive was created by the most celebrated of the chapter's legal disputes, known as the Whiston Matter, between 1849 and 1874 (LP34).[7]

The four remaining groups of chapter records are all relatively small. The charity records include providers' accounts, covering the period 1699–1819 (C1/1–60) and a few papers relating to Kent charities with which the chapter had some involvement: Watt's Charity, Lady Clerke's Charity, Mrs Knight's Charity, Robert Gunley's Charity, Paul Bairstow's School at Trottiscliffe, and St Bartholomew's Hospital (C2–12). The sacrist had the cure of souls within the cathedral precinct and the records of his office include the cathedral registers of baptisms, marriages, burials and offertories (S1–5). There is a small group of, mostly nineteenth century, records relating to the King's School (KS1–54). The chapter clerks' papers include a bundle of deeds and accounts for Lady Clerke's Charity at Cliffe (CC1) and letter books for the period 1878–1922 (CC2).

Two related deposits in the Medway Studies Centre at Strood are the antiquarian notes of the Revd Canon Sidney Wheatley (1869–1951), vicar of St Margaret's, Rochester, who was also an honorary canon of the cathedral, and the papers of Emil Godfrey, the former surveyor of the fabric to the dean and chapter of Rochester, for the period 1951–67.[8]

Nigel Yates

---

6 LP 1–18, 21, 23–9, 35–40, 43–55 relate to lesser legal issues involving the dean and chapter.
7 Dealt with above, pp. 121–3.
8 These are catalogued as DE53/1 and DE209 respectively.

Appendix C

Priors and Deans of Rochester

No firm succession of priors can be established before 1225. The last prior, Walter Boxley *alias* Phillips became the first dean in 1541.

Priors

1225–39	Richard Derente (Darenth)
1239–42	William Hoo
1242–52	Alexander Glanville
1252–62	Simon de Clyve
1262–83	John de Rainham (deposed)
1283–92	Thomas de Wouldham, Bishop of Rochester 1292–1317
1292–4	John de Rainham (re-elected)
1294–1301	Thomas Shelford
1301–14	John Greenstreet
1314–19	Hamo de Hethe, Bishop of Rochester 1319–52
1320–1	John de Westerham
1321–33	John de Spelderhurst
1333–52	John de Sheppey I, Bishop of Rochester 1352–60
1352–61	Robert de Southfleet
1361–80	John Hertlepe (Hartlip)
1380–1419	John de Sheppey II
1419–45	William Tonbridge
1445–60	John Clyve *alias* Cardon
1460–?	Richard Pecham
c1468–75	William Woode
?–1494	Thomas Bourne
1494–1509	William Bysshope
1509–32	William Fressell
1532–8	Lawrence Dan *alias* Mereworth
1538–40	Walter Boxley

Deans

1541–70	Walter Phillips
1570–2	Edmund Freake, Bishop of Rochester 1572–5, Norwich 1575–84 and Worcester 1584–91
1572–81	Thomas Willoughby
1581–91	John Coldwell, Bishop of Salisbury 1591–6
1592–1611	Thomas Blague
1611–15	Richard Milborne, Bishop of St Davids 1615–21 and Carlisle 1621–4
1615–20	Robert Scott
1621–4	Godfrey Goodman, Bishop of Gloucester 1624–40
1624–39	Walter Balcanquall

1639–42	Henry King, Bishop of Chichester 1642–69
1642–44	Thomas Turner
1660	Benjamin Lany, Bishop of Peterborough 1660–3, Lincoln 1663–7 and Ely 1667–75
1661–70	Nathaniel Hardy
1670–3	Peter Mews, Bishop of Bath and Wells 1673–84 and Winchester 1684–1706
1673–88	Thomas Lamplugh, Bishop of Exeter 1676–88* and Archbishop of York 688–91
[1676–88	John Castilion]*
1688	Simon Lowth **
1689–1706	Henry Ullock
1706–23	Samuel Pratt
1724–32	Nicholas Claggett, Bishop of St Davids 1732–42 and Exeter 1742–6
1732–43	Thomas Herring, Bishop of Bangor 1738–43,* Archbishop of York 1743–7 and Canterbury 1747–57
1743–4	William Barnard, Bishop of Raphoe 1744–7 and Derry 1747–68
1744–65	John Newcombe
1765–7	William Markham, Bishop of Chester 1771–7, Archbishop of York 1777–1807
1767–75	Benjamin Newcombe
1775–9	Thomas Thurlow, Bishop of Lincoln 1779–87 and Durham 1787–91
1779–82	Richard Cust
1782–1802	Thomas Dampier, Bishop of Rochester 1802–8 and Ely 1808–12
1802–8	Samuel Goodenough, Bishop of Carlisle 1808–27
1808–20	William Beaumont Busby
1820–70	Robert Stevens
1870	Thomas Dale
1870–87	Robert Scott
1887–1904	Samuel Reynolds Hole
1904–13	Ernald Lane
1913–28	John Storrs
1928–32	Reginald Thomas Talbot
1932–7	Francis Underhill, Bishop of Bath and Wells 1937–43
1937–43	Ernest Morell Blackie
1943–59	Thomas Crick
1959–66	Robert William Stannard
1966–78	Stanley Woodley Betts
1978–89	John Robert Arnold
1989–	Edward Frank Shotter

* retaining the Deanery of Rochester *in commendam*. Patrick Mussett, however, casts doubt on Lamplugh's *commendam*, noting that Arb2, f. 78, records Charles II's patent giving the deanery to Castilion and the mandate for installation, both dated 13 November 1676, and stating that the deanery was vacant following Lamplugh's nomination to the see of Exeter. Evidence from the chapter acts suggests that Castilion carried out the function of dean, including presiding at chapter meetings, for significant parts of the period 1676–88, though evidence from the financial records suggests that at least some of the income of the deanery was being split between Castilion and Lamplugh.

** Lowth was nominated by the Crown and instituted by the bishop, who then advised the chapter not to install him on the grounds that Lowth did not have the necessary degrees stipulated by the statutes. The chapter accepted the advice and the bishop annulled the institution. See above, pp. 97–8.

Guide to Further Reading

Detailed references to the manuscript and printed sources for the history of Rochester Cathedral are provided in the footnotes to each chapter. This guide is therefore confined to works in two categories: recent general studies of cathedral history and specific studies of other cathedrals with which the history of Rochester Cathedral may be compared and contrasted.

Publications in the first of these categories are fairly limited. There is no study of English monastic cathedrals comparable with Kathleen Edwards, *The English Secular Cathedrals in the Middle Ages*, Manchester 1949, 2nd edn 1967. There are, however, chapters on the cathedral monasteries in David Knowles, *The Monastic Order in England*, Cambridge 1940, 2nd edn 1963, and *The Religious Orders in England*, Cambridge 1948–59, volumes 1 and 3. For the post-Reformation period the most important recent monographs are:

S.E. Lehmberg, *The Reformation of Cathedrals: Cathedrals in English Society 1485–1603*, Princeton 1988
D. Marcombe and C.S. Knighton, eds, *Close Encounters: English Cathedrals and Society since 1540*, Nottingham 1991
P.L.S. Barrett, *Barchester: English Cathedral Life in the Nineteenth Century*, London 1993
S.E. Lehmberg, *Cathedrals Under Siege: Cathedrals in English Society, 1600–1700*, Exeter 1996

The lack of more general publications has, to some extent, been compensated for by the large number of specialist monographs on individual cathedrals:

G.E. Aylmer and R. Cant, eds, *A History of York Minster*, Oxford 1977
F. Bussby, *Winchester Cathedral 1079–1979*, Southampton 1979
Francis Woodman, *The Architectural History of Canterbury Cathedral*, London 1981
L.S. Colchester, ed., *Wells Cathedral: A History*, Shepton Mallet 1982
Suzanne Eward, *No Fine but a Glass of Wine: Cathedral Life at Gloucester in Stuart Times*, Salisbury 1985
P. Mussett and P.G. Woodward, *Estates and Money at Durham Cathedral 1660–1985*, Durham 1988
Michael Swanton, ed., *Exeter Cathedral: A Celebration*, Crediton 1991
David Welander, *The History, Art and Architecture of Gloucester Cathedral*, Stroud 1991
Thomas Cocke and Peter Kidson, *Salisbury Cathedral: Perspectives on the Architectural History*, London 1993
Eric Fernie, *An Architectural History of Norwich Cathedral*, Oxford 1993
D.M. Owen, ed., *A History of Lincoln Minster*, Cambridge 1994
Mary Hobbs, ed., *Chichester Cathedral: An Historical Survey*, Chichester 1994

Patrick Collinson, Nigel Ramsay and Margaret Sparks, eds, *A History of Canterbury Cathedral*, Oxford 1995

Ian Atherton, Eric Fernie, Christopher Harper-Bill and Hassell Smith, eds, *Norwich Cathedral: Church, City and Diocese 1096–1996*, London 1996

For those interested in medieval art and architecture the British Archaeological Association has so far published volumes of conference transactions covering the following cathedrals: Worcester (1978), Ely (1979), Durham (1980), Wells (1981), Canterbury before 1220 (1982), Winchester (1983), Gloucester (1985), Lincoln (1986) and Exeter (1991).

Glossary of Technical Terms

Abacus   The horizontal slab on top of a capital (q.v.).

Aisle   A low, narrow space paralleling nave, quire or transept from which it is separated by an arcade.

Arcade   A series of arches supported by shafts, columns or piers; when applied to a wall surface, called a *blind arcade*.

Ashlar   Masonry cut to form an oblong block with (five) flat surfaces at right angles.

Augmentations   Department created by Henry VIII to administer the dissolution of the monasteries and the revenues resulting therefrom.

Barrel   A type of vault in which an arch (semi-circular or pointed) is extended as a single concave plane; also known as tunnel (vault).

Bay   The area between one vertical support and the next, or the space bounded by any four such elements.

Billet   An ornamental motif consisting of short half-cylindrical bars of stone spaced at regular intervals, in one to three rows.

Boss   A projecting carved block of stone marking the juncture of any two ribs in a vault.

Buttress   An exterior vertical element projecting from a wall to stabilise or strengthen it.

Capital   The block on top of a shaft, column or pier which increases the load bearing area of the support and generally effects a transition from round to rectangular, often given an ornamental form and carved decoration.

Chamfer   A diagonal cutting away of the right angle between two planes.

Choir   *See* **Quire**

Chorepiscopus   A bishop without a diocese who assists another. The institution was severely censured by reformers of the church and soon afterwards widely abandoned.

Chrism   The oil blessed by the bishop for use by his clergy, pre-eminently at baptism and for extreme unction.

Clerestory   A row of windows placed high up in a wall, just under the ceiling or roof.

Column   A round vertical support composed of a single piece of stone (monolithic) or layers (drams).

Congé d'élire   Royal licence to a cathedral chapter to elect a bishop.

Corbel   A stone projecting from the face of a wall, used to support wall shafts relating to the springing of a vault or in a series as under an eaves (corbel table).

Crossing   The area, generally square in plan, created by the intersection of nave (q.v.) and transept (q.v.), defined by four large piers (q.v.) over which a tower is often placed.

Crypt   A low space totally or partly below ground level, usually vaulted with many supports.

Cushion   A form of capital in which the sides of the block are each carved with a large scallop creating the transition from the circular base to the oblong top.

Cusp   The point or apex formed by two adjacent foils or lobes as in a trefoil or quatrefoil; used in tracery within arches (*cusping*) or within foils or lobes (*subcusping*).

Diaper A repetitive pattern, flat or in slight relief, used as surface decoration, composed of any one of numerous motifs, such as squares, diamonds, scallops.

Dog-tooth An ornamental motif consisting of four petal-or leaf-like forms arranged as the angles of a pyramid.

Fine Capital sum paid to the landlord by a new or renewing tenant.

Gable The wall, usually triangular in shape, closing the end of a double pitched roof.

Gallery Usually the second level or storey of an elevation, between the arcade (q.v.) and clerestory (q.v.), open to the nave by large arches; generally the vaults of the aisle serve as its floor, the space being covered by a lean-to roof, rising from a short or tall exterior wall with windows (the absence of an exterior wall results in a false-gallery).

Groin A vault formed by the intersection of two barrel vaults at right angles to each other, thus creating four curving triangular surfaces; the line where their curving places met is the groin which crosses the bay diagonally creating an 'x' pattern.

Higan Household, commonly also the clergy of a church.

Impost The horizontal plane above which the curve of an arch departs from a vertical jamb, usually marked by a projecting course of masonry.

Label A projecting moulding placed over and following the curve of an arch, originally to throw off water but also used decoratively on interiors; also called dripstone or hoodmould.

Lancet A single narrow window with a pointed arch.

Light One of the subdivisions of a traceried window defined by vertical mullions (q.v.).

Mullion The vertical bars of stone in a (traceried) window.

Muniments Archives

Nave The central tall and wide space of a church, often but not always flanked by aisles (q.v.); also used to refer to the entire arm of the church west of the transept (q.v.).

Newel Stair A spiral stair with a central post (built of coursed masonry).

Obit Liturgical annual celebration of the day of death of a benefactor of a church.

Oculus A round opening.

Pallium A vestment conferred by the Pope on specially favoured bishops, which came to be largely confined to archbishops by the tenth century.

Pier A large vertical support constructed of coursed ashlar masonry; may be round, square or cruciform in shape often with pilasters or shafts added to any of its surfaces.

Pilaster A broad flat-faced vertical projection from a wall plane, often used as a respond (q.v.).

Piscina A basin, usually in a wall niche, supplied with a drain, for washing mass vessels.

Plinth A projecting course or courses of masonry, of various heights, used at ground or floor level under walls, shafts, columns or piers.

Presbytery The section of the church between the quire (q.v.) and the high altar.

Quatrefoil A decorative shape composed of four three-quarter circles (foil or lobe, often inscribed in a larger circle; often an important element in tracery design at the top (head) of a window).

Quire That section of the (monastic) church containing the stalls, where the service is sung; architecturally loosely used to refer to that part of the church east of the crossing (q.v.).

Respond A vertical projection from a wall surface, in a variety of shapes (i.e. pilaster, shaft, or a combination of), as a response to a free standing column or pier, on an aisle wall or at the end of an arcade (q.v.).

Rib An arch of stone constructed before and to aid the support of a stone vault; in the simplest type (quadripartite) two diagonal ribs take the place of groins.

Sacring Consecrating.

Sarum Salisbury.

Scallop Also known as a cushion capital (q.v.) but more generally refers to a type in which the sides of the capital block are carved with two or more scallop motifs.

Scotia A concave moulding of semi-circular profile, often used between two tori (q.v. *torus*) as a base for a shaft, column or pier.

Sexpartite A form of ribbed (q.v.) vault in which the diagonal ribs are supplemented by a transverse rib, intersecting them at the crossing and thereby creating six compartments as opposed to four (*quadripartite* q.v.).

Shaft A thin column of stone, either coursed and bonded into the wall or, made from separate cylindrical pieces of various lengths.

Spandrel The roughly triangular area or surface between two adjacent arches.

Stiff-leaf A type of foliage decoration, emphasising the stems and knobby leaves.

String-course A horizontal course of masonry projecting from a wall; of various profiles, usually used to mark levels.

Sulung Standard assessment of land for various royal burdens in Kent up to and beyond the Norman Conquest, replacing the hides and carrucates of other parts of England. It should not be taken as a measurement of area.

Torus A convex moulding of semi-circular profile, often used in conjunction with a scotia (q.v.) to form a base for a shaft, column or pier.

Tracery Bars of stone sub-dividing a window opening into smaller units of various and varying shapes.

Transept A nave-like space (tall and wide) of which the axis runs north-south (perpendicular to the main axis of the church from entrance to sanctuary).

Trefoil A decorative shape composed of three three-quarter angles; generally placed under an arch as in *blind arcading* or *tracery* (q.v.).

Turret A miniature or small tower-like form, often used to terminate or cap an angle buttress or stair vice.

Tympanum The place – usually a flat surface but sometimes receiving sculpture – between two sets of arches (generally one arch spanning two or more smaller ones) or an arch and a lintel.

Vault An arched construction of stone forming a ceiling; of several types; barrel, groin, ribbed (q.v.).

Vice The shaft of a spiral-stair.

Volute A type of capital in which the angles of the block are emphasised by leaf forms ending in a knob-like projection under the abacus (q.v.).

Water-holding A form of base moulding employing the combination of torus/scotia/torus, in which the scotia is nearly horizontal, thus, when used externally, likely to catch or hold water.

Index

Offices held in the diocese and cathedral of Rochester are indicated in **bold**. Dates (of appointment, unless otherwise shown) are given only where this more precise identification is necessary. Place names are in Kent unless otherwise stated, and counties are those existing before 1974. Bishops and peers are indexed under their family names after 1500; earlier persons are generally indexed under their forenames.

The indexer wishes to record his indebtedness to the editors and his fellow contributors for their assistance.

C.S. Knighton

son John, vicar of Lamberhurst, 96, 97
Grant, Lindy, writer, 166n.70
'Grantly, Dr, archdeacon of Barchester', 122&n.26
Gratian, canonist, 218
grave-goods, 2
Gravesend, rural deanery, 118
Gravesend, 122
Greatrex, Joan, writer, 50n.143
Greaves, John, **almsman**, 67
Greek, study of, 67, 103&n.68, 104, 126
Greenwich, 130
    cathedral organ in tavern, 76
Gregory I, St, pope, 1, 2, 8, 218
Gregory IX, pope, 36
Gregory, Robert, canon [*later* dean] of St Paul's, 127–8
Grey, Thomas, **monk, gospeller**, 58
Griffith, John, **canon**, 116, 127, 148
    wife, 127
Griffith, Maurice, **archdeacon, canon, bishop**, 55, 63, 64
Griffiths, John, **headmaster**, 104
Grindal, Edmund, archbishop of Canterbury, 73
Guernsey, 64
Gundulf, **bishop, founder**, 5, 8, 10, 11–15, 16, 19&n.89, 20, 22, 23, 30, 57
    anniversary, 23, 48&n.125
    benefactions, 14n.57, 15&n.62, 19&n.90
    bible, 217, 219–20
    building, 150–1, 153, 155n.24, 157n.32, 167, 168, 172n.90, 208
        for Gundulf's Tower *see also* Rochester Cathedral: fabric
    career, 11, 15, 17
    deputy to archbishop, 21
    division of estates, 14–15
    foundation of Chatham Hospital, 18n.84, ?92
    knight service, 21n.106
    Life, 15, 16, 18
    liturgical acts, 16, 21
    military engineer, 11, 13, 127
Gunley, Robert, charity, 227
Gunning, G., artist, 165n.68
Guy, –, surveyor, 186, 187
Guy, George, tenant, 83
Guy's Hospital, 227

Hacket, John, bishop of Coventry and Lichfield, 81–2
Haddenham, Bucks, church/rectory, 23, 95, 227
    estates, 226
    manor, 12–13, 14, 15, 24, 39
    rent, 26
Hadleigh, Suff, 70
Hadrian, abbot of Canterbury, 2
Haesten, Danish chief, 6

Haimo, sheriff of Kent, men of, 13, 17
Haimo [fitz Hamo], steward to Henry I, benefactor, 13
Haimo fitz Vitalis, brother, **monk**, 17
Hales, John, builder, 189–90
Halling, estates, 7
    manor, 27
    ordinations at, 49
    vicarage, 96
Halstow, High, 86
Hamo de Hethe, **prior, bishop**, 49
    benefactions, 32
    building, 35–6, 129, 182, 210–11, 212
    disputes with monks, 33, 35
    nepotism, 34
Hamo *see also* Haimo
Harbledown, secular college proposed, 31
'Harding, Septimus, precentor of Barchester Cathedral', 122
Hardy, Nathaniel, **dean**, 91
Harmer, John Reginald, **bishop**, 129, 131
Harris, John, **canon**, 91, 92, 221
Harrison, Frederick, writer, 115–16
Harrison, William, vicar of St Nicholas, Rochester, 67
Harrison, William Bagshaw, **minor canon**, 96
Hartlip, rectory, 40
    vicarage, 95, 95–6
Hartlip (surname) *see* John
Harvey, John Hooper, writer, 183n.[119]
Harwood, Thomas, carpenter/timber agent, 191
    widow, 109
Hasted, Edward, writer, 113, 185, 195, 196
Hastings, family, earls of Pembroke, 37
Hattfield, Edward, **chamberlain**, 51
Hawkins, Edward, **canon**, provost of Oriel, 116–17, 126, pl. 9(b)
Hawkins, Joanna, 108
Hayte, Walter, **canon, treasurer**, 63, 72
Heath, Nicholas, **bishop**, 57, 58, 60
Heath, Philip, and father, **lay clerks**, 65
Heather, Elizabeth, widow, 111
Helyas, **prior**, 29n.2
Hendle, Walter, solicitor of Augmentations, 58
Henniker, Anne, Baroness Henniker, tomb, 198
Henry I, king, 11, 20n.97, 23
    benefactions, 13, 15, 23, 39
    charter, 14–15&n.61
    present at consecration of cathedral, 23
Henry II, king, 27, 31
Henry III, king, 36
    charter, 35
Henry VII, king, 39
Henry VIII, king, **founder**, 53, 54n.166, 57–60, 68–9, 95, 99n.141, 100, 106
    educational foundations, 66, 102, 121
    library, 66, 219